The Rorschach: A Comprehensive System, in two volumes
by John E. Exner, Jr.
Theory and Practice in Behavior Therapy
by Aubrey J. Yates
Principles of Psychotherapy
by Irving B. Weiner
Psychoactive Drugs and Social Judgment: Theory and Research
edited by Kenneth Hammond and C. R. B. Joyce
Clinical Methods in Psychology
edited by Irving B. Weiner
Human Resources for Troubled Children
by Werner I. Halpern and Stanley Kissel
Hyperactivity
by Dorothea M. Ross and Sheila A. Ross
Heroin Addiction: Theory, Research and Treatment
by Jerome J. Platt and Christina Labate
Children's Rights and the Mental Health Profession
edited by Gerald P. Koocher
The Role of the Father in Child Development
edited by Michael E. Lamb
Handbook of Behavioral Assessment
edited by Anthony R. Ciminero, Karen S. Calhoun, and Henry E. Adams
Counseling and Psychotherapy: A Behavioral Approach
by E. Lakin Phillips
Dimensions of Personality
edited by Harvey London and John E. Exner, Jr.
The Mental Health Industry: A Cultural Phenomenon
by Peter A. Magaro, Robert Gripp, David McDowell, and Ivan W. Miller III
Nonverbal Communication: The State of the Art
by Robert G. Harper, Arthur N. Wiens, and Joseph D. Matarazzo
Alcoholism and Treatment
by David J. Armor, J. Michael Polich, and Harriet B. Stambul
A Biodevelopmental Approach to Clinical Child Psychology: Cognitive Controls and
Cognitive Control Theory
by Sebastiano Santostefano
Handbook of Infant Development
edited by Joy D. Osofsky
Understanding the Rape Victim: A Synthesis of Research Findings
by Sedelle Katz and Mary Ann Mazur
Childhood Pathology and Later Adjustment: The Question of Prediction
by Loretta K. Cass and Carolyn B. Thomas
Intelligent Testing with the WISC-R
by Alan S. Kaufman
Adaptation in Schizophrenia: The Theory of Segmental Set
by David Shakow
Psychotherapy: An Eclectic Approach
by Sol L. Garfield
Handbook of Minimal Brain Dysfunctions
edited by Herbert E. Rie and Ellen D. Rie
Handbook of Behavioral Interventions: A Clinical Guide
edited by Alan Goldstein and Edna B. Foa
Art Psychotherapy
by Harriet Wadeson
Handbook of Adolescent Psychology
edited by Joseph Adelson
Psychotherapy Supervision: Theory, Research and Practice
edited by Allen K. Hess

Continued on back

EXCUSES

EXCUSES

MASQUERADES IN
SEARCH OF GRACE

C. R. SNYDER
RAYMOND L. HIGGINS
RITA J. STUCKY

Department of Psychology
The University of Kansas

BF
637
.E95
S68
1983

A WILEY-INTERSCIENCE PUBLICATION

JOHN WILEY & SONS

New York • Chichester • Brisbane • Toronto • Singapore

Library of Congress Cataloging in Publication Data:

Snyder, C. R.
   Excuses: masquerades in search of grace.

   (Wiley series on personality processes, ISSN 0195-4008)
   "A Wiley-Interscience publication."
   Includes bibliographies and index.
   1. Excuses—Psychological aspects.   I. Higgins,
Raymond L.   II. Stucky, Rita J.   III. Title.   IV. Series.
[DNLM: 1. Defense mechanisms.   2. Self concept.   WM 193
S675e]

BF637.E95S68   1983   158   83-6615
ISBN 0-471-87702-6

Printed in the United States of America

10 9 8 7 6 5 4 3 2

To all those who really deserved a good excuse,
but didn't have one . . .

Series Preface

This series of books is addressed to behavioral scientists interested in the nature of human personality. Its scope should prove pertinent to personality theorists and researchers as well as to clinicians concerned with applying an understanding of personality processes to the amelioration of emotional difficulties in living. To this end, the series provides a scholarly integration of theoretical formulations, empirical data, and practical recommendations.

Six major aspects of studying and learning about human personality can be designated: personality theory, personality structure and dynamics, personality development, personality assessment, personality change, and personality adjustment. In exploring these aspects of personality, the books in the series discuss a number of distinct but related subject areas: the nature and implications of various theories of personality; personality characteristics that account for consistencies and variations in human behavior; the emergence of personality processes in children and adolescents; the use of interviewing and testing procedures to evaluate individual differences in personality; efforts to modify personality styles through psychotherapy, counseling, behavior therapy, and other methods of influence; and patterns of abnormal personality functioning that impair individual competence.

IRVING B. WEINER

University of Denver
Denver, Colorado

Preface

Like Rodney Dangerfield, excuses "don't get no respect." Often they are thought to be foolish and easily understood tactics that *other* people use to "cover their asses." We even laugh at them, just as we laughed at comedian Steve Martin's punch line "Well, excuuuuuuuuuuuuuuuse me!" Perhaps our most charitable appraisal of excuses is that they are humorous. The social scientist who studies excuses runs the risk of inviting reactions similar to Senator William Proxmire's "Golden Fleece Awards."

Against this backdrop of negative sentiment, however, we have increasingly come to respect the subtlety, complexity, effectiveness, and pervasiveness of excuses. And, of course, they are not used just by other people. You probably use them. We certainly do, although after months of raising our own as well as our colleagues' consciousness of them, we find them more and more difficult to get away with. Excuses are not all good, by any means, but they are not all bad either. We have reached these and other conclusions in the process of developing a descriptive model of excuses and performing research on them over the last years.

A great number of people have made valued contributions to this book. Included in this list are Robert M. Arkin, C. Daniel Batson, William R. Bowerman, Benjamin Braginsky, Philip Brickman (now deceased), Robert B. Cialdini, John M. Darley, Anthony G. Greenwald, John H. Harvey, Fritz Heider, Robert Hogan, B. Kent Houston, William Ickes, Edward E. Jones, George Kellas, Kevin D. McCaul, E. Jerry Phares, Catherine A. Riordan, Joseph F. Rychlak, Harold A. Sackeim, Barry R. Schlenker, Abraham Tesser, Gifford Weary, Thomas Ashby Wills, and Beatrice A. Wright. Our department chairpersons, Lawrence S. Wrightsman and, later, Michael D. Storms, provided a supportive atmosphere for this project. Special thanks are due to Timothy W. Smith, who generated an intellectual spark at the inception of this project.

The positive impact of our excuse research group is also felt throughout this book. These "excuseologists" include John Anderson, Robert Augelli, JoAnn Basgall, Erik Kilgren, Robin Lewis, Tom Locke, Kathy Minick, Rick Mehlman, Cheryl Newburg, Tom Nowak, David Roth, and Eidell Wasserman. Our assistants, Debbi Wensel and Judy Williams, have patiently facilitated the completion of the various technical aspects of the book. Additionally, we wish to thank our editor at Wiley, Herb Reich, who shared our view that a theory-based book-length manuscript on excuse-making was worth nurturing. This project was aided by a grant (Number 3727-60-0038) from the University of Kansas Graduate School Research Fund to the first author.

Finally, a full dose of gratitude is extended to all those people who have had to put up with having resident "experts" on excuses. To our colleagues, friends, and especially our families, please (to borrow a term) *excuse* us, and thank you.

C. R. SNYDER
RAYMOND L. HIGGINS
RITA J. STUCKY

Lawrence, Kansas
August 1983

Acknowledgments

We wish to thank each of the following sources for permission to reprint or use material in this book:

Drawing by Richter; © 1981, The New Yorker Magazine, Inc.

Drawing by Lorenz; © 1982, The New Yorker Magazine, Inc.

Drawing by John Trever; © 1981, *Albuquerque Journal,* Permission of Field Newspaper Syndicate.

Drawings by Schulz; © 1979, 1981, 1982, United Feature Syndicate, Inc.

Drawing by Harris; 1982, the Register and Tribune Syndicate, Inc.

Lyrics by Paul Simon from "Ace in the Hole:" © 1979, Paul Simon, reprinted by permission.

Data presented in Table 1 of Chapter 4 from M. Zuckerman, "Attribution of Success and Failure Revisited, or: The Motivational Bias Is Alive and Well in Attribution Theory." *Journal of Personality,* 1979, **47,** 245–287; © 1979, Duke University Press (Durham, North Carolina).

Data presented in table of Chapter 4 from D. H. Bennett, and D. S. Holmes, "Influence of Denial (situation redefinition) and Projection on Anxiety Associated with Threat to Self-Esteem." *Journal of Personality and Social Psychology,* 1975, **32,** 915–921; © 1975, American Psychological Association, reprinted by permission of the senior author.

Quotations presented in Chapter 4 by V. C. Hammond, *The Saturday Evening Post,* Fall 1972, **244,** p. 89; © 1972, The Saturday Evening Post Company.

Quotations presented in Chapters 8 and 9 by Alfred Adler, appearing in H. L. Ansbacher and R. R. Ansbacher, *The Individual Psychology of Alfred Adler.* New York: Harper & Row, 1967; these quotations are reproduced courtesy of the estate of Alfred Adler.

Figure 1 of Chapter 8 from A. H. Maslow, *Toward a Psychology of Being.* Copyright © 1968 by D. Van Nostrand Company; reprinted by permission of Van Nostrand–Reinhold Company, New York, New York.

Figure 2 of Chapter 8 from I. D. Yalom, *Existential Psychotherapy.* Copyright © 1980 by Basic Books, Inc.; reprinted by permission of Basic Books, Inc., New York, New York.

Figure 3 of Chapter 8 from A. Bandura, *Social Learning Theory.* Copyright © 1977 by Prentice-Hall, Inc.; reprinted by permission of Prentice-Hall, Inc., Englewood Cliffs, New Jersey.

Contents

EXCUSES

CHAPTER 1

Browsing Through
the Excuses Costume Shop

He said, "Who told you that you were naked? Have you eaten of the tree which I commanded you not to eat?" The man said, "The woman whom thou gavest to be with me, she gave me fruit of the tree, and I ate." Then the LORD God said to the woman, "What is this that you have done?" The woman said, "The serpent beguiled me, and I ate."

GENESIS 3:11–13 REVISED STANDARD VERSION

If we were to search the world and find a person without faults, we might know, for the first time, a person who does not make excuses. The rest of us, being imperfect, are not always happy with ourselves. We are tempted by and succumb to excuse-making as a way of living with our flaws. If we listen closely, we can easily discover a never-ending parade of excuses in our friends, spouses, co-workers, leaders, children, and ourselves. Lurking in our memories and on the tips of our tongues is a constant stream of "Who me?," "I didn't do it," "It's only a game," "Well, she asked for it," "It was fate," "I couldn't help it," or "I didn't mean to"—to recite but a few.

Reflecting for a moment, one is likely to recall hearing a wide variety of excuses, both exotic and mundane. Picture, for example, the following situation: We are watching a tennis match or baseball game, and it has become obvious that one side is not even close. Listen carefully, and a barrage of subtle and not so subtle "explanations" begin to surface. The loser begins to limp or rub an elbow. Someone complains about the sun. Someone else complains about the referee or points out the home team advantage or notes that the fans haven't been supportive.

If unfair play or poor judging or new rules or dead balls or greased palms or floating elbows or simple tripping aren't to blame for the outcome, there is always God, fate, or dumb luck, as can be seen in the following statement by a basketball coach after his team lost: "This isn't an excuse . . . but perhaps it was meant to be for them. It seemed like three or four times they would put up shots and the ball just wouldn't get away from the rim without going in" (*Lawrence Journal World*, March 8, 1981, p. 16). Coaches may be the acknowl-

"And please protect me from the appearance of wrongdoing."

Drawing by Lorenz; © 1982 The New Yorker Magazine, Inc.

edged experts, but it appears that everyday incidents such as these can inspire creative excuse-making in nearly anyone.

It is interesting to note that excuses appear in a wide variety of situations, including those times when we do something we shouldn't, when we don't do something we should, when we do something badly, and when we are caught redhanded. All that is really required of a situation to make it prime ground for excuse-making is that it put us in a bad light.

Sticky situations that reflect negatively on us are to be found everywhere, and excuses are made about virtually everything. Popular arenas are school appearances, social faux pas, parties, dieting, sports, weight, indiscretions, paying bills, being late, personality quirks, failing to write letters, lack of cleanliness (or godliness), bad jokes, bad ideas, bad habits, sex, taxes, marriages, divorces, drinking, attitudes—the list goes on and on. Excuse-making, like death, is a great equalizer. No matter the age ("I'm too old/young to know better"), ethnic group ("What do you expect from a black/white/ Puerto Rican?"), occupation ("All musicians are overly emotional"), or position in life ("Do you think I'd have done it if I were rich?"), excuses are widely used and received. In this vein, one is reminded of the saying among military people: "Excuses are like anuses—everybody's got one."

LOOK IN THE MIRROR

Chances are good that you have had substantial involvement with excuses in your life. You have heard them from the friend who came over and dropped

your most expensive wine glass on the floor, from the date who sulked all evening and wanted to go home early, from the woman who dropped cigarette
ashes on your new Persian rug, from your parents, from your teachers, from
your President, your friends, your kids, your mate, your co-workers, the gro-
cery store checker, the dry cleaner attendant, and the photo developer's clerk.
You can probably remember hearing an excuse this very day. In fact, chances
are good that you made at least one yourself. The chances are even better that
today you excused yourself in your continual interior dialogue. Right about
now, if you allow yourself to look at your own excuse-making, you may be
doing an interesting thing—making excuses about your excuses!

As long as we are not perfect, excuses will abound, for they appear whenever
we look in a mirror and see an imperfect image of ourselves. All of us can recall
the feeling of vulnerability we experience when we discover differences between who we usually *think* we are and the less than acceptable reality of who
we are. Even when *we* are able to face the image in that mirror, there are painful times when others are not so tolerant. It is inevitable that, from time to time,
our carefully hidden flaws will be exposed. Caught undressed in these ways, it
is easy to remember how we clothe ourselves in many different social and private masks. We all understand that we keep secrets about who we "really" are,
but most of the time we try to act as though we have nothing to hide. In fact, we
are actors in a social masquerade, donning masks designed to make the image
of ourselves appealing. Excuses occur when our masks slip a bit, showing
something unsavory underneath; they then become part of the masquerade, allowing us to repair the chinks in our masks that come with long use. Not only
do we pretend we are not wearing masks, but we also pretend we are not repairing them through excuse-making.

It is obvious that excuses are a very common part of our day-to-day lives,
but we seem to have a notion that excuses are one of those, well, not quite polite things to talk about. Indeed, our ability to ignore excuses is so pervasive
that theories of excuse-making have been relatively absent in both folk wisdom
and more formal study of human behavior. Because excuses are such a universal experience, however, it seems important to bring them into the limelight.

WHAT IS AN EXCUSE?

Although excuses often are seen as some sort of social anomaly with no explanation or utility, we believe that they do have a purpose. More specifically, excuses are especially designed to work to our advantage. If we look closely at the
situations where excuses are most prevalent, we can see that they are used
when things are not going well. We can observe that excuses occur close upon
the heels of, simultaneous with, or even before some sort of predicament.

There are three things that are necessary for excuse-making to occur. The
first is that we do something that is attributable to us. A second element of the

excuse-making context is that the act has a negative flavor and we do not want to be associated with it. The third essential component is an observer. For one reason or another, observers have some sort of authority over us. We care what they think of us, and we want them to think good things. We believe that if they think negatively of our actions (or inactions), they will also think negatively of us. While the observer (the audience) is often outside ourselves (teachers, parents, peers, friends, or enemies), each of us also possesses an internal observer—and it is to this entity that many of our excuses are directed.

Put all these assumptions together, and we arrive at the following definition of excuses: *Excuses are explanations or actions that lessen the negative implications of an actor's performance, thereby maintaining a positive image for oneself and others.* This definition is a framework for a theoretical model of excuse-making as well as some rather detailed discussion of a wide variety of excuses and their implications. But first, let us spend a few moments considering the sorts of things that might fit under this definition of excuse-making.

SOME COMMON EXCUSES

I Didn't Do It

One very common excuse-making type is of the "I didn't do it" school. Included in this group of excuses is a wide range of possibilities all designed to negate the fact that you have anything to do with the bad thing that happened.

Denial

Among the most rudimentary of excuses is the admission that something happened, with an assertion that we didn't have anything to do with it. These denials are often called lies. "I didn't do it" is a prize-winner in this category. "I didn't do it" gains many points for style when performed with the accompanying gestures that involve shaking the head, shrugging the shoulders, and then throwing out the hands with a look of concerned confusion.

Alibis

A slightly more sophisticated form of lying is "I didn't know anything about it," which is really the beginning of an alibi. "How *could* I be having an affair, I've been working at the office all of the time." In the case of alibis, the accused feigns total ignorance or argues the physical impossibility of having been involved. The unwritten statement is "I *couldn't* have done it, I don't even know about it (or I wasn't even there)."

Blaming

The group of "I didn't do it" excuses is greatly enhanced by the simple addition of another possible culprit. Excuses in this category vary widely, but all have in

"I blame my parents, and the previous Administration."

common the proverbial pointing finger. Persons in this position may point in a specific direction for blame: "The butler did it," "The dog ate it," "The kids broke it." Or they may blame in a vague way: "I didn't do it, and I don't know who did" (with the implication that *somebody* else did). Sometimes people do both, as is the case in the following statement by a psychotherapy client of one of the authors: "It's like this. If it's not my fault, it's her fault, and if it's not her fault, it's still not my fault."

It Wasn't So Bad

"It wasn't so bad" excuses all have in common an attempt to make it appear that the bad performance wasn't as bad as it seemed.

Minimization

A frequent excuse in this category is direct minimization. "It was only a little piece of cake," "I only hit him once," or "It's only 45 minutes late." It isn't that a transgression didn't occur, but rather that it wasn't so bad. Even when confessing their sins, people may minimize or leave out the grizzly details of the acts they committed: "Father, I fought with my brother," rather than, "Father, I tried to stab my brother in the hand with scissors."

Justification

Another group of "It wasn't so bad" excuses are justifications and/or reasons. In civil society, reasons have long held the advantage as excuses because of their obvious reasonableness. Used with proper finesse, the reason may not even have the double characteristic of being a lie. If they aren't already true, they are excellent things to talk ourselves into actually believing ("No, I'm not angry with you for wrecking the car, it's just that I've had a long day," "Joey hit me first," or "It's for your own good"). While justifications are typically reasonable to their user, they sometimes appear ludicrous to the audience. For example, consider this statement by Adolf Hitler (cited in Myers, 1979, p. 200):

> I have said and done all that I could; I have made proposal after proposal to Britain; likewise to France. These proposals were always ridiculed—rejected with scorn. However, when I saw that the other side intended to fight, I naturally . . . forged a powerful weapon of defense.

One other advantage of some "reasons" is that they frequently not only help get the user out of a tight squeeze, but they also can, with practice, be used as a method of simultaneously gaining positive points. Not only, we rationalize, are we not to blame, but we really should be thanked ("We aren't endangering people with our nuclear power plant, we are improving the quality of their lives").

Derogation

A third type of "It wasn't so bad" excuse can be called derogation. In derogation, we downgrade the setting, the critic, or the victim with such statements as "The test was too tricky," "The professor doesn't know as much about anatomy as *I* do," or "Of course I assaulted her. With that low-cut blouse and sleazy walk, she was asking for it." This sort of excuse has been used to rationalize burning witches and heretics, using capital punishment, and killing Vietnamese women and children (i.e., "Gooks").

Yes, But . . .

The last major category of excuses we address here is exceptionally common. In this category, two early and usually covert admissions are made: "I did it" and "I was bad." These admissions form the "yes" part of the "Yes, but . . ." excuse. The subsequent focus is on the word "but."

I Couldn't Help It

The most pervasive form of "Yes, but" is probably, "Yes, but I couldn't help it." These are excuses that appeal to some sort of force other than the will: "He ran away and was gone for a year. When he came back home he told me the silly story of being captured by pirates on Lake Michigan, and kept in chains so he could not write me" (Masters, 1962, p. 159). Of particular popularity in this group of excuses are appeals to "demon rum," "media violence," and both physical and mental illness. Being possessed by the devil is also a good excuse here (i.e., "The Devil made me do it"). Likewise, there are appeals to luck or fate or the hand of God or the past. In common parlance these excuses take such forms as "What do you expect from a Virgo?," "It was obviously meant to be," "It was the booze talking," or, more disturbingly, "I was selected by God to kill!" The implication is that you, of course, would not have done what you just did if it hadn't been for powerful outside forces that temporarily rendered your will power or judgment ineffective.

I Didn't Mean To

In addition to "Yes, but" excuses that seek to reduce the sense of the person's choice in doing the evil deed, there is a second category involving intentionality called "I didn't mean to." "I didn't mean to's" are usually accompanied by an apology: "I'm sorry, I didn't mean to trip and spill hot coffee down the back of your neck and all over your new shirt," "I didn't mean to make her cry," or, one of the worst, "I was only joking." "I didn't mean to's" are designed to appeal to the klutz in all of us. The well-intentioned nice guy or gal who is always saying or doing the wrong thing is hard to hate. The bumbling fool is making a distinction between ignorant incompetence and maliciousness, with the implication that he or she really isn't a bad sort.

It Wasn't Really Me

Finally, in the "Yes, but" category of excuses is a group called "It wasn't *really* me." In this group are excuses that are designed to split off different parts of the self. For example, people may argue that they didn't really do it, instead it was their "mood," their "forgetfulness," their "temper," or their "sensitivity." The message is that the "real" person would never do such a thing.

A PREVIEW OF THE EXCUSE MASQUERADE

It is appropriate to close this introductory chapter with a glimpse of what is to come in subsequent pages. Chapter 2 is devoted to background regarding excuse-making, and we will see how excuses relate to philosophical issues. Chapter 3 introduces a theory of excuse-making and a model for understanding what excuses do and how they work. Chapters 4 and 5 examine excuses from the perspective of timing. Chapter 4, for example, is a discussion of research involving excuses formed after the evil deed is done, while Chapter 5 involves a review of the literature for what we call anticipatory excuses—setting up protection even before the dastardly act. In Chapter 6 we explore the question of who may be especially prone to excuse-making.

The remaining chapters address some of the wider implications of excuse-making. A discussion of the development of the capacity for excuse-making in the individual appears in Chapter 7. Chapters 8 and 9 involve the identification and treatment of dysfunctional excuses. The final chapter presents a discussion of the value of excuse-making as a social force, and a recognition that excuse-making is an institutional as well as individual phenomenon.

REFERENCES

Lawrence Journal World, March 8, 1981, p. 16.

Masters, E. L. *Spoon River anthology.* New York: Collier-Macmillan, 1962.

Myers, R. A. *Excuses, excuses: Or, how to get out of doing practically everything.* New York: Bell Publishing Company, 1979.

CHAPTER 2

The Philosophical Backdrop to the Excuse Masquerade

In certain historical periods the dilemmas of life become more pronounced, more difficult to live with, and harder to resolve. Our period, the middle of the twentieth century, is one such time.

ROLLO MAY, *Psychology and the Human Dilemma*

Excuses and excuse-makers are almost everywhere. The full impact and meaning of excuses, however, are not obvious in a discussion of everyday excuses. Although it is certainly true that excuses belong in the worlds of social faux pas and legal scrapes, they are not limited to the mundane aspects of life. We shall posit excuse-making as a fact of human behavior, rooted in basic philosophical beliefs about human existence. For this discussion, the seemingly day-to-day excuses are temporarily replaced with those that involve more weighty matters. Indeed, it is our view that everyday excuses are a continuous reminder of the more fundamental issues in which they are grounded.

In the biblical myth, for example, the first free act of humankind (Adam and Eve's sampling of the apple) was not accompanied with a sense of pride and accomplishment but, rather, with an excuse. Since Adam and Eve, human actions have been separated from the actors unwilling to carry the weight or responsibility for their bad performances. This process of separation is the process of excuse-making.

Excuse-making is not only a basic human issue, but it has particular relevance in our time. Ours is a time when human acts have vast significance, and when we can see ever so clearly the effects of our past actions. The threat of nuclear war is a common symbol of that fact; we are the first species of animal possessing the capacity to obliterate itself.

To complicate matters further, the issues in our age are rarely so starkly good and evil as is the case of nuclear war. The increased rate of change, the proliferation of differing values, and the dismantling of societal norms combine to provide us with exceedingly ambiguous roles (Yankelovich, 1981). In the midst of this uncertainty, the temporary solution of excuse-making is very

9

"PAY NO ATTENTION. IT'S PROBABLY JUST A SUPREME ACT OF LEGITIMATE SELF-DEFENSE."

By John Trever; © 1981 Albuquerque Journal. Permission of Field Newspaper Syndicate.

tempting. The existential and social themes that underpin the phenomenon of excuse-making are explored next.

THE CORE PHILOSOPHICAL ISSUES

"I did not."
"You did too."
"I did not."
"You did too."
"Well, you made me."
"I did not."

This brief interchange comes courtesy of early childhood memories. Its commonness bespeaks the relevance of excuse-making, which, as we indicated, is inextricably embedded in the scripts of human action. But why is this the case? A starting point involves an examination of the issues of determinism and choice.

Determinism and Choice

Do human beings actually *act?* Must they—can they—make choices between this action and that?

Determinism

The word determinism has Latin roots meaning to set limits on events. Determinism occurs when "there are factors in a circumstance which constrain it, make certain alternatives impossible, or necessarily bring about some outcome" (Rychlak, 1979, p. 33). Pure determinism as a philosophical assumption implies that all events occur out of the necessity of factors outside of a person's control. Another way of stating this is to say that an individual's purposes or intentions do not account for what occurs. Instead, even intentions and desires are "caused" by other factors.

Throughout the recorded history of Western civilization, there have been philosophies suggesting that we have little or no choice and free will (Yalom, 1980). In early Greek life this lack of choice was expressed as "necessity," or fate. Fate, for example, was thought to govern particularly those actions that people believed were under their own control (Berofsky, 1966). In this way, the Gods kept people from becoming too powerful. The concept of predestination was prevalent during the medieval period. Predestination held that events were determined prior to their occurrence, through divine intervention. During the aforementioned historical periods, the belief in God's knowledge of the past and future conflicted with the concept of individual will: If God knows what is to happen, how do we have the choice? And why should we be held responsible for sin?

Eventually, the emphasis on divine law and order was replaced by the "scientific" viewpoint. Freud gave determinism a grounding in psychology: "The deeply noted belief in psychic freedom and choice is . . . quite unscientific and must give ground before the claim of a determinism which governs mental life" (cited in May, 1969, p. 180). In more recent times, people have been likened to machines who act out (output) behaviors in response to the situation (input). Although behaviorists may vary in their position on the issues of intention and purpose, behaviorism is still generally conceptualized as a deterministic philosophy (Skinner, 1974).

Choice

In contrast to determinism, "to be free is to be without constraint, open to alternatives, and not only bound by a fixed course" (Rychlak, 1979, p. 10). If individuals have freedom, they purportedly exercise (whether they know it or not) the faculty of choice or free will. As long as nothing absolutely forces us to act in a particular fashion, our actions are typically perceived as manifestations of our choices. Indeed, there is considerable research suggesting that people actively seek to maintain a sense of choice (Brehm, 1966; Brehm & Brehm, 1981).

The notion of pure choice has been advocated by the existentialists. As Lachalier puts it (1949, p. 172), "We achieve a destiny which we have chosen." The existentialists point out, however, that choice is an awesome thing. The human being is not only free, but is "doomed to freedom" (Sartre, 1956, p. 633). Since the individual's actions are wholly free, nothing is taken as a "given." The essence of this view is that through freely chosen acts, the individual constructs a self for whom he or she is the sole author. Paradoxically, the process of self construction can be freeing, but it also is something we can never escape. In this context, individuals have no choice about the fact that they have free choice.

The Practical Solution

As we have briefly seen, the existence of choice is a question that has interested people for centuries (see Ryle, 1949, 1980, for a discussion of the dilemma inherent in the choice issue). A simple solution to the dilemma is not forthcoming, however. The belief in human freedom is still achieved through an act of faith, as is the belief in determinism, because these issues involve noncumulative "evidence." Slightly more sophisticated arguments have evolved on one side or the other, and new language to express the difficulty is invented, but the conflicts involving choice and determinism raise questions for which final answers cannot be discovered. It is instead an issue which, in its continuous tension, becomes a theme of human existence in general and of our own lives in particular. Try as we might, we can never really "know" beyond any reasonable doubt whether we delude ourselves by thinking we are free or delude ourselves by thinking we are not.

As long as we examine the conflict from the perspective of philosophical purity, that is, force ourselves to select either the choice or determinism position, we may make little progress in understanding our own behavior. If we view the conflict from the practical level, however, it appears that we operate with the assumption that our actions are both determined and free (see Ryle, 1980). It is obvious that we operate with certain physical, economic, and social limitations. For example, if we wish to move long distances over water without the aid of a boat, we are very quickly forced to face the facts of our physical limitations. If we decide upon the boat to help us, we must operate within financial constraints. And if we feel limited by financial constraints, we might consider walking into a bank to take the money we want, except that for most of us this idea dies in the face of social and legal considerations. Still, provided that we operate within practical limitations, we are free to pursue our desires.

From this perspective, our freedom is bordered by those things that are determined, but it does exist. The challenge to the individual is to maximize freedom in the face of those things that are fixed. Over time, we are likely to enact the choice–determinism debate within our lives, leaning at first to one side of the continuum and then to the other. And we are surrounded by people who have differing beliefs about the matter of choice. Perhaps we have been frustrated both by people who say that they can't take control of their lives and by those who constantly point out the limits to their possibilities. Equally exasperating are those people who assert that they are in absolute control of their existences and act without consideration of practical matters. The former people are stifling and constrained, the latter are worrisome and heedless of potential catastrophe.

The issue of determinism versus choice comes alive when applied to the vagaries of everyday life. We arrive (often without awareness) at a position on the matter for most of the major and minor activities of our lives. Typically, we think of those acts that we consciously choose as being free and those that we "just do" as being determined. However, this is a simplistic solution. In fact, we are continuously assessing the number of possibilities open to us and testing the limitations. Each act is an individual case that is examined on the basis of its unique merits. The solution or, rather, the final decision we make about the freeness versus determinedness of an event is rarely stated, and probably is frequently open to question if it were articulated.

While the dilemma remains unresolved at the philosophical and personal levels, a fairly consistent stance is taken by society. We see few instances where deterministic concepts are accepted in everyday life (Kemeny, 1959). Rather, society is constructed largely on the opposite assumption, that people are capable of choice. Of course, there are frequent appeals to the notion that we simply act out the lines, and hence the lives, we have been given. But even when we believe we have no free will, we recognize that our society operates as if we do.

Responsibility and Freedom

What is it about the choice–determinism issue that makes it so compelling? Why does it seem to be so important to philosophers and lay people alike? The answer lies with the issue of responsibility.

The Freedom–Responsibility Link

Advocates of both choice and determinism agree that without choice people are not free and "unless the individual is free to constitute the world in any number of ways, then the concept of responsibility has no meaning" (Yalom, 1980, p. 200). Or to state it another way, acting freely (choice) is a necessary precondition for responsibility (Berofsky, 1966; Franklin, 1968; Sartre, 1956; Toffler, 1970). If there is no choice, persons should not be held responsible for their acts because these acts are not really their *own*. They belong instead to some outside causal factor. Responsibility, then, according to Sartre (1956, p.

640), is the "consciousness of being the uncontested author of an event or object."

The Advantage of Choice

There are many choices for what we do, who we are, and what sort of lifestyle we lead. The range of options includes decisions both for the large framework of our lives and who we become and for the small framework of what we wish to do in this moment. The advantage to choice is that we are free to be how and what we wish to be. Indeed, Fritz Perls (1969) believed that the assumption of responsibility enhances one's life. In his words: "Taking responsibility for your life and being rich in experience and ability is identical. And what I hope to do is . . . make you understand how much you gain by taking responsibility for every emotion, every movement you make, every thought you have" (p. 65).

The Disadvantage of Choice

The ironic disadvantage to responsibility is that once given a possibility, we *must* choose. In fact, as long as it is decided that we have some measure of choice, we are held responsible whether we "take" the choice or not. Choice is a two-edged sword. We are free to choose, but we are bound to be responsible for our choices. If we are indeed the authors of acts over which we have choice, then we must answer the question: Why? Why did we have the priorities that we had? Why did we choose this act rather than that? It is not surprising, then, that we continuously assess the situations we encounter and our own behaviors. For unless we can *excuse* ourselves by claiming that we really have no choice, we will be held accountable. Paul Tillich's (1952, p. 52) explanation is quite clear: "Man's being is not only given to him but demanded of him. He is responsible for it; literally, he is required to answer, if he is asked, what he had made of himself."

Responsibility and Practicality

In the light of accompanying responsibility, it appears that the issues of choice and determinism are weighty ones. Envision, for a moment, a world with no legal or moral accountability and it becomes obvious that societies cannot afford to entertain the notion that people have no choice or responsibility. Indeed, the abstract concept of responsibility has been inextricably woven into the concrete reality of our legal and moral institutions throughout history.

Kafka's (1937) *The Trial* exemplifies the human reality of being perpetually in court, and as such illustrates the inherent sense of responsibility that people feel. The protagonist awakens one day to find that he is "guilty." What the charge may be is irrelevant. In accepting the surrealistic situation and offering no fight, the protagonist demonstrates the feeling of being judged responsible (and guilty) for his actions in an ultimate sense. While it is infrequent that anyone actually demands that we justify our existence, we are continuously asked to do so symbolically. Each justification of a particular behavior can be seen as a microcosmic reenactment of the larger scenario.

THE MODERN DILEMMA

The dilemmas involving determinism, choice, and responsibility have plagued humankind since the beginnings of civilization, but our present age appears to be one in which these issues have taken on a new and more urgent meaning. Excuse-making may be rampant throughout all levels of our society partly because it allows us to handle these important dilemmas. The factors that have enhanced the inherent problems of responsibility are the proliferation of choices, the increase of responsibility, and the loss of individual power in our society. We turn to a discussion of these issues next.

The Proliferation of Choices

In this section, we suggest that one of the most compelling antecedents to excuse-making is that people appear to have more freedoms than ever before. With more freedom, people make a larger number of choices and hence encounter an expansion of situations and acts in need of justification.

More Arenas

In recent times, Western society has experienced a rapid growth in choices deriving from the dissolution of external domination in many spheres. Choices that were once made for people have come under the purview of the individual. One striking example is the way in which metaphysical issues have been dislodged from the authority of a few ecclesiasts and placed in the hands of the individual. By virtue of the Protestant Reformation, we were empowered to make our own choices among religious preferences.

No longer are all of us baptized at birth and permanently (barring catastrophe) endowed with membership into the universal (Catholic) church. Instead, metaphysical individualism has grown to such a degree that individuals increasingly choose not one of the prepackaged set of meanings from any number of religious groups but a religious identity and belief system of their own design. Alternatively, we may choose to deemphasize the importance of "religious" issues altogether, so that ecclesiastical freedom is freedom from religion, rather than freedom to choose a religious belief system (Fromm, 1941). When issues of human purpose and meaning are no longer answered by religious dogma, the individual chooses from a range of possibilities as infinite as his or her imagination. Metaphysical individualism, then, represents an incredible expansion of human freedoms, albeit one that often is frightening in its scope.

Since the medieval period, philosophical self-determination has had a practical counterpart in the increase of political self-determination. The right to rule was once a matter of divine providence, and it was lodged in the hierarchy of the church or in the rights of absolute monarchs. In the midst of the political upheavals evidenced by the French and American revolutions and the introduction of political democracy, however, the notion evolved that the individual had the right to the rule over self. Since that time, the number of persons included in the liberation from divinely sanctioned authority has increased by at least two times, as slaves and women were added to the ranks of human beings with the right to choose.

Finally, it is not only new external realms that have expanded our possibilities—much of our exploration into new territories has involved the internal world. Psychology, once taught as a course in departments of philosophy, has grown into an entity of its own. With Freud's introduction of the unconscious, the exploration of the inner world represented a new frontier (Freud, 1952). In Freud's theory, consciousness is merely the tip of the iceberg, while the unconscious aspect of the human mind is the seedbed of all ideas and actions. At first, the unconscious was viewed as being basically immutable, and as such it provided a set of limitations on conscious choice. But the modern trend has been to focus increasingly on the capacity of choice in internal matters.

A profusion of new therapies, personality theories, and therapists has emerged to emphasize the fact that we are capable of choice and change. If we point to our unconscious as an explanation for our actions, an existential therapist is likely to demand, "Whose unconscious is it, anyway?" If we write to "Dear Abby" to complain of our difficulties, she is likely to enjoin us to change, via the help of a "trained professsional." While the freedoms gained by choice in internal matters often are ambiguous, and the limitations of internal freedom have not been discovered, it is a general belief that we have freedom to change our personalities, indeed, our very selves. What was once attributable to the shape of our faces, the bumps on our heads, or the humors of our bodies has become a matter of choice.

More Acts

While psychological, political, and metaphysical freedoms represent new and previously untapped arenas for exercising individual choice, some of the growth of freedom is related to the arenas in which choices were always made. Perhaps most striking is the increased choice for the individual person in the day-to-day decisions of social life. The pressure toward freedom in the past century has escalated to a point where the choices of everyday life at times boggle the senses, leaving us unsure of where to turn (Yankelovich, 1981).

The constraints of religious and political structures were carried through the Victorian period by strict cultural standards or norms. In recent years, however, social norms have given way to a culture that Yalom (1980) calls "compulsively permissive." He states:

> Structure, ritual, and boundaries of every type are being relentlessly dismantled ... Today's patient has to cope more with suppressed freedom than with suppressed drives. No longer pushed from within by what he or she "must" or "ought" to do, the patient has to cope with the problem of choice—with what he or she wants to do. (p. 224)

We are encouraged to coin an already aging phrase—"do your own thing"—and we are somehow expected to figure out what that is. Many previously unacceptable, even unthinkable ways of relating to others are now permitted by society. Popular magazines are filled with articles like "Should You Live with a Man?," "The Lesbian Alternative," "Having a Baby on Your Own," and "Group Marriage: Pros and Cons." Values have multiplied to such an extent that for nearly every conceivable human behavior, it is usually possible to find groups of people who think it is sick or it is admirable (Menninger, 1973).

The expansion of social roles has provided new responsibilities. The workaday accountant can become a physical fitness enthusiast at home and can spend weekends in the midst of the disco scene. With each of the seemingly ever-increasing number of interests, jobs, and activities that can be pursued, there is an accompanying identity or role. While a description of your occupation used to suffice as an answer to a question about who you are, such a description rarely answers that question today. From codified law, or the will of God, or strict Victorian mores, we have developed exceedingly ambiguous scripts of acceptable behaviors over which few people agree (Yalom, 1980). Many individuals are in the odd situation of going from role to role where the expected behaviors not only are different but may be diametrically opposite.

We also have more choices regarding physical issues. Should we spend our vacations under the surface of the ocean, skiing down the side of a mountain, or hanging from a bit of aluminum and nylon, simulating the action of birds? As a species, do we leave the surface of the earth or imbed ourselves deeply inside it? Our technology affords us choices only dreamt by the physical masters of past ages. With a drop of glue we can stick together a car and a crane; with the flick of the wrist, satellite transmitters enable us to see events halfway around the earth. We are increasingly transcending the traditional limits of physical existence.

To confuse matters further, our American society seems to offer choices at a mundane and banal level. Which deodorant shall we choose? Which car? What shall we do when confronted by an entire aisle of the supermarket devoted to brightly colored boxes of breakfast cereal? And once we have chosen our cereal, which of five kinds and sizes of milk will accompany it? We often come dangerously close to a preoccupation with this level of choice—an essentially meaningless one. If we were to take advertising totally seriously, our identities would be related to the brands of toothpaste and hairspray that we purchase.

Writing Our Own Lines

If we hide in the aforementioned choices, aided by the latest consumer report (if prudence is part of the image that we seek to construct), it is for good reason. There are no paths to guide us through the maze of alternatives at the more far-reaching levels of our lives. Without the safe, though stifling hand of external authority, we are caught, whirling and lost, in a vortex of choices. In despair, Karl Menninger asks, "Where, indeed, did sin go? What became of it?" (1973, p. 15). Perhaps if we knew what was sinful, we would have some notion of which way to turn. Rollo May (1969, p. 185) describes the problem as follows: "This new freedom occurs just at the time when the values which normally serve as a basis for choice are most in chaos, when there is confusion approaching bankruptcy in outward guidance . . . the gift of freedom, yes; but the burden of the individual is tremendous indeed." In short, both human and environmental barriers have eroded to the point that the possibilities facing each individual are enormous. To the question "What are we to do?," there are few clear answers. In Toffler's (1970, p. 259) words, "As we hurdle into tomorrow, millions of ordinary men and women will face emotion-packed options so unfamiliar, so untested, that past experience will offer little clue to wisdom."

Which Audience?

As we contemplate the scripts we desire for ourselves, we must also consider the audience for whom the play (our behavior) is designed. Our once concrete critics—the external authority of church, state, and family—have lost their exclusive power. The critics have not disappeared, however; they have mushroomed along with our choices. Moreover, they have become largely invisible (Fromm, 1941). We now must decide whether to play to any number of observers: conscience, common sense, physical or psychic health, normality, public opinion, and so on. According to McHale (1966, p. 3):

> The most uniform cultural contexts are typically primitive enclaves. The most striking feature of our contemporary "mass" culture is the vast range and diversity of its alternative cultural choices . . . The "mass," on even cursory examination, breaks down into many different "audiences."

The Responsibility Crisis

The significance of the growth of choices, as described in the previous section, is that we are responsible for each of them. As we make more choices in more arenas in front of more observers, the responsibility becomes increasingly burdensome. We have become progressively liberated, but we have also suffered the backlash of accountability that follows the euphoria of newly found freedom. The crisis of responsibility is a crisis of liberation (Fromm, 1941). While some would say that our culture is overwhelmed by permissiveness so pervasive that it is detrimental (Menninger, 1973), others claim instead that we are only suffering from the shock waves inherent in awakening to our own range of choices and possibilities (Yankelovich, 1981). What is less controversial is that the issue of responsibility is a central one in a culture reeling from the effects of Watergate, pollution, and welfare. Yalom (1980, p. 253) editorializes, "Responsibility awareness has come of age in America."

We have learned to claim that we are taking responsibility, for we know that we cannot get away with a blanket disclaimer for our actions. But we do not yet possess the gumption, or the masochism, to stand up freely and claim responsibility for all that we do. Further, our sense of responsibility has expanded because we may have to consider events occurring far away and far into the future, as well as those that have more import than the normal everyday choices of life.

Events Far Away

In previous generations, news of world events was sporadic and slow. Even in societies that had highly developed communication networks, information was transmitted in oral or written form to a privileged elite (McLuhan, 1964). These modes of communication were far less involving than the information channels of modern mass media. The present generation is often painfully cognizant of world events as portrayed on television, and we may feel a sense of participation in and responsibility for them. In fact, we are occasionally admonished to remember that we have some personal responsibility for events that occur thousands of miles away (McLuhan, 1964; Toffler, 1970).

Notions linked to the advent of the mass media, such as the "global village," "spaceship earth," and the "shrinking planet" (McLuhan, 1964), focus on the idea that the world is our community—one for which we are responsible. The information available to us through mass media enables us to be more knowledgeable than ever before, but there is a problem of responsibility, succinctly described by Maslow (1968, p. 66): "Often it is better not to know, because if you *did* know, then you would have to act and stick your neck out." Many of us simply refuse to watch. It is painful to be informed. Yet even when we do not know the specifics, we are plagued by the vague discomfort that we should be doing something about what is "going on."

Events Far in the Future

In addition to our sense of responsibility for events that are physically remote, we have also come to feel a sense of responsibility for the temporally remote world of future generations. It was not long ago that the prevailing belief was one of optimism. Our predecessors felt that the human species would naturally evolve to a pleasant end. However, we live in an age in which we recognize the lingering consequences of the choices made by these previous generations, and we have a foreboding of the enduring legacy of our own lives. We have established supremacy over nature, but we have bequeathed eroded resources, serious pollution, and the loss of much of the beauty and dignity of nature. We have developed a highly advanced medical technology, only to find ourselves prolonging the lives of a world population that often cannot be fed. Neither the utopias nor the doomsdays predicted by decison-makers of previous generations occurred. Instead, our enduring lesson is that the decisions we make now may (in the long run) affect factors we never thought to take into consideration.

We are just on the threshold of realizing the amazing interconnectedness of things. No longer are we able to explain events in a linear causality mode of reality. We sense that things we do can have startling effects years from now, but we do not know what the effects may be (see Merton, 1957, on latent consequences). Hence we are saddled with responsibility from the newly found knowledge that the world of causality is exceedingly complex. We are responsible for those things that we cause to happen. But how are we to know all of the ramifications of our actions? We feel a keen sense of responsibility for unknown events to come.

Big Events

The crisis of responsibility is not only caused by our feeling of participation in events far away in space or time. These concepts help explain the scope of our responsibility crisis, but they still do not capture the sense of urgency that we often feel. This sense comes instead from the "bigness" of many of the issues with which we struggle. Wars, terrorism, starvation, and injustice are the fare of the mass media information system—and these are the things for which we may feel responsible. We are told that we must begin to take responsibility for the actions of our government, and that involvement is necessary for survival in the nuclear age.

Our age is such that we often feel a sense of urgency to our commitments. The stakes of world events seem greater than before. While previous generations were able to feel that the positive course of events could be improved by individual contributions, we are more likely to feel that the only way the world can be saved from certain destruction is through group intervention that depends, in some mysterious way, on our personal effort. May (1969, p. 183) gives a voice to our dilemma: "God made form out of chaos and we have made chaos out of form, and it is a rare human being who is not, in some secret place in his heart, scared to death that we shall not be able to turn chaos into form again before it is too late." In a very real sense, our decisions about nuclear energy, war, famine, resources, and life styles *are* urgent. The decisions that the world faces *are* momentous, and we *are* involved, as individuals, as localities, and as governments.

The increase of personal freedom does nothing to reduce the responsibility crisis; rather, it only serves to magnify it. We are held responsible for each of the many aspects of everyday life: our sex lives, our eating habits, our transportation, our political or nonpolitical views, our morality, our jobs, our parenting or nonparenting, our choice of friends, our leisure activities, what we eat, how we heat our houses, and what religious beliefs we develop, to name but a few. In addition to our actions, we may feel responsible for our inactions, our tacit participation in events across the globe, and our decisions that may affect future generations in profound ways. The sad fact, however, is that we may be suffering from an excess of possibilities and have found that too much freedom and too many choices can be just as entrapping as too few (Fromm, 1941; May, 1969). We are overburdened with options. We can construct ourselves nearly any way we wish, and we are free to pursue any number of hobbies or lifestyles, but the responsibility and necessity for self-justifications inherent in those choices can be crippling.

Catch-22

Why do we feel that we are forced to *be* responsible but that we cannot *take* it? The answers involve yet another twist in the paradoxes of choice and responsibility—that we are at the same time powerful and powerless.

Response-Ability

Responsibility, sensibly defined, implies more than authorship or recognition of limitations. It also implies that one has the power to choose at least one other alternative. The paradox of responsibility assumption in our era, however, is that it is not consistently accompanied by real abilities to make a difference. We are held responsible for world events that we, as individuals, may have little ability to change. Even if we *wanted* to "take" responsibility, to get involved and fight for one cause or another, we would quite likely find that the requisite power seldom is associated with our responsibility.

Power and Technology

At the same time that we acknowledge responsibility for the things we have little ability to affect, we are surrounded by evidence of the power of the human race. Humankind may have the power to (relatively effortlessly) control the temperature of homes, but it is a member of this same species who feels powerless to face the electric company regarding an error in the bill or an increase in the rates. We enjoy the miracle of private transportation, but many of us are helpless if our cars stall on the road. As a world superpower, the United States must face a growing dependency on smaller countries which, by virtue of their natural resources, have the capacity to severely impair our industries.

Just as the individual is feeling powerless and plagued by self doubts about his own decisions, he is, at the same time, assured that modern man can do anything

... Our curious predicament is that the same processes which make modern man so powerful—the magnificent development of atomic and other kinds of technical energy—are the very processes which render us powerless. (May, 1969, pp. 183–184)

Technology, then, in the growing set of responsibility paradoxes, is a two-edged sword. Not only does it provide us with the power to effect great changes, but it often robs the individual of the self-sufficiency necessary to undertake the changes. Once again, the individual is saddled with distressing responsibilities over which he or she often has little power.

Power and Numbers

While the individual is urged to accept responsibility that he or she may not truly be able to take, it is equally disastrous for the individual to avoid that dilemma by giving up. Zbinden (1970, p. 25) sums up the difficulty this way:

The ubiquity of the masses ... the constant presence and pressure of large numbers, ... makes it more difficult for the individual to have confidence in the power of personal values and choices. He sees himself faced with huge anonymous organizations, national and international complexes, structures with an impersonal bureaucracy, and above all, with the steadily growing power of the state. He loses the courage to act on his own. Instead of undertaking responsible action himself, he leaves it to the collective authorities, which oust and usurp the authority of the individual conscience.

Frequently people see themselves as smaller than life, as a cog in a machine, as a nameless/faceless number, as a statistic, as a blind consumer, as a set of demographics, or as a passive recipient of the constant barrage of media input that renders them paralyzed (Mander, 1978). Consider, for example, the woman who was unable to exercise her choice to turn off her television. She became so enthralled with the machine that she actually ended up shooting it in order to free herself from its clutches (Krasner, 1977). When asked "What does your T.V. teach you?," she replied, "The purpose of life is for machines to tell people what to do . . ." (p. 56).

While the act of shooting one's television is an extreme attempt to reassert personal power, and mass media are not the only power-eroding institution, the point becomes clear. Now, perhaps more than ever, our lives can be programmed. Easily and painlessly, we can give up our power of self-determination to the collective external powers. People who cannot use their freedom of self-determination, even at the opportunity of planning an evening at home without the comforting company and decision-making of a television, have become frighteningly prevalent in our society. People who wish to lay claim to their freedom of choice and self-determination will find themselves first battling their tendency to shirk the burdens of choice. Even if they are successful in finding this powerful freedom on the individual scale, they may find themselves powerless to have any real impact on the larger decision-makers of our society. What is one voice to the legislature, the oil companies, the utilities, or the automobile industry? As a species, we are capable of more self-determination than ever before, yet the powers of the individual to influence the decisions of society, a community, a neighborhood, or even a household are smaller than ever. There is more and more responsibility, but we have in many ways less power to meet the demands of increased freedom and responsibility. This is Catch-22.

The Masquerade Solution

Modern people experience the frustration of being given a large part in the middle of the stage, without being given the lines necessary to act out the part; moreover, they aren't told what the play is all about. They even have to decide this for themselves. There are more and more choices, yet many of the choices have no real meaning. Our deliberations are likely to occur among choices that are artificially expanded. It is wonderful that we have the choice of religious beliefs, but it is ridiculous to call picking one dishwashing detergent over another a matter of real choice. When we expend our energies making meaningless decisions, we allow ourselves to be lulled away from the more critical issues of life. And who are we to please with our choices? Is the audience made up of ourselves, the power companies, the factories for which we work, public opinion, or science? The choices are staggering, the responsibilities are sometimes overwhelming, and our power to meet the demands is, in many ways, smaller than ever. Caught in the crisis of freedom and responsibility, between choice and the erosion of power to make choices, it is no surprise that we are prone to latch onto the easily accessible solution of excuse-making.

Excuses in the Controversy

It is not our purpose to resolve the controversy of determinism and free will (as suggested earlier, this is an impossible task); rather, it is our aim to point out the continued ambivalence we have regarding the issue of freedom. Do we have free choice? Must we *really* accept the responsibility for everything? The extent of our ambivalence is made salient by the continued prevalence of the determinism–choice debate throughout history. At the core of this ambivalence, excuses have their place. Although we do not fully accept that we are determined, we also do not accept that we are free, for

> the full acceptance of responsibility for one's actions broadens the scope of guilt by diminishing escape hatches. With excuses the individual can rely on such alibis as "I didn't mean it," "It was an accident," "I couldn't help it," "I followed an irresistible impulse." (Yalom, 1980, p. 227)

Unable to land comfortably either on the side of determinism with its lack of freedom or on the side of choice with its legacy of responsibility and guilt, humankind continues to find its way in the midst of ambivalence. It is in this very ambivalence that excuses flourish. Excuses have the magical power, temporarily at least, to relax the distinction between things for which we may or may not be responsible. Excuses are one way of both recognizing and attempting to reconcile our ambivalence over having and taking responsibility.

The Scope of Ambivalence

Excuses involve more than our ambivalence over particular, discrete events in time. The full impact of excuse-making can be felt when we see that, at a fundamental level, we may deny our responsibility and excuse ourselves from virtually *everything*. In short, we "constitute the world in such a way that it appears independent of our construction" (Yalom, 1980, p. 222). How do we do this? We do it by denying our self-creating abilities. Becker (1973, p. 23) describes this constrained person in this way:

> He accepts the cultural programming that turns his nose wherever he is supposed to look. He uses all kinds of techniques, which we call "character defenses." He learns not to expose himself, not to stand out, he learns to imbed himself in otherpower, . . .

As Becker implies, a prevalent method of avoiding creative capacity and subsequent responsibility is through the appeal to a larger power. Fromm (1941) calls the process of excuse-making an "escape from freedom" and declares that authoritarianism is one such method of escape. In his view, authoritarianism is the "tendency to give up the independence of one's own individual self in order to acquire the strength which the individual self is lacking" (p. 161). In fact, the appeal of determinism (irrespective of its veracity) is precisely this: it takes our freedom and, with it, the burden of responsibility. The lack of acceptance of the determinism notion in the everyday practical world, however, leaves us with responsibility.

Getting off the Hook

Our society typically operates with the assumption that we are responsible for our behavior. Yet even when we are clutched in the throes of this dilemma, we are not helpless. We back against the wall only to find that the wall is a door opening to a secret avenue of escape and temporary respite from the onslaught. Even though we are "guilty," excuses give us amnesty.

While our existence often is confusing, we can continue to act, confident in the knowledge that we can return over and over to excuses as a temporary solution. In rare cases, such as physical or emotional illness, we may be excused from making an appearance. More frequent is the excuse designed for a particularly bad performance, and these occur at every level. We excuse ourselves and other people, and we even excuse institutions. Without the grace of excuses in our world, perhaps we would be too frightened to act at all. Once excused, we are able to try again.

REFERENCES

Becker, E. *The denial of death.* New York: Free Press, 1973.

Berofsky, B. (Ed.), *Freewill and determinism.* New York: Harper and Row, 1966.

Brehm, J. W. *A theory of psychological reactance.* New York: Academic Press, 1966.

Brehm, S. S., & Brehm, J. W. *Psychological reactance: A theory of freedom and control.* New York: Academic Press, 1981.

Franklin, R. L. *Freewill and determinism: A study of rival conceptions of man.* London: Routledge and Kegan Paul, 1968.

Freud, S. A general introduction to psychoanalysis. In R. M. Hutchins (Ed.), *Great books of the western world* (Vol. 54). Chicago: Encyclopedia Britannica, 1952.

Fromm, E. *Escape from freedom.* New York: Holt, Rinehart & Winston, 1941.

Kafka, F. *The trial.* New York: Knopf, 1937.

Kemeny, J. G. *A philosopher looks at science.* Princeton, N.J.: Van Nostrand, 1959.

Krasner, P. Hypnotic age regression of a television addict. *Coevolution Quarterly,* 1977, **16,** 53.

Lachalier, J. *Psychologie et metaphysique.* Presse: Universitaire de France, 1949.

Mander, J. *Four arguments for the elimination of television.* West Caldwell, N.J.: William Morrow, 1978.

Maslow, A. H. *Toward a psychology of being.* New York: Van Nostrand-Reinhold, 1968.

May, R. *Love and will.* New York: Dell, 1969.

McHale, J. Education for real. *World Academy of Art and Science Newsletter,* Transnational Forum, June 1966, p. 3.

McLuhan, M. *Understanding media: The extensions of man.* New York: New American Library (published by permission of McGraw-Hill), 1964.

Menninger, K. *Whatever became of sin?* New York: Bantam Books (published by arrangement with Hawthorne), 1973.

Merton, R. K. *Social theory and social structure.* Glencoe, Ill.: Free Press, 1957.

Perls, F. *Gestalt therapy verbatim.* Lafayette, Calif.: Real People Press, 1969.

Rychlak, J. *Discovering free will and personal responsibility.* New York: Oxford, 1979.

Ryle, G. *The concept of mind.* New York: Barnes & Noble, 1949.

Ryle, G. *Dilemmas.* Cambridge: Cambridge University Press, 1980. (first published in 1954)

Sartre, J. *Being and nothingness.* (Translated by Hazel Barres.) New York: Philosophical Library, 1956.

Skinner, B. F. *About behaviorism.* New York: Vintage, 1974.

Tillich, P. *The courage to be.* New Haven, Conn.: Yale University Press, 1952.

Toffler, A. *Future shock.* New York: Bantam Books, 1970.

Yalom, I. D. *Existential psychotherapy.* New York: Basic Books, 1980.

Yankelovich, D. *New rules: Searching for self-fulfillment in a world turned upside down.* New York: Random House, 1981.

Zbinden, H. *Conscience.* Edited by The Curatorium of the C. G. Jung Institute, Zurich. (Translated by R. F. C. Hull and Ruth Horine.) Evanston, Ill.: Northwestern University Press, 1970.

CHAPTER 3

Theory of Excuses: Positive Images for Others and Self

The goal of this chapter is to familiarize the reader with the basic model of excuse-making. Before posing a definition of excuses, we suggest that people are motivated to maintain a positive image of themselves. Without this "good show" motivation, excuses would rarely visit our lives. Although our positive self-images are essential, they do not always lead tranquil existences. In the second section we explore those instances in which our positive self-image may be threatened because we are held responsible for some sort of negative activity. Under the threat of a "bad review," excuses come to life. In the third section we define and clarify how excuses help to lessen the "bad review" and thereby preserve one's positive self-image. Finally, we detail the various dimensions that characterize excuse-making.

A GOOD SHOW: POSITIVE IMAGES FOR THE AUDIENCE

All the world's a stage
And all the men and women are merely players.
WILLIAM SHAKESPEARE, *As You Like It*

All the world is not, of course, a stage,
but the crucial ways in which it isn't
are not easy to specify.
ERVING GOFFMAN, *The Presentation of Self in Everyday Life*

In this section we describe those oftentimes vain actors whose self-images take center stage.

Self-Images Defined

In the theater of the mind, images of oneself are played.* Like any theater, there are three basic components to the self-image—the actor (in this case, oneself), the performance (how one behaved in a particular situational setting), and the audience (a combination of others and oneself). The self-image is thus defined as an actor's mental picture of his or her performance in a particular situation before an audience. This definition of self-image as a private representation of oneself in delimited areas differs from previous, more encompassing definitions. For example, Miller, Galanter, and Pribram (1960) define the image as "all the accumulated, organized knowledge that the organism has about itself and its world" (p. 17). Self-image in the present context entails a cognitive encoding process in which a relatively large sequence of events involving one's performance *in a given situation* is condensed into a shortened form. Encoded self-images are similar to what the cognitive psychologists term "chunking" or "clustering," wherein a person stores complex and lengthy information in an abbreviated format (McCauley & Kellas, 1974; Melton & Martin, 1972; Neisser, 1967). Unlike the encoding of information in general, however, it should be emphasized that images, as defined in this book, consistently focus on one important and often fascinating object—*oneself.*

Self-images typically are formed along a few important identity continuums. While these undoubtedly vary across people, it is likely that such identity continuums as unintelligent–intelligent, incompetent–competent, unfriendly–friendly, and lazy–hard-working, among others, are fairly common. The principal identity continuums may facilitate the person's self-image-formation process in that they provide a structure for organizing, interpreting, and simplifying a complex set of information. Furthermore, the important identity continuums for a given person probably guide the formation of a self-image. In this vein, Markus (1977) demonstrated that individuals who had well-defined and important self-relevant identity continuums in their lives (what she called self-schemata) (1) were self-confident in predicting their future actions, (2) made decisions and judgments about themselves easily and quickly, and (3) were very resistant to changing their views about themselves on their self-relevant dimensions. Similar findings have been generated by other researchers (Mischel, 1973; Rogers, Rogers, & Kuiper, 1979; Turner, 1978).

In facilitating the self-image formation process, it is assumed that one or a

---

* This analogy between the theater and the mind is based on a more general analogy between the theater and life, a very old and generally accepted analogy. It is acknowledged by such major philosophers as Plato and Hobbes; moreover, it is highlighted in the writings of famous writers such as Shakespeare and Cervantes (Schlenker, 1980). For a full discussion of this theater–life analogy, the reader is directed to Brisset and Edgleys' *Life as Theater: A Dramaturgical Sourcebook* (1975), Burns' *Theatricality: A Study of Convention in the Theatre and in Social Life* (1973), Evreinoff's *The Theatre in Life* (1927), and Goffman's *The Presentation of Self in Everyday Life* (1959).

few identity continuums are especially important because they allow a person to maintain a positive image of himself or herself. A person may be resistant to changing his or her views on an important identity dimension because that dimension has repeatedly been associated with a positive self-image for the person. This is not meant to suggest, however, that a person's identity continuums and accompanying self-image may not at times be threatened. As we describe in detail throughout the rest of this book, our cherished positive self-images are periodically assaulted. Indeed, this latter phenomenon is the precursor to excuse-making.

The multitude of self-images that a person has about himself or herself on important identity continuums generates what various theorists have called the "self-concept." As Schlenker (1980, p. 95) put it, "One's self-concept and social identity are composed of numerous interrelated images of oneself; each image is discrete yet part of the whole." Just as self-images form a shorthand way of summarizing one's performance in particular situational contexts, the self-concept is an encapsulation and integration of many self-images. Throughout this book, therefore, we emphasize the role of self-images as the building blocks to a person's self-concept.

Good Review Motives

People generally seek a favorable review in the theater of the mind. Achieving and maintaining a positive self-image have been postulated as important motivational variables throughout the history of psychology. Although the terminology utilized by different theorists and researchers may vary, a common underlying idea is that people attempt to maximize their *self-esteem.* Stanley Coopersmith (1967) provided the following apt definition of self-esteem:

> By self-esteem we refer to the evaluation the individual makes and customarily maintains with regard to himself: it expresses an attitude of approval or disapproval, and indicates the extent to which the individual believes himself to be capable, significant, successful and worthy. In short, self-esteem is a *personal* judgment of worthiness that is expressed in the attitudes the individual holds toward himself. (pp. 4–5)

Thus self-esteem reflects the value judgment that a person makes about self-images in particular and the self-concept in general. Self-images and the larger self-concept thus provide the structural content and self-esteem determines the affective and cognitive value or flavor. Further, the motivation to maximize self-esteem biases the self-image and self-concept toward the positive or favorable perspective.

For many years the notion of the maintenance of self-esteem as a basic motivation has been the focus of personality and psychotherapy theorists, and in recent years this idea has captured the attention of social psychologists who emphasize attributions in their explanations of behavior. Since this book embraces both of these perspectives, it is appropriate at this point to briefly review the self-esteem literature.

Personality and Psychotherapy Self-Esteem Theorists

The proponents of the self-esteem motive could populate a *Who's Who* in psychology. William James provided early notions of the self-esteem motive in his *Principles of Psychology* (1890), where he posited that self-esteem maintenance was a "fundamental instinctive impulse" that manifests itself in our dress, possessions, behavior toward others, and so on. For James, a sense of self-esteem is achieved when one's perceived outcomes match or exceed one's perceived reality constraints.

Four noted psychodynamic theorists—Alfred Adler, Karen Horney, Harry Stack Sullivan, and Erich Fromm—all relied on self-esteem as a motivational variable. The most striking example of this emphasis is found in the work of Adler (1927; see also Ansbacher & Ansbacher, 1956), who believed that a feeling of inferiority often develops in a child and subsequently fuels the search for a sense of esteem and competence in the adult. In fact, one of the reasons Adler broke off from his mentor Freud in 1911 was his theoretical emphasis on the power of inferiority feelings in motivating behavior aimed at increasing self-esteem (Janis, Mahl, Kagan, & Holt, 1969). Horney (1945, 1950) saw the motivation toward and achievement of self-esteem as a means of providing an antidote for underlying feelings of anxiety. In a similar vein, Sullivan (1947, 1953) suggested that people maintain their sense of self-esteem in order to minimize the anxiety that may accompany interpersonal rejection or personal feeling of distress. What Sullivan called "security operations" served primarily as a means of bolstering a person's self-esteem. For Erich Fromm (1941, 1947), the person seeks a sense of self-esteem through social relationships that are characterized by mutual respect, acceptance, trust, and freedom of expression. Although Adler, Horney, Sullivan, and Fromm may differ somewhat in their particular versions of how self-esteem maintenance operates, they all emphasize the profound psychological difficulties that accompany a lack of self-esteem. For these four theorists, therefore, as self-esteem goes so goes psychological health.

Other personality theorists also integrated the self-esteem motive into their theories. Gordon Allport (1937), for example, asserted that the defense of the ego and the accompanying maintenance of self-esteem was "nature's oldest law" (p. 170). Allport believed that the need for self-esteem may be innate. Carl Rogers (1951) distinguished between the admiration that a person seeks from external audiences ("the need for positive regard") and the admiration for the internal audience of oneself ("self-regard"). Self-regard is seen as growing out of initial external audience concerns. Rogers conceptualized the self-esteem need as developing universally because of either genetic or environmental factors. Abraham Maslow (1968) provided yet another perspective on self-esteem needs. He posited that people initially respond to lower-order survival needs (e.g., food, water, shelter, physical protection) and later pursue higher needs, one of which is self-esteem (e.g., affection, self-esteem, and self-actualization).

Overall, the motivation to maximize self-esteem has been described by many past and present personality theorists and researchers (see Hall & Lindzey, 1978, for review). Similarly, recent theory on the formation of one's self-concept has emphasized the importance of the self-esteem maximization process (see Epstein, 1973; Wells & Marwell, 1976; Wylie, 1974, 1979). As support for this theory, personality researchers have consistently found that people are highly acceptant of self-esteem–enhancing (positively worded) psychological feedback (Collins, Dmitruk, & Ranney, 1977; Jones, 1973; Mosher, 1965; Snyder, 1978; Snyder & Shenkel, 1976; Snyder, Shenkel, & Lowery, 1977). Self-esteem enhancement also has been demonstrated in the social comparison of abilities, especially when the self-image is threatened (see Gruder, 1977; Wills, 1981); moreover, self-esteem maintenance has been linked to uniqueness-seeking needs of people (see Snyder & Fromkin, 1980).

Research indicates that given the constraints of a particular person's talents and the situation, that person will often attempt to claim an image that garners him or her maximal social approval and esteem in the eyes of an external audience (Jones, 1964; Jones & Wortman, 1973; Leary & Schlenker, 1981; Schlenker, 1975b, 1980). A related body of research suggests that after an initial unexpected success, people will reject their success if they are going to again have to perform in the same arena and it appears that they will do more poorly (see Aronson & Carlsmith, 1962; Mettee, 1971). This "taking a dive" phenomenon suggests that it is not just pure hedonism that motivates people, but it is the motivation to preserve one's self-image that is important. Finally, cognitive psychologists have begun to echo personality researchers' emphasis on self-esteem maintenance. For example, Ulric Neisser (1981) performed a fascinating analysis of John Dean's memory of his role in Watergate, concluding that Dean's testimony to the Senate Watergate Investigating Committee, compared to the subsequently published tapes, often reflected a distorted and enhanced positive self-image.

Social Psychological Attributional Theorists

Since the early 1970s there has been an explosion of social psychological research within the general framework of attribution approaches to self and interpersonal perception (see Harvey, Ickes, & Kidd, 1976, 1978, 1981; Harvey & Smith, 1977; Harvey & Weary, 1981). Attribution theories, at the most basic level, involve the process of trying to understand the causes of events (e.g., "Why did that happen?"). Attributions, then, consist of reasons that people have for their behaviors as well as the behaviors of others. Fritz Heider (1944,

1958) provided the intellectual spark that ignited the interest in attributional explanations of events. Throughout his work, Heider noted that attributions about events (especially as they pertain to oneself) may be influenced by a person's self-esteem needs. For example:

> It is obvious that the tendency to keep the ego level high must play a role in attribution. Since origins are assimilated to acts attributed to them, an act of low value, when attributed to the ego, will lower the ego level, and an act of high value will raise it. However, this will happen only when the stimulus conditions are so strong as to enforce the attribution, that is, if there can be no doubt that the own person is the source. Often, the possibility of different organization will exist. Then the tendency to raise the ego level will structure the causal limits in such a way that only good acts and not bad ones are attributed to the own person. (Heider, 1944, pp. 368–369)

Although Heider acknowledged the potential importance of the esteem motive in forming attributions, early researchers tended to emphasize more cognitive or information-processing types of attribution (e.g., Bem, 1972; Jones & Nisbett, 1972; Kelley, 1967). Within a context of controversy regarding the relative importance of esteem-motivated (what we will call "hot") attributions compared to cognitive (what we will call "cold") attributions (see Miller & Ross, 1975; Nisbett & Ross, 1980), the preponderance of evidence since the mid-1970s has been in favor of esteem-motivated attributions (for reviews see Arkin, Cooper, & Kolditz, 1980; Zuckerman, 1979).

Recent research provides strong and consistent support for the tendency to maintain self-esteem by internalizing credit for positive outcomes and externalizing blame for bad outcomes. In a review of 38 studies in which people worked on achievement tasks alone or in pairs, Zuckerman (1979) found that 27 studies (71%) showed people taking more responsibility for success than failure and only two studies (5.3%) showed the reverse pattern. Similar findings have been generated in group studies where people take more responsibility for a successful group's performance than an unsuccessful group's performance (Forsyth & Schlenker, 1977; Iso-Ahola, 1977; Schlenker, Soraci, & McCarthy, 1976).

Two studies are noteworthy on this topic because they were conducted as specific tests to rule out the esteem-motivated attributional explanation, and they were conducted by researchers (i.e., Miller & Ross, 1975) who had previously argued against the esteem-motivated model of attribution. In a study by Miller (1976), the research participants' performance (success vs. failure) and level of self-esteem involvement (low vs. high) were manipulated. People in the low self-esteem involvement condition were told they had worked on a new and untested measure; people in the high self-esteem involvement condition were told that they had worked on an established and valid measure of social perception. Further, people in the success condition were told that they had done well and people in the failure feedback condition were told that they had done poorly. In support of the esteem motivated explanation, high as compared to low self-esteem involvement people assumed *more* responsibility for their success performances and *less* responsibility for their failure performances. In a second study by Sicoly and Ross (1977), research participants were initially given failure or success feedback and then attributed their responsibility for their performance. Next they were asked to judge the accuracy of feedback given to them by a confederate who either gave them more or less responsibility than they had given themselves previously. The researchers assumed that research participants would rate confederate feedback as being more accurate when it served to maintain self-esteem. In support of the esteem-motivated explanation, research participants who were given more responsibility for failure and less responsibility for success rated the feedback as less accurate than research participants who were given less responsibility for failure and more responsibility for success. These two studies, plus those showing that the external attribution of failure and the internal attribution of success correlates with positive emotional states (e.g., Nicholls, 1975; Riemer, 1975; Weary, 1980), reveal that esteem is integrally involved in the attributional process.

It is best to turn again to Heider (in Harvey, Ickes, & Kidd, 1976, p. 16) for a summary of the "hot" attribution perspective: "One is inclined to attribute to oneself good things, but one suffers when one has to attribute to oneself something that is not good." A variety of labels have emerged to describe this phenomenon, including *attributional egotism* (Snyder, Stephan, & Rosenfield, 1978; Snyder & Wicklund, 1981), *egocentric attributions* (Ross & Sicoly, 1979; Schlenker & Miller, 1977), *ego-defensive attributions* (Miller, 1976), *self-serving attributional bias* (Bradley, 1978; Riess, Rosenfeld, Melburg, & Tedeschi, 1981; Weary, 1979), *subjective competence attributions* (Bowerman, 1978), and *beneffectance* (Greenwald, 1980). The last two concepts, subjective competence and beneffectance, suggest that perceptions of personal competence are inextricably bound up with the motive to maintain one's self-esteem. The idea that people seek to achieve a sense of competence and control in their lives has been a focus of nonattribution theory (see Bandura, 1973; White, 1959); moreover, recent attributional research tends to support this need (Bercheid, Graziano, Monson, & Dermer, 1976; Langer, 1975; Miller, Norman, & Wright, 1978; Wortman, 1976). Furthermore, it has been suggested that a sense of control or competence may contribute to an overall level of esteem (Schlenker, 1980, p. 90). As Miller and Norman (1975) note, "An effectance motive is but one of a number of manifestations of the pervasive need to view oneself 'positively.' " (p. 513). Finally, recent reinterpretations of the cognitive dissonance phenomenon imply that people attempt to reduce their perceived inconsistencies in the service of self-esteem maintenance (Aronson, 1969; Berkowitz, 1980).

In a wide spectrum of experimental settings involving many different activities performed by research participants, therefore, it appears that people are found to form attributions in a manner that *maintains* their sense of self-esteem. It should be emphasized, however, that the "maintenance" of self-esteem involves both the enhancement of esteem and the protection of esteem. Enhancement reflects those instances where we especially internalize credit for success. Relevant research shows that people who are given success as compared to neutral (or average) feedback tend to make internal attributions (e.g., Fitch, 1970; Kuiper, 1978; Schlenker et al., 1976; Wolosin, Sherman, & Till, 1973). Protection reflects those instances where we especially externalize responsibility for failure. Relevant research indicates that people who are given failure as compared to neutral (or average) feedback tend to make external attributions (e.g., Larson, 1977; Lefcourt, Hogg, Struthers, & Holmes, 1975; Schlenker, 1975a; Schlenker et al., 1976; Wolosin et al., 1973). Perhaps the role of attribution in the service of self-esteem is best summarized by William Saroyan (cited in Myers & Ridl, 1979, p. 89), who noted, "Every man is a good man in a bad world—as he himself knows."

Audience Issues: Positive Images for Whom?

The self-image as a mental picture of oneself is governed in part by audience issues. Although a self-image is generated by a person, that image may reflect that person's concerns of how (1) an *external* audience may react, (2) the *internal* audience of oneself may react, or (3) *both* external and internal audiences may react. It is necessary at this point to turn to a discussion of these audience issues in order to more clearly understand the process of image-information.

Playing to the Audience Without

A vivid example of a concern for the external audience comes in the comment of entertainer Sammy Davis, Jr.: "As soon as I go out of the door of my house in the morning, I'm on, Daddy, I'm on" (cited in Burns, 1973, p. 37). This sentiment is not a new one, however. In fact, the role of self-images for external audiences relates to a centuries-old notion that a person puts on a mask for the audience. Moreover, the derivation of the terms *person* and *personality* can be traced to the Latin *persona,* the mask that a character wears in a play. Different masks may thus appear for different audiences.

William James provided an early insight into this perspective. In 1890 (Vol. 1, p. 294) James wrote:

> A man has as many social selves as there are individuals who recognize him and carry an image of him in their mind ... But as the individuals who carry the images form naturally into classes, we may practically say that he has as many different social selves as there are distinct groups of persons about whose opinions he cares.

While the James quotation suggests that a person may adopt a chameleonlike multiple self, it also illustrates the more general fact that a person has a continuous concern for his or her image as others may perceive it.

Although the term impression management has rather Machiavellian connotations, perhaps in part through the popularity of such books as *One-Upmanship* (Potter, 1962), *Looking Out for Number One* (Ringer, 1977), and *The Selling of the President 1968* (McGinniss, 1970), it should be emphasized that some concern for one's self-image for an external audience is probably necessary for functioning effectively in interpersonal relations and society. In fact, this assertion formed the basis of Cooley's (1902/1922) and Meads' (1934) symbolic interaction perspective. Symbolic interaction stresses the necessity of "stepping into another person's shoes" and seeing oneself as others do. Other people become a "looking-glass" from which we may garner a reflected appraisal of ourselves. To borrow Cooley's (1902/1922) words, "As we see our face, figure and dress in the glass . . . so in imagination we see in another's mind some thought of our appearance, manners, aims, deeds, character, friends and so on, and are variously affected by it" (p. 184). The "looking-glass self" thus reflects our view of how others see and judge us. Overall, therefore, symbolic interactionism emphasizes the reflective capabilities of people, the existence of selves, the importance of social influences in the development of self and standards, and the ability of people to take the social perspective into account.

Along similar lines, it is noteworthy that several contemporary theories rely in part on an external audience appraisal mechanism that is consistent with the symbolic interactionism perspective. For example, in Buss' (1980) *public self consciousness* and Wicklund's (Duval & Wicklund, 1972; Wicklund, 1975) *objective self-awareness*, the individual becomes concerned with how he or she appears to others. Likewise, Alexander's (Alexander & Knight, 1971; Alexander & Lauderdale, 1977; Alexander & Sagatum, 1973) *situated identities*, and Biddle and Thomas' (1966; Thomas, 1968) *role* theories emphasize how situations in particular, or roles in general, elicit a sensitivity to how other people may perceive us.

Perhaps the most prominent proponent of impression management for an external audience has been Erving Goffman (1955, 1959, 1963, 1967). Goffman characterized social interactions as being very similar to a theatrical performance in which a person is concerned with acting out a "line" for the benefit of an audience. One goal of successfully acting out one's lines, and thereby maintaining "face," is to sustain a positive image of oneself; more important, by maintaining "face" Goffman suggests that social interaction can continue because others know what to expect of us. In regard to this latter point, Goffman believes that social interaction is predicated on the assumption that participants are concerned with how their peers may perceive them. This underlying premise has guided impression management theory in general, as well as impression management as it relates to excuselike behaviors in particular (see Jellison, 1977, on the process of "social justification").

Playing to the Audience Within

While symbolic interactionism emphasizes how people initially react to an external audience, it also suggests that a person internalizes the standards of external audiences. Over time, the developing child learns to anticipate how external audiences may react to his or her words and deeds. This phenomenon is obviously related to the socialization process. As such, the looking-glass self becomes a constant fixture in the theater of the mind. That is, we rarely are totally unconcerned with how others would judge us. Self-images may be for oneself, but our past experience with external audiences molds our self concerns.

The internalization of external audience guidelines is at the core of theory and research dealing with moral development. There are three general theoretical perspectives pertaining to moral development. First, there is Freud's (1927) well-known psychoanalytic system, involving the *id, ego*, and *superego*. The superego consists of the ego ideal (the person one would like to be) and the conscience (a censor to one's personality). Important early external audiences in a child's upbringing—teachers, siblings, and especially parents—have an impact in the formation of the internal superego audience. In this vein, Freud considered the introjection of parental authority to be a primary process in the development of the superego.

A second perspective on the internalization of external audiences involves cognitive theories of moral development. The two major proponents of this cognitive viewpoint are Jean Piaget and Lawrence Kohlberg. For Piaget (1926, 1932/1965), the developing child goes from a concrete to an abstract level of reasoning. In regard to moral development, the child initially is seen as undergoing the *heteronomous* stage in which rules are accepted because they come from external authorities; subsequently, the child undergoes the *autonomous* stage in which the external rules are internalized and yet subject to modification to fit a situation. Expanding on Piaget's two-stage theory, Kohlberg (1963, 1968) suggested that there are three general stages (preconventional, conventional, and postconventional) through which a child progresses. First, in the *preconventional* level the child is preoccupied with hedonistic self-gratification; next, in the *conventional* level, the child is preoccupied with maintaining the expectations of important external audiences; finally, in the *postconventional* level a person refines the general value of honoring human welfare (this value purportedly may be defined independently of societal influences).

The third perspective on the internalization of audiences is generated by the social learning theorists. Notable within this perspective is Albert Bandura, whose early work suggested that individuals would directly imitate (i.e., "copy") behavior that they had seen. Bandura (1977) more recently expanded the modeling concept to include *abstract* modeling, which consists of the observing person viewing another person's behavior and subsequently internalizing the behavior so that similar behaviors and attitudes may be elicited on the part of the observer. Over time, the child will supposedly develop a *self-censure* mechanism whereby the internalized moral principles serve to delimit his or her actions. The social learning position has also pointed out, however, that on occasion the self-censure mechanism is overridden by exonerative moral reasoning. In this case, the person finds justifications for his or her behavior (see Bandura, 1973).

Playing to the Audiences Without and Within: Revolving Images

The previous discussion suggests that we often are concerned with our self-image for an external audience. At the same time, it appears that developmental viewpoints all suggest that we internalize the external audience and consequently cultivate private internal concerns for our self-image. Whether the audience is a public external or a private internal one, however, it is likely that a similar esteem-maintenance motive is operative. Research on this topic reveals that people are prone to esteem-maintenance behaviors under public and private conditions. In one test of this issue, Riess et al. (1981) measured causal attributions for good or bad performances on a "social-intelligence test." In a private condition, people responded on a bogus pipeline "electromyograph" (see Jones & Sigall, 1971; Quigley-Fernandez & Tedeschi, 1978, for validity information on this approach) that was supposedly "capable of measuring the intensity and direction of people's true attitudes and feelings by detecting implicit muscle potentials and galvanic skin responses" (Riess et al., 1981, p. 227). (It was reasoned and corroborated by a manipulation check that people would respond with their private causal attributions on this lie-detectorlike bogus pipeline.) In a public condition, people merely responded with their causal attributions on the same apparatus, but no mention of its purported lie-detector capabilities was made. Results showed that the only effect was caused by performance feedback, such that people internalized success feedback and externalized failure feedback. This finding further corroborates the self-esteem–maintenance process described in the previous section, "Good Review Motives." What is especially relevant for the present discussion, however, is that people equally maintained this esteem under public and private conditions. In another study examining attributions after failure, Arkin, Appelman, and Burger (1980) found that public and private condition subjects both made image-protecting attributions, but this tendency was increased for the public as compared to private (bogus pipeline) condition. Likewise, Weary (1980) and Frey (1978) report that public relative to private conditions tend to intensify the esteem-maintenance pattern of attributions. Overall, these studies suggest that people are very concerned with maintaining a positive image for both the internal and external audiences, and that on occasion the self-presentational motives (see Baumeister, 1982; Weary & Arkin, 1981) aimed at the external audience may amplify the esteem-maintenance process.

Although it may be feasible to empirically disentangle those instances in which the audience concerns are internal or external, or to ascertain when the external audience may be predominant to the internal audience influences, and there may be individual differences such that a few people primarily attend to either the internal or external audience (Greenwald, 1982; Hogan, 1982), it nevertheless appears that most of us typically wish to maintain a positive self-image for the internal audience of ourself and the external audience of others. In fact, the instances in which *purely* external or internal audience concerns prevail may be relatively rare.

A more common state, and one that is a cordial bedfellow to the looking-glass self notion, is that a person is simultaneously concerned with external and internal audiences. This interaction of external and internal audiences is perhaps inevitable. Indeed, a careful analysis of the psychoanalytic roots of neurotic and moral anxiety reveals the interaction of internal and external audiences. Although neurotic and moral anxiety are typically viewed as being derived solely from internal concerns, both types of anxiety have to reflect both internal and external audience issues. For example, neurotic anxiety is defined as the conflict between instinctual desires (id) and reality constraints (ego); moreover, moral anxiety is defined as the conflict involving the id, the ego, and the idealized personal standards of the superego (Freud, 1927, 1965). The constraining factor in this model, the reality-oriented ego, is based on an internalization of external standards. Thus the neurotic and moral anxieties, which play a critical role in the generation of psychodynamic defense mechanisms, are actually manifestations of both internal and external audience concerns. Additionally, newer theories of personality that emphasize socialization needs, such as Hogan's (1982) socioanalytic theory, suggest that the individual is mindful of both internal and external audience reactions. In more recent attributional terms, Weary and Arkin (1981) reached a similar conclusion, "attributions that serve one's public presentation may affect, through the reactions of others (real or imagined), one's private self-evaluation. Conversely, one's self-image may influence one's strategic causal analyses" (pp. 242–243).

Consistent with the aforementioned logic, we propose that in everyday settings people usually are concerned with *revolving self-images.* As shown in Figure 3.1, a person's self-image "revolves" so as to appear to both the external and the internal audience. Of course, the self-image is not revolving in a technical sense, but in the moment by moment concern with one's image, the audience may quickly switch from the external to internal, and vice versa. To push the "revolving" self-images idea further, it may be the case that external and internal audiences alternate so quickly that the two audiences fuse. In this instance, the shaded area of the illustration represents a combination of self-images for both the external and internal audiences.

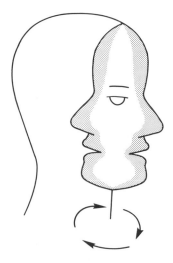

Figure 3.1.   Revolving images.

BAD REVIEWS: WHEN THE SELF-IMAGE IS THREATENED

Understanding excuse-making obviously involves more than assuming that people are motivated to maintain their positive self-images. This "good review" motive provides the underlying impetus for excuse-making, but it is the threat to the positive self-image that actually unleashes the excuse-making process. In this section we turn to a discussion of the issues that pertain to a threat to our positive image.

Actors and Their Performances: A Model

People are connected to their actions by a *responsibility linkage.* As such, the actor–responsibility link–performance chain represents the basis for a self-image that a person forms of himself or herself. When the performance is a poor one, and the person is seemingly responsible for that bad performance, the self-image is threatened. The elements of this sequence are illustrated in Figure 3.2. This diagram suggests at least two principal elements that contribute to a threatening self-image, the negative performance and the responsibility link. (Another element that contributes to a threatening self-image reflects the individual differences in the actor that may predispose him or her to a "bad review" and excuse-making. A detailed discussion of such individual difference factors is deferred to Chapter 6.) A negative performance represents any action or behavior on the part of a person that falls below the standards that have

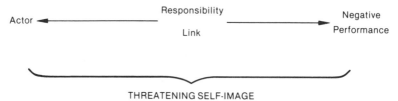

THREATENING SELF-IMAGE

Figure 3.2.   The threatening self-image.

been established as being typical for that person or people in general (see Snyder, 1972; Snyder & Katahn, 1970, 1973; Suls & Miller, 1977; Thibaut & Kelly, 1959). The responsibility linkage represents information indicating that a person is accountable for a particular bad performance. In the aforementioned discussion of a bad performance and responsibility, it is important to note that occurrences that have nothing to do with the actor's behavior may occasionally contribute to the bad performance. For example, the reputation, status, or deeds of ancestors (e.g., the actor was born a "bastard" or a member of a low social class) or one's physical characteristics (e.g., features) may be considered to fit the general definition of a negative performance. Even though these events or features are not caused by the person's own actions, the actor may be held responsible. Overall, the more negative the performance, and the more obviously an actor is linked to that bad performance, the greater should be the threat to a person's self-image. Issues pertinent to the impact of a bad performance and the responsibility connection related to that bad performance are addressed at this point.

Bad Performance Issues

In this section we briefly explore factors that influence the negativeness of the bad performance.

Clarity of Standard

The clearer the standard for a particular performance, in terms of either societally or personally determined guidelines, the more that a potential performance may be perceived as concretely falling below the standard (Jellison, 1977). Greater negativity of performance is therefore probable under conditions of clear standards. Increasingly poorer performances occur when the actor generates a performance that falls further below the clearly established standards.

Intentionality

In the degree to which an actor purposefully engages in an activity that has a bad outcome, that performance is seen as more negative. Research related to this point suggests that an intended negative action is viewed more negatively than an unintended one (Riordan, 1982; Rotenberg, 1980). This intentionality dimension is, not surprisingly, also given considerable weight in criminal law where crimes committed "on purpose" are viewed very negatively (Darley & Zanna, 1982). A first related issue is that consistently bad performances are seen as more negative, perhaps in part because the perpetrator intended to repeat the ill deed. A second related issue is that performances that do not attain the moral standards held by a person or by society may be seen as worse than performances that are merely seen as incompetent or ineffective (Jones, 1981); thus incompetence or lack of effectiveness may be unintentional, whereas moral transgressions are not. A third related issue pertains to the foreseeability of the negative action. If the actor could not reasonably be expected to anticipate the negative outcome, then the "bad" performance is viewed less severely (Shaw, 1968; Shaw & Reitan, 1969; Shaw & Sulzer, 1964; Sulzer & Burglass, 1968). Within the legal profession, this foreseeability issue is central to the issue of negligence (Darley & Zanna, 1982). Obviously, "accidents" are pertinent to the foreseeability issue.

Harming Others versus Self

Another rule of thumb is that perpetrating physical harm to another person is generally seen as worse than harming oneself; moreover, the same principle generally applies to inflicting psychological harm.

Actuarial Rarity

The worse a particular activity, the less it may be perceived as occurring in the general population. Related research suggests that people perceive increasingly negative feedback as being less applicable to the population in general (Snyder & Shenkel, 1976).

Importance of Part

Another general defining characteristic of a bad performance relates to how important the particular activity may be to a person's overall self-concept. Feedback on activities that reflect important self-relevant identity continuums for a person (see Markus, 1977, on self-schemata) should be emotionally charged for that person. If a particular performance seemingly contradicts an important self-image that a person may hold of himself or herself, the performance is phenomenologically experienced as being negative and distressing (Aronson, 1968; Carson, 1969; Walster, Walster, & Bercheid, 1978). A related point is inherent in Festinger's (1957) original theorization about cognitive dissonance, wherein he suggested that dissonance should be aroused especially in those areas involving important cognitions in a person's life. Recent writings on dissonance assert that this aroused state should result primarily in those domains where a person feels ego-involved (Greenwald & Ronis, 1978; Wicklund & Brehm, 1976). For example, a psychology professor should be primed to accentuate the severity of an editorial review of his latest book but may not exhibit such sensitivity to his colleagues' disparaging comments about his dress.

Similarly, activities that represent "running engagements" in which a person will continue to have an investment in the same activity (e.g., our psychologist writing books or an actress who has just received feedback on her first-night performance of a potentially long-running play) should enhance the perceived importance and thus the threat inherent in a "part."

Power of the Critic

One factor that may intensify the threat of negative feedback is the perceived expertness of the critic. For example, Aronson, Turner, and Carlsmith (1963) demonstrated that a highly expert source may influence attitude change more than a source that has low expertise. Similarly, Halperin, Snyder, Shenkel, and Houston (1976) report that negative personal feedback is accepted more readily when it is from a high status source, and Snyder and Newburg (1981) found that negative feedback is better remembered when it is delivered by a high as compared to low status source. A second factor related to the power of a critic pertains to the feedback recipient's perceived similarity to the critic. Persuasion research suggests that feedback from a "critic" with whom we perceive some similarity results in accommodation of the feedback (Bercheid, 1966; Bettinghous, 1968). Finally, the greater the number of the critics, and the more unanimity that they share, the more pervasive should be the subsequent conformity behavior (Allen, 1965; Asch, 1956, 1963; Kiesler & Kiesler, 1969). Overall, therefore, one inference from the aforementioned literature is that the factors that enhance acceptance of feedback, persuasion, and conformity may also intensify the negativity and associated threat of a "bad" performance.

The Responsibility Connection

A bad review entails more than a bad performance per se. Another necessary component of a bad review is that the person (actor) is perceived as being responsible for the bad performance (Tedeschi & Riess, 1981). The attributional theory of the social psychologist Harold Kelley provides a useful framework for understanding the responsibility link. Kelley's theory is variously known as a covariance or an analysis of variance model in that it emphasizes the causes that appear to vary with an effect over time. If one of several causes appears to fluctuate with a particular effect, it is inferred that the effect should be attributed to the particular cause. Kelley (1967, 1971, 1973) expanded on Heider's notions of dispositional (person) or situational causes of behavior by suggesting that three kinds of information (consensus, consistency, and distinctiveness) are relevant in forming attributions about people. Each of these kinds of information may facilitate a person being held responsible for a particular activity (in the present context, a bad performance). In the subsequent presentation, Kelley's theoretical ideas regarding consensus, consistency, and distinctiveness apply to the attributional responsibility for bad performances assigned both to others and to oneself (see Harvey & Smith, 1977; Stevens & Jones, 1976).

Consensus

One type of information is consensus, or the extent to which others in the same performance situation as the person (actor) would behave, or have behaved, similarly (Kelley, 1967). The *lower* the consensus, the greater is the degree to which an actor is held responsible for a bad performance. For example, a baseball player who strikes out three times in a row is viewed as being more responsible for his poor batting performance when his teammates have gotten base hits rather than striking out also.

Consistency

A second type of information is *consistency,* which reflects how the person (actor) is seen as behaving in the same performance situation over time (Kelley, 1967). The *higher* the consistency, the greater is the degree to which an actor is held responsible for a bad performance. Consider again our baseball player. If he has been striking out for several games rather than in just one game, he will be viewed as being especially responsible for his bad batting performance.

Distinctiveness

A third type of information is *distinctiveness,* which represents how the person (actor) behaves in other performance situations (Kelley, 1967). The *lower* the distinctiveness, the greater is the degree to which an actor is held responsible for a bad performance. In the case of the batter who has been striking out frequently, if he has also been doing poorly in his handball and tennis games, he may be seen as the source of his poor performances (thereby not only being a bad baseball batter, but a poor athlete).

The most extreme case would occur when all these types of information converge to provide the maximal responsibility link to a bad performance. In this case of low consensus, high consistency, and low distinctiveness, the actor may be linked strongly to his or her bad performances. Research exploring the aforementioned "responsibility" attributions (i.e., to the person) generally supports the predictions when all three types of information are available (Major, 1980, McArthur, 1972; Orvis, Cunningham, & Kelley, 1975; Ruble & Feldman, 1976). Additionally, when all three types of information are not available (e.g., only consensus, and not consistency and distinctiveness information), people nevertheless appear to make the attributions that would be predicted if all three types of information were available (Kulik & Taylor, 1980; Major, 1980; Orvis et al., 1975; Wells & Harvey, 1977). In fact, Kelley (1972) suggested that people may employ *causal schemas* in those more typical daily instances where all three types of information (consensus, consistency, and distinctiveness) are not available. A causal schema is conceptualized as a "shorthand" method of assigning responsibility. Thus because of previous experience and knowledge of causes of behavior, people may assign responsibility for a bad performance without garnering the complete attributional contributing information.

One other theory is also worthy of mention because it suggests that responsibility for an action may be differentially linked to an actor depending on the circumstances. Jones and Davis (1965) introduced the concepts of category- and target-based expectancies. Category-based expectancies are similar to Kelley's consensus information in that we purportedly attribute greater responsibility to the actor who is doing something different from his or her membership group of peers; target-based expectancies are similar to Kelley's consistency information in that we attribute greater responsibility to the actor who has performed the same action over time. (It is interesting to note that Jones and his colleagues [e.g., Jones & McGillis, 1976] also suggested similarities between the original category- and target-based expectancy model and Kelley's model.)

The Responsibility–Bad Performance Interaction

Theoretically, the responsibility connection and bad performance factors should be interrelated. In other words, the worse the performance, the more likely that the actor should be held accountable by society for that performance. Consistent with this general proposition, research indicates that people who engage in activities that have increasingly more negative impact on others are seen by observers as having more responsibility for their actions. In a review of this general question, Burger (1981) concluded that the overall results of 22 relevant studies reliably support the responsibility–negative performance relationship. These results are consistent with Kelley's (1972) proposal that people may make attributions of others so as to maintain a sense of control in the environment. Thus the observer may serve as the "watchdog" of society by forming stronger attributions of responsibility as people engage in progressively more negative actions.

Research findings suggest that there are three qualifying points that must be considered in order to understand the general relationship between responsibility and negative performance described in the preceding paragraph. Each of these qualifications suggests circumstances in which an *observer* will not hold an actor more responsible for more negative actions. First, it appears that the observer must perceive the actor as being free *not* to behave in the particular negative fashion (Harvey, Harris, & Barnes, 1975; Kruglanski & Cohen, 1973). Without freedom, the actor's behavior may be perceived as (1) the same as anyone in the same situation (high consensus); (2) different from how she or he normally would behave in that situation (low consistency), and (3) different from how she or he would behave in different situations (high distinctiveness). In legal terms, the more the actor is seen as performing under *duress,* the less he or she is held as being responsible. Second, the observer evidently must see the actor as being different psychologically or behaviorally from the observer (Burger, 1981; Chaikin & Darley, 1973; McKillip & Posavac, 1972, 1975; Shaver, 1970). When the observer feels similar to the actor, then the actor's behavior may be seen as the same as anyone (including the observer) in the same situation (high consensus). Third, the observer should not be psychologically involved in the situation (Burger, 1981; Chaikin & Darley, 1973; Shaver, 1970; Walster, 1966). When the observer becomes psychologically involved and seemingly identifies with the actor in the situation, then the actor's behavior may be seen as the same as anyone (including the observer) in the same situation (high consensus).

In the previous examples, it is important to note that the very factors that serve to diminish or increase an actor's responsibility for more negative acts (i.e., the actor's lack of freedom, actor–observer similarity, and an observer's identification with the actor's situation) can be easily translated into consensus, consistency, and distinctiveness notions. Just as the consensus, consistency, and distinctiveness variables may define the interactive nature of the responsibility linkage and the bad performance that is so threatening to a person's image (see Shaw & Reitan, 1969; Shaw & Tremble, 1971), these variables also serve the potential excuse-making actor. Once the threat to the image has occurred, the masquerade of excuses is close behind. Thus the probability of a person making an excuse should be positively related to the negativity of the performance and one's responsibility for that performance.

MAINTAINING SELF-IMAGES: THE "ROLE" OF EXCUSES

Definition and Expanded Model

Excuses are explanations or actions that lessen the negative implications of an actor's performance, thereby maintaining a positive image for oneself and others.*

---

* On occasion an actor's performance may be sufficiently negative that society will impose sanctions (e.g., a fine, prison sentence, loss of job). When such dire consequences may be associated with a bad performance, the actor should especially aim his or her excuse at the appropriate external audience. In such circumstances, though, the actor is not concerned *solely* with the external audience. In fact, even in the face of punishment, actors may in part respond with excuses aimed at the internal audience of oneself. Whether the audience is primarily external or internal, however, the basic principle of excuse-making is the same— *maintain one's positive image.* Further, it should be noted that negative performances in which there are dire consequences are actuarially uncommon. For most of us, our negative performances are probably best described as being in the "moderate" range. Although we deal with excuses related to such moderate negative performances through most of this book, it is the case that the present model also applies to excuses made for extremely negative performances (see also discussion of "Excuses and the Law" in this chapter).

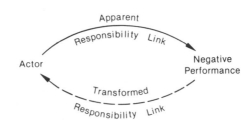

THREATENING SELF-IMAGE

Figure 3.3.   The components of the excuse-making model.

To understand excuses, it is appropriate at this point to look at the expanded diagram of the excuse-making model (see Figure 3.3). This model contains three components—the apparent responsibility link, the negative (or bad) performance, and the transformed responsibility link—that influence the actors' self-image. The responsibility link described in the previous section on "bad reviews" actually consists of both an apparent and a transformed responsibility link. The *apparent* responsibility link represents the initial information that connects the actor with a bad performance, and the *transformed* responsibility link represents subsequent information that may modify the extent to which an actor is perceived as being accountable for a bad performance. Additionally, the apparent responsibility link typically reflects physical "evidence" that connects an actor with a negative performance, whereas transformed responsibility usually reflects psychological evidence that corroborates or refutes the physical evidence. As such, apparent responsibility may be equated with a person's causality contribution to a bad performance. Interestingly, the derivation of the word *excuse* appears to be related to the apparent responsibility notion. *Excuse* comes from *ex* (from) and *causa* (cause), and an excuse indeed does lessen the actor's causal responsibility for a bad performance. In an "intuitive lawyering" (see Hamilton, 1980) or a "man as lawyer" (see Fincham & Jaspars, 1980) sense, the apparent responsibility link establishes whether the actor actually engaged in the nefarious deed. Thus apparent responsibility encompasses the necessary conditions that must exist before any further assignment of responsibility can be pursued (D'Arcy [1963] calls these qualifying circumstances). Once the apparent responsibility issue is resolved (e.g., the actor admits to having "done it"), the transformed responsibility excuse tactics may be activated. The transformed responsibility excuses seek to lessen the sense of condemnation for a particular "bad" performance; other writers have advocated similar concepts, labeling them as accounts (Schlenker, 1980), quantifying circumstances (D'Arcy, 1963), sanctions (Hamilton, 1980), or social justifications (Jellison, 1977).

While excuse-making obviously may occur in the context of the transformed responsibility link, it is also the case that excuse-making may occur in the apparent responsibility component and the bad performance component. In fact, excuse-making episodes often relate to at least two and sometimes all three of the components. For example, consider a 10-year old boy named Spencer who just received a BB gun for his birthday. Spencer goes "hunting" with his friends, and he shoots a dog. When confronted with this bad performance, he pleads, "I didn't do it," thus invoking an excuse aimed at lessening the apparent responsibility link. When his dad breaks through this excuse by telling Spencer that he saw him do it, Spencer then argues, "It wasn't so bad because I only shot a dog." This ploy involves an attempt to lessen the badness of the performance. When his dad tells him that animals are living beings like people and shouldn't be shot, Spencer tries a third excuse as he asserts, "But everyone else was shooting at the dog too, and I thought it was OK." This excuse is aimed at lessening the transformed responsibility for Spencer's dog shooting performance.

Lessening Apparent Responsibility ("I didn't do it")

The first component of this excuse-making model is comprised of strategies for lessening the apparent responsibility. Since actors are held especially accountable for actions that they are directly perceived as having produced (see Shaw & Sulzer, 1964; Turner, 1968), a fundamental tactic for preserving one's self-image is to break the apparent responsibility link between oneself and a bad performance.

Innocence

In legalistic jargon, the actor attempts to demonstrate his or her innocence of the "charge," or the bad performance (see Fitzgerald, 1962, and Hart, 1968, for discussions of innocence and denial of allegation in the legal system). Perhaps an alibi may be employed to prove that the actor was not even physically present at the bad performance situation. Or if the actor was obviously physically present at a bad performance, it may be argued that he or she was not the one who actually performed the ill deed (e.g., "just an innocent bystander"). This innocence tactic is similar to denial.

Blaming

Often the issue may not be that a person was the sole physical agent responsible for a bad performance, but rather that the actor was partially responsible for the performance (whether or not he or she actually perpetrated the act). If there is some possibility of establishing one's lack of responsibility for a particular predicament, this excuse tactic may be solidified by identifying something external to blame. Following failure, the blame may fall on external objects (e.g., Bowerman, 1981) or people (e.g., Ryan, 1972; Schlenker & Miller, 1977).

In some instances, however, it is difficult to defuse the apparent responsibility link because it may be nearly impossible to refute the fact that one engaged in the negative performance. Thus although defenses of innocence are appealing because of their simplicity and their power to absolve a person from responsibility, seldom can they be employed with total success. The subsequently described excuse-making strategies are called upon much more frequently.

Reframing Performances ("It's really not so bad")

A second component to the present excuse-making model is made up of excuse strategies that entail attempts on the part of the actor to lessen the perceived negativity of the "bad" performance by engaging in redefinition strategies.

See No Evil, Hear No Evil

A first type of reframing ploy involves strategies suggesting that the actor doesn't comprehend the potential badness of an action. This strategy can be accomplished in several ways. In research on helping, for example, it was found that the nonhelping actor may "see" no real need to render aid (e.g., Latané & Darley, 1970; Latané & Rodin, 1969). Or the actor may perceptually distort (lessen) the negativity of his actions. As a case in point, research participants in a study by Brock and Buss (1962) shocked a confederate but later reported that the shocks weren't actually painful. Schlenker (1980, p. 144) provides other relevant examples, such as "a student who cheats explains that it didn't affect anyone else's grade; a child points out that the broken lamp was old and needed replacement anyway; . . . a businessman describes an embarrassing faux pas as a minor flub not worthy of comment." (Recall how the Nixon administration in the early stages of Watergate dismissed the whole event as a mere "third-rate burglary.")

In another ploy, the actor may contend that the object (victim) involved in his or her bad performance is rather unimportant. Sykes and Matza (1957) provided early evidence of this general condemning the victim phenomenon among juvenile delinquents, and in subsequent years Lerner (1970, 1980) documented the derogation of victim process among a variety of populations. Again, Schlenker (1980, p. 144) captures the essence of this logic:

> It might be explained that the victim was only a Nazi, criminal, communist, prostitute, Black, Jew, or whatever. Each society and subgroup within a society usually has a list of the types of people who can be "justifiably" mistreated because they are supposed to be inferior, unworthy, potentially dangerous, unimportant, or simply not the kind of people that "decent" citizens should be concerned about (Scott & Lyman, 1968). Thus, it is argued that the event emerges as being less negative in its consequences.

Manipulating Standards for "Bad" Performance

A second type of reframing reflects attempts by the actor to change the standards so as to yield a more positive personal image. Here the actor may attack the clarity of the standards, or argue that "expectations were set too high." A related version of the latter ploy is to customize the standards to fit one's performances. Or the actor may acknowledge that the performance appears to be a bad one, but that it really should be seen as one relatively minor negative event in the context of a much larger positive set of goals or activities. This type of thinking has been called *embedding* (Jellison, 1977) or *exonerative moral reasoning,* and examples unfortunately abound. Wrightsman and Deaux (1981, p. 220) write:

> Executioners in Nazi Germany did not believe that they were doing anything morally wrong; instead, they justified their crimes by claiming service to a higher moral good, in this case the Aryan culture. Parents who severely beat their children often use a similar exonerative strategy—they were not trying to hurt the child, but it was for the child's own good. In one case in Indianapolis in 1978, the worthy goal was allegedly to teach the child to spell *butterfly,* but the child's death cut the lesson short.

Derogating the Sources of Negative Feedback

A third type of reframing involves maneuvers aimed at discrediting the veracity of the sources of negative feedback. For example, research has consistently shown that after negative feedback, people will derogate the testing instrument (e.g., Clair & Snyder, 1979; Snyder & Clair, 1976; Snyder & Shenkel, 1976) and the other people involved in the situation (Aronson & Worchel, 1966; Mettee & Aronson, 1974).

Lessening Transformed Responsibility ("Yes, but . . .")

If the apparent responsibility link is clearly established (the actor definitely did it) and the performance is clearly seen as bad (it definitely does not meet the actor's, and to an extent society's standards), then the actor should invoke a variety of excuse-making maneuvers to transform his or her responsibility to a lower level. Thus although excuses aimed at the transformed responsibility link may never totally disentangle the actor from a bad performance, they do diminish the threat to one's image. In this vein, the philosopher J. L. Austin (1961/1970) writes, "Few excuses get us out of it completely: the average excuse, in a poor situation, gets us only out of the fire into the frying pan—but still, of course, any frying pan in a fire" (p. 177).

Consensus Raising

A first means of lessening the transformed responsibility for a bad performance is to engage in consensus-raising excuses. As noted in the previous discussion of

Kelley's consensus concept, a person is held more responsible for his or her actions when the consensus is *low*. Thus one means of lessening the transformed responsibility is to generate excuses that would suggest that anyone in the same situation would also perform as poorly as did the actor. There are several excuse strategies that may be employed to argue for this high consensus state of affairs. The plea that "everyone else was doing it" has been applied to a variety of negative performances, and as such it may have become a standard phrase in the excuse repertoire of most teenagers. If most everyone is doing "it" (whatever "it" may be), the inherent logic is that the particular perpetrator of the act (i.e., the one who asserts that "he or she was the only one caught") should be seen as less responsible.

Yet another version of this type of consensus excuse is the "most people do even worse than I did" ploy (this process is similar to what Jellison [1977] calls contrasting). The idea here is to suggest that anyone would do poorly in a given situation, and probably many people would perform *even* more poorly than did the actor. It is also often argued in this type of excuse that a negative performance which is actuarially frequent should not be viewed negatively. This rationale is consistent with research suggesting that the negativity of feedback about oneself is correlated with the perception that the feedback is seen as being relatively uncommon for most other people (see Snyder & Shenkel, 1976). Not surprisingly, therefore, research generally reveals that people who are given negative feedback tend to invoke the justification that "everyone else is doing it" (this is similar to such concepts as "defensive projection"—see Bramel, 1963; Holmes, 1978; Steiner, 1968; or "attributive projection"—see Holmes, 1981; Sherwood, 1981).

Consensus raising is also inherent in excuses based on the "merely following orders" or coercion rationale. In this type of excuse, the actor argues that he or she had no choice but to go along with another person's (often a "superior") commands to behave in a certain way. Within the legal context, such excuse tactics would fall within the law of agency, which deals with a superior's responsibility for a subordinate's actions. Implicitly, this transformed responsibility interpretation implies that anyone in the same circumstances also would have "followed orders" and in this sense the consensus is raised. If a performance is particularly bad, research has shown that actors will say they had little choice and were forced to behave in a particular negative manner (Brock & Buss, 1962, 1964). Whenever the actor can externalize the blame for a bad performance, therefore, some degree of consensus raising is probably an integral part of the excuse. This externalization process is also inherent in appeals, after failure, to the difficulty of the task or luck. Task difficulty and luck are popular tactics after failure (see Zuckerman, 1979, for review); by invoking these consensus-raising external factors, the excuse-making actor is suggesting that these factors would cause most everyone to fail also.

Consistency Lowering

A second means of lessening the transformed responsibility for a bad performance is to engage in *consistency-lowering excuses*. If a bad performance is seen as being consistently poor over time, then the actor will be held maximally responsible. Thus the transformed responsibility connection may be weakened by excuse ploys suggesting that the one bad performance is highly inconsistent from the actor's usual performances. In other words, the actor may assert that he or she had an "off night" and thus should not be held accountable for a highly unusual event. (This excuse is particularly seductive in that we all may have had an "off night," and the excuse-maker may play on our sympathy.) Recent theory and research support the idea that people may at times employ inconsistent self-presentations in order to divest themselves of the responsibility associated with their potential bad performances. For example, one theory suggests that people seek a sense of *attribute ambiguity* and thereby at times may behave inconsistently so they will have several potential reasons for their behavior (Snyder & Wicklund, 1981). Given a bad performance, the actor can take advantage of this "ambiguity" to achieve the most benign sense of transformed responsibility. A similar underlying excuse mechanism is inherent in *self-handicapping* theory, which suggests that people may adopt a self-label that promotes inconsistency-related excuses (Jones & Berglas, 1978; Snyder & Smith, 1982). For example, the person with a "drinking problem" (the handicap) may be expected to engage in occasional (i.e., inconsistent) bad performances without being held totally responsible.

Other consistency-lowering tactics may involve lowered effort. In other words, after (or before) a "failure," the actor may announce that he or she "Didn't really try" (i.e., the person implicitly suggests that on other occasions in the same setting, he or she has, or could, perform much better when exerting full effort). Research supports the existence of this reduced effort excuse (Miller, 1976). Additionally, the excuse-maker may employ the intentionality concept to buttress the consistency-lowering process. That is, the actor may assert that he or she did *not* intend for the bad performance to occur, but that unforeseen consequences developed (see Schlenker, 1980, p. 41). (As noted previously, the legal system also gives a good deal of weight to intentions in determining the guilt of the accused person.)

Distinctiveness Raising

A third means of lessening the transformed responsibility for the bad performance is to engage in distinctiveness-raising excuses. Here the task for excuse-makers is to demonstrate that they may have had a poor performance in a particular situation, but in most other different situations or roles they perform well. In other words, the excuse-maker seeks to split the person who may have performed poorly in a particular situation from the "real" person who does well in a variety of other situations. Goffman (1971) describes this splitting process as forming the basis for most *apologies* in that the "good" self is separated from the "bad" self that participated in the poor performance. Further, it may not be unusual to hear such a person close this particular apology by asserting, "I promise, give me another chance and I'll show you the real me!"

Many of the aforementioned excuses aimed at the transformed responsibility connection actually may simultaneously raise the consensus and distinctiveness and lower the consistency. For purposes of exposition we have presented excuses in the context of their major transformed responsibility attribution process. However, most excuses lessen responsibility in several ways. For example, the excuse of coercion not only elevates consensus, but a coerced person certainly has a legitimate reason to suggest that the bad performance did not represent his or her normal performance in that particular situation (consistency lowering) or other situations (distinctiveness raising). Or consider our heavy drinker whose "off night" lowers consistency. The alcohol also facilitates the splitting of the "bad" person from the "real," good (nondrunk) person (distinctiveness raising); furthermore, most anyone's act may be expected to bomb when the actor is "bombed" (consensus raising). In these examples, it should be apparent that the reduction of the transformed responsibility may also make the bad performance itself seem less offensive. Additionally, it is occasionally the case that the transformed responsibility excuse may be obvious even at the time of the ill deed (e.g., the actor is obviously drunk); in this example the excuse may actually operate at both the apparent and transformed linkages. When it comes to self-image protection, therefore, a good excuse goes a long way.

Exceptions That Aren't Totally ("When modesty is the best policy")

Although the bulk of evidence shows that people will attempt to deny or lessen their responsibility for a bad performance, there is a small body of research showing that people sometimes (1) accept responsibility for their poor performance (e.g., Ames, 1975; Beckman, 1973; Feather & Simon, 1971; Ross, Bierbrauer, & Polly, 1974), or (2) moderate their tendencies to make externalizing excuses for their failures (Arkin et al., 1980; Arkin, Gabrenya, Appelman, & Cochran, 1979). This research seemingly flies in the face of the present excuse theory in that people are not entirely preserving their positive self-images. It is relevant to briefly explore these studies in order to ascertain their impact on the proposed excuse-making phenomenon.

The Teacher Studies

A first type of situation in which modesty may prevail is when the actor's role expectations or social norms dictate that he or she take responsibility for a failure (Tetlock, 1980). A good example is that of teachers, who are expected to assume responsibility for students' poor performance. Not surprisingly, there-fore, several initial studies showed that teachers attributed responsibility for student failure to themselves. For example, Beckman (1973) reported that teachers assumed responsibility for increasingly poorer performance by stu-dents in a laboratory teaching task. Similarly, Ross et al. (1974) found that teachers took responsibility for students' poor performance on a spelling task; moreover, Ames (1975) showed that teachers assumed responsibility for stu-dent failure even when the students' initial probability of success was rated as low. After considering the aforementioned counterdefensive behavior of teach-ers, Weary and her colleagues (Weary-Bradley, 1978; Weary & Arkin, 1981) reasoned that these studies actually reflect instances in which actors intuitively know that an external audience will view them more positively when they ac-cept blame for failure. Consistent with this logic, Tetlock (1980) found that ob-servers rated the teacher who takes responsibility for student failure more posi-tively than the teacher who avoids responsibility (see also Shovar & Carlston, 1979). Apparently, these studies reflect an instance in which the concerns for an external audience reaction may override those related to the internal audience. As long as the external audience is salient, therefore, teachers may preserve their self-image by not making an excuse. It is an interesting and as yet un-tested proposition, however, to speculate that teachers may privately engage in the usual excuse-making avoidance of responsibility for students' failure when they are not under the scrutiny of an observing external audience (i.e., an ex-perimenter who views their attributions in the aforementioned studies).

The Invalidation Studies

A second type of situation in which modesty may prevail occurs when there is some source that may invalidate the actor's excuse-making. There are several experimental examples of this phenomenon. Arkin et al. (1980, Experiment 2) investigated attributions following success and failure through a regular paper-and-pencil technique and through a bogus pipeline technique (the lie–detector-like device). They found that the usual externalizing of failure oc-curred, but that this was less pronounced under the pipeline compared to paper-and-pencil technique condition. In other words, people still tended to make excuses, but did so in a less marked fashion when they were hooked to the lie-detector device. Additionally, two studies suggest that very intense scru-tiny by observers diminishes the typical excuselike attributional pattern (Arkin et al., 1979; Wells, Petty, Harkins, Kagehiro, & Harvey, 1977). Overall, the in-validation studies are consistent with the idea that people are concerned about embarrassment that follows when a debunking source is present (see Goffman, 1955; Modigliani, 1971).

The present "exceptions" to the posited excuse-making process all share a common and seemingly paradoxical theme: It is sometimes more efficacious to preserve one's positive image by lessening or eliminating excuse-making. Even these exceptions, however, may not be totally inconsistent with excuse-making. For example, in the "teacher studies," it has yet to be demonstrated whether the teachers privately engage in excuse-making. Further, it should be emphasized that the "invalidation studies" suggest circumstances where excuse-making may be lessened although not necessarily eliminated. Future research is obviously needed on the boundaries of excuse-making so that we may better understand when and where excuses *won't* be made following failure. An important focus of these boundary-defining future studies may be people's concern with the defensibility and perceived effectiveness of their excuse-making maneuvers (see Schlenker, in press; Schlenker & Leary, 1982; Snyder, in press).

Excuses and Related Frameworks

Before concluding this section on the "role" of excuses, it may be worthwhile to briefly examine the relationship of the present excuse model to other existing frameworks. The two frameworks that appear most relevant are defense mechanisms and legal systems.

Excuses and Defense Mechanisms

Defenses typically are conceived as mechanisms whereby the ego is called upon to justify a bad performance (e.g., A. Freud, 1948). Since, as we argued previously, the ego by necessity reflects "revolving self-images" for both internal and external audiences, there are obvious audience similarities in defense and excuse mechanisms. Furthermore, it is useful to describe the similarities between excuses and the particular defense mechanisms of rationalization and projection. Theoretical explanations of rationalization usually emphasize its image protection role (Kalish, 1970; Laughlin, 1970). For example, rationalization has been defined as "a widely used adaptive technique that functions to enable individuals to maintain self in situations that otherwise might be intolerable . . . by: (1) justifying and finding socially acceptable reasons for beliefs and actions and (2) softening the impact of failure and disappointment" (Bernard & Huckins, 1978, p. 293). In regard to the defense mechanism of projection, protection of the self-image is also critical. In this vein, Freud (1924/1956) posited that people were unaware of possessing the undesirable characteristic that they projected onto other people. This common definition emphasizing denial or repressionlike processes has been labeled *classical projection.* Unfortunately, there is little empirical support for the existence of such classical projection processes (see for reviews Holmes, 1968, 1978). A second type of projection, known as *attributive projection,* reflects a process whereby the person is aware of possessing an undesirable characteristic and thereby "defensively" ascribes (projects) this characteristic onto other people.

Unlike classical projection, there is empirical support for the attributive projection process (see for reviews Holmes, 1968, 1978, 1981; Sherwood, 1981). Overall, therefore, it should be acknowledged that the present excuse-making model does resemble the particular psychodynamic defense mechanisms of rationalization and attributive projection.

Given the fact that there are similarities in the present excuse-making model and the defense mechanism notions, one should naturally ask why a new model is desirable. One reason for the development of the present excuse model is that it provides a larger framework for analyzing self-image protecting maneuvers. For example, projection is examined in Chapter 4 as just one subcategory of excuse-making. A second reason for the development of the present excuse model was the belief it may lend itself more easily to empirical scrutiny than the psychoanalytic notions that have historically been difficult to translate into operational tests. Likewise, the present excuse model is based on "commonsense" attributional principles of the thoughts and actions of people, whether or not such people evidence psychopathology; thus excuse-making may be applied logically to the full range of people. Although we obviously believe that there are advantages to the present excuse-making model, we also acknowledge the contribution of defense mechanism concepts such as rationalization and projection. Indeed, the theory and rich clinical tradition of these previous concepts helped to refine the present excuse-making model.

Excuses and the Law

If the present excuse model is to be advocated instead of a more traditional defense mechanism model, the reader may at this point question the necessity of an excuse model relative to a legal framework. Certainly it is the case that the legal system is based on a detailed description of the validity of various types of "excuses" (Darley & Zanna, 1982). There are at least two areas, however, where the differences in emphasis between the excuse and legal models should be noted. First, the focus of the legal system typically is to assign responsibility for the "crime" in order to determine the defendant's punishment (fine, sentence). The focus of the excuse model, however, is on the way in which the actor assigns (lessens) responsibility primarily to preserve his or her self-image and secondarily to diminish the actual punishment. Second, within the legal model, the emphasis is on the perceptions of an external audience (the jury) in determining the guilt and culpability of the defendant. The present excuse model, on the other hand, employs the "revolving images" notion in which the actor is at once concerned with internal and external audience reactions.

Despite these distinctions, it should be obvious that there is a great deal of overlap between the present psychological excuse theory and the legal framework. In point of fact, the present excuse model may represent a more basic theory regarding the behavior of people in predicaments, and as such it may translate easily to the legal level. That is to say, while the legal system empha-sizes the physical sentence as determined by an external audience (the jury or judge), the underlying assignment of responsibility may be based on an intui-tive understanding of how each person preserves his or her self-image through excuses. In fact, one potential result of the present psychological model of ex-cuses may be a better understanding of how psychological and legal concepts are interrelated. This stance has been taken by recent theorists within psychol-ogy (e.g., Darley & Zanna, 1982; Fincham & Jaspars, 1980; Hamilton, 1978, 1980), and in various places throughout this book we note the similarities be-tween our psychological terminology and the related legal terminology.

THE SHOW WITHIN THE SHOW: FURTHER DIMENSIONS OF EXCUSE-MAKING

In the previous section we defined the excuse-making model and described the general components that determine its operation. Beyond this general model, however, it is also possible to discern further dimensions along which the ex-cuse masquerade can be analyzed. The major dimensions that further define excuse-making are (1) the degree of awareness that the actor has of the excuse, (2) the extent to which the excuse is avowed (verbally reported) or self-evident (physically manifested), (3) the effectiveness of the excuse in terms of main-taining a positive image and the pervasiveness (or number) of situations in which it works, and (4) whether the excuse is employed before or after a bad performance. Each of the dimensions is elaborated at this point.

Awareness

The first dimension is the degree to which the actor is aware that he or she is engaging in excuse-making activities. Given a negative performance, the actor should feel the need to protect his or her self-image. Since excuses are a princi-pal weapon in the armamentarium one calls upon when the image is threat-ened, it would appear that some initial sense of awareness should occur. Fur-ther, the strategic use of excuse-making should sometimes be within awareness. However, if the threat is one that the actor has encountered repeatedly, or if the individual has a long history of employing the excuse, it may be that the asso-ciated excuse-making becomes automatic in nature. Like most things that we learn, we are at first very aware of the process, but over time we may perform the act out of habit. Thus, like habits, excuse-making may progressively recede from awareness.

It should be noted that the preceding habit explanation implicitly suggests that excuses are not motivated actions; this position is consistent with the view that habits are motiveless actions (e.g., Tedeschi & Riess, 1981). Alternatively, however, we may lack an awareness of our excuse-making and this may be motivated by our desire to maintain image. The theoretical literature and recent empirical evidence on the concept of *self-deception* provides an interesting and relevant framework for an analysis of excuse-making as sometimes reflecting a motivated unawareness. In this vein, philosophers have suggested that self-deception involves a motivated lying to oneself (see Camus, 1956; Fingarette, 1969; Sartre, 1958). Sartre (1958, p. 49) describes this seeming paradox: "The one to whom the lie is told and the one who lies are one and the same person, which means that I must know in my capacity as deceiver the truth which is hidden from me in my capacity as the one deceived. Better yet I must know the truth very exactly in order to conceal it more carefully."

Psychologists have also advocated the importance of the self-deception concept. Hilgard (1949) stated that self-deception is inherent in all defense mechanisms; Mischel (1974) described self-deception as the core concept in the "neurotic paradox"; Murphy (1975) suggested that self-deception is imbedded in the perceptual defense process.

Elaborating on recent assertions that people often are unaware of their cognitions (see Hilgard, 1977; Nisbett & Wilson, 1977), Gur and Sackeim (1979) added impetus to the self-deception notion by arguing, and empirically demonstrating, that a lack of awareness may at times be a motivated behavior. The criteria for self-deception are intriguing when applied to excuse-making. First, Gur and Sackeim (1979) suggest that self-deception entails a person simultaneously holding two opposite beliefs. In the case of excuses, persons could believe that they had or had not made an excuse. Second, self-deception involves the person not being aware of holding one of the beliefs. With excuses, for example, persons may believe that they have not made an excuse. Third, self-deception reflects a motivated process as to which belief is held in awareness; the belief that is held in awareness provides a psychological gain. Returning to the topic of excuses, it is more psychologically satisfying and conducive to esteem to believe that one has not made an excuse.

Before leaving this section on awareness, it is relevant to note that the definition of an excuse offered previously does *not* imply that it must be false. People can subjectively bias their interpretations of events (i.e., prefer one explanation over another for self-image reasons) without those interpretations necessarily being objective errors (i.e., deviations from some objective criterion for truth). Thus although excuses invariably are biased interpretations of events, they are not invariably errors. In a large number of situations we have no objective criterion for determining the truthfulness of varying explanations, especially when these alternative explanations appear to fit the facts of the incident equally well (Schlenker, 1981). Within the context of this book, excuses are employed as an inclusive and nonpejorative term to include various explanations for "bad" performances. The actor, as we noted earlier, prefers to call such explanations reasons rather than excuses. Indeed, it should not be esteem enhancing to see oneself as an "excuse-maker." In addition to the states of very high and very low awareness of excuse-making described in this section, it is also likely that there is an intermediate level of awareness regarding one's excuse-making (Schlenker, 1982). This state of intermediate awareness is characterized by the actor's cognitive processing of the believability of the explanation in the eyes of people (including the actor). Frequently the actor concludes that the explanation "seems" to be true, and as such it attains the status of a reason. If the explanation for a "bad performance" is not believable, it may regress in status to a "mere excuse."

Avowal versus Self-Evidence

The individual who has undergone, or anticipates undergoing a bad performance may verbally cite his or her excuse, or the excuses may be physically manifested. The former avowed excuses are self-reported by the actor and often are corroborated only by that actor's testimony; the latter self-evident excuses represent overt actions or actual physical activities that are publicly observable (Snyder & Smith, 1982). As an example, imagine a basketball player who is shooting very poorly. The avowed excuse of having a sore shoulder (told to a sports writer before or after the game) may be somewhat convincing, but having to wear a shoulder harness that is visible to all the spectators at the game is even more convincing. Self-evident excuses thus may have the added advantage of naturally acting to detach the actor from a bad performance; that is, the actor may not even have to actively avow the excuse. Very often there is a blend of avowed and self-evident excuses; moreover, in the extent to which the actor can have his or her avowed excuses corroborated by others, the excuse may become more effective.

Effectiveness and Pervasiveness

The effectiveness of an excuse refers to the degree that the excuse lessens the responsibility link (and perhaps the perception of the bad performance itself), thereby maintaining a positive image. A variety of researchers suggest that the effectiveness of the excuse must be matched to the negativeness of the bad performance (Goffman, 1971; Schlenker, 1980; Scott & Lyman, 1968). For example,

> The excuse "I forgot what time it was" is usually effective in explaining why one was embarrassingly late for the party. It will not work for a doctor whose patient died in the emergency room while waiting for the doctor's arrival. The justification "It didn't really matter" might be expected to explain why one ran over a frog; it should not be expected to explain why one ran over a child. (Schlenker, 1980, p. 151)

The worse the performance, therefore, the greater should be the effectiveness of the excuse employed to lessen that actor's responsibility.

The pervasiveness of an excuse refers to the variety of performance situations in which the excuse may be employed. For example, having a headache may explain why one did poorly in a job interview, but it should not serve as an excuse for how one acts in other situations. However, being chronically depressed could serve as an excuse in a wide variety of interpersonal, academic, and vocational arenas. The effectiveness and pervasiveness dimensions are stressed in a discussion of maladaptive excuse-making in Chapter 8.

When the Excuse Appears

Traditionally, the lay person's view of excuses is that they appear *after* the actor has committed the bad performance. That is, once the actor perceives that he or she has performed poorly, a barrage of excuses may be activated in order to maintain a positive image. This temporal conceptualization of excuses as occurring after a bad performance has also been discussed by professionals from various disciplines, including philosophy (Austin, 1961/1970), law (Hart, 1968), sociology (Goffman, 1971; Scott & Lyman, 1968), and psychology (Schlenker, 1980). Here we refer to this type of excuse-making as *retrospective* excuses. Retrospective excuses are of sufficient importance that we devote an entire chapter to them (see Chapter 4).

Since people often have the ability to predict that an upcoming situation may result in a bad performance on their part, it is also likely that excuses are employed *before* the actual bad performance. Many of the excuses employed after a bad performance may also appear as a *disclaimer* before a potential bad performance (Tedeschi & Riess, 1981). For example, "I didn't really try" may become "I won't really try." The idea that excuses may be employed before a potential bad performance is rooted in the early work of Alfred Adler (1913, 1927, 1929, 1931), and more recently has been articulated under the general heading of self-handicaps (see Berglas & Jones, 1978; Jones & Berglas, 1978; Smith, Snyder, & Handelsman, 1982; Snyder & Smith, 1982). As noted earlier in this chapter, self-handicaps are excuses established before a potential bad performance that serve to lessen the actor's eventual responsibility for his or her performance. In this book we refer to excuses that occur before a potential bad performance as *anticipatory* excuses, and Chapter 5 details recent theoretical and empirical developments related to this type of excuse.

REVIEW: THE SHOW GOES ON

The premise that we have adopted throughout this chapter is that actors are concerned with maintaining their positive self-images; further, these positive self-images are assumed to be, in most instances, as much for the actor as they are for the audience. When "bad reviews" enter, as they seem to for most of us, the actor is painfully aware of the link to an activity that threatens his or her positive self-image. In such circumstances excuses diminish one's responsibility for the negative activity, as well as lessen the perceived negativeness of the act. If successful, the excuse masquerade maintains one's positive image. Perhaps "the show goes on" precisely because excuses enable the cast of actors to preserve their positive self-images for future performances.

REFERENCES

Adler, A. *Individual psychologische behandlung der neurosen.* In D. Sarason (Ed.), *Jahreskurse für arztliche fortbildung.* Munich: Lehmann, 1913.

Adler, A. *The practice and theory of individual psychology.* New York: Harcourt, 1927.

Adler, A. *Problems of neuroses: A book of case-histories.* London: Kegan Paul, Trench, Truebner, & Co., 1929.

Adler, A. *What life should mean to you.* Boston: Little, Brown, 1931.

Alexander, C. N., & Knight, G. W. Situated identities and social psychological experimentation. *Sociometry,* 1971, **34,** 65–82.

Alexander, C. N., & Lauderdale, P. Situated identities and social influence. *Sociometry,* 1977, **40,** 225–233.

Alexander, C. N., & Sagatum, I. An attributional analysis of experimental norms. *Sociometry,* 1973, **36,** 127–142.

Allen, V. L. Situational factors in conformity. In L. Berkowitz (Ed.), *Advances in experimental social psychology* (Vol. 2). New York: Academic Press, 1965.

Allport, G. W. *Personality: A psychological interpretation.* New York: Holt, 1937.

Ames, R. Teachers' attributions of responsibility: Some unexpected counterdefensive effects. *Journal of Educational Psychology,* 1975, **67,** 668–676.

Ansbacher, H. L., & Ansbacher, R. R. (Eds.), *The individual psychology of Alfred Adler.* New York: Basic Books, 1956.

Arkin, R. M., Appelman, A. J., & Burger, J. M. Social anxiety, self-presentation, and the self-serving bias in causal attributions. *Journal of Personality and Social Psychology,* 1980, **38,** 23–35.

Arkin, R. M., Cooper, H., & Kolditz, T. A statistical review of the literature concerning the self-serving attribution bias in interpersonal influence situations. *Journal of Personality,* 1980, **48,** 435–448.

Arkin, R. M., Gabrenya, W. K., Jr., Appelman, A. S., & Cochran, S. T. Self-presentation, self-monitoring, and the self-serving bias in causal attribution. *Personality and Social Psychology Bulletin,* 1979, **5,** 73–76.

Aronson, E. Dissonance theory: Progress and problems. In R. P. Abelson, E. Aronson, W. J. McGuire, T. M. Newcomb, M. J. Rosenberg, & P. H. Tannenbaum (Eds.), *Theories of cognitive consistency: A sourcebook.* Chicago: Rand McNally, 1968.

Aronson, E. The theory of cognitive dissonance: A current perspective. In L. Berkowitz (Ed.), *Advances in experimental social psychology* (Vol. 4). New York: Academic Press, 1969.

Aronson, E., & Carlsmith, J. M. Performance expectancy as a determinant of actual performance. *Journal of Abnormal and Social Psychology,* 1962, **65,** 178–182.

Aronson, E., Turner, J., & Carlsmith, M. Communicator credibility and communicator discrepancy as determinants of opinion change. *Journal of Abnormal and Social Psychology,* 1963, **67,** 31–36.

Aronson, E., & Worchel, P. Similarity vs. liking as determinants of interpersonal attractiveness. *Psychonomic Science,* 1966, **5,** 157–158.

Asch, S. E. Studies of independence and conformity: A minority of one against a unanimous majority. *Psychological Monographs,* 1956, **70** (9 Whole No. 416).

Asch, S. E. Effects of group pressure upon the modification and distortion of judgements. In M. H. Guetzkow (Ed.), *Groups, leadership, and men.* New York: Russell & Russell, 1963. (Original copyright, Pittsburgh: Carnegie Press, 1951.)

Austin, J. L. *Philosophical papers* (2nd ed.). New York: Oxford University Press, 1970. (Originally published in 1961.)

Bandura, A. *Aggression: A social-learning analysis.* Englewood Cliffs, N.J.: Prentice-Hall, 1973.

Bandura, A. *Social-learning theory.* Englewood Cliffs, N.J.: Prentice-Hall, 1977.

Baumeister, R. F. A self-presentational view of social phenomena. *Psychological Bulletin,* 1982, **91,** 3–26.

Beckman, L. Teachers' and observers' perceptions of causality for a child's performance. *Journal of Educational Psychology,* 1973, **65,** 198–204.

Bem, D. J. Self perception theory. In L. Berkowitz (Ed.), *Advances in experimental social psychology* (Vol. 6). New York: Academic Press, 1972.

Bercheid, E. Opinion change and communicator–communicatee similarity and dissimilarity. *Journal of Personality and Social Psychology,* 1966, **4,** 670–680.

Bercheid, E., Graziano, W., Monson, T., & Dermer, M. Outcome dependency: Attention, attribution, and attraction. *Journal of Personality and Social Psychology,* 1976, **34,** 978–989.

Berglas, S., & Jones, E. E. Drug choice as a self-handicapping strategy in response to noncontingent success. *Journal of Personality and Social Psychology,* 1978, **36,** 405–417.

Berkowitz, L. *A survey of social psychology.* New York: Holt, Rinehart & Winston, 1980.

Bernard, H. W., & Huckins, W. C. *Dynamics of personal adjustment.* Boston: Holbrook Press, 1978.

Bettinghaus, E. P. *Persuasive communication.* New York: Holt, Rinehart & Winston, 1968.

Biddle, B. J., & Thomas, E. J. (Eds.), *Role theory: Concepts and research.* New York: Wiley, 1966.

Bowerman, W. R. Subjective competence: The structure, process and function of self-referent causal attributions. *Journal for the Theory of Social Behaviour,* 1978, **8,** 45–75.

Bowerman, W. R. Applications of a social psychological theory of motivation to the language of defensiveness and self-justification. In M. M. T. Henderson (Ed.), *1980 Mid-America linguistic conference papers.* Lawrence: University of Kansas Linguistics Department, 1981.

Bradley, G. W. Self-serving biases in the attribution process: A reexamination of the fact or fiction question. *Journal of Personality and Social Psychology,* 1978, **36,** 56–71.

Bramel, D. A. Selection of a target for defensive projection. *Journal of Abnormal and Social Psychology,* 1963, **66,** 318–324.

Brisset, D., & Edgley, C. *Life as theater: A dramaturgical sourcebook.* Chicago: Aldine, 1975.

Brock, T. C., & Buss, A. H. Dissonance, aggression and evaluation of pain. *Journal of Abnormal and Social Psychology,* 1962, **65,** 197–202.

Brock, T. C., & Buss, A. H. Effects of justification for aggression in communication with the victim on post-aggression dissonance. *Journal of Abnormal and Social Psychology,* 1964, **68,** 403–412.

Burger, J. M. Motivational biases in the attribution of responsibility for an accident: A meta-analysis of the defensive-attribution hypothesis. *Psychological Bulletin,* 1981, **90,** 496–512.

Burns, E. *Theatricality: A study of convention in the theatre and in social life.* New York: Harper & Row, 1973.

Buss, A. *Self-consciousness and social anxiety.* San Francisco: Freeman, 1980.

Camus, A. *The fall.* New York: Vintage Books, 1956.

Carson, R. C. *Interaction concepts of personality.* Chicago: Aldine, 1969.

Chaikin, A. L., & Darley, J. M. Victim or perpetrator? Defensive attribution of responsibility and the need for order and justice. *Journal of Personality and Social Psychology,* 1973, **25,** 268–275.

Clair, M. S., & Snyder, C. R. Effects of instructor-delivered sequential evaluative feedback upon students' subsequent classroom related performance and instructor ratings. *Journal of Educational Psychology,* 1979, **71,** 50–57.

Collins, R. W., Dmitruk, V. M., & Ranney, J. T. Personal validation: Some empirical and ethical considerations. *Journal of Consulting and Clinical Psychology,* 1977, **45,** 70–77.

Cooley, C. H. *Human nature and the social order* (rev. ed.). New York: Scribner's, 1922. (Originally published in 1902.)

Coopersmith, S. *The antecedents of self-esteem.* San Francisco: Freeman, 1967.

D'Arcy, E. *Human acts.* New York: Oxford University Press, 1963.

Darley, J. M., & Zanna, M. P. Making moral judgements. *American Scientist,* 1982, **70,** 515–521.

Duval, S., & Wicklund, R. A. *A theory of objective self-awareness.* New York: Academic Press, 1972.

Epstein, S. The self-concept revisited: Or a theory of a theory. *American Psychologist,* 1973, **28,** 404–416.

Evreinoff, N. *The theatre in life.* New York: Benjamin Bloom, 1927.

Feather, N. T., & Simon, J. G. Attribution of responsibility and valence of outcome in relation to initial confidence and success and failure of self and other. *Journal of Personality and Social Psychology*, 1971, **18**, 173–188.

Festinger, L. *A theory of cognitive dissonance*. Evanston, Ill.: Row, Peterson, 1957.

Fincham, F. D., & Jaspars, J. M. Attribution of responsibility: From man the scientist to man as lawyer. In L. Berkowitz (Ed.), *Advances in experimental social psychology* (Vol. 13). New York: Academic Press, 1980.

Fingarette, H. *Self-deception*. London: Routlege & Kegan Paul, 1969.

Fitch, G. Effects of self-esteem, perceived performance, and choice on causal attributions. *Journal of Personality and Social Psychology*, 1970, **16**, 311–315.

Fitzgerald, P. *Criminal law and punishment*. New York: Oxford University Press, 1962.

Forsyth, D. R., & Schlenker, B. R. Attributing the causes of group performance: Effects of performance quality, task importance, and future testing. *Journal of Personality*, 1977, **45**, 220–236.

Freud, A. *The ego and the mechanisms of defense*. London: Hogarth Press, 1948.

Freud, S. *The ego and the id*. London: Hogarth Press, 1927.

Freud, S. Further remarks on the defense neuropsychoses. In *Collected papers of Sigmund Freud* (Vol. 1). London: Hogarth Press, 1956. (Originally published in 1924.)

Freud, S. *New introductory lectures on psychoanalysis*. New York: Norton, 1965.

Frey, D. Reactions to success and failure in public and in private conditions. *Journal of Experimental Social Psychology*, 1978, **14**, 172–179.

Fromm, E. *Escape from freedom*. New York: Rinehart, 1941.

Fromm, E. *Man for himself*. New York: Rinehart, 1947.

Goffman, E. On facework. *Psychiatry*, 1955, **18**, 213–231.

Goffman, E. *The presentation of self in everyday life*. Garden City, N.Y.: Doubleday-Anchor, 1959.

Goffman, E. *Stigma: Notes on the management of spoiled identity*. Englewood Cliffs, N.J.: Prentice-Hall, 1963.

Goffman, E. *Interaction ritual: Essays on face-to-face behavior*. Garden City, N.Y.: Doubleday, 1967.

Goffman, E. *Relations in public*. New York: Basic Books, 1971.

Greenwald, A. G. The totalitarian ego: Fabrication and revision of personal history. *American Psychologist*, 1980, **35**, 603–618.

Greenwald, A. G. Ego task analysis: An integration of research on ego involvement and self-awareness. In A. H. Hastorf & A. M. Isen (Eds.), *Cognitive social psychology*. New York: Elsevier-North Holland, 1982.

Greenwald, A. G., & Ronis, D. L. Twenty years of cognitive dissonance: Case study of the evolution of a theory. *Psychological Review*, 1978, **85**, 53–57.

Gruder, C. L. Choice of comparison persons in evaluating oneself. In J. M. Suls & R. L. Miller (Eds.), *Social comparison processes: Theoretical and empirical perspectives*. Washington, D.C.: Hemisphere, 1977.

Gur, R. C., & Sackeim, H. A. Self-deception: A concept in search of a phenomenon. *Journal of Personality and Social Psychology*, 1979, **37**, 147–169.

Hall, C. S., & Lindzey, G. *Theories of personality* (3rd ed.). New York: Wiley, 1978.

Halperin, K., Snyder, C. R., Shenkel, R. J., & Houston, B. K. Effects of source status and message favorability on acceptance of personality feedback. *Journal of Applied Psychology,* 1976, **61,** 85–88.

Hamilton, V. L. Who is responsible? Toward a social psychology of responsibility attribution. *Social Psychology,* 1978, **4,** 316–318.

Hamilton, V. L. Intuitive psychologist or intuitive lawyer? Alternative models of the attribution process. *Journal of Personality and Social Psychology,* 1980, **39,** 767–772.

Hart, H. L. A. *Punishment and responsibility: Essays on the philosophy of law.* New York: Oxford University Press, 1968.

Harvey, J. H., Harris, B., & Barnes, R. D. Actor-observer differences in the perceptions of responsibility and freedom. *Journal of Personality and Social Psychology,* 1975, **32,** 22–28.

Harvey, J. H., Ickes, W. J., & Kidd, R. F. (Eds.), *New directions in attribution research* (Vol. 1). Hillsdale, N.J.: Lawrence Erlbaum Associates, 1976.

Harvey, J. H., Ickes, W. J., & Kidd, R. F. (Eds.), *New directions in attribution research* (Vol. 2). Hillsdale, N.J.: Lawrence Erlbaum Associates, 1978.

Harvey, J. H., Ickes, W. J., & Kidd, R. F. (Eds.), *New directions in attribution research* (Vol. 3). Hillsdale, N.J.: Lawrence Erlbaum Associates, 1981.

Harvey, J. H., & Smith, W. P. *Social psychology: An attributional approach.* St. Louis: C. V. Mosby Company, 1977.

Harvey, J. H., & Weary, G. *Perspectives on attributional processes.* Dubuque, Iowa: W. C. Brown Company, 1981.

Heider, F. Social perception and phenomenal causality. *Psychological Review,* 1944, **51,** 358–374.

Heider, F. *The psychology of interpersonal relations.* New York: Wiley, 1958.

Heider, F. A conversation with Fritz Heider. In J. H. Harvey, W. J. Ickes, & R. F. Kidd (Eds.), *New directions in attribution research* (Vol. 1). Hillsdale, N.J.: Lawrence Erlbaum Associates, 1976.

Hilgard, E. R. Human motives and the concept of the self. *American Psychologist,* 1949, **4,** 374–382.

Hilgard, E. R. *Divided consciousness: Multiple controls in human thought and action.* New York: Wiley, 1977.

Hogan, R. A socioanalytic theory of personality. In M. Page & R. Dienstbier (Eds.), *Nebraska Symposium on Motivation.* Lincoln: University of Nebraska Press, 1982.

Holmes, D. S. Dimensions of projection. *Psychological Bulletin,* 1968, **69,** 248–268.

Holmes, D. S. Projection as a defense mechanism. *Psychological Bulletin,* 1978, **85,** 677–688.

Holmes, D. S. Existence of classical projection and the stress reducing function of attributive projection: A reply to Sherwood. *Psychological Bulletin,* 1981, **90,** 460–466.

Horney, K. *Our inner conflicts.* New York: Norton, 1945.

Horney, K. *Neurosis and human growth.* New York: Norton, 1950.

Iso-Ahola, S. Immediate attributional effects of success and failure in the field: Testing some laboratory hypotheses. *European Journal of Social Psychology,* 1977, **7,** 275-296.

James, W. *The principles of psychology* (Vols. 1 & 2). New York: Holt, 1890.

Janis, I. L., Mahl, G. F., Kagan, J., & Holt, R. R. *Personality: Dynamics, development, and assessment.* New York: Harcourt, Brace, & World, 1969.

Jellison, J. M. *I'm sorry I didn't mean to and other lies we love to tell.* New York: Chatham Square Press, 1977.

Jones, E. E. *Ingratiation.* New York: Appleton-Century-Crofts, 1964.

Jones, E. E. Personal communication, 1981.

Jones, E. E., & Berglas, S. Control of attributions about the self through self-handicapping strategies: The appeal of alcohol and the role of underachievement. *Personality and Social Psychology Bulletin,* 1978, **4,** 200-206.

Jones, E. E., & Davis, K. E. From acts to dispositions: The attribution process in person perception. In L. Berkowitz (Ed.), *Advances in experimental social psychology* (Vol. 2). New York: Academic Press, 1965.

Jones, E. E., & McGillis, D. Correspondent inferences and the attribution cube: A comparative reappraisal. In J. H. Harvey, W. J. Ickes, & R. F. Kidd (Eds.), *New directions in attribution research* (Vol. 1). Hillsdale, N.J.: Lawrence Erlbaum Associates, 1976.

Jones, E. E., & Nisbett, R. E. The actor and observer: Divergent perceptions of the causes of behavior. In E. E. Jones, D. Kanouse, H. H. Kelley, R. E. Nisbett, S. Valins, & B. Weiner (Eds.), *Attribution: Perceiving the causes of behavior.* Morristown, N.J.: General Learning Press, 1972.

Jones, E. E., & Sigall, H. The bogus pipeline: A new paradigm for measuring affect and attitudes. *Psychological Bulletin,* 1971, **76,** 349-364.

Jones, E. E., & Wortman, C. *Ingratiation: An attributional approach.* Morristown, N.J.: General Learning Press, 1973.

Jones, S. C. Self and interpersonal evaluations: Esteem theories vs. consistency theories. *Psychological Bulletin,* 1973, **79,** 185-199.

Kalish, R. A. *The psychology of human behavior.* Belmont, Calif.: Brooks/ Cole, 1970.

Kelley, H. H. Attribution theory in social psychology. In D. Levine (Ed.), *Nebraska Symposium on Motivation* (Vol. 15). Lincoln: University of Nebraska Press, 1967.

Kelley, H. H. *Attribution in social interaction.* New York: General Learning Press, 1971.

Kelley, H. H. Causal schemata and the attribution process. In E. E. Jones, D. Kanouse, H. H. Kelley, R. E. Nisbett, S. Valins, & B. Weiner (Eds.), *Attribution: Perceiving the causes of behavior.* Morristown, N.J.: General Learning Press, 1972.

Kelley, H. H. The process of causal attribution. *American Psychologist,* 1973, **28,** 107-128.

Kiesler, C. A., & Kiesler, S. B. *Conformity.* Reading, Mass.: Addison-Wesley, 1969.

Kohlberg, L. Moral development and identification. In H. Stephenson (Ed.), *Child psychology* (62nd yearbook of the National Society for the Study of Education). Chicago: University of Chicago Press, 1963.

Kohlberg, L. The child as a moral philosopher. *Psychology Today,* 1968, **2**(4), 24-30.

Kruglanski, A. W., & Cohen, M. Attributed freedom and personal causation. *Journal of Personality and Social Psychology,* 1973, **26,** 245–250.

Kuiper, N. A. Depression and causal attributions for success and failure. *Journal of Personality and Social Psychology,* 1978, **36,** 236–246.

Kulik, J. A., & Taylor, S. E. Premature consensus on consensus? Effects of sample-based versus self-based consensus information. *Journal of Personality and Social Psychology,* 1980, **38,** 871–878.

Langer, E. J. The illusion of control. *Journal of Personality and Social Psychology,* 1975, **32,** 311–328.

Larson, J. R. Evidence for a self-serving bias in the attribution of causality. *Journal of Personality,* 1977, **45,** 430–441.

Latané, B., & Darley, J. M. *The unresponsive bystander: Why doesn't he help?* New York: Appleton-Century-Crofts, 1970.

Latané, B., & Rodin, J. A lady in distress: Inhibiting effects of friends and strangers on bystander intervention. *Journal of Experimental Social Psychology,* 1969, **5,** 189–202.

Laughlin, H. P. *The ego and its defenses.* New York: Appleton-Century-Crofts, 1970.

Leary, M. R., & Schlenker, B. R. The social psychology of shyness. In J. T. Tedeschi (Ed.), *Impression management theory and social psychological research.* New York: Academic Press, 1981.

Lefcourt, H. M., Hogg, E., Struthers, S., & Holmes, C. Causal attributions as a function of locus of control, initial confidence, and performance outcomes. *Journal of Personality and Social Psychology,* 1975, **32,** 391–397.

Lerner, M. J. The desire for justice and reaction to victims. In J. R. Macauley and L. Berkowitz (Eds.), *Altruism and helping behavior.* New York: Academic Press, 1970.

Lerner, M. J. *The belief in a just world: A fundamental delusion.* New York: Plenum, 1980.

Major, B. Information acquisition and attribution processes. *Journal of Personality and Social Psychology,* 1980, **39,** 1010–1023.

Markus, H. Self-schemata and processing information about the self. *Journal of Personality and Social Psychology,* 1977, **35,** 63–78.

Maslow, A. H. *Toward a psychology of being* (2nd ed.). New York: Van Nostrand, 1968.

McArthur, L. A. The how and what of why: Some determinants of consequences of casual attribution. *Journal of Personality and Social Psychology,* 1972, **22,** 171–193.

McCauley, C., & Kellas, G. Induced chunking: Temporal aspects of storage and retrieval. *Journal of Experimental Psychology,* 1974, **102,** 260–265.

McGinness, J. *The selling of the president 1968.* New York: Pocket Books, 1970.

McKillip, J., & Posavac, E. J. Attribution of responsibility for an accident: Effects of similarity to the victim and severity of consequences. *Proceedings of 80th Annual Convention of the American Psychological Association,* 1972, **7,** 181–182.

McKillip, J., & Posavac, E. J. Judgments of responsibility for an accident. *Journal of Personality,* 1975, **43,** 248–265.

Mead, G. H. *Mind, self, and society.* Chicago: University of Chicago Press, 1934.

Melton, A. W., & Martin, E. *Coding processes in human memory.* Washington, D.C.: V. H. Winston, 1972.

Mettee, D. R. Rejection of unexpected success as a function of the negative consequences of accepting success. *Journal of Personality and Social Psychology,* 1971, **17,** 332–341.

Mettee, D. R., & Aronson, E. Affective reactions to appraisal from others. In T. L. Huston (Ed.), *Foundations of interpersonal attraction.* New York: Academic Press, 1974.

Miller, D. T. Ego involvement and attribution for success and failure. *Journal of Personality and Social Psychology,* 1976, **34,** 901–906.

Miller, D. T., & Norman, S. A. Actor–observer differences in perceptions of effective control. *Journal of Personality and Social Psychology,* 1975, **31,** 503–515.

Miller, D. T., Norman, S. A., & Wright, E. Distortion in person perception as a consequence of the need for effective control. *Journal of Personality and Social Psychology,* 1978, **36,** 598–607.

Miller, D. T., & Ross, M. Self-serving biases in the attribution of causality: Fact or fiction? *Psychological Bulletin,* 1975, **82,** 213–225.

Miller, G. A., Galanter, E., & Pribram, K. H. *Plans and the structure of behavior.* New York: Holt, Rinehart & Winston, 1960.

Mischel, T. Understanding neurotic behavior: From "mechanism" to "intentionality." In T. Mischel (Ed.), *Understanding other persons.* Totowa, N.J.: Rowman & Littlefield, 1974.

Mischel, W. Toward a cognitive social learning reconceptualization of personality. *Psychological Review,* 1973, **80,** 252–283.

Modigliani, A. Embarrassment, face work, and eye contact: Testing a theory of embarrassment. *Journal of Personality and Social Psychology,* 1971, **17,** 15–24.

Mosher, D. L. Approval motive and acceptance of "fake" personality test interpretations which differ in favorability. *Psychological Reports,* 1965, **17,** 395–402.

Murphy, G. *Outgrowing self-deception.* New York: Basic Books, 1975.

Myers, D. G., & Ridl, J. Can we all be better than average? *Psychology Today,* 1979, **12,** 89–98.

Neisser, U. *Cognitive psychology.* New York: Appleton-Century-Crofts, 1967.

Neisser, U. John Dean's memory: A case study. *Cognition,* 1981, **9,** 1–22.

Nicholls, J. G. Causal attributions and other achievement related cognitions: Effects of task outcome, attainment value, and sex. *Journal of Personality and Social Psychology,* 1975, **31,** 379–389.

Nisbett, R. E., & Ross, L. *Human inference: Strategies and shortcomings of social judgement.* Englewood Cliffs, N.J.: Prentice-Hall, 1980.

Nisbett, R. E., & Wilson, T. D. Telling more than we know: Verbal reports on mental processes. *Psychological Review,* 1977, **84,** 231–259.

Orvis, B. R., Cunningham, J. D., & Kelley, H. H. A closer examination of causal inference: The role of consensus, distinctiveness, and consistency information. *Journal of Personality and Social Psychology,* 1975, **32,** 604–616.

Piaget, J. *The language and thought of the child.* New York: Harcourt, Brace, 1926.

Piaget, J. *The moral judgment of the child.* New York: Free Press, 1965. (Originally published in 1932.)

Potter, S. *Three-upmanship: The theory and practice of gamesmanship. Some notes on lifemanship: One-upmanship.* New York: Holt, Rinehart & Winston, 1962.

Quigley-Fernandez, B., & Tedeschi, J. T. The bogus pipeline as a lie detector: Two validity studies. *Journal of Personality and Social Psychology,* 1978, **36,** 247–256.

Riemer, B. S. Influence of causal beliefs on affect and expectancy. *Journal of Personality and Social Psychology,* 1975, **31,** 1163–1167.

Riess, M., Rosenfeld, P., Melburg, V., & Tedeschi, J. T. Self-serving attributions: Biased private perceptions and distorted public descriptions. *Journal of Personality and Social Psychology,* 1981, **41,** 224–231.

Ringer, R. J. *Looking out for number one.* New York: Harper & Row, 1977.

Riordan, C. A. Intent, consequences, and locus of control: Some more effects on judgments following harmdoing. Unpublished manuscript, University of Missouri–Rolla, 1982.

Rogers, C. R. *Client-centered therapy: Its current practice, implications, and theory.* Boston: Houghton Mifflin, 1951.

Rogers, T. B., Rogers, P. J., & Kuiper, N. A. Evidence for the self as a cognitive prototype: The "false alarms" effect. *Personality and Social Psychology Bulletin,* 1979, **5,** 53–56.

Ross, L., Bierbrauer, G., & Polly, S. Attribution of educational outcomes by professional and non-professional instructors. *Journal of Personality and Social Psychology,* 1974, **29,** 609–618.

Ross, M., & Sicoly, F. Egocentric biases in availability and attribution. *Journal of Personality and Social Psychology,* 1979, **37,** 322–336.

Rotenberg, K. Children's use of intentionality in judgements of character and disposition. *Child Development,* 1980, **51,** 282–284.

Ruble, D. N., & Feldman, N. S. Order of consensus, distinctiveness, and consistency of information and causal attributions. *Journal of Personality and Social Psychology,* 1976, **34,** 930–937.

Ryan, W. *Blaming the victim.* New York: Vintage Books, 1972.

Sartre, J. P. *Being and nothingness: An essay on phenomenological ontology* (Translated by H. Barnes.). London: Methuen, 1958.

Schlenker, B. R. Group members' attributions of responsibility for prior group performance. *Representative Research in Social Psychology,* 1975, **6,** 96–108. (a)

Schlenker, B. R. Self-presentation: Managing the impression of consistency when reality interferes with self-enhancement. *Journal of Personality and Social Psychology,* 1975, **32,** 1030–1037. (b)

Schlenker, B. R. *Impression management: The self-concept, social identity, and interpersonal relations.* Monterey, Calif.: Brooks/Cole, 1980.

Schlenker, B. R. Personal communication, 1981.

Schlenker, B. R. Personal communication, 1982.

Schlenker, B. R. Translating actions into attitudes: An identity-analytic approach to the explanation of social conduct. In L. Berkowitz (Ed.), *Advances in experimental social psychology*. New York: Academic Press, in press.

Schlenker, B. R., & Leary, M. R. Social anxiety and self-presentation: A conceptualization and model. *Psychological Bulletin*, 1982, **92**, 641–669.

Schlenker, B. R., & Miller, R. S. Egocentrism in groups: Self-serving biases or logical information processing? *Journal of Personality and Social Psychology*, 1977, **35**, 755–764.

Schlenker, B. R., Soraci, S., & McCarthy, B. Self-esteem and group performance as determinants of egocentric perceptions in cooperative groups. *Human Relations*, 1976, **29**, 1163–1176.

Scott, M. B., & Lyman, S. M. Accounts. *American Sociological Review*, 1968, **33**, 46–62.

Shaver, K. G. Defensive attribution: Effects of severity and relevance on the responsibility assigned to an accident. *Journal of Personality and Social Psychology*, 1970, **14**, 101–113.

Shaw, M. E. Attribution of responsibility by adolescents in two cultures. *Adolescence*, 1968, **3**, 23–32.

Shaw, M. E., & Reitan, H. T. Attribution of responsibility as a basis for sanctioning behavior. *British Journal of Social and Clinical Psychology*, 1969, **8**, 217–226.

Shaw, M. E., & Sulzer, J. L. An empirical test of Heider's levels in attribution of responsibility. *Journal of Abnormal and Social Psychology*, 1964, **69**, 39–46.

Shaw, M. E., & Tremble, T. R. Effects of attribution of responsibility for a negative event to a group member upon group process as a function of the structure of the event. *Sociometry*, 1971, **34**, 504–514.

Sherwood, G. G. Self-serving biases in person perception: A reexamination of projection as a mechanism of defense. *Psychological Bulletin*, 1981, **90**, 445–459.

Shovar, N., & Carlston, D. *Reactions to attributional self-presentation.* Paper presented at the Midwestern Psychological Association, Chicago, 1979.

Sicoly, F., & Ross, M. Facilitation of ego-biased attributions by means of self-serving observer feedback. *Journal of Personality and Social Psychology*, 1977, **35**, 734–741.

Smith, T. W., Snyder, C. R., & Handelsman, M. M. On the self-serving function of an academic wooden leg: Test anxiety as a self-handicapping strategy. *Journal of Personality and Social Psychology*, 1982, **42**, 314–321.

Snyder, C. R. Effects of comparison level feedback on classroom-related verbal learning performance. *Journal of Educational Psychology*, 1972, **63**, 493–499.

Snyder, C. R. The "illusion" of uniqueness. *Journal of Humanistic Psychology*, 1978, **18**, 33–41.

Snyder, C. R. The excuse: An amazing grace? In B. R. Schlenker (Ed.), *Self and identity: Presentations of self in social life*. New York: McGraw-Hill, in press.

Snyder, C. R., & Clair, M. S. Effects of expected and obtained grades on teacher evaluation and attribution of performance. *Journal of Educational Psychology*, 1976, **68**, 75–82.

Snyder, C. R., & Fromkin, H. L. *Uniqueness: The human pursuit of difference.* New York: Plenum, 1980.

Snyder, C. R., & Katahn, M. The relationship of state anxiety, feedback, and ongoing self-reported affect to performance in complex verbal learning. *American Journal of Psychology*, 1970, **83**, 237–247.

Snyder, C. R., & Katahn, M. Comparison levels, test anxiety, ongoing affect, and complex verbal learning. *American Journal of Psychology*, 1973, **86**, 555–565.

Snyder, C. R., & Newburg, C. L. The Barnum effect in groups. *Journal of Personality Assessment*, 1981, **45**, 622–629.

Snyder, C. R., & Shenkel, R. J. Effects of "favorability," modality, and relevance upon acceptance of general personality interpretations prior to and after receiving diagnostic feedback. *Journal of Consulting and Clinical Psychology*, 1976, **44**, 34–41.

Snyder, C. R., Shenkel, R. J., & Lowery, C. R. Acceptance of personality interpretations: The "Barnum effect" and beyond. *Journal of Consulting and Clinical Psychology*, 1977, **45**, 104–114.

Snyder, C. R., & Smith, T. W. Symptoms as self-handicapping strategies: The virtues of old wine in a new bottle. In G. Weary & H. L. Mirels (Eds.), *Integrations of clinical and social psychology*. New York: Oxford University Press, 1982.

Snyder, M. L., Stephan, W. G., & Rosenfield, D. Attributional egotism. In J. H. Harvey, W. J. Ickes, & R. F. Kidd (Eds.), *New directions in attribution research* (Vol. 2). Hillsdale, N.J.: Lawrence Erlbaum Associates, 1978.

Snyder, M. L., & Wicklund, R. A. Attribute ambiguity. In J. A. Harvey, W. J. Ickes, & R. F. Kidd (Eds.), *New directions in attribution research* (Vol. 3). Hillsdale, N.J.: Lawrence Erlbaum Associates, 1981.

Steiner, I. D. Reactions to adverse and favorable evaluations of oneself. *Journal of Personality*, 1968, **36**, 553–564.

Stevens, L., & Jones, E. E. Defensive attribution and the Kelley cube. *Journal of Personality and Social Psychology*, 1976, **34**, 809–820.

Sullivan, H. S. *Conceptions of modern psychiatry*. Washington, D.C.: William Alanson White Foundation, 1947.

Sullivan, H. S. *The interpersonal theory of psychiatry*. New York: Norton, 1953.

Suls, J. M., & Miller, R. L. (Eds.), *Social comparison processes: Theoretical and empirical perspectives*. Washington, D.C.: Hemisphere, 1977.

Sulzer, J. L., & Burglass, R. K. Responsibility attribution, empathy and punitiveness. *Journal of Personality*, 1968, **36**, 272–282.

Sykes, G., & Matza, D. Techniques of neutralization: A theory of delinquency, *American Sociological Review*, 1957, **22**, 664–670.

Tedeschi, J. T., & Riess, M. Verbal strategies in impression management. In C. Antaki (Ed.), *The psychology of ordinary explanations of social behavior*. London: Academic Press, 1981.

Tetlock, P. E. Explaining teacher explanations of pupil performance: A self-presentation interpretation. *Social Psychology Quarterly*, 1980, **43**, 283–290.

Thibaut, J. W., & Kelley, H. H. *The social psychology of groups*. New York: Wiley, 1959.

Thomas, E. J. Role theory, personality, and the individual. In E. F. Borgatta & W. W. Lambert (Eds.), *Handbook of personality theory and research*. Chicago: Rand McNally, 1968.

Turner, R. G. Self-consciousness and speed of processing self-relevant information. *Personality and Social Psychology Bulletin,* 1978, **4**, 456–460.

Turner, R. H. The self-conception in social interaction. In C. Gordon & K. J. Gergen (Eds.), *The self in social interaction.* New York: Wiley, 1968.

Walster, E. Assignment of responsibility for an accident. *Journal of Personality and Social Psychology,* 1966, **3**, 73–79.

Walster, E., Walster, G. W., & Bercheid, E. *Equity: Theory and research.* Boston: Allyn & Bacon, 1978.

Weary, G. Self serving attributional biases: Perceptual or response distortions? *Journal of Personality and Social Psychology,* 1979, **37**, 1418–1420.

Weary, G. An examination of affect and egotism as mediators of bias in causal attributions. *Journal of Personality and Social Psychology,* 1980, **38**, 348–357.

Weary, G., & Arkin, R. M. Attributional self-presentation. In J. H. Harvey, W. Ickes, & R. F. Kidd (Eds.), *New directions in attribution research* (Vol. 3). Hillsdale, N.J.: Lawrence Erlbaum Associates, 1981.

Weary-Bradley, G. Self-serving bias in the attribution process: A reexamination of the fact or fiction question. *Journal of Personality and Social Psychology,* 1978, **36**, 56–71.

Wells, G. L., & Harvey, J. H. Do people use consensus information in making causal attributions? *Journal of Personality and Social Psychology,* 1977, **35**, 279–293.

Wells, G. L., Petty, R. E., Harkins, S. G., Kagehiro, D., & Harvey, J. H. Anticipated discussion of interpretation eliminates actor-differences in the attribution of causality. *Sociometry,* 1977, **40**, 247–253.

Wells, L. E., & Marwell, G. *Self-esteem: Its conceptualization and measurement.* Beverly Hills, Calif.: Sage Publications, 1976.

White, R. W. Motivation reconsidered: The concept of competence. *Psychological Review,* 1959, **66**, 297–333.

Wicklund, R. A. Objective self-awareness. In L. Berkowitz (Ed.), *Advances in experimental social psychology* (Vol. 8). New York: Academic Press, 1975.

Wicklund, R. A., & Brehm, J. W. *Perspectives on cognitive dissonance.* Hillsdale, N.J.: Lawrence Erlbaum Associates, 1976.

Wills, T. A. Downward comparison principles in social psychology. *Psychological Bulletin,* 1981, **90**, 245–271.

Wolosin, R. J., Sherman, S. J., & Till, A. Effects of cooperation and competition on responsibility attribution after success and failure. *Journal of Experimental Social Psychology,* 1973, **9**, 220–235.

Wortman, C. B. Causal attributions and personal control. In J. H. Harvey, W. J. Ickes, & R. F. Kidd (Eds.), *New directions in attribution research* (Vol. 1). Hillsdale, N.J.: Lawrence Erlbaum Associates, 1976.

Wrightman, L. S., & Deaux, K. *Social psychology in the 80s* (3rd ed.). Monterey, Calif.: Brooks/ Cole, 1981.

Wylie, R. C. *The self-concept: A review of methodological and measuring instruments* (Vol. 1, rev. ed.). Lincoln: University of Nebraska Press, 1974.

Wylie, R. C. *The self-concept: Theory and research on selected topics* (Vol. 2, rev. ed.). Lincoln: University of Nebraska Press, 1979.

Zuckerman, M. Attribution of success and failure revisited, or: The motivational bias is alive and well in attribution theory. *Journal of Personality,* 1979, **47,** 245–287.

CHAPTER 4

Retrospective Excuses: Masquerades for the Past

Definition

Retrospective excuses are explanations or actions, *generated after a previous bad performance*, that lessen the negative implications of the performance and thereby also serve to maintain a positive self-image for oneself and others. This definition of retrospective excuses should be viewed in the context of the phenomenological field seen in Figure 4.1. The actor in this scenario senses that he or she has done something that may be construed as a bad performance. The knowledge of having previously generated a poor performance is kindled by feedback from external or internal sources (i.e., one is given feedback by another person that the performance isn't up to societal standards, or the person realizes that the performance isn't up to internal standards); moreover, the sense of bad performance often may be ignited by both external and internal sources. If the actor experiences any responsibility for a bad past performance, the self-image is threatened. Something has to be done about the threatening image, and this "something" often takes the form of the retrospective excuse masquerade.

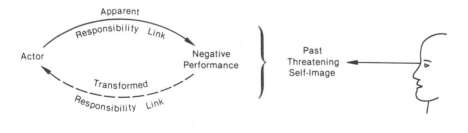

Figure 4.1. The components of the retrospective excuse-making model.

Examples

The following examples reflect actual events and participants. These case studies are presented to give the reader a taste of the breadth of excuse-making words and deeds.

CASE 1.   WITNESSES TO THE KITTY GENOVESE MURDER

At 3:20 A.M. on March 13, 1964, Catherine (Kitty) Genovese parked her car in the lot at the Kew Gardens railroad station in Queens, New York. After noticing a man in the nearby parking lot, she became nervous and hurried toward a police telephone box. The assailant overtook Ms. Genovese, slashing her with a knife. Kitty Genovese pleaded several times for help; nearby lights went on and windows were raised. A man from an adjacent apartment yelled "Let that girl alone!" The assailant apparently became frightened and returned to his car. There were 38 witnesses to this incident, yet none of them called the police. After the lights in the apartment building windows were turned off, the attacker returned to repeatedly stab Ms. Genovese, who was struggling to get to her apartment building. She screamed, "I'm dying!" Again, lights went on, windows were opened, and the assailant ran to his car. Still, none of the witnesses called the police. Ms. Genovese crawled to the door of her apartment building, only to find that her assailant had returned. He knifed her again and again, and Kitty Genovese died some 35 minutes after she had gotten out of her car. Since it took the police only two minutes to arrive at the scene, if any of the 38 witnesses had called, the murder would have been prevented.

Why hadn't the witnesses helped in some way? Basically, all people implicitly or explicitly asserted, "It wasn't my responsibility." In fact, one witness thought the whole incident was just a lovers' quarrel (Rosenthal, 1964). It is relevant to examine the excuses offered by the witnesses in this example in terms of the dimensions mentioned previously in the theory chapter. Both the more general "It wasn't my responsibility" and the specific "lovers' quarrel" excuses are verbally avowed by the witnesses. Seemingly, these witnesses may have had some awareness of their excuse-making. These excuses were applied only to the Kitty Genovese murder, and as such were low in pervasiveness. Finally, the degree to which these excuses "worked" (i.e., were effective) for the witnesses is not clear; certainly the public furor over the witnesses' lack of helping behavior suggests that these excuses did not function for the external audience.

CASE 2.   THE SOLDIERS AT THE MY LAI MASSACRE

Three platoons of U.S. troops entered the small South Vietnamese village of My Lai on March 16, 1968. A platoon led by Lt. William Calley, Jr. killed hundreds of innocent and nonresisting villagers.

Calley then turned his attention back to the crowd of Vietnamese and issued an order: "Push all those people in the ditch." Three or four GIs complied. Calley struck a woman with a rifle as he pushed her down. Stanley remembered that some of the civilians "kept trying to get out. Some made it to the top . . ." Calley began shooting and ordered Meadlo to join in. Meadlo told about it later: "So we pushed our seven to eight people in with the big bundle of them. And so I began shooting them all. So did Mitchell, Calley . . . I guess I shot maybe twenty-five or twenty people in the ditch . . . men, women, and children. And babies." (Hersch, 1970, p. 63)

And how do the soldiers excuse such behavior? The excuses were many. One version was that the "Gooks" were inferior people, hardly human. Another notion was that the Vietnamese had done the same thing to American women and children. Yet another tack was that they were "merely following orders." These excuses are verbalized (avowed), apply only to the "war" situation (low pervasiveness), and were in varying degrees successful in lessening the soldiers' responsibility (low to high effectiveness). It may be argued that this excuse rationale was beyond awareness. Certainly the "Gooks" epithet was introduced in the soldiers' basic training and reinforced by the commanding officers in Vietnam. The "following orders" excuse may not have been totally within awareness for similar reasons.

CASE 3. WHEN PROPHECY FAILS

In September 1964, a certain Marion Keech reported that she had received a prophecy from a distant planet called Clarion. She revealed that the superior beings from Clarion had visited Earth in their flying saucers, and they had seen severe fault lines in the crust of the Earth. They purportedly informed Mrs. Keech that a great flood was imminent, and it would spread from the Arctic Circle to the Gulf of Mexico, engulfing the West Coast of the United States. Mrs. Keech's mission was to warn the world of the impending watery catastrophe. In a brief time, Mrs. Keech attracted a group of followers who prepared for "the end," which has not yet arrived.

And how did Mrs. Keech respond to the fact that the great flood didn't materialize on the predicted date? She gave the following explanation:

Well, all right. Suppose they gave us the wrong date. Well, this only got into the newspapers on Thursday and people had only 72 hours to get ready to meet their maker. Now suppose it doesn't happen tonight. Let's suppose it happens next year or two or three years from now. I'm not going to change one bit. I'm going to sit here and write and maybe people will say it was this little group spreading light here that prevented the flood. Or maybe if it's delayed for a couple of years there'll be some time to get people together. I don't know. All I know is that the plan has never gone astray. (Festinger, Riecken, & Schachter, 1965, p. 166)

Along the previously described excuse dimensions, Mrs. Keech engaged in extensive verbalization (avowal) regarding the failure of her predictions. Her "reasons" for the unfulfilled predictions were highly specific to each situation (low pervasiveness). On several occasions when the damp disaster did not occur, the excuses generated by Mrs. Keech and her followers appeared to elicit some sense of relief (moderate effectiveness). As Mrs. Keech and her followers became progressively immersed in their "mission," they seemed to have less awareness of the excuses that they made "when the prophecy failed."

CASE 4.   THE "NOT TRYING" HIGH SCHOOL STUDENT

Jack was a 17-year-old adolescent who lived in a middle class family in a suburb of a large city. A quiet person who enjoyed reading, Jack had generally performed well in school (As and Bs) prior to the beginning of high school. Upon entering high school, he was full of energy and enthusiasm for his studies. He took college preparatory courses, but for the first time in his educational career he found that not every course was "easy."

It is at this point that Jack began to develop his excuse repertoire. He singled out math and chemistry courses as being "impossible." At least this is what his parents began to hear. After a few relatively poor grades in these courses (Cs), he lamented that the tests weren't fair in that they weren't over the readings or the lectures. As his grades deteriorated in these two courses, for the first time Jack also began to say negative things about his teachers, describing them as being the cause of all his problems. By his junior year, Jack's grades were Ds and Fs, and he repeatedly noted that he "wasn't really trying." Behaviorally, he ceased to study and passionately pleaded that high school just wasn't the place for him. When last seen, Jack was on the verge of dropping out of high school and was very invested in not being invested in school. In this case study, Jack not only verbalized his no-effort excuse (avowal), but he eventually behaviorally stopped trying (self-evident). Although this "not trying" ploy may have started in awareness, over time it appears to have become automatic. This excuse did allow Jack some relief from the responsibility of performing poorly in school (moderate effectiveness), and "not trying" may serve Jack in other arenas in addition to academics (high pervasiveness).

In these four case studies the principal characters all espouse their excuses after it is apparent that they have had a bad performance of some sort. The point of these examples is to illustrate the diverse arenas that precipitate excuse-making, as well as to show just a few of the many forms that retrospective excuses take. These examples, and others, are discussed further throughout this chapter. As outlined in the previous theory chapter, excuses work in three possible (sometimes interrelated) ways: lessening the apparent responsibility, reframing the performance, and lessening the transformed responsibility. Each of these three types of retrospective excuse-making is described in subsequent sections.

LESSENING APPARENT RESPONSIBILITY

Retrospective excuses of the apparent responsibility type attempt to sever the causal connection between the actor and the bad performance. If successful, this type of excuse is very effective because the actor is seemingly free of *any* responsibility for the bad performance. Ranging from simple "I didn't do it" to more complex blaming ploys, apparent responsibility excuses often are called upon first when our self-image is threatened. Indeed, if there is no "smoking gun" in our hand, we initially may set out to establish total innocence.

Innocence ("It wasn't me")

Several years ago, Chuck Berry, one of the fathers of rock and roll music, wrote and sang a song entitled "It Wasn't Me." This song reflects the essence of the innocence plea: the protagonist repeatedly finds himself in several jams, and through the refrain exclaims to anyone who will listen "It wasn't me. It must have been someone, though. It wasn't me."

The innocence plea is one of the more rudimentary excuse tactics. If the facts support the actor's "excuse," then the excuse is obviously based on the "truth"; if the facts do not support the "excuse," then it is often perceived as a lie. In the latter case, the "liar" may or may not be aware of the fact that he or she is lying. Although it is more common to consider the lie as a conscious, purposeful act that is motivated to gain a reward or avoid a punishment (see Bok, 1979), we argued in Chapter 3 that an excuse may or may not be beyond awareness. At one extreme rests the psychopathic liar—a person seemingly content in knowingly denying culpability for an ill deed. For other cases, however, if people have chronically employed excuses of denial (i.e., "It wasn't me"), over time they may actually cease to perceive any link between themselves and a "bad" performance. In the clinical realm, certain people appear to dissociate themselves from their actions. In the previous discussion, therefore, it is important to highlight the fact that the "I didn't do it" excuse may vary in terms of the actor's awareness, even when some objective criterion establishes the actor's link to the bad performance.

At the legal level, the "It wasn't me" assertion does not suffice. An alibi helps in court; so too does an alibi help at the psychological level. If the actor can demonstrate to self and others that he or she was somewhere other than the purported place where the bad performance occurred, then the responsibility link is obviously broken. Alibis, in this context, serve as physical evidence that may be particularly convincing to the audience of oneself and others. Not only may the actor assert that "It wasn't me," but the alibi corroborates this excuse.

Sometimes it helps if the excuse-maker can demonstrate "who it was." It is here that the actor can further solidify the excuse by blaming someone or something else for the bad performance. Excuse-making through blaming is addressed next.

Blaming ("It wasn't me, it was the . . .")

If it "wasn't me," the adroit excuse-maker will often go on to point out just who it was that was responsible for the bad performance. By pinning it on someone or something else, the excuse-maker has further disconnected himself or herself from having any apparent responsibility for the negative action. Consider the following examples; each represents a slight variation on the same "It wasn't me, it was the . . ." theme.

"The Computer Did It"

Expanding on the earlier work of Austin (1961) and Bolinger's (1975) concept of "syntactic exploitation," Bowerman (1981) suggested that the very structure of language can nicely serve the potential excuse-maker. Among several examples cited by Bowerman, one is noteworthy because the excuse-making writer attempts to suggest that the computer was responsible for a mistake. After an important error appeared in a directory of mental health care providers, the editor of that directory sent the following letter to all directory subscribers:

> Dear Directory Buyer:
> It was intended that members in private practice would be identified with a dagger symbol in the 1978 Directory's Geographic Index. However, due to reversed logic in the typesetting contractor's computer program, the dagger symbols were omitted for the private practitioners and were assigned in some instances to licensed persons who are not in private practice. (Cited in Bowerman, 1981, p. 29)

This mistake is seemingly in the province of the editor, but watch what happens. In the first sentence, the editor switches the focus away from himself by noting "It was intended . . ." instead of "I intended . . ." After altering the focus in the first sentence, the second sentence locates the origin of the problem as the computer (or some unidentified programmer). In two sentences, the editor has convicted the defenseless computer. This syntactic exploitation highlights the power of language as a vehicle for excuse-making. (Perhaps all of the English courses that we take in high school and college enhance our excuse-making potential.)

"That Dummy Did It"

People sometimes find themselves in group situations where there is a possibility for either a successful or an unsuccessful "group" performance. Research relevant to this point suggests that members of groups that have failed see themselves as less responsible for the failure than their partner (Johnston, 1967) or the "average" group member (Schlenker, 1975; Wolosin, Sherman, & Till, 1973); further, this bias occurs even when the group member knows that he or she was a member of the majority who determined the outcome that was deemed unsuccessful (i.e., majority group members assign themselves the same low level of responsibility as do minority group members after a failure) (Schlenker & Miller, 1977). In these studies, the group members apparently are adopting the "It wasn't me" excuse strategy. For example, in a study by Schlenker and Miller (1977), members of failed groups blamed "the poorest group member" for the unsuccessful performance. Although logically each person in the failure group contributed to the failure, the failed group member ascribed blame to "some other dummy" in his or her group. Those who are familiar with group dynamics, from families to bureaucracies, undoubtedly can testify to this phenomenon.

"They Lost" (CORFing)

The preceding subsection suggests that when a group fails, members dissociate themselves, but there are some circumstances when group membership is not clearly defined. In certain circumstances, the individual can alter the extent to which he or she appeared to be associated with a group. After a group "failure," it should follow, therefore, that persons should respond so as to make it appear less likely that they were associated with the failed group. Robert Cialdini coined the term BIRGing as shorthand for the phenomenon of "basking in reflected glory." BIRGing reflects the phenomenon whereby the individual associates with positive or attractive groups and *distances himself or herself from negative or unattractive groups* (see Cialdini, Borden, Thorne, Walker, Freeman, & Sloan, 1976, p. 370fn.; Richardson & Cialdini, 1981, p. 43).

Three experiments were performed to test this BIRGing hypothesis. In a first study, it was reasoned that students at large universities should be more prone to exhibit the connection with "their" school on Mondays following a football victory than on Mondays following a loss. Apparel identifying the university—jackets, sweaters, buttons, and tee shirts displaying the school name, nickname, or mascot—was covertly counted every Monday in sections of introductory psychology courses at Arizona State, Louisiana State, Ohio State, Notre Dame, Michigan, Pittsburgh, and Southern California universities. As predicted, there were more affiliative displays on Mondays after victories than on Mondays after defeats. Unfortunately, the authors do not report the incidence of wearing school identifying apparel on "control" days when the team did not play; by comparing the incidence of apparel wearing on days after a team victory or defeat to this baseline group, a better estimate could be made as to whether students were basking (i.e., wearing more school identifying apparel after a "victory" day than a normal day) and/or distancing themselves (i.e., wearing less school identifying apparel after a "loss" day than a normal day).

Nevertheless, the results do suggest that some combination of basking and distancing allows the student to alter his or her association with a failing team.

In a second study, Cialdini et al. sought to further document BIRGing through language. Students were called by a purported "Regional Survey Center" under the guise of a survey concerning campus issues. The students initially answered a series of questions about the campus, and half were told they had done well and the other half were told they had done poorly. Next, half of the students were asked to recall the results of a game where the football team had won and the other half of the students were asked to recall the results of a game where the team had lost. Results showed that students described the victorious games in terms of "we won" and the lost games in terms of "they lost." More important, this effect was largely due to the responses of students who initially were told they had done poorly on the campus survey. In other words, if one is already feeling unsuccessful, the tendency to associate oneself with a successful group and distance oneself from an unsuccessful group may be heightened; indeed, in this latter set the more common verbiage (86% of the respondents) was "they lost." (A third Cialdini et al. study further corroborated the "we won/they lost" phenomenon.)

For all of those instances where we may see the fans of championship teams announcing to the everpresent television camera "We're Number 1," it should be realized that there are far more excuse-making fans (they may merely call themselves "spectators") of poor teams who assert "they lost" or "they're losers." The index finger pointing skyward ("We're Number 1") may very quickly arc downward to point out who is to blame when the team loses ("They lost").* Perhaps BIRGing needs to be yoked with a new logical corollary: "CORFing" (Cutting Off Reflected Failure).† Thus although BIRGing and CORFing may both tap a more general "maintenance" of self-esteem process, BIRGing appears to reflect an *enhancement* of esteem process (for related research see Fitch, 1970; Kuiper, 1978; Schlenker, Soraci, & McCarthy, 1976; Wolosin et al., 1973) and CORFing may relect a *protection* of esteem process (for related research see Larson, 1977; Lefcourt, Hogg, Struthers, & Holmes, 1975; Schlenker, 1975).

---

* An old saying asserts that "Victory has a hundred fathers and defeat is an orphan." Actually, it appears to be the case that people will ascribe the lineage of a defeat to some identifiable other person or persons. If defeat is an orphan, therefore, it clearly is not because the blaming person doesn't try to find it a good home.

† Cialdini and Richardson (1980) proposed another phenomenon related to basking. They suggest that one additional means of maintaining a positive personal image is to *blast* a publicly known opponent. In two studies, Cialdini and Richardson (1980) show that after a personal failure on a task, subjects enhance the quality of their university (basking) and devalue the quality of a rival university (blasting).

The Art of Savage Discovery

Yet another means of slicing one's potential ties to an unfortunate outcome is to *blame the victim.*

Zero Mostel used to do a sketch in which he impersonated a Dixiecrat Senator conducting an investigation of the origins of World War II. At the climax of the sketch, the Senator boomed out, in an excruciating mixture of triumph and suspicion, "What was Pearl Harbor *doing* in the Pacific?" (Ryan, 1972, p. 3)

In a slashing indictment of American social action programs, William Ryan (1972) introduced the concept of the "art of savage discovery" in his book *Blaming the Victim.* Ryan argues that a recurring pattern of social action programs is to identify the victims as being different and strange from the rest of us; this difference is perceived as barbarian or savage. "Savage discovery," therefore, is a primary process in blaming the victim. In this process we treat social problems (i.e., disease, poverty, mental illness) as a manifestation of the individual deviance in the special problem groups of people. Ryan (1972) writes, "We cannot comfortably believe that *we* are the cause of that which is problematic to us; therefore, we are almost compelled to believe that *they*—the problematic ones—are the cause and this immediately prompts us to search for deviance" (pp. 12–13).

While the actors in the aforementioned scenario may perceive themselves as thoughtful, humanistic persons who are striving to help others, the "savage discovery" process clearly places the blame in "those people"; if social programs fail, it is not because of the pitfalls inherent in the overall societal structure, but it is because the participants have somehow failed. This sounds like the CORFing process mentioned in the preceding subsection; the apparent responsibility is on "them." In reference to the actors in these circumstances, Ryan (1972) notes: "They are, most crucially, rejecting the possibility of blaming, not the victims, but themselves. They are all unconsciously passing judgments on themselves and bringing in a unanimous verdict of Not Guilty" (p. 28).

Before moving on to discuss other excuse-making strategies, it may be useful to consider the lessening of apparent responsibility in terms of the awareness, avowal/self-evident, and effectiveness/pervasiveness dimensions. The easiest analysis along these lines pertains to the fact that the various innocence and blaming strategies are typically verbalized (avowed). (Some assert this is not always true, however, citing the classic looks of innocence [self-evident] found in children.) It appears that the use of language may be especially relevant to various blaming strategies, including such bodies of research as "The Computer Did It," "CORFing," and "Savage Discovery." The innocence tactics occasionally may be successful, especially if they are buttressed with blaming; as such, these techniques may be of moderate to high effectiveness. Since the innocence and blaming avowals are relatively circumscribed in that they pertain to a particular event, they probably are low in pervasiveness. The awareness issue is a more difficult one. Although it appears to be obvious (at least from an outside observer's view) that the actor is making an excuse when pleading innocence, the actual state of affairs for the actor who engaged in blaming suggests some lack of awareness. Blaming may become such an ingrained process that it thereby loses its conscious level of processing; moreover, some of the blaming strategies such as CORFing and savage discovery may be beyond awareness because the actor may never conceptualize that he or she is actually employing an excuse.

REFRAMING PERFORMANCES

If the actor is not able to effectively cut the ties to a bad performance, the next set of excuse-making strategies is aimed at lessening the negativity of the performance itself. The reframing of the "bad" performance so that it may be seen in a more positive light may take several forms.

See No Evil, Hear No Evil

This general type of reframing ploy is based on the premise that the actor doesn't "comprehend" the negativity of his or her own actions. The emphasis in the "See no evil, hear no evil" types of reframing is on the actor's perception of the particular events that seemingly constitute a "bad" performance. Consider the following subcategories.

The Kitty Genovese Murder Studies

The murder of Kitty Genovese, Case 1 at the beginning of this chapter, sent ripples throughout American society in general and the social sciences in particular in the spring of 1964 (Latané & Darley, 1969; Milgram, 1977). A. M. Rosenthal (1964), the city editor who was in charge of the *New York Times* coverage of this murder, offered the following comment: "It was not her life or her dying that froze the city, but the witnessing of her murder—the choking fact that thirty-eight of her neighbors had seen her stabbed or heard her cries, and not one of them, during that hideous half hour, had lifted the telephone in the safety of his own apartment to call the police and try and save her life" (p. 74).

The media synopsis of the cause of this phenomenon was "apathy." (There were subsequent books, plays, movies, and television specials exploring the Kitty Genovese murder and apathy in urban residents [Latané and Darley, 1969].) This apathy label, however, actually clouds the understanding of the witnesses' responses. They were apathetic only in the sense that they did not intervene in the murder; however, the witnesses report having experienced a combination of fascination and distress as they watched the stabbing, and as they wrestled in subsequent days and weeks with the fact that they didn't help. Recall that one witness interpreted the murder as merely a "lovers' quarrel"; this sounds suspiciously like reframed excuse-making. Indeed, the witnesses' reported perceptions of the events suggest that there was no need to call the police, and therefore the witnesses' "bad" nonhelping performance is reframed.

The Kitty Genovese murder case spawned a series of noteworthy studies by John Darley, Bibb Latané, and their colleagues. This research on bystander apathy (i.e., the lack of helping responses) consistently demonstrates that an individual is more likely than the person in a group context to respond to an emergency (Darley & Latané, 1968; Latané & Darley, 1968; Latané & Rodin, 1969; Schwartz & Clausen, 1970).

Why do people in groups not seem to help in laboratory and real-life settings? Latané and Darley (1970) suggest that nonhelpers appear to "see" the emergency as not being an emergency. This "See no evil, hear no evil" tack may be a reframing excuselike maneuver. Consider, for example, some experimental findings. In a study described as "Where there's smoke there's (sometimes) fire," Latané & Darley (1968) had male research participants wait in a room either alone or in conditions where there were two and three other persons. While completing a questionnaire, smoke suddenly began to flow into the room through a vent in the wall. The "smoke" was "finely divided titanium dioxide produced in a stoppered bottle and delivered under a slight air pressure through the vent" (p. 217). Results showed that the research participant was *more* willing to report the smoke when in the room alone as compared to group conditions. In the present reframing context, however, it is revealing to note the behaviors of the people who didn't report the fire. First, the people who didn't report the smoke appeared to take longer to actually notice the "smoke." Second, in reference to this non–help-seeking group, Latané and Darley write, "They uniformly said that they had rejected the idea that it was a fire" (p. 219). Some said it was steam or air conditioning vapors, and others thought it was smog. Sequentially, therefore, the reframing excuse-maker in this experiment may assert that he didn't spot the emergency very quickly and when he did see it, he didn't interpret it as an emergency.

In another study, often known as "The lady in distress" experiment, Latané and Rodin (1969) had male research participants wait alone or with another person. From an adjacent room, a woman was heard to fall with a loud crash; a moment later she screamed, "Oh my God, my foot . . . I . . . I . . . can't move it. Oh my ankle . . . I . . . can't get this . . . thing . . . off me" (p. 192). In actuality, the accident was staged through a tape-recording, and the variable of interest was help rendered. Again, the research participants in the alone condition were more prone to offer aid. But what about those who didn't respond? This is surely a bad performance in that the person did not offer help to another human being who was in distress. Those who did not offer help did not see it this way, however. On the contrary, they did "not seem to believe that they had behaved callously or immorally" (p. 197); rather, among the noninterveners, 59% said they weren't sure what had happened, 46% said they didn't think it was serious, and 25% thought other people would help.

The nonhelper's response that "others will help" forms the basis of the "diffusion of responsibility" hypothesis, which posits that a person feels less responsible when acting as a member of a group than when acting alone. A final step in the interpretive phase of a helping (or nonhelping) response, according to Latané and Darley (1970), involves the actor's appraisal of personal responsibility. The nonhelpers purportedly do not perceive the need to render aid because they assert that there are others present who can or will help. Through diffusion of responsibility, therefore, the actor in a group setting further suggests that he or she does not "sense" much personal responsibility (see Mynatt & Sherman, 1975; Schwartz, 1968).

Although the Kitty Genovese studies portray an extreme situation in which help is not rendered, the principle may apply to less severe circumstances. The older brother who is admonished for not helping his sister is heard to plea, "But Mom, I didn't even hear Sissy cry"; the husband who does not help his wife feed or change the baby in the middle of the night says, "Hon, I didn't even hear the kid during the night." Somehow, therefore, it appears that there are enormous amounts of day-to-day things that are not "seen," "heard," or generally "comprehended" as really demanding the excuse-maker's action.

The Choice-Harm Deescalator Studies

In the Kitty Genovese studies, it is the lack of action which generates the "bad" performance that necessitates perceptual reframing. In other instances, however, it may be an overt action that necessitates the excuse-maker's reframing. Studies within this framework often vary the actor's sense of choice of performing an act that may harm another person so as to investigate the actor's perception of the negativity of his or her actions. Results generally suggest that under higher choice conditions in which the actor believes that he or she willingly chose to perform an action, the actors tend to *underestimate* the negativity of their action. This set of findings is, for our present purposes, called the *choice-harm deescalator* effect.

In perhaps the earliest test of this phenomenon, Brock and Buss (1962) had research participants administer "painful" shocks to male and female victims (experimental confederates who, of course, actually received no shocks) under voluntary and nonvoluntary choice conditions. The voluntary choice condition was achieved by emphasizing the fact that "it's entirely up to you whether or not you stay and give the shocks" (p. 198), while the nonvoluntary choice condition gave the research participants no choice. Results revealed that the greater choice on the part of the "aggressing" research participant yielded a perceived minimization of the pain of the shock; moreover, under choice conditions (for the male "victim"), the greater the magnitude of the shocks delivered, the greater was the minimization of the pain. (This pattern of results was replicated in a subsequent study by Buss and Brock [1963].)

Related studies generally support the "choice–harm deescalator" effect in attitude change studies (Calder, Ross, & Insko, 1973; Riess & Schlenker, 1977); these studies show that people who willfully advocate an attitude that may be either insincere (e.g., Calder et al., 1973) or produce aversive consequences for another person (e.g., Riess & Schlenker, 1977) actually change their attitudes to match those that they had initially argued for. In other words, if we have willfully chosen to say something that may be construed as negative, we will in time actually come to believe in what we said. Thus an insincere statement is reframed as sincere, and a statement that may have aversive consequences is perceived as being less aversive. Therefore, among those who openly admit to having chosen to say or do something, that "something" will be seen through rose-colored glasses. As such, the choice–harm deescalator at times may have visited many of our lives. Do any of the following sound familiar? "Oh, come on, it didn't hurt that much." "It's better than it seems." "Yes, I thought of it, and give it a chance and you'll see it isn't such a bad idea."

The Victim Derogation Studies

Actors who perform actions that harm others often respond by derogating their victims. The slaughtered North Vietnamese at My Lai 4 became "Gooks" who were hardly seen as human ("They don't even value human life"); the woman who is raped is portrayed as a "whore" who "really was asking for it"; the assaulted homosexual is a "fag" who "had gotten out of place"; and so on. The language of derogation suggests that certain victims are "fair game." The derogation of the victim transforms him or her into an "object" that is seemingly deserving of injury (Goffman, 1952; Roebuck, 1964; Sykes & Matza, 1957). Or, if the victim doesn't deserve the actor's injurious assault, at least it is seen as a relatively neutral event to harm someone who is inferior or unimportant (Scott & Lyman, 1968). History is replete with examples of this phenomenon, and it should therefore come as no surprise that laboratory research has consistently documented the victim derogation reframing strategy.

The early studies relevant to this victim derogation topic indicate that once a person has performed a harmful action toward another person, that person will come to dislike the victim (e.g., Berkowitz, Green, & Macauley, 1962; Davis & Jones, 1960; Glass, 1964). This effect appears to be especially prevalent when the actor chooses to engage in a harmful activity such as delivering negative verbal feedback to another person over a microphone (Davis & Jones, 1960) or delivering electric shock to another person (Glass, 1964). (These victim derogation studies showing the importance of the actor's choice are reminiscent of the "choice–harm deescalator" described in the previous section.) The typical explanation of these results is in terms of dissonance reduction: it is less dissonant if the actor believes that he or she has harmed a bad person rather than a good one (Bercheid & Walster, 1969). Since dissonance theory is increasingly viewed as being motivated by self-esteem maintenance (Aronson, 1969; Berkowitz, 1980), the similarities between the excuse and dissonance explanations are obvious.

Melvin Lerner and his colleagues have more recently construed victim derogation as evidence for the "just world hypothesis" that people "get what they deserve" (Lerner, 1980; Lerner & Miller, 1978.)* In a usual paradigm, the research participant views a fellow subject who is being given shock by the experimenter (actually the other subject is a confederate who is receiving no shocks). Findings indicate that the research participants consistently derogate the victim even though they are not the ones delivering the shocks (e.g., Lerner, 1971; Lerner & Matthews, 1967; Lerner & Simmons, 1966). A study by Cialdini, Kenrick, and Hoerig (1976) is noteworthy in this series because it suggests that when the actor feels more responsible for the shock-induced pain in the other person, that actor engages in much more derogation of the "victim." In fact, when the actor felt no responsibility for the delivery of the shocks, the victim derogation effect disappeared in this latter study. This finding reveals that it may not be the "just world hypothesis" that is motivating people to derogate, but it may be a simple justification process (Cialdini et al., 1976). Thus the excuse-related explanation appears to be the more parsimonious and plausible one.

Manipulating Standards for "Bad" Performance

Another set of reframing approaches emphasizes the role of the standards that are applied to judge performances. If the person senses a bad performance based on one conception of a standard, the excuse-maker may go to work on the standards themselves in order to generate a more benevolent picture of his or her deeds. The variations in this type of reframing approach follow.

Attacking the Clarity of the Standard

The basis of this type of reframing is that the actor argues, after a seeming bad performance, that the original standards by which the performance was judged are not clear. Such rhetoric as "We really just didn't know what to expect," "There is no clearcut yardstick to judge this sort of thing," "The precedents aren't straightforward," and "I didn't know it had to be 10 pages long" may be

---

* This "get what they deserve" notion is reminiscent of the old "eye for an eye" adage. A good example is former President Nixon's rationale for authorizing the deception and burglary involved in acquiring the psychiatric records of Daniel Ellsberg. Nixon believed that he was repaying Ellsberg for his previous treachery (Bok, 1979, p. 132). Interestingly, this is the same logic invoked by confidence men (Goffman, 1952; Roebuck 1964) and delinquents (Sykes & Matza, 1957).

heard. Consider again the perspective of the leaders of the group, cited in the earlier examples section, who portended the end of the world by flood in 1954. After the first flood failed to materialize, Mrs. Keech argued that they may have been given the wrong date for the flood ("It's certainly coming, mind you, but we just may have the wrong timing"). It was suggested that the "messages" were hard to read and didn't establish absolute timetables. On another occasion after a spaceship had not come to pick up the faithful followers, the co-leader of the movement, Dr. Armstrong, notified the press that the spacemen possibly would pick them up, but the messages made no promises as to the exact time and place (Festinger et al., 1956, p. 188). This "When prophecy fails" example also may illustrate a general phenomenon wherein persons who engage in new or unusual activities may have a built-in excuse in that they can reason that there really are no clearly defined standards or expectations.

Lowering Expectations Relevant to Standards

The idea that is inherent in this type of reframing ploy is to lower the expectations and therefore the standards relevant to a performance. This is a recalibration process of sorts, in which the actor attempts to convince himself or herself and external audiences that the previous standards were "just set too high." "I'm not perfect" (and often the corollary, "Nobody's perfect"), "Let's be more realistic about this," "I can't always win," and "You expect too much out of me" may be invoked by the excuse-making actor.

It should be noted that consensus information often is employed by the excuse-maker to lower the *transformed* responsibility; however, such information also can be utilized to reframe the negative performance by lowering standards. (Although several of the consensus excuses described in the subsequent section on transformed responsibility may also serve to reframe the standards by a lowering process, only one or two consensus examples will be described in this subsection.) If "everyone is doing it," the aversiveness of the act should somehow be lessened. There is some empirical support for the fact that positive actions are seen as more prevalent in the general population (Snyder & Shenkel, 1976). Whatever the "it" that "everyone is doing," the excuse-making actor implicitly reasons that the standards should be yoked to prevalent behaviors. Whether it is marijuana smoking, premarital sex, low academic performance, unemployment, income-tax evasion, speeding, corner-cutting, and so on, the standards regress to the public norms. A related reframing strategy is contrasting (Jellison, 1977), whereby the actor argues that "most people would do worse even than I did." Surely, the excuse-maker reasons, the standards need to be lowered if this is the case.

Customizing: Tailoring the Standards to Fit

"It's no fair to change the rules after the game has started," according to the familiar schoolyard saying. It may not be fair, but the adroit excuse-maker can try it when it looks as though his or her outcomes aren't measuring up. Customizing, as defined here, reflects the process whereby the person seeks to change the rules or standards so as to generate a more positive view of his or her words or deeds. As an example, recall George Orwell's (1946) classic *Animal Farm*. The animals overthrew their cruel owner, Mr. Jones, and took over the running of the farm. It was to be an oasis where animals worked in harmony for their shared welfare. Commandments were written on the side of the barn so as to exhibit the new libertarian standards for all to see. Included in the commandments are "No animal shall sleep in a bed," "No animal shall drink alcohol," "No animal shall kill another animal," and "All animals are equal" (p. 33). As the pigs took over the administration of the farm, however, the standards were seemingly violated. When the pigs began to sleep in the beds in Farmer Jones' house, the other animals protested and pointed to the commandment written on the barn. Mysteriously, it now read "No animal shall sleep in a bed *with sheets.*" Since the pigs didn't use sheets, their behavior was permissible. After various "transgressions" by the pigs, the other commandments seemed to reveal that the transgressions weren't transgressions after all: "No animal shall drink alcohol *to excess*"; "No animal shall kill any other animal *without cause.*" As the story ends with the farm being run in a far more "inhumane" fashion than when Mr. Jones was the owner, the pigs had eradicated all the commandments except one, written in bold print: "ALL ANIMALS ARE EQUAL, BUT SOME ANIMALS ARE MORE EQUAL THAN OTHERS."

Obviously, language plays a key roll in the customizing technique. The following examples, collected by V. C. Hammond (1972, p. 89), illustrate customizing at work.

> He is henpecked, you are uxorious, I am married to a fine little woman whose opinions I respect.
> His son is a bum, yours is a hippie, mine is trying to find himself.
> He is pugnacious, you are contentious, I stand up for rights.
> He is sneaky, you are crafty, I am subtle.
> She is a tramp, you are a flirt, I have a warm, affectionate nature.
> She is slovenly, you are untidy, I like a house with a nice lived-in look.
> She is hidebound, you are old-fashioned, I revere tradition.
> She is childish, you are immature, I am young at heart.
> She is erratic, you are eccentric, I am capricious.

Exonerative Moral Reasoning

This type of reframing tactic involves the embedding (see Jellison, 1977) of a particular event within some other context. The excuse-maker reasons that a seemingly bad performance should be considered in the larger context of a more general standard. Consider, as an example, the comments of the bombardier of the airplane that dropped the atomic bomb on Hiroshima. The explosion is believed to have killed close to 100,000 people and injured many thousands more. On the thirtieth anniversary of this event, the bombardier commented, "I'm not proud of killing all those people, but I'm proud of saving all the lives we did" (*The Kansas City Star,* 1975, p. 4B). When former President Harry Truman was asked how he could order a bombing that resulted in such devastating destruction of human life, Truman instantly snapped back that many more lives were *saved* by the bombing (Snyder, 1982). Interestingly, the Japanese people purportedly accepted the "necessity" of the bombing of Hiroshima, but they offer the perplexing question "But why did you have to bomb Nagasaki?" (Wright, 1982).

Other examples of exonerative moral reasoning include Nazi executioners who were exterminating Jews in the service of the higher Aryan culture; parents who beat their children in order to "socialize" them; governments who send armed "observers" to "make the world safe" for democracy, communism, or whatever; social scientists who may temporarily deceive research participants during an experiment in order to further science or the understanding of people; and physicians who withhold information from a dying patient in order to "prevent suffering." A brief story involving exonerative moral reasoning may serve as an apt close to this subsection. On April 10, 1981, a 33-year-old man named Orval Wyatt Lyod killed his mother-in-law with an axe. His explanation was that he heard a noise in the garage and thought it was a large raccoon hunting for food. The raccoon was his mother-in-law.

Derogating the Sources of Negative Feedback

Another class of reframing strategies emphasizes assaults on the sources who generate the negative feedback. If these sources can be discredited or maligned, the veracity of their negative feedback is challenged. With the negative feedback thus questioned, the person has accomplished a reframing of the "bad" performance. The actor can derogate one or both of two general sources of negative feedback: (1) the test or instrument used to derive the feedback, and (2) the evaluating person who gives the feedback. We turn to these two types of derogation at this point.

Derogating the Evaluative Instrument

To turn a twist on an old saying, "It's a poor worker, but a good excuse-maker, who faults his or her tools." This excuse-making strategy questions the quality or "diagnosticity" of a test in providing any useful information. Relevant research suggests that this instrument derogation occurs only after the test has generated negative rather than positive feedback.

A good example of this instrument derogation phenomenon may be found in students' evaluations of the tests that they take in school. One reliable finding in this area is that students who do poorly on an exam also give the exam low marks. The deprecations flowing from the failed student include such classics as "It was way too picky," "That exam has all trick questions," "It was too long (or short, or multiple choice . . .)." A study by Snyder and Clair (1976) illustrates this phenomenon. Students initially heard a 20-minute lecture, after which they completed a 20-question fill-in-the-blank exam over the information covered in the lecture. Next, the students were returned their scored exams in which an A, B, or C was marked at the top (people in actuality were randomly assigned to one of the three grade conditions). Finally, the students completed a modified version of the Teacher Assessment Blank (Holmes, 1971), which taps, among other factors, perceptions regarding the clarity of the test. Results revealed that the lower the grade, the lower were the ratings of the test clarity. For anyone who has ever taught (or been taught), these results will come as no surprise.

Personality tests may also undergo the instrument derogation effect when the feedback recipient receives negative feedback. In a paradigm that is generally known as "Barnum effect" or the "acceptance phenomenon" (see Snyder, Ingram, & Newburg, 1982; Snyder, Shenkel, & Lowery, 1977, for reviews), research participants initially took a projective test (the Rorschach) and then waited for "their" feedback (Snyder & Shenkel, 1976). The diagnostician who had scored the projective test then gave the person "his" or "her" test results. In actuality, all people received either a positively worded or a negatively worded personality interpretation. As one of the dependent measures, feedback recipients rated their "faith in psychological tests as a means of gaining accurate information about themselves." As expected, those who received the negative feedback reported having less faith in tests than those who received positive feedback. In a replication of this study, Snyder and Clair (1977) asked an even more pointed question: "How much faith do you have in psychological tests such as ink-blots?" In two studies, persons who had received negative feedback reported having less faith in the inkblots than did people who received positive feedback. It's a bad test, then, that gives us bad feedback.

Derogating the Evaluative Person

In a wide variety of experimental situations, the actor who receives negative feedback will respond by engaging in some form of derogation of the evaluator who generates or delivers the feedback (Jones, 1973; Mettee & Aronson, 1974; Snyder & Clair, 1976). (One is reminded of the stories about the unfortunate messenger who brings bad news, only to find that the king or emperor has him killed.) In the general area of teacher evaluation, it has become almost axiomatic to note that students who receive lower grades will deprecate the teacher's performance (Anikeef, 1953; Clair & Snyder, 1979; Holmes, 1972; Snyder & Clair, 1976; Stewart & Malpass, 1966). In the Snyder and Clair (1976) study described in the previous section, the students who received the lower grades generated the poorer overall instructor ratings; moreover, they perceived the instructor's presentations and level of motivation as being weak. An additional finding was that the students who expected higher grades rated the instructor more poorly. It was as if the high expectations set up circumstances wherein the obtained grades could only "fall below" expectations. And who is to "pay" in this disappointment set? The answer is the teacher, who is criticized for not having "taught" the students who thought they were going to do very well.

Research pertaining to personality feedback also suggests that the recipients of negatively worded as compared to positively worded feedback will derogate the skills of the diagnostician. In the Snyder and Shenkel (1976) study described previously, the research participants who received either positive or negative feedback were also asked to rate "How skillful is your diagnostician in deriving personality interpretations of people?" Those who received the negative personality feedback rated the diagnostician as far less skillful. These results have been replicated in two subsequent studies (Snyder & Clair, 1977).

In another body of literature within the interpersonal attraction paradigm, results indicate that an evaluator who gives the actor negative rather than positive feedback is reviewed more negatively (Aronson & Worchel, 1966; Berkowitz & Green, 1962; Griffit & Guay, 1969; Jones & Panitch, 1971; Shrauger & Jones, 1968; Skolnick, 1971). A study by Skolnick (1971) is representative of these interpersonal attraction studies. The research participant initially was (1) placed in a situation with seven strangers and was supposed to form impressions of them, (2) informed that he would take two performance tests and then the group would be divided into two groups that would compete for a prize, and (3) asked to write a note about another person in the group and in that note comment on his general feelings about the person as well as his desire to have the person on his team. The experimenters surreptitiously manipulated the notes so that some research participants received notes stating that the other person didn't want him on his team (the negative interpersonal feedback). The findings showed that the sender of the negative note was rated much lower than the sender of the positive note. In short, we don't like an evaluator who doesn't like us. In this reframing process, the excuse-making actor has diluted the negativity of the feedback by discrediting the evaluator.

The aforementioned studies provide consistent information supporting the fact that the actor, following negative feedback, derogates the evaluator. There is at least one study, however, that takes this question one step further by examining the potential stress-reducing effects of derogating the evaluator. In a study by Burish and Houston (1979), subjects initially were given stressful failure feedback regarding their performance on an achievement test, and then were either allowed or not allowed to derogate the test examiner. In the "derogation" condition,* subjects were told that examiners can have a significant in-

---

* Burish and Houston (1979) call this "derogation" condition causal projection. The term causal projection is related to what has been called "complementary projection" within psychoanalytic theory. Definitionally, causal projection "refers to the process by which a person

fluence on how people perform on achievement tests, and then were asked to (1) list all the things the examiner did "which could have caused you or anyone else to do poorly on the test," (2) "rate the extent to which the examiner made her nervous and anxious," and (3) "select from a list of 14 adjectives [taken from the Hostility Scale of the MAACL] those which best described the examiner" (Burish & Houston, 1979, p. 64). In a "no-derogation" control condition, subjects were given no mention of the examiner's potential role, nor were they allowed to rate the examiner on the three dimensions. The dependent measures of interest in this study were state measures of anxiety, depression, and hostility taken before and after the "derogation–no-derogation" manipulation. Relative to the no-derogation condition subjects, the derogation condition subjects reported significantly less increase in anxiety, depression, and hostility.* Thus the derogation of the examiner served to lessen the threatening impact of the "bad" performance. Indeed, a poor performance on an achievement test may not be so "bad" when the examiner can be derogated.

A final issue in regard to the present section on reframing strategies pertains to an analysis of these excuses in terms of the avowal, effectiveness, and awareness dimensions. The previously mentioned excuse strategies aimed at reframing one's bad performances are all verbalized (avowed). At least one of the tactics, customizing, appears to call for special verbal acrobatic skills. Although a great number of studies demonstrate that actors invoke reframing strategies after bad performances, there is little research revealing the effectiveness of these strategies in maintaining the actor's image. However, there is at least one empirical study showing the stress-controlling influence of derogation. This finding, coupled with the highly consistent and reliable generation of reframing ploys *after failurelike experiences,* suggests that reframing must serve the actors well. Thus it is the case that reframing excuses are probably in the moderate to high range in terms of their effectiveness. Although many of the reframing tactics were elicited in specific situations, in principle they appear applicable to similar situations (low to high pervasiveness). For example, derogation can be employed only in a particular situation, or it can be applied across a variety of situations. It should also be obvious that the actor's level of awareness can vary considerably in reframing strategies. Some widely employed tactics, such as derogating the source of negative feedback, appear to be good candidates for

---

attributes the cause of his/ her feelings, behaviors, or personality characteristics onto a non-veridical source outside of himself or herself" (Burish & Houston, 1979, p. 58). As such, causal projection operationally is synonymous with derogation of the evaluator as it is employed in the present context of reframing type of excuse strategies.

* Two previous studies by Houston and his colleagues (Bloom & Houston, 1975; Burish, Houston, & Bloom, 1978) did not find any stress reducing effect related to the derogation of the evaluator, but Burish and Houston (1979) offer a variety of methodological reasons for the lack of effects in their previous studies.

excuses within awareness. Even those tactics, however, when used chronically, may recede from awareness. Many of the other reframing strategies may not be within the immediate awareness of the excuse-maker, especially since such maneuvers as the "See no evil" ones probably are not even conceptualized as excuses. Further, given the potential effectiveness of these reframing strategies, they may take on the status of a reason for the actor; in this sense, the awareness is clouded further.

LESSENING TRANSFORMED RESPONSIBILITY

If the actor acknowledges the apparent responsibility for a bad performance (yes, he or she did it), and the performance is indeed a bad one in that it does not meet personal or societal standards (yes, it was bad), a threatening self-image is still playing in the theater of the mind. The masquerade is not over, however. On the contrary, the excuse-maker can call on a myriad of transformed responsibility strategies that will lessen personal responsibility. A verbal parade of "yes, buts" is generated to suggest that the actor should be held far less responsible than it seems. The excuse masquerader is in full regalia at this point.

Consensus Raising

The common theme of this type of excuse strategy is that almost anyone would behave in the same way the actor did in a particular situation. If the actor can demonstrate that others have behaved or would behave similarly, the "psychological" responsibility for the particular actor is lessened.

Task Difficulty and Luck

Bernard Weiner and his colleagues (Weiner, Frieze, Kukla, Reed, Rest, & Rosenbaum, 1971) proposed that a person may attribute his or her success or failures on achievement-related tasks to internal factors such as ability and effort and to external factors such as task difficulty and luck. (Actually, Weiner also proposed that attributions may be characterized by a temporary–stable dimension and an intentionality dimension. These additional factors do not add to the present discussion of excuse-making and are therefore not addressed.) Task difficulty attributes relate to elevated consensus because it may be reasoned that if a task is difficult, then *anyone* would do poorly on it. Similarly, when "bad luck" or fate is invoked as an explanation, each can at times engulf anyone.

A fairly large body of research has tested the task difficulty and luck types of attributions after success or failure on a variety of achievement-related tasks. For example, people have been given success and failure feedback on such tasks as anagrams (Davis & Davis, 1972), cryptograms (Larson, 1977), sensory discrimination (Stevens & Jones, 1976), social perceptiveness (Miller, 1976), and college exams (Simon & Feather, 1973). Although there are a few instances in which people do not engage in the excuselike strategy of giving task difficulty and luck external attributions after a failure rather than the internal attributions of ability and effort, the overall analysis of some 29 studies relevant to this topic suggests that the external attributions are more prevalent after failure feedback (Zuckerman, 1979). As can be seen in Table 4.1, it appears that when failure subjects are compared to success subjects, they attribute their performances more to the image-protecting external task difficulty and "bad" luck factors, and success subjects attribute their performances more to image-enhancing internal ability and elevated effort factors (this effort issue will be addressed more fully in a subsequent section on consistency lowering).

The consensus component of the task difficulty and luck attributions should be obvious to the reader. Consider just two examples: "That test was so hard that no one could have done well," and "That guy's serve was so good today, nobody could have beaten him." In these task difficulty excuses, the negativity of the performance is presented as being directly caused by the difficulty of achieving an adequate performance in that situation. The implicit reasoning

TABLE 4.1. Number of Studies Exhibiting Causal Attributions to External Factors and Internal Factors on Achievement-Related Tasks as a Function of Success/Failure Attributional Pattern[a]

Success/Failure Attributional Pattern	Causal Attribution Factor			
	Internal		External	
	Ability	Effort	Task Difficulty	Luck
Significantly higher attribution of success than of failure subjects to factor	14	13	3	1
No difference in attributions of failure and success subjects to factor	10	3	6	13
Significantly higher attribution of failure than of success subjects to factor	3	1	9	15

[a] Data are taken from Zuckerman, 1979; note that the incompletely cited results of a 1976 Miller study in the original Zuckerman review are corrected in the present table.

would maintain that *any* actor given the same circumstances would produce the same poor performance. Such is also the case when the classic nebulous external factors of "bad luck" and fate are given as excuses. We laugh at Lucy, but only because she may be less subtle than we are.

Coercion

The perpetrators of the My Lai 4 killings, from private on up to U.S. Army Lieutenant Calley, suggested that they were "merely following orders." Adolf Eichmann, who oversaw the extermination of 6 million Jews in Nazi Germany, argued at his trial that he was doing what he was told by his superiors. These cases are shocking in the transparency of the excuses, and the reader may take solace in the fact that these examples are extreme. The underlying coercion rationale, however, may exist in common day-to-day excuses such as "I *had* to do it," "My Mom made me do it," "You told me to do it." By invoking coercion and suggesting that he or she had no choice, the actor is employing the consensus-raising logic that anyone in the same circumstances would have behaved in the same fashion.

Perhaps the most well-known studies dealing with the general topic of coercion are those on obedience that were conducted by Stanley Milgram (1963, 1965). In the original study, 40 males of various ages and occupations from the New Haven, Connecticut area were paid to participate in a research project at Yale University. The subject was instructed that his job was to teach the learner a list of word-pair associates, and that the experimenter was interested in the effects of punishment on learning. The subject then saw a learner (who was really a confederate) strapped to a chair with electrodes attached to his wrist. The electrodes purportedly delivered the electric shocks that were to be administered by the subject when the learner gave an incorrect answer. The subject was told to administer an increasingly higher shock, going from 15 volts ("slight shock") to 450 volts ("Danger: Severe Shock"), whenever the learner made a mistake on the paired associated task. In actuality the learner, who was in a separate room, did not receive any shocks; moreover, the learner gave standardized responses (via tape-recorder) at various shock levels. At 300 volts, the learner pounded on the walls, screamed in protest, and shortly thereafter ceased to respond. If the subject turned to the experimenter for advice, the experimenter merely gave standardized responses to the effect that the subject should continue. To the surprise of Milgram and others (e.g., psychiatrists) who had been asked to predict the subjects' *obedience* in giving shock, 26 of the 40 subjects, or 65%, gave 450 volts. Thus a situation evidently can impel normal people to engage in behavior that is destructive to other people. Indeed, Milgram (1974) argues that we cannot count on "human nature" to prevent such aggressive interpersonal behavior.

If "human nature" cannot be counted on to prevent such aggressive behavior, it *can* be counted on to deliver excuses. For anyone who has watched the film of the original obedience study, it is fascinating to listen to the subjects as they explain why they shocked another human being with 450 volts. Their reason is always that they were made to do it: "The experimenter made me do it." This is a coercion appeal in its most basic form.

Before leaving the present topic, it is relevant to introduce a term that further defines the coercion excuse rationale. Several studies show that after a person has apparently delivered painful electric shocks to another person, the greater the perceived harm, the more the subject will assert that he or she had no choice (Brock & Buss, 1962, 1964; Harvey, Harris, & Barnes, 1975). We will call this phenomenon the *harm–choice deescalator,* since greater harm apparently results in a lessening of perceived choice or freedom on the part of the transgressing actor. The harm–choice deescalator appears to be the temporal sequalae to the choice–harm deescalator described in a previous section of this chapter. Thus if people are given a choice and go ahead and harm another person, they diminish the perceived harm (the choice–harm deescalator); then if people generate greater harm to another person, they diminish their perceived choice (the harm–choice deescalator).

Misery Loves Company

This well-known saying appears to capture the essence of consensus-raising excuse-making. If the actor is threatened by a bad performance, that actor may be expected to argue that other people also have had bad performances. By suggesting that other people would also do poorly *in the same situation,* the excuse-maker is cutting personal responsibility and in turn placing the responsibility in the situation. Whether the researchers call this process "scapegoating" or "projection," the consensus-raising excuse is present through a *threat-derogation* process (Wills, 1981, p. 251). After a strong ego threat (the bad performance), threat derogation takes the form of the actor devaluing and derogating other people in the same circumstances, and in so doing implicitly raising the consensus for his or her ill deeds.

In studies of "scapegoating" (also called "hostility generalization" or "displaced aggression"), the bad performance typically first involves failure feedback on an intellectual task, and this failure is sometimes accompanied by severe criticism and ridicule from the experimenter; the subject then is allowed to make ratings of target people who are *not* related to the provoking experimenter or evaluator. (The reader should refer back to the previous section for a discussion of derogations of the evaluator.) In a review of the studies within this general paradigm, Wills (1981) reports a consistent pattern of results wherein the ego-threatened as compared to non–ego-threatened subjects devalue both high and low status target persons across a number of different personality traits.

Perhaps the best known "misery loves company" type of excuse has been explored under the rubric of *projection.* Generally speaking, projection is defined as the process whereby the person ascribes personal shortcomings to others in order to avoid a psychological threat. Since Freud introduced the projection concept as a mechanism of defense, the initial theory and psychoanalytically oriented writing centered upon *classical projection,* which purportedly reflects the process in which the actor is unaware of possessing a negative characteristic that is ascribed to others. Freud's (1895/1966) conceptualization of this "classical" projection was that it served "to fend off an idea that is incompatible with the ego by projecting its substance into the real world" (p. 270).* This definition of projection is not relevant to the present excuse-making model which posits that the person is aware of the "bad review"; moreover, research on classical projection has generally failed to demonstrate any convincing evidence for its existence (for reviews see Holmes, 1968, 1978, 1981). Indeed, Sherwood (1982) implied that the criterion of "lack of awareness" of possessing a negative characteristic may render an experimental analysis of "classical" projection as being difficult, if not impossible to achieve. Therefore, classical projection is not addressed further.

Contrary to classical projection, however, research has consistently demonstrated the existence of *attributive projection* (for reviews see Holmes, 1968, 1978, 1981; Sherwood, 1981). In attributive projection, the actor is fully aware of possessing the particular characteristic that is ascribed to other people. The people either are or are not given negative personality feedback, and they are then allowed to make ratings of some other person or persons. The usual findings are that the threatened person who is given a more negative feedback also perceives other people more negatively. Further, it should be emphasized that the threatened person usually generates more negative ratings of *both* "desirable" and "undesirable" other persons (e.g., Bramel, 1962, 1963; Edlow & Kiesler, 1966; Holmes, 1976, cited in Holmes, 1978). Thus the threatened persons may use all target ("positive" and "negative") people when they are seek-

---

* An analysis of Freud's original writings pertaining to "classical" defensive projection gives the reader the impression that Freud was not so much concerned with elucidating the concept of defensive projection per se; rather, Freud appears to invoke defensive projection somewhat inconsistently in the service of explicating other phenomena such as paranoia (Freud, 1895/1966; 1896/1953), taboos related to death (Freud, 1913/1955), hysterical phobias (Freud, 1915/1957), and extreme jealousy (Freud, 1922/1955).

ing to heighten the consensus for their personality weaknesses. This projectionlike process appears to be very similar to the results found in the "scapegoating" studies; this similarity of results should not be surprising in light of the fact that the methodologies in the "scapegoating" and "projection" studies are comparable (Wills, 1981, 1982). In fact, the threat-derogation hypothesis may reflect a parsimonious explanation for both bodies of literature.

Implicit in the threat-derogation hypothesis is the fact that threatened people are raising consensus in order to preserve their self-images. Additional studies, however, have been conducted to directly test the stress-reduction, or image-maintenance, function of attributive projection. There are four studies whose methodologies provide sound tests of the stress-reduction role of projection (Bennett & Holmes, 1975; Burish & Houston, 1979; Holmes & Houston, 1971; Zemore & Greenough, 1973) and two studies whose methodologies render the results as being uninterpretable (Heilbrun, 1978; Stevens & Reitz, 1970). Since the stress-reducing role of projection is crucial to an understanding of the self-image maintenance of consensus-raising excuse-making, and because there are precious few studies that go beyond the demonstration of the existence of excuses to actually establish their stress-reduction role, each of these four studies is discussed in some detail. (Some of the conditions and variables in these studies are not discussed because they are not directly relevant to the projection–stress-reduction issue.)

In an early study, Holmes and Houston (1971) gave one group of females feedback that they were maladjusted ("students receiving this feedback should be seen immediately in the Health Center or Counseling Center", p. 209), and a second group was given feedback that they were well-adjusted. Next, the subjects were given a form with the names of three of their friends, and they were asked how maladjusted the friends would be if they took the same test. Results showed that maladjustment feedback subjects projected significantly more pathology onto their friends than did the control ("well-adjusted") subjects. Thus the projection phenomenon was demonstrated. However, the maladjustment subjects did not self-report any more anxiety reduction than the control group. This finding obviously does not support the stress-reduction effect of projection. Nevertheless, one additional internal analysis provided some indication of the stress-reduction role of projection; more specifically, within the maladjustment group, the high as compared to low projectors evidenced slightly more anxiety reduction ($p < .12$, one-tailed).

In another projection study, female college students took a vocabulary test which was called the "Wide Range Vocabulary Test" (Bennett & Holmes, 1975, p. 917). In a manipulation of the first variable, the researchers informed the failure feedback subject that she had performed at a level that was 55% of that which she estimated; the no-failure feedback subject was told that the experimenters were merely "testing out the test" and that the subject did not even have to put her name on the test, nor would she receive feedback. Subsequent manipulation checks revealed that the failure–no-failure feedback was very successful in generating differential levels of stress. Immediately after completing the test, subjects completed a state measure of anxiety known as the Affect Adjective Checklist (AACL; Zuckerman, 1960). Next the subjects were administered one of the two instructions of the projection condition variable. In the projection condition, after the completion of the first AACL, subjects were given a form with the names of three friends whom the subject had identified earlier. The subject was then asked to rate the percentile for each of the three friends if they were to take the test. This procedure allowed the subject to project her failure onto her friends. (Recall that in excuse terms, the assertion that others would also do poorly on the tasks externalizes the responsibility by suggesting that it is the situation that is causing the poor performance, not the person.) In the no-projection technique condition, the subjects were given no forms on which to project their friends' performance, nor was any mention of the friends made. Finally, all subjects completed the AACL for a second time in order to ascertain differential anxiety reactions as a function of failure versus no-failure feedback and projection versus no-projection techniques.

The results of the Bennett and Holmes study demonstrated that projection did occur; failure projection condition subjects estimated that their friends would have scores at the 57th percentile, while the nonfailure projection condition subjects estimated their friends' scores at 73rd percentile. Thus after experiencing failure, people were more prone to assert that their friends would fail also. The results pertaining to anxiety are shown in Table 4.2. Generally, the findings provide clearcut support for the anxiety-reducing role of projection. For example, after failure feedback, projection condition subjects reported less anxiety than subjects who had no postfailure projection technique; moreover, the no-failure projection condition subjects did not report a significantly lower anxiety level than the failure projection condition subjects. Overall,

TABLE 4.2.   Postcoping Mean Adjusted AACL Anxiety Scores Adjusted for Initial AACL Scores as a Function of Failure Condition (Failure vs. No Failure) and Projection Condition (Projection vs. No Technique)[a]

Failure Condition	Projection Condition	
	Projection	No Technique
Failure	5.96_{bc}	7.98_a
No failure	4.46_{cd}	3.74_d

[a] Taken from Bennett & Holmes, 1975, p. 919.
Note: Any two means that do not share the same subscript differ at the .10 level of significance.

therefore, the Bennett and Holmes results suggest that failure feedback people do project, and this projection appears to reduce their reported anxiety level.

In a more recent study that is similar to that of Bennett and Holmes, Burish and Houston (1979) again tested the stress-reduction role of projection. After initially completing state measures of anxiety, depression, and hostility, female college students took a test labeled as the "Advanced College Achievement Test," which was described as "an important test because it has been found to be highly predictive of intelligence and success in upper-level college courses" (Burish & Houston, 1979, p. 63). The description contributed to a high stress condition, which was further accentuated by giving the subjects feedback that they had performed at 55% of how they had estimated they would perform. The low stress feedback subjects were not told that they were taking an important test, nor were they told that they would receive any feedback on their performance. Manipulation checks showed that both the high and low stress groups increased in anxiety from before to after taking the test, but the high stress group evidenced significantly greater increases. After taking the test but before they received feedback, the experimenters introduced the second variable, projection versus no-projection conditions. Subjects in the projection condition were allowed to rate how poorly three of their friends would have performed on the same tasks, while subjects in the no-projection condition were not given this opportunity. (The authors do not report any checks on the projection variable.) Finally, all subjects again completed state measures of anxiety, depression, and hostility. Results indicated that the projection condition subjects experienced significantly less increase in anxiety than the no-projection condition subjects. (No changes in the depression and hostility measures were obtained.) Further, the anxiety-inhibition effect for the projection group appeared to occur for both the high and low stress groups (since both groups were found to increase after taking the test, it follows that projection would operate to inhibit anxiety arousal for both groups). Again, these results suggest that projection may help the person to handle the anxiety attached to failure feedback.

A final study to be addressed in this section varies methodologically from the previously mentioned projection studies. In an experiment by Zemore and Greenough (1973), male college students in two high threat conditions were initially informed that they had been selected because they had shown themselves to be extremely high on femininity and low on masculinity in a previously administered questionnaire; a third no-threat condition was comprised of males who were given no mention of their previous test results. Manipulation checks supported the contention that the subjects in the two high threat conditions were more anxious than were subjects in the low threat condition. Next, the projection/no-projection instructions were introduced. The high threat projection and low threat projection condition subjects were asked to rate another student on a masculinity–femininity dimension after listening to a tape-recording of the other student making responses to a TAT card. The high threat–no-projection condition subjects worked on a distractor task involving crossing out words from a string of letters.

The projection effect was demonstrated in that the high threat projection subjects attributed more femininity to the other subject than did the low threat projection subjects. The last phase of this experiment involved two measures of anxiety reduction. A first self-report anxiety measure did not reveal any differential anxiety reduction for the three groups. However, a second measure did reveal varying levels of anxiety-reductionlike activity in the three groups. In this measure, subjects were allowed to select a preferred level of exercise, going from very low (what 10-year-olds pick) to very high (what weightlifters pick), on a hand dynamometer. Zemore and Greenough predicted that the high threat subjects who had projected femininity had already reduced their anxiety and thus, not needing to compensate, they should choose a lower level of exercise than subjects who had been threatened and not allowed to project femininity. (Some support is given to this inferential anxiety reduction role of choice of exercise level in a study by Holmes [1971a], where males who were anxious as compared to males who were not anxious about their masculinity did "compensate" by selecting higher levels of exercise.) As predicted, the high threat projection and low threat projection condition subjects selected *lower* exercise levels than did the high threat–no-projection condition. This study is noteworthy because it employs an anxiety-reduction measure other than the usual self-report scales. Although Zemore has not published subsequently on this topic, the reader should note that he was not able to replicate the previous results. The reason for this lack of replication has been debated (see Holmes, 1981; Sherwood, 1981).

Although there are occasional unexpected findings in the "misery loves company" studies cited in this section, the full portfolio of studies provides consistent support for the fact that (1) projectionlike measures are generated more after ego-threatening feedback, and (2) projection serves to alleviate the stress associated with the threat. By asserting that anyone would do poorly in the same situation, the excuse-maker is firmly placing the responsibility on the situation and not on himself or herself. The commonness of this consensus-raising ploy transcends age and socioeconomic barriers. The young boy caught cheating on an exam moans, "But everybody was doing it"; the retired couple found shoplifting food plead, "Everyone in our boarding house has to do it"; the poor woman who is distorting family information for welfare benefits argues, "A lot of others do the same thing"; the affluent businessman explains his tax evasion by asserting, "Most people cut corners on their taxes."

Misery Loves More Miserable Company

The previous section suggests that the actor who has undergone a bad review will "project" his or her failure onto other people. In the process of threat derogation, the actor casts aspersions on other target people. If, after negative feedback, the actor is given a choice as to whether he or she wishes to derogate a high or low status target person (or persons), studies have consistently demonstrated that the lower status person is the preferred target of the derogation (Kaufmann & Feshbach, 1963a,b; Stricker, 1963). These results add further to the "misery loves company" studies by suggesting that "misery loves more miserable company" when there is a potential choice of many target persons.

The studies mentioned in the previous paragraph may represent a "have your cake and eat it too" approach on the part of the excuse-maker; that is, the actor not only raises the consensus and thus externalizes the responsibility for the behavior but also suggests that there are others who are even worse than he or she. This is similar to what Jellison (1977) calls "contrasting." Perhaps an even more clearcut demonstration of this phenomenon may be derived from experiments in the social comparison paradigm. In this literature, results have revealed that an ego-threatened actor will seek out comparison information with others who are worse off than the actor (see Gruder, 1977; Wills, 1981, for reviews). An exemplary study may illustrate this "misery loves more miserable company" effect. Hakmiller (1966) gave female college students (in groups of six) a purported personality test, whereafter the students received feedback that they had hostility toward their parents. In the high threat condition this hostility was described as maladjusted, while in a low threat condition it was described as manifesting a certain level of maturity. After receiving her score showing high hostility, each subject was allowed to select one other person's score in the group of six. Noteworthy is the fact that 95% of the high threat people selected someone who had a worse score than they had; moreover, the high threat subjects selected the "worst off" person in the group more than did the low threat subjects. Finally, it should be emphasized that the high threat people reported a significant lowering of their anxiety level after garnering comparison information about the worst off person. These latter results suggest that the inherent consensus raising excuselike tact of identifying "even more miserable company" may serve to maintain one's self-image.

Consistency Lowering

A consistently "bad" performance may be the worst nightmare that can haunt an actor. To counteract this scenario, the adroit excuse-maker attempts to establish the fact that a "bad" performance is unusual for him or her in that situation. Temporary inconsistency is embraced because it suggests that the actor "had an off night (game, test, etc.)" or that "It was just an accident." Implicitly, the actor suggests to internal and external audiences that he or she should not be held totally accountable for "just one bad performance." In one form, this consistency lowering excuse ploy suggests that the actor "never intended for it to happen that way" (intentionality); another strategy involves such rhetoric as

"I didn't really try" (effort expenditure). The roles of intentionality and effort expenditure in the service of lowering consistency are described next.

Intentionality ("I didn't mean to . . .")

Jones and Davis (1965) have hypothesized that dispositional as compared to situational attributions regarding an actor (i.e., "he is hostile" vs. "he is not hostile, but was provoked by the situation") will occur more frequently when the actor's actions are perceived as being intentional in nature. (The legal system implicitly adopts a similar emphasis on the elusive intentionality variable in an attempt to ascribe degree of responsibility for a crime.) There are several empirical studies that support this logic. For example, Rotenberg (1980) reported that a boy who purposefully, rather than accidentally, hurt another child with a ball was perceived as being less "friendly" and more "aggressive." Likewise, cross-cultural studies reveal that people are held more responsible for unintended negative actions that were foreseeable compared to those that were unforeseeable (Shaw, 1968; Shaw & Reitan, 1969; Shaw & Sulzer, 1964; Sulzer & Burglass, 1968). Inherent in intentionality, therefore, is the concept that an actor would consistently perform negatively in the same situation over time *because he or she intends to do so.*

The good excuse-maker, of course, intuitively "knows" the aforementioned literature without ever having read any of the studies. In this regard, one of the earliest childhood scripts is "I didn't mean to." Lack of intentionality in adults may take several forms. For example, excuse-makers may directly assert unintentionality through a lack of forethought or unforeseen consequences (Schlenker, 1980); additionally, excuse-makers may indirectly suggest unintentionality by employing "insanity," "drunkenness," or a "fit of rage" plea (Tedeschi & Riess, 1981). Obviously, unintentionality excuses may vary from the relatively straightforward and simple types ("I didn't mean to") to highly complex ploys (temporary insanity).

Effort ("I didn't try")

Although in a previous section we discussed the excuse potential in attributions to the *external* factors of task difficulty and luck, it should be apparent that at times an *internal* factor under the control of the actor may nicely serve an excuse role. Effort is a case in point. Birney, Burdick, and Teevan (1969) write:

> One way of reducing the significance of a performance as an indicator of an underlying skill is to reject responsibility for the performance. Some well-worn techniques that we seem to recognize only when other people use them are the claims that fatigue, bad luck, distraction, and not-trying were the primary causes of nonattainment. There is little one can do about bad luck and fatigue except to try to convince oneself and others that they are operative. But not-trying is within the control of the individual, and we would expect a person who is particularly

fearful of experiencing self-devaluation not to put out a maximum of effort when involved in an achievement task. (p. 215)

In the wake of a bad performance, the actor may reason that he or she didn't really exert any effort (see Case 4 described at the beginning of this chapter). This consistency-lowering excuse strategy suggests that the one bad performance was just that—one bad performance that was caused by lowered effort; implicitly, the excuse-maker suggests that if he or she "really tried," then on future occasions the performance would be much better. Thus it is not the case that the person is dumb, incompetent, or physically uncoordinated (the more central and important image-related concepts), but merely that the person didn't try. Lowered effort may therefore increase the ambiguity as to the actual underlying cause of the poor performance (Snyder & Wicklund, 1981).

The lowered effort strategy has been investigated in research over the last 30 years. In perhaps the earliest statement of this lowered effort gambit, Lazarus, Deese, and Osler (1952) wrote, "A subject in an experiment may stop work so that, even if he fails in the eyes of the experimenter, he can justify his failure to himself on the grounds that he really didn't try" (p. 312). Research relevant to this topic consistently has shown the lowered-effort excuselike phenomenon. In a review of some 17 studies in which people are given success or failure feedback about their performance on a variety of tasks, 13 studies show that failure condition subjects report significantly lower effort than do the success condition subjects (Zuckerman, 1979).

One exemplary study may highlight the lowered effort after failure phenomenon. Miller (1976) had male and female college students initially complete a bogus social perceptiveness test (SPS) involving two case studies and questions over the cases. In order to manipulate high or low involvement, the half of the subjects in the high involvement condition were informed that "the SPS was a well established social perceptiveness test and had been administered to well over 10,000 people in various walks of life" (p. 902); the half of the subjects in the low involvement condition were told that the "SPS had only been developed recently by a psychologist at the subject's university and that its usefulness was still very much in doubt" (p. 902). Later, the experimenter returned the subject's scored test, and the half of the subjects in the success condition were told they had done very well (80%), while the half of the subjects in the failure condition were told they had done poorly (20%). Finally, the subjects completed several questions, including the effort item asking "How hard did you try on the SPS?" (7-point response scale). Results showed that the failure condition subjects reported working significantly less hard on the SPS test than did the success subjects. Further, within the failure condition subjects, the high involvement condition subjects reported expending significantly less effort than did the low involvement condition subjects. These findings suggest that not only may failure evoke verbalized lowered effort, but failure on an important task may especially foster the "I didn't try" excuse. Such results are entirely consistent with the general model of excuse-making as described in Chapter 3.

Distinctiveness Raising

A third excuse tactic for lessening the transformed responsibility involves attempts to raise the distinctiveness of the bad performance in a particular situation. Unlike consistency lowering wherein the actor seeks to establish that he or she would not behave in the same unacceptable fashion in the same situation over time, in distinctiveness raising the actor suggests that there are *other* arenas where he or she does well. Implicitly, the excuse-maker may employ the *idiosyncrasy credits* that he or she may have established in other positive interactions with other people or society (see Hollander, 1958, 1964). Because of the previously established idiosyncrasy credits reflecting a sense of competence and status, the "transgressing" actor may be "allowed" to violate personal or social norms (Hollander, 1976; Hollander & Willis, 1967; Wiggins, Dill, & Schwartz, 1965). To cash in idiosyncrasy credits and thereby increase the distinctiveness of a bad performance when one is in a jam, the actor may divert attention to his or her good points or may split the bad performance from the otherwise "good" person. In fact, the excuse-making actor may employ both diversion and splitting tactics.

Attention Diversion

If a person has performed poorly in one arena, that person may call attention to his or her feats in other arenas. Relevant research reveals that when the failings or weaknesses of people are revealed publicly, those people appear to compensate by presenting themselves very positively on unrelated dimensions (Baumeister & Jones, 1978). As an example, consider the man who does not receive a promotion in his job and asserts to himself and others that he has had better success in other arenas, being a good father, amateur athlete, and so on. Indeed, if the actor has compiled a substantial number of idiosyncrasy credits, he or she may switch focus to these assets. Although the actor in this scenario is still held somewhat accountable for a bad performance, the responsibility is diluted as one ponders the other "virtues." If there is a "benefit of the doubt" to be garnered, the attention diverting actor will be first in line.

Splitting

The emphasis in this type of distinctiveness-raising technique is on separating the person who performed badly in a particular situation from the "good" person who is present in most other situations. Goffman (1971) implies that apologies may serve a splitting function in that the apologizing speaker often suggests that he or she is really a "good" person in other situations. Several concepts related to apologies may be interpreted as attempts by the actor at splitting the "bad" part from the much larger "good" characteristics. If the actors are full of remorse, for example, they may be seen as being less responsible for their bad actions. In this vein, juries have been shown to be more lenient with defendants who report greater remorse (Austin, Walster, & Utne, 1976; Kalven & Zeisel, 1966). Further, if the transgressing actors can demonstrate that they have suffered because of their transgressions, there is both applied (i.e., jury decisions) and experimental laboratory research demonstrating that the actors are viewed less negatively (Austin et al., 1976; Bramel, Taub, & Blum, 1968). (The principal defendants in Watergate exhibited the "suffering" logic.) Finally, research reveals that a person who harms another person will attempt to make restitution to the victim (Bercheid & Walster, 1967; Schmitt & Marwell, 1972; Walster & Prestholdt, 1966). This restitution may be yet another way of asserting that the actor is actually a "good" person. These apologies often are conceptualized as being primarily for the benefit of the external audiences, but within the present context we assert that in part they are aimed at convincing the internal audience of oneself that generally the actor is "good."

Triple and Double Plays

In the foregoing discussion of tactics for lessening transformed responsibility, the roles of consensus- and distinctiveness-raising and consistency-lowering were presented separately. In reality, however, consensus, consistency, and distinctiveness excuses may all simultaneously interact in order to lessen the transformed responsibility. When all three processes are involved in lessening the transformed responsibility, the excuse-making actor is completing a "triple play." Two examples illustrate this fact. First, consider the high school student who fails an exam; by offering the excuse that the exam was too hard (task difficulty), not only is consensus raised ("Most anyone would do poorly on that exam"), but consistency is lowered ("I've done better on previous exams in that course"), and distinctiveness is raised ("I'm doing fine in my exams in other courses"). Or imagine the soldier who harms an innocent civilian and then offers the excuse that he was ordered to do so; this coercion logic raises consensus ("Anyone would have done the same"), lowers consistency ("I haven't done it previously when I wasn't ordered"), and raises distinctiveness ("I certainly am not an aggressive person in other areas of my life").

In some instances, the consistency-lowering and distinctiveness-raising excuses are inextricably interwoven. For example, the actor who offers the excuse "I didn't mean to" for his or her bad performance lowers the consistency of the behavior in a given situation and raises the distinctiveness by suggesting that in this and other situations he or she did not intend for a bad performance. Likewise, when a person attempts to split the bad person who committed the ill deed from the good person inside, that actor is both raising distinctiveness and lowering consistency by asserting that such behavior is *not* representative of him or her in the given situation or in other situations. The actor who simultaneously invokes two transformed responsibility factors such as consistency lowering and distinctiveness raising is, in the present context, engaging in a "double play."

Before leaving this section on transformed responsibility, it is relevant to consider these excuses on the avowal/self-evident, effectiveness/pervasiveness, and awareness dimensions. Overall, it is obvious that the consensus- and distinctiveness-raising and consistency-lowering transformed responsibility excuses are based on the verbal (avowed) tactics of the actor. In fact, excuses that lessen the actor's transformed responsibility call on such classic phrases as "I was unlucky," "It was too hard," "Everybody does it," "Most people do worse," "I didn't mean to," and "I didn't try." Generally, the research also suggests that this type of excuse-making does protect the actor's self-image (high effectiveness). In regard to pervasiveness, it appears that the actor applies transformed responsibility excuses to specific bad performance situations; however, it should be emphasized that wide-ranging situations have been shown to evoke similar excuses and as such the given strategy may apply to several arenas (high pervasiveness). As with the other types of excuse strategies, it appears that tactics aimed at lessening the transformed responsibility may reflect varying degrees of awareness on the part of the actor. Since many of the transformed responsibility excuses necessitate a psychological understanding of human nature (e.g., appeals to "misery loves company," "task difficulty and luck," and "I didn't really try, or mean to"), it follows that their application reflects some awareness by the actor. Indeed, given the sheer number, prevalence, and seeming success of these "Yes, but . . ." transformed responsibility excuses, they may have become part of the social fabric of our day-to-day existence. Through habit, therefore, we may lose complete awareness of such excuses. Although there are certainly motivational reasons for not being aware of our excuse-making, the present research on transformed responsibility has yet to address this issue.

THE DIRTEing PROCESS: DIRECTING INTERNAL RESPONSIBILITY TO EXTERNAL

The foregoing description of strategies that lessen the apparent responsibility, reframe the performances, and lessen the transformed responsibility illustrate the utility of an attributional framework in understanding retrospective excuse-making. Throughout the various strategies, a common attributional process often emerges: after a bad performance the actor seeks to move the responsibility from himself or herself to outside sources. This postfailure directing of internal responsibility to external sources (DIRTEing) represents a recurring excuse-related theme.

The DIRTEing process is rather obvious in the various excuse strategies aimed at lessening the apparent responsibility. In a multitude of blaming ploys, the actor denies that he or she had anything to do with the bad performance by directing the blame to someone or something else. The excuse-maker rarely points to himself or herself; the more common tactic is to pin "it" (the bad performance) on something external.

Although it may be less obvious, the DIRTEing process also often operates in some performance reframing excuse strategies. For example, by arguing that "everyone is doing it," the actor has lowered the otherwise burdensome high standards; consensus raising thus suggests that there must be some situational factor that is causing so many to do so poorly. Similarly, in derogating either the evaluative instrument or person, the actor is asserting that external forces are the source of the problem. Moreover, several of the "see no evil, hear no evil" ploys suggest that the other persons (often called the victim) "deserved" what they got.

Many of the excuses that lessen the transformed responsibility also trade on the DIRTEing process. The most obvious examples are the excuses involving the task difficulty rationale; it's not the person but rather the difficult task that purportedly caused the poor performance. Likewise, coercion-based excuses place the responsibility spotlight clearly on external causative factors. Finally,

as noted in the previous paragraph, the high consensus excuse implies that there has to be something in the situation that is causing all people to fail.

Although the DIRTEing concept obviously does not succinctly underlie all of the many retrospective excuse strategies that have been detailed in this chapter, it can be seen that DIRTEing is most certainly in the repertoire of the adroit excuse-maker. Perhaps it is appropriate to close this chapter with another glimpse of Lucy, the consummate professional at DIRTEing.

REFERENCES

Anikeef, A. M. Factors affecting student evaluation of college faculty members. *Journal of Applied Psychology,* 1953, **37,** 458–460.

Aronson, E. The theory of cognitive dissonance: A current perspective. In L. Berkowitz (Ed.), *Advances in experimental social psychology* (Vol. 4). New York: Academic Press, 1969.

Aronson, E., & Worchel, P. Similarity vs. liking as determinants of interpersonal attractiveness. *Psychonomic Science,* 1966, **5,** 157–158.

Austin, J. L. A plea for excuses. In J. L. Austin (Ed.), *Philosophical papers.* London: Oxford University Press, 1961.

Austin, W., Walster, E., & Utne, M. K. Equity and the law: The effect of a harmdoer's "suffering in the act" on liking and assigned punishment. In L. Berkowitz & E. Walster (Eds.), *Advances in experimental social psychology* (Vol. 9). New York: Academic Press, 1976.

Baumeister, R. F., & Jones, E. E. When self-presentation is constrained by the target's knowledge: Consistency and compensation. *Journal of Personality and Social Psychology,* 1978, **36,** 608–618.

Bennett, D. H., & Holmes, D. S. Influence of denial (situation redefinition) and projection on anxiety associated with threat to self-esteem. *Journal of Personality and Social Psychology,* 1975, **32,** 915–921.

Bercheid, E., & Walster, E. When does a harm-doer compensate a victim? *Journal of Personality and Social Psychology,* 1967, **6,** 435–441.

Bercheid E., & Walster, E. *Interpersonal attraction.* Reading, Mass.: Addison-Wesley, 1969.

Berkowitz, L. *A survey of social psychology.* New York: Holt, Rinehart & Winston, 1980.

Berkowitz, L., & Green, J. A. The stimulus qualities of the scapegoat. *Journal of Abnormal and Social Psychology,* 1962, **64,** 293–301.

Berkowitz, L., Green, J. A., & Macaulay, J. R. Hostility catharsis and the reduction of emotional tension. *Psychiatry,* 1962, **25,** 23–31.

Birney, R. C., Burdick, H., & Teevan, R. C. *Fear of failure.* New York: Van Nostrand-Reinhold, 1969.

Bloom, L. J., & Houston, B. K. An experimental investigation of the effectiveness of complementary projection for reducing anxiety. *Journal of Clinical Psychology,* 1975, **31,** 525–529

Bok, S. *Lying: Moral choice in public and private life.* New York: Vintage Books, 1979.

Bolinger, D. *Aspects of language* (2nd ed.). New York: Harcourt Brace Jovanovich, 1975.

Bowerman, W. R. Applications of a social psychological theory of motivation to the language of defensiveness and self-justification. In M. M. T. Henderson (Ed.), *1980 Mid American linguistic conference papers.* Lawrence: University of Kansas Linguistics Department, 1981.

Bramel, D. A dissonance theory approach to defensive projection. *Journal of Abnormal and Social Psychology,* 1962, **64,** 121–129.

Bramel, D. Selection of a target for defensive projection. *Journal of Abnormal Psychology,* 1963, **66,** 318–324.

Bramel, D., Taub, B., & Blum, B. An observer's reactions to the suffering of his enemy. *Journal of Personality and Social Psychology,* 1968, **8,** 384–392.

Brock, T. C., & Buss, A. H. Dissonance, aggression and evaluation of pain. *Journal of Abnormal and Social Psychology,* 1962, **65,** 197–202.

Brock, T. C., & Buss, A. H. Effects of justification for aggression and communication with the victim on postaggression dissonance. *Journal of Abnormal and Social Psychology,* 1964, **68,** 403–412.

Burish, T. G., & Houston, B. K. Causal projection, similarity projection, and coping with threat to self-esteem. *Journal of Personality,* 1979, **47,** 57–70.

Burish, T. G., Houston, B. K., & Bloom, L. J. Effectiveness of complementary projection in reducing stress. *Journal of Clinical Psychology,* 1978, **34,** 200–206.

Buss, A. H., & Brock, T. C. Repression and guilt in relation to aggression. *Journal of Abnormal and Social Psychology,* 1963, **66,** 345–350.

Calder, B. J., Ross, M., & Insko, C. A. Attitude change and attitude attribution: Effects of incentive, choice, and consequences. *Journal of Personality and Social Psychology,* 1973, **25,** 84–99.

Cialdini, R. B., Borden, R. J., Thorne, A., Walker, M. R., Freeman, S., & Sloan, L. R. Basking in reflected glory: Three (football) field studies. *Journal of Personality and Social Psychology,* 1976, **34,** 366–375.

Cialdini, R. B., Kenrick, D. T., & Hoerig, J. H. Victim derogation in the Lerner paradigm: Just world or just justification? *Journal of Personality and Social Psychology,* 1976, **33,** 719–724.

Cialdini, R. B., & Richardson, K. D. Two indirect tactics of impression management: Basking and blasting. *Journal of Personality and Social Psychology,* 1980, **39,** 406–415.

Clair, M. S., & Snyder, C. R. Effects of instructor-delivered sequential evaluative feedback upon students' subsequent classroom-related performance and instructor ratings. *Journal of Educational Psychology,* 1979, **71,** 50–57.

Darley, J. M., & Latané, B. Bystander intervention in emergencies: Diffusion of responsibility. *Journal of Personality and Social Psychology,* 1968, **8,** 377–383.

Davis, K. E., & Jones, E. E. Changes in interpersonal perception as a means of reducing cognitive dissonance. *Journal of Abnormal and Social Psychology,* 1960, **61,** 402–410.

Davis, W. L., & Davis, D. E. Internal–external control and attribution of responsibility for success and failure. *Journal of Personality*, 1972, **40**, 123–136.

Edlow, D. W., & Kiesler, C. A. Ease of denial and defensive projection. *Journal of Experimental Social Psychology*, 1966, **2**, 177–193.

Festinger, L., Riecken, H. W., & Schachter, S. *When prophecy fails.* Minneapolis: University of Minnesota Press, 1965.

Fitch, G. Effects of self-esteem, perceived performance, and choice on causal attributions. *Journal of Personality and Social Psychology*, 1970, **16**, 311–315.

Freud, S. Further remarks on the defense neuropsychoses. In *The collected papers of Sigmund Freud* (Vol. 1). London: Hogarth Press, 1953. (Originally published in 1896.)

Freud, S. Totem and taboo. In *The complete psychological works of Sigmund Freud* (Vol. 1). London: Hogarth Press, 1955. (Originally published in 1913.)

Freud, S. Some neurotic mechanisms in jealousy, paranoia, and homosexuality. In *The complete psychological works of Sigmund Freud* (Vol. 18). London: Hogarth Press, 1955. (Originally published in 1922.)

Freud, S. The unconscious. In *The complete psychological works of Sigmund Freud* (Vol. 14). London: Hogarth Press, 1957. (Originally published in 1915.)

Freud, S. Extracts from the Fliess papers. In *The complete psychological works of Sigmund Freud* (Vol. 1). London: Hogarth Press, 1966. (Originally published in 1895.)

Glass, D. C. Changes in liking as a means of reducing cognitive discrepancies between self-esteem and aggression. *Journal of Personality*, 1964, **32**, 531–549.

Goffman, E. On cooling the mark out: Some aspects of adaptation to failure. *Psychiatry*, 1952, **15**, 451–463.

Goffman, E. *Reactions in public.* New York: Basic Books, 1971.

Griffit, W., & Guay, P. "Object" evaluation and conditioned affect. *Journal of Experimental Research in Personality*, 1969, **4**, 1–8.

Gruder, C. L. Choice of comparison persons in evaluating oneself. In J. M. Suls & R. L. Miller (Eds.), *Social comparison processes: Theoretical and empirical perspectives.* Washington, D.C.: Hemisphere, 1977.

Hakmiller, K. L. Threat as a determinant of downward comparison. *Journal of Experimental Social Psychology*, 1966, **2**, (Supplement 1), 32–39.

Hammond, V. C. *The Saturday Evening Post*, Fall 1972, **244**, p. 89.

Harvey, J. H., Harris, B., & Barnes, R. D. Actor–observer differences in the perceptions of responsibility and freedom. *Journal of Personality and Social Psychology*, 1975, **32**, 22–28.

Heilbrun, A. B. Projective and repressive styles of processing aversive information. *Journal of Consulting and Clinical Psychology*, 1978, **46**, 156–164.

Hersch, S. *My Lai 4: A report on the massacre and its aftermath.* New York: Vintage Books, 1970.

Hollander, E. P. Conformity, status, and idiosyncrasy credit. *Psychological Review*, 1958, **65**, 117–127.

Hollander, E. P. *Leaders, groups, and influence.* New York: Oxford University Press, 1964.

Hollander, E. P. *Principles and methods of social psychology.* New York: Oxford University Press, 1976.

Hollander, E. P., & Willis R. H. Some current issues in the psychology of conformity and non-conformity. *Psychological Bulletin,* 1967, **68,** 62–76.

Holmes, D. S. Dimensions of projection. *Psychological Bulletin,* 1968, **69,** 248–268.

Holmes, D. S. Compensation for ego threat: Two experiments. *Journal of Personality and Social Psychology,* 1971, **18,** 234–237. (a)

Holmes, D. S. The teaching assessment blank: A form for student assessment of college instructors. *Journal of Experimental Education,* 1971, **39,** 34–38. (b)

Holmes, D. S. Effects of grade and disconfirmed grade expectations on students' evaluations of their instructor. *Journal of Educational Psychology,* 1972, **63,** 130–133.

Holmes, D. S. Attribution (projection) of one's undesirable traits. Self-defense or person perception? Unpublished manuscript, University of Kansas, 1976.

Holmes, D. S. Projection as a defense mechanism. *Psychological Bulletin,* 1978, **85,** 677–688.

Holmes, D. S. Existence of classical projection and the stress-reducing function of attributive projection: A reply to Sherwood. *Psychological Bulletin,* 1981, **90,** 460–466.

Holmes, D. S., & Houston, B. K. The defensive function of projection. *Journal of Personality and Social Psychology,* 1971, **20,** 208–213.

Jellison, J. M. *I'm sorry I didn't mean to, and other lies we love to tell.* New York: Chatham Square Press, 1977.

Johnston, W. A. Individual performance and self-evaluation in a simulated team. *Organizational Behavior and Human Performance,* 1967, **2,** 309–328.

Jones, E. E., & Davis, K. E. From acts to dispositions: The attribution process in person perception. In L. Berkowitz (Ed.), *Advances in experimental social psychology* (Vol. 2). New York: Academic Press, 1965.

Jones, S. C. Self and interpersonal evaluations: Esteem theories versus consistency theories. *Psychological Bulletin,* 1973, **79,** 185–199.

Jones, S. C., & Panitch, D. The self-fulfilling prophecy and interpersonal attraction. *Journal of Experimental Social Psychology,* 1971, **7,** 356–366.

Kalven, J., & Zeisel, H. *The American jury.* Boston: Little, Brown, 1966.

Kansas City Star, August 3, 1975, p. 4B.

Kaufmann, H., & Feshbach, S. Displaced aggression and its modification through exposure to antiaggressive communications. *Journal of Abnormal and Social Psychology,* 1963, **67,** 79–83. (a)

Kaufmann, H., & Feshbach, S. Influence of antiaggressive communications upon response to provocation. *Journal of Personality,* 1963, **31,** 428–444. (b)

Kuiper, N. A. Depression and causal attributions for success and failure. *Journal of Personality and Social Psychology,* 1978, **36,** 236–246.

Larson, J. R. Evidence for a self-serving bias in the attribution of causality. *Journal of Personality,* 1977, **45,** 430–441.

Latané, B., & Darley, J. M. Group inhibition of bystander intervention in emergencies. *Journal of Personality and Social Psychology,* 1968, **10,** 215–221.

Latané, B., & Darley, J. M. Bystander "apathy." *American Scientist,* 1969, **57,** 244–268.

Latané, B., & Darley, J. M. *The unresponsive bystander: Why doesn't he help?* New York: Appleton-Century-Crofts, 1970.

Latané, B., & Rodin, J. A lady in distress: Inhibiting effects of friends and strangers on bystander intervention. *Journal of Experimental Social Psychology,* 1969, **5,** 189–202.

Lazarus, R. S., Deese, J., & Osler, S. F. The effects of psychological stress upon performance. *Psychological Bulletin,* 1952, **49,** 293–317.

Lefcourt, H. M., Hogg, E., Struthers, S., & Holmes, C. Causal attributions as a function of locus of control, initial confidence, and performance outcomes. *Journal of Personality and Social Psychology,* 1975, **32,** 391–397.

Lerner, M. J. Justice, guilt, and veridical perception. *Journal of Personality and Social Psychology,* 1971, **20,** 127–135.

Lerner, M. J. *The belief in a just world: A fundamental delusion.* New York: Plenum, 1980.

Lerner, M. J., & Matthews, P. Reactions to suffering of others under conditions of indirect responsibility. *Journal of Personality and Social Psychology,* 1967, **5,** 319–325.

Lerner, M. J., & Miller, D. T. Just world research and the attribution process: Looking back and ahead. *Psychological Bulletin,* 1978, **85,** 1030–1051.

Lerner, M. J., & Simmons, C. Observer's reaction to the "innocent victim": Compassion or rejection? *Journal of Personality and Social Psychology,* 1966, **4,** 203–210.

Mettee, D. R., & Aronson, E. Affective reactions to appraisal from others. In T. L. Houston (Ed.), *Foundations of interpersonal attraction.* New York: Academic Press, 1974.

Milgram, S. Behavioral study of obedience. *Journal of Abnormal and Social Psychology,* 1963, **67,** 371–378.

Milgram, S. Some conditions to obedience and disobedience to authority. *Human Relations,* 1965, **18,** 57–76.

Milgram, S. *Obedience to authority.* New York: Harper & Row, 1974.

Milgram, S. *The individual in a social world: Essays and experiments.* Reading, Mass.: Addison-Wesley, 1977.

Miller, D. T. Ego involvement and attributions for success and failure. *Journal of Personality and Social Psychology,* 1976, **34,** 901–906.

Mynatt, C., & Sherman, S. J. Responsibility attribution in groups and individuals: A direct test of the diffusion of responsibility hypothesis. *Journal of Personality and Social Psychology,* 1975, **32,** 1111–1118.

Orwell, G. *Animal farm.* New York: Harcourt Brace Jovanovich, 1946.

Richardson, K. D., & Cialdini, R. B. Basking and blasting: Tactics of indirect self-presentation. In J. T. Tedeschi (Ed.), *Impression management theory and social psychological research.* New York: Academic Press, 1981.

Riess, M., & Schlenker, B. R. Attitude change and responsibility avoidance as modes of dilemma resolution in forced-compliance situations. *Journal of Personality and Social Psychology,* 1977, **35,** 21–30.

Roebuck, J. The "short con man." *Crime and delinquency,* July 1964, 240–246.

Rosenthal, A. M. *Thirty-eight witnesses.* New York: McGraw-Hill, 1964.

Rotenberg, K. Children's use of intentionality in judgments of character and disposition. *Child Development,* 1980, **51,** 282–284.

Ryan, W. *Blaming the victim.* New York: Vintage Books, 1972.

Schlenker, B. R. Group members' attributions of responsibility for prior group performance. *Representative Research in Social Psychology,* 1975, **6,** 96–108.

Schlenker, B. R. *Impression management: The self-concept, social identity, and interpersonal relations.* Monterey, Calif.: Brooks/ Cole, 1980.

Schlenker, B. R., & Miller, R. S. Egocentrism in groups: Self-serving biases or logical information processing. *Journal of Personality and Social Psychology,* 1977, **35,** 755–764.

Schlenker, B. R., Soraci, S., & McCarthy, B. Self-esteem and group performance as determinants of egocentric perceptions in cooperative groups. *Human Relations,* 1976, **29,** 1163–1176.

Schmitt, D. R., & Marwell, G. Withdrawal and reward allocation as responses to inequity. *Journal of Experimental Social Psychology,* 1972, **8,** 207–221.

Schwartz, S. M. Words, deeds, and the perception of consequences and responsibility in action situations. *Journal of Personality and Social Psychology,* 1968, **10,** 232–242.

Schwartz, S. M., & Clausen, G. T. Responsibility, norms, and helping in an emergency. *Journal of Personality and Social Psychology,* 1970, **16,** 249–310.

Scott, M. B., & Lyman, S. M. Accounts. *American Sociological Review,* 1968, **33,** 46–62.

Shaw, M. E. Attribution of responsibility by adolescents in two cultures. *Adolescence,* 1968, **3,** 23–32.

Shaw, M. E., & Reitan, H. T. Attribution of responsibility as a basis for sanctioning behavior. *British Journal of Social and Clinical Psychology,* 1969, **8,** 217–226.

Shaw, M. E., & Sulzer, J. L. An empirical test of Heider's levels in attribution of responsibility. *Journal of Abnormal and Social Psychology,* 1964, **69,** 39–46.

Sherwood, G. G. Self-serving biases in person perception: A reexamination of projection as a mechanism of defense. *Psychological Bulletin,* 1981, **90,** 445–459.

Sherwood, G. G. Consciousness and stress reduction in defensive projection: A reply to Holmes. *Psychological Bulletin,* 1982, **91,** 372–375.

Shrauger, J. S., & Jones, S. C. Social validation and interpersonal evaluations. *Journal of Experimental Social Psychology,* 1968, **4,** 315–323.

Simon, J. G., & Feather, N. T. Causal attribution for success and failure at university examinations. *Journal of Educational Psychology,* 1973, **64,** 46–56.

Skolnick, P. Reactions to personal evaluations: A failure to replicate. *Journal of Personality and Social Psychology,* 1971, **18,** 62–67.

Snyder, C. R., & Clair, M. Effects of expected and obtained grades on teacher evaluation and attribution of performance. *Journal of Educational Psychology,* 1976, **68,** 75–82.

Snyder, C. R., & Clair, M. S. Does insecurity breed acceptance? Effects of trait and situational insecurity on acceptance of positive and negative diagnostic feedback. *Journal of Consulting and Clinical Psychology,* 1977, **45,** 843–850.

Snyder, C. R., Ingram, R. E., & Newburg, C. L. The role of feedback in help-seeking and the therapeutic relationship. In T. A. Wills (Ed.), *Basic processes in helping relationships.* New York: Academic Press, 1982.

Snyder, C. R., & Shenkel, R. J. Effects of "favorability," modality, and relevance on acceptance of general personality interpretations prior to and after receiving diagnostic feedback. *Journal of Consulting and Clinical Psychology,* 1976, **44,** 34–41.

Snyder, C. R., Shenkel, R. J., & Lowery, C. R. Acceptance of personality interpretations: The "Barnum effect" and beyond. *Journal of Consulting and Clinical Psychology,* 1977, **45,** 104–114.

Snyder, M. L., & Wicklund, R. A. Attribute ambiguity. In J. H. Harvey, W. Ickes, & R. F. Kidd (Eds.), *New directions in attribution research* (Vol. 3). Hillsdale, N.J.: Lawrence Erlbaum Associates, 1981.

Snyder, R. L. Personal communication of questions she asked President Truman as part of her high school class' visit to the President Truman Library in the Fall of 1963. February 1982.

Stevens, H., & Reitz, W. An experimental investigation of projection as a defense mechanism. *Journal of Clinical Psychology,* 1970, **26,** 152–154.

Stevens, L., & Jones, E. E. Defensive attribution and the Kelley cube. *Journal of Personality and Social Psychology,* 1976, **34,** 809–820.

Stewart, C. T., & Malpass, L. F. Estimates of achievement and ratings of instructors. *Journal of Educational Research,* 1966, **59,** 347–350.

Stricker, G. Scapegoating: An experimental investigation. *Journal of Abnormal and Social Psychology,* 1963, **67,** 125–131.

Sulzer, J. L., & Burglass, R. K. Responsibility attribution, empathy and punitiveness. *Journal of Personality,* 1968, **36,** 272–282.

Sykes, G. M., & Matza, D. Techniques of neutralization: A theory of delinquency. *American Sociological Review,* 1957, **22,** 664–670.

Tedeschi, J. T., & Riess, M. Predicaments and impression management. In C. Antaki (Ed.), *Ordinary explanations of social behavior.* London: Academic Press, 1981.

Walster, E., & Prestholdt, P. The effect of misjudging another: Overcompensation or dissonance reduction? *Journal of Experimental Social Psychology,* 1966, **2,** 85–97.

Weiner, B., Frieze, I., Kukla, A., Reed, I., Rest, S. A., & Rosenbaum, R. M. Perceiving the causes of success and failure. In E. E. Jones, D. E. Kanouse, H. H. Kelley, R. E. Nisbett, S. Valins, & B. Weiner (Eds.), *Attribution: Perceiving the causes of behavior.* Morristown, N.J.: General Learning Press, 1971.

Wiggins, J. A., Dill, F., & Schwartz, R. D. On "status liability." *Sociometry,* 1965, **28,** 197–209.

Wills, T. A. Downward comparison principles in social psychology. *Psychological Bulletin,* 1981, **90,** 245–271.

Wills, T. A. Personal communication. March 1982.

Wolosin, R. J., Sherman, S. J., & Till, A. Effects of cooperation and competition on responsibility attribution after success and failure. *Journal of Experimental Social Psychology,* 1973, **9,** 220–235.

Wright, J. Personal communication. February 1982.

Zemore, R., & Greenough, T. Reduction of ego threat following attributive projection. *Proceedings of the 81st Annual Convention of the American Psychological Association,* 1973, **8,** 343–344.

Zuckerman, M. The development of an affect adjective check-list for the measurement of anxiety. *Journal of Consulting Psychology,* 1960, **24,** 457–462.

Zuckerman, M. Attribution of success and failure revisited, or: The motivational bias is alive and well in attribution theory. *Journal of Personality,* 1979, **47,** 245–287.

CHAPTER 5

Anticipatory Excuses: Masquerades for the Future

As seen in Chapter 4, people may employ retrospective excuses for bad performances that have already occurred. Often, however, a person may predict that an upcoming performance is going to be a bad one. To some degree, we are all amateur fortune tellers who are constantly engaged in guessing what the future holds for us. Unlike the circus fortune tellers whose crystal balls tend to predict only positive future happenings (see Snyder & Shenkel, 1975), most people have some ability to foresee their impending bad performances. Almost everyone probably has one or more personal or professional arenas that portend possible negative performances. We naturally seek to anticipate these bad performance arenas so that we may be prepared for them, and one means of preparing for a potential bad performance is to invoke *anticipatory excuses*.

Definition

Anticipatory excuses are explanations or actions, *generated prior to an expected bad performance*, that serve to lessen the negative implications of an actor's

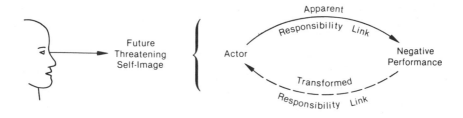

PRESENT   FUTURE

TIME LINE

Figure 5.1. The components of the anticipatory excuse-making model.

subsequent performance and thereby also serve to maintain a positive self-image for the actor or others. Consider this definition of anticipatory excuses in the context of the phenomenological field illustrated in Figure 5.1. The person, perhaps because of previous experience in situations that are similar to the upcoming one, foresees that he or she will be held responsible as the actor who is linked to a bad performance. This overall image is a threatening one, and anticipatory excuse-making may be called upon to preserve the actor's positive self-image. Although it would be an overstatement to suggest that "an ounce of anticipatory excuses is worth a pound of retrospective excuses," it is probably accurate to assert that anticipatory excuses are a very effective means of preserving an actor's positive self-image.

Examples

The following examples illustrate anticipatory excuses in action.

CASE 1. THE "INJURED" ATHLETE

Chuck Rooker is a pitcher on his high school baseball team. Sometimes he is a good pitcher; he throws hard, has a sharp-breaking curve ball, and has control of his pitches. At other times he is a very bad pitcher; he does not throw hard, his curve hangs, and he is wild. In short, he is erratic. Further, Rooker has no way of easily predicting when he will have a good or bad pitching performance. After one particularly poor showing, Rooker's coach came to the mound to take him out and to bring in a relief pitcher. Rooker was rubbing his right arm slightly, and the coach asked him if it hurt. He said it was a little sore. As the two walked back to the dugout, the coach told Rooker that his poor performance was probably due to a sore arm. Thereafter, Chuck Rooker became a "sore-arm" pitcher. He complained about the pain in his arm during practice, and made special mention of it when he was warming up before a game in which he was to be the starting pitcher. In those instances when he pitched well, he was able to garner extra praise because he did it in spite of his sore arm; in those instances when he pitched poorly, he could hold "that sore arm" as being responsible. The "sore arm" had become a recognized excuse that absolved Chuck Rooker from responsibility for his bad performances. His image was protected by the excuse before he threw the first pitch of a game!

   In terms of the dimensions of excuse-making described in the previous theory chapter, our sore-armed pitcher is verbally employing his excuse (avowal) and by also rubbing his "sore" arm when he gets in a jam, the spectators may "see" his excuse (self-evident). Since Rooker purposefully utilizes this excuse, it is probably within awareness. Further, this sore-arm excuse disarms the responsibility rather well (high effectiveness), but does so only for Rooker's pitching performance (low pervasiveness), that is, a sore arm doesn't excuse poor academic or social performance.

CASE 2. THE "TOO-TIRED" LOVER

Jason Parker placed a great deal of emphasis on his sexual prowess, and revelled in his nickname "Good Time." After a college playboy existence in which Parker energetically sustained his reputation, he married one of the members of his "harem." Although Jason had never experienced impotence, he became more and more preoccupied with this possibility. To guard against this "bad" performance that was especially threatening to his self-image, Parker began to generate a variety of excuses for not having sexual intercourse with his wife. His favorite line was to assert that he was "too tired." Tired as this cliche may be, it protected Jason Parker from his fantasized bad sexual performance.

This "too-tired" excuse obviously is a verbalized one (avowed), but as Jason Parker began to overwork himself, he actually became physically tired (self-evident). Although this excuse may have begun in awareness, over time Parker began to live his excuse so that it may have receded from awareness. Certainly his excuse allowed him some relief from the responsibility of performing sexually (moderate effectiveness), but over time it has the possibility of developing into an excuse that may "work" in a variety of situations (high pervasiveness).

CASE 3. THE PROCRASTINATOR

Susan Lindley was a first-year law student at a well-known midwestern law school. Throughout high school and college, she had waited until the last few hours to cram for an important exam or to write term themes. Much to Susan's continued amazement, her performance on the tests and term papers was very good. Although she did not admit it to anyone, she was terrified that she wouldn't do well in school. Since she came from a family of professionals (her mother was a physician and her father was a political science professor), it was expected that she would do well academically. The sense of fear about her academic performance intensified when Susan entered law school. Within this pressured context in which her entire course grade rested on her performance on lengthy semester final exams, Susan Lindley continued her procrastination pattern. This time, however, her last minute cram sessions didn't work; she failed most of her courses. After flunking out of law school, for the first time she publicly invoked the excuse potential inherent in her procrastination. She told her parents and herself, as well as her psychotherapist, that she had not really failed. Rather, she just had not tried. Later in therapy, she began to unravel the underlying motivation for her procrastination: if she truly applied herself and did not do well, then the self-image that she was intellectually gifted would be completely shattered.

Susan's procrastination was verbalized (avowed) and observable (self-evident) in that she did not study until the last minute before an impending deadline. Interestingly, in psychotherapy she became increasingly aware of her excuse; perhaps because of a general previous lack of insight or the long-term nature of her procrastination pattern, she may have been relatively unaware of its excuse-making role. The procrastination did provide some relief from the responsibility of performing poorly in school (moderate effectiveness), but it was not employed in other areas of Susan Lindley's life (low pervasiveness).

CASE 4. THE EXCUSE MACHINE

In 1982, a Texas inventor and entrepreneur named Mason Zelazny began to market a pay telephone device called "What's Your Excuse." By depositing a dollar in this machine, the caller can get one of a dozen background recordings that corroborate the caller's excuse. Favorite excuse background noises include car engines roaring and machinery grinding (the "My car broke down and I'm at the shop" excuse), airplanes flying overhead and arrival and departure messages (the "My plane is going to be late" excuse), hospital waiting room sounds (the "I had a little accident" excuse), thunder, lightning, and pouring rain (the "I'd hate to venture out in this weather" excuse), and so on. Excuse booths are evidently becoming popular since they are appearing in various locations in major urban settings throughout the United States (reported in the *New Republic*, May 19, 1982, p. 43).

These excuse booths represent verbalized (avowed) excuses that are supported by the physical evidence of the appropriate sound effects (self-evident). The booths obviously are patronized by persons who know that they are making an excuse (awareness). These excuse booth excuses should work only in one particular circumstance (low pervasiveness), and the degree to which they actually reduce the responsibility for a bad performance is uncertain. At best, such excuses may lessen the responsibility for the external audience. Even this goal may be undermined, however, by the popularity of the booths. For example, after relaying a background sound effect augmented excuse to his wife, a husband turned off the "Excuse in Use" sign and stepped out of the booth. His wife was waiting in line to place an excuse call to him.

In these examples, as with the others reported later in this chapter, the individual plants his or her excuse well before the potential bad performance. As with excuses in general, these anticipatory excuses act in three possible ways by lessening the transformed responsibility, reframing the performance, or lessening the transformed responsibility. We turn to a discussion of each of these types of anticipatory excuse in subsequent sections of this chapter.

LESSENING APPARENT RESPONSIBILITY

Anticipatory excuses that are aimed at lessening the apparent excuse link seek to establish the fact that the actor didn't have *anything* to do with the upcoming bad performance. This is a powerful excuse, if successful, in that it can almost completely break the responsibility link between the actor and a potential bad performance.

Avoidance of "Bad" Performance Arena

If a "bad" performance looms imminent for a person, one potential excuse strategy is to avoid the performance arena that appears risky. By withdrawing from this evaluative arena, the actor will not have to face the harsh lights of the critics (oneself and others). Consider, for example, the politician who sees (through polling or intuition) that he will not do well in the upcoming primaries and dramatically withdraws his name from the ballot. Does he say that he did this because he could foresee his defeat? Usually not. Rather, he suggests that there is too much mudslinging involved in the race, or too much money being poured into his opponent's campaign fund, or that the campaign is just too hard on his family and he needs to spend more time with them. These reasons sound laudable, but at a deeper level they each merely represent window-dressing on his withdrawal excuse strategy. On the dimensions of excuse-making, this politician's excuse may be characterized as (1) avowed (he said it) as well as self-evident (he actually withdrew), (2) within awareness (he strategically used it), and (3) moderate in effectiveness (it does to some degree get him off the responsibility hook) and low in pervasiveness (withdrawal acts only to excuse our politician from responsibility in this situation).

Excuses that operate through avoidance are similar to what Anna Freud called *ego restriction*. Ego restriction reflects a defense wherein the person anticipates a lowered sense of self-esteem, often because of a situation involving an invidious comparison with another's performance. This avoidance excuse is illustrated in Anna Frued's psychoanalytic treatment of a young boy. One day both Freud and the boy were drawing. She writes:

> Suddenly . . . he glanced at what I was doing, came to a stop and was evidently upset. The next moment he put down his pencil, pushed the whole apparatus (hitherto jealously guarded) across to me, stood up and said, "You go on doing it; I would much rather watch." Obviously, when he looked at my drawing, it struck him as more beautiful, more skillful or somehow more perfect than his own and the comparison gave him a shock. He instantly decided that he would not compete anymore, since the results were disagreeable, and thereupon he abandoned the activity which, a moment ago, had given him pleasure. He adopted the role of the spectator, who does nothing and so cannot have his performance compared with that of someone else. By imposing this restriction on himself the child avoided a repetition of the disagreeable impression. (Freud, 1936, p. 101)

More recent excuse-making avoidance behavior is found in the experimental data flowing out of the achievement motivation paradigm. For example, within the context of competitive achievement-related situations, many males generally tend to resist participating in activities where they may do poorly relative either to others or to a clear set of standards (see Atkinson, 1957, for an early statement, and Atkinson & Feather, 1966, for a more recent review). This phenomenon initially was labeled the *motive to avoid failure,* and it subsequently has been corroborated and relabeled *fear of failure* (see Birney, Burdick, & Teevan, 1969, for review). In related research, it has been shown that people tend to withdraw more from competitive activities as their probability of success is successively lowered (to 50%), and this withdrawal type of excuse is more prevalent among people who are relatively uncertain their ability (Conelley, Gerard, & Kline, 1978). Finally, what have been called privacy needs (see Altman, 1975) may be, in part, generalized avoidance strategies whereby we may maintain our self-esteem by retreating from evaluative public arenas (Westin, 1970).

Based on the aforementioned examples, clinical literature, and empirical results, it appears that avoidance may be a rudimentary and fairly common type of anticipatory excuse.

Blaming Through Framing

A second general means of lessening apparent responsibility is to get someone else to take the blame for a bad performance. In the language of the streets, the actor can "frame" someone else. Although a person "behind the scenes" may orchestrate the ill deed, it is the highly visible "hired" actor that takes the responsibility. Thus the real perpetrator of the bad action, the person behind the scene, offers the excuse that he or she had "nothing to do with it." The most obvious example in this type of anticipatory excuse-making is an extreme one—the use of a hit man to murder or threaten another person.

Although the hit man example represents an instance where the buyer of the services is using the inherent excuse primarily to avoid physical punishment (potentially having to serve a prison sentence), it is also possible that an analogous excuse-making process can serve to protect one's positive self-image. In business, for example, *hatchet people* ("consultants") may be hired to come into an organization and fire the workers who are not performing well. The consultant makes the tough decision to terminate various employees. This is an awkward and messy process, and the boss can assert that it was not his or her decision to fire people, but that the consultant did it. (This is of course not the case because the boss typically hired the consultant on a temporary basis.) Further, the bosses may continue to assert that they are "nice people" and if there were anything they could do they would try to do it to keep their fired employees.

In this example, it appears that the boss is very aware of the use of the hatchet man as an excuse. In many instances, however, we may not be as fully aware that we are attempting to get someone else to "take the rap" for a potentially negative performance and in doing so maintaining our self-image. In this vein, if an impending event is truly threatening, a fairly common response may be to try to entice someone else to do it. For example, as children on Halloween night we wanted someone else in our gang to "soap old man Barker's door"; as teenagers we wanted another peer to "buy the beer"; as a parent we may want our partner to "discipline the children"; and so on. In these instances we do not wish to see ourselves as a destructive child, an alcoholic teenager, or a punitive parent. Unlike the rare Harry Truman who wanted "the buck to stop here," therefore, an impending negative or risky performance would prompt many among us to want "the buck to stop *there*" (see Feldman-Summers, 1977, for an analysis of "buckpassing"). This philosophical dodge reflects the essence of the "blaming through framing" anticipatory excuses that are aimed at lessening the apparent responsibility linkage.

REFRAMING PERFORMANCES

If the excuse-maker is not able to avoid the anticipated bad performance situation, the next excuse strategy is to reframe the performance so that it will not seem so negative. The anticipatory tactics typically employed to effect this reframing process are discussed under one of the following three strategies: (1) see no evil, hear no evil; (2) manipulating standards for "bad" performance; and (3) derogating the sources of negative feedback.

See No Evil, Hear No Evil

As described previously in the chapter on retrospective excuses, the "see no evil, hear no evil" excuse-reframing tactic rests on the premise that the actor doesn't "comprehend" that he or she has done, or is about to do, something that may be construed as a bad performance. In the present anticipatory sense, the actor generates the "see no evil, hear no evil" excuses before potentially image threatening events. In fact, the anticipatory excuse may actually come to influence the actor's perception of his or her world, and channel subsequent actions (Schlenker, in press).

No Problem, No Help

As an example of this latter point, consider the repercussions of the Kitty Genovese studies. Although these studies focused on people after they had not rendered aid to another person, the retrospective excuses could obviously flavor a person's perception of those who do and do not need help. For an urban dweller, for example, the human figure slumped in the gutter is seen not as a person really needing help but as a bum or drunk; people assaulting each other are perceived as having a "family quarrel"; and so on. Indeed, the guiding set may be to "mind my own business."

Victim Derogation

The perceptual distortion may also result on occasions when the actor may knowingly engage in activities that may detrimentally influence another person or persons. As noted in the previous chapters, whenever there are victims generated by our activities, these performances are seen as very negative. In this set, the actor attempts to somehow lessen the importance of the victim. Although the derogation of victim type of excuse-making is often employed retrospectively when one has harmed another person (see Chapter 4), a person who repeatedly may bring harm to other people may derogate the victim in an anticipatory fashion.

Prejudice enables the actor to believe that he or she does not need to be concerned about the victim because that victim is somehow less than human. Depending on one's upbringing, one or more of the following may be justifiable targets or victims: Jews, Blacks, Indians, Communists, Nazis, WASPs, prostitutes, ex-convicts, and so on (Harding, Proshansky, Kutner, & Chein, 1969; Scott, & Lyman, 1968). Indeed, every culture probably has a subset of people who are seen as inferior (Lerner, 1980), and the mere membership in a particular subgroup may render them as being deserving of their bad fortune (Kelman, 1973).

A related prejudicial phenomenon is revealed in persons who argue that "All _____ are the same." Whatever the fill-in-the-blank (e.g., homosexuals) may be, the prejudiced actor has a monolithic view of the entire group for which a particular action appears. The inherent excuse logic is that "If they are all the same," it won't hurt as much to harm one or a few of them. (Recall President Reagan's alleged comment, "If you've seen one redwood you've seen them all.")

In those instances where the actor does not already derogate the victim, it may be the case that a particular bureaucracy will operate to "teach" the excuse. For example, basic training camps in the military commonly teach the foot soldier that the enemy is not really a human being and as such there should be little concern about this subhuman victim. Pejorative names such as "Japs" and "Gooks" serve to further this indoctrination.

The "see no evil, hear no evil" reframing excuses may actually, over time, reflect a certain lack of awareness as the person seemingly "views" no bad performance. These excuses are verbalized (avowed), and they often are applied to specific situations (low pervasiveness). The degree of effectiveness of such excuses is not known at this time.

Manipulating Standards for "Bad" Performance

Reframing excuses of this type are aimed at the standards for a performance. The idea is to rework the standards in some way so that they will provide a more charitable view of oneself. Variants on this tactic are treated next.

Attacking the Clarity of the Standard

Just as one can suggest that there were no clear standards for performance after one has failed, this strategy also may be advocated before one fails. If the outcome is in doubt, the excuse-making actor may spew forth a series of lawyerlike assaults on the lack of clarity of the rules or guidelines. Such rhetoric as "We haven't been told the rules," or "It's unclear how we will be evaluated" may be heard.

Lowering Expectations Relative to Standards

If the standards for performance are very clear, then the anticipatory excuse-maker may try another approach. As noted in the previous theory chapter, a bad performance is defined as one that does not meet one's level of expectation. Given the case where the expectations are based on one's past accomplishments in similar situations as well as society's norms on the same or similar situations, it may be necessary at times to lower our (and society's) expectations as to what constitutes a good performance. This is a psychological "recalibration" process of sorts in which the yardstick markers regarding performance may be temporarily changed.

Consider the young basketball coach who is hired for her first university head coaching job. She has had a superb record of coaching winning teams in high school and small colleges, and she thus is selected for the job at a major university that has a tradition of winning teams. Our coach looks over her recruits and her returning players and then examines the upcoming schedule. Her assessment of her players is that they appear to be low on talent, while the opposition looks very strong. The upcoming season portends to be a tough one at best, and a nightmare at worst. This forecast calls for some changing of expectations on the part of the coach. She tells herself, the alumni, and the press that "just staying competitive" will be the goal for the next year. When pushed by a reporter, the young coach asserts that a .500 season would represent a magnificent accomplishment given the circumstances. The resetting of expectations, as shown in this example, is a fairly prevalent anticipatory excuse utilized by people who are new to a performance setting. Whether it is a new administration in the local school system, or the President of the United States, the idea upon entering the office is to lower the level of a "good" performance.

Customizing: Tailoring the Standards to Fit

Somewhat related to the previously discussed standard-lowering reframing strategy are attempts to reshape the standards so that they actually define our performance as a success. If we see that things are not going to go well for us according to the present rules, then the soon-to-fail actor may seek to rework those rules. Lemaine and his colleagues (Jamous & Lemaine, 1962; Lemaine, 1966) performed several experiments that support the "customizing" concept. In one naturalistic study, Lemaine examined the behavior of children in summer camps. The children were offered a prize for building the best hut in the woods. One group of children, selected at random, was given the appropriate supplies to build the hut and a second group was given the appropriate supplies to make a garden. When this latter group saw that they were doomed to failure in the hut-building contest, they successfully sought to have the rules changed so that garden growing could also win a prize. Although in commonsense terms this may appear merely to be a clever piece of bargaining, the failure group has, upon closer inspection "customized" the standards so that they are not losers; in fact, the garden growers actually become winners.

Exonerative Moral Reasoning

In this type of reframing approach, the actors try to emphasize the big picture, or the larger, more positive context of their actions. For example, Robin Hood wasn't "stealing," but redistributing the wealth. Or, as a soldier kills another human being in combat, the context of this action suggests that it is good in that it protects democracy, the state, or whatever. Consider the crew of the bomber plane that dropped the atomic bomb that was to kill over 80,000 people at Hiroshima. It is noteworthy to examine the perspective of one crew member going into this bombing raid; he asserted that the bombing would actually save lives by shortening the war (*The Kansas City Star,* 1975).

Although the harm to human beings is obviously far less than the Hiroshima example, it should be emphasized that scientists sometimes employ exonerative moral reasoning to justify any psychological or physical risks that research participants may undergo in their experiments (Bok, 1979; Greenberg, 1981; Milgram, 1964). These scientists argue that the long-range benefits of their research will outweigh any short-term risks to the research participants. As a final example, consider parents who spank their children repeatedly. Before each spanking, the parent makes a speech to the effect that "This is for your good."

The reframing excuses that manipulate the standards for a bad performance are all self-reported (avowed). Most of these tactics appear to be within the awareness of the person, although because of repeated use they may recede somewhat from awareness. Also, it could be argued that a typical person does not conceptualize these various maneuvers as excuses, and in this sense they are not within awareness. It is difficult to estimate the extent to which these strategies are employed across different situations (the pervasiveness issue); they certainly could be applicable to a variety of potential failure situations. Finally, the effectiveness of these reframing tactics remains an open question.

Derogating the Sources of Negative Feedback

If the person anticipates an arena where he or she may not do well, that person may attempt to derogate the setting and its evaluative components. By discrediting the sources of potentially negative feedback, the person thus reframes any subsequent "bad" performance. This can be accomplished by derogating the setting and its evaluation agents (i.e., evaluative persons or instruments).

Derogating the Setting

The essence of this type of excuse is that the actor attempts to demonstrate that an impending performance situation is not a legitimate one. One common ploy here is to indicate that the performance is just not a very important one. Professional athletes often suggest to a television interviewer that an upcoming championship game is "just another game." This may appear to the listener to be a transparent charade, but in point of fact it may be a well-ingrained strategy that is utilized so frequently that the actor is not aware of its full excuse potential. At an adaptive level, moreover, this type of excuse may enable the actor to not get overly stressed by the importance of the particular upcoming performance situation.

Another related means of derogating a particular setting is to suggest that it will not be a test of something that is important to oneself. If the person convinces himself or herself (and the external audience) that the performance arena was not a valued one, then the level of performance becomes less important. For example, a college professor who prides herself on her research and her teaching has difficulty in the latter area in that she can't seem to talk coherently to large groups of people. Accordingly, she extols the importance of a college professor's research activities and generally dismisses teaching (except for perhaps a small seminar) as an indicant of one's overall professional worth. Further, when she teaches a large course she is quick to point out to the students and her colleagues that the course is not important to her. (For those who can remember teachers who began their courses with such an "I'm not interested in teaching this course" soliloquy, it may be of some solace to suggest that these professors *were* interested but were actually making anticipatory excuses.)

Derogating the Critics

In this type of anticipatory excuse the actor asserts that there is no person or instrument available to adequately rate the impending performance. Implicit in this derogation is the fantasy on the part of an actor that there are people or evaluative instruments (e.g., tests) that will generate an adverse judgment of his or her performance. Thus in the present context, "critics" are defined as people and instruments that are recognized for their potential to generate image-threatening feedback.

Consider first the reactions that we have to people who serve as critics. It is probably no coincidence that many well-known personages, including Sir Winston Churchill, Mark Twain, Gustave Flaubert, Lord Byron, Benjamin Disraeli, and Samuel Taylor Coleridge deplored the behavior of critics. In the words of Shelley (*Fragments of Adonias*, 1821, cited in Bartlett, 1968, p. 528): "Reviewers, with some rare exceptions, are a most stupid and malignant race. As a bankrupt thief turns thief-taker in despair, so an unsuccessful author turns critic."

The derogation of people who serve as critics probably occurs throughout many different walks of life. The factory worker questions the foreman's skill at examining his work; the high-school sophomore berates her English teacher's ability to critique her papers; the 10-year-old boy says his parents are "dumb" because they haven't learned the "new" math that is tormenting him; the husband tells his wife that she just hasn't been under the same type of stress that he has undergone at work and thus can't "understand" his problems. In all of these instances, an individual who may give negative feedback about our impending performance is characterized as being less than competent. A critic thus cut off at the knees is far less threatening and the excuse has done its job.

Although the previous discussion centers on the reactions to people as the "critics," the same inferences may be drawn for the derogation of instruments that serve a "critic" role. The worried applicant to graduate school berates the validity of the Graduate Record Examination; the student blasts multiple choice (or essay) exams as a measure of what she knows. Wherever we may find testing instruments that provide important evaluative feedback, it is probably safe to surmise that there also will be some people who question such tests.

In considering the previous discussion, it should be noted that there is a large body of research (see Chapter 4) showing that people will derogate critics (whether defined as people or instruments), but the degree to which people do this in anticipation of a bad performance is at this point an unexplored issue in empirical research. It is unlikely, however, that people constrain their critic derogation to postfailure situations; future research probably will reveal that these derogation tactics are also highly prevalent in anticipatory failure situations.

"Critic" derogation is a verbal tactic (avowed) that seemingly should be within the awareness of the person. Again, however, it may be the case that the person is aware that he or she is derogating the critic, but this may not be conceptualized as an excuse. Critic derogation is often specific to a threatening situation (low pervasiveness), although we may know a person or two who invokes it in anticipation of many different evaluative situations (high pervasiveness). Finally, given the prevalence of derogation, it seemingly must maintain the self-image (moderate to high effectiveness).

LESSENING TRANSFORMED RESPONSIBILITY

Perhaps the most prevalent anticipatory excuses are those that are aimed at diminishing the transformed responsibility for an upcoming negative performance. This type of anticipatory excuse should occur when it appears to the actor that he or she will be obviously yoked to a bad performance, and when it is difficult to directly reframe the bad performance so that it appears less negative. Similar to the description of retrospective transformed responsibility excuses given in Chapter 4, in an anticipatory sense the person generally admits that "Yes, I will do it, and yes it will be bad, but . . ." These "buts" represent the extenuating circumstances that the actor generates in order to reduce the extent to which he or she will be held accountable. Most people have a closet full of anticipatory excuse masquerades, and we turn to a discussion of them at this point. Transformed responsibility excuses are analyzed in terms of their consensus-raising, consistency-lowering, and distinctiveness-raising properties.

Consensus Raising

The basis of this type of anticipatory excuse is the actor's belief that most people would do as poorly (or maybe even worse) in an upcoming performance arena. By suggesting that most people would behave similarly in the impending situation, the actor has diminished his or her personal "psychological" responsibility.

Everyone Is Doing It

An obvious consensus-raising tactic is based on the "everyone is doing it" logic. The essence of this strategy is "Oh hell, everyone else would do it in this situation." Consider a middle-aged couple who purchased a special chair for their living room. The chair arrives and they love it. However, as time passes they get progressively more concerned when the bill (say for $350.00) from the furniture store does not arrive. One, two, three, and four weeks pass; the weeks turn into months and there is still no bill. The man and woman continually talk over their unusual dilemma, and they conclude that anyone in their shoes would just go right ahead and enjoy their free chair. In fact, a neighbor suggests that they would be fools to alert the furniture store to the fact that the bill was not sent. The couple never does correct the billing mistake and the consensus excuse has lessened their responsibility.

Researchers suggest that actors sometimes assume a greater consensus to their actions than may be the case. That is, actors believe their behaviors are more common than they are. This phenomenon has been called *attributive projection* (Holmes, 1968), *egocentricity* (Heider, 1958), and the *false consensus effect* (Ross, Greene, & House, 1977). What is relevant to the excuse-making process is the fact that people will especially invoke this consensus rationalization when their image is threatened (see Bramel, 1963; Holmes, 1968, 1978; Steiner, 1968).

In the "everyone is doing it" strategies, the anticipatory excuse is verbalized (avowed). There is a body of research, however, that suggests that people may behaviorally (i.e., self-evidently) seek the company of others in anticipation of a threatening situation. In a paradigm variously known as the "fear-affiliation" effect (see Wills, 1981) or the "misery loves miserable company" effect (Schachter, 1959), the research participants are told that they will be receiving either painful electric shocks (the "high anxiety" condition) or painless shocks (the "low anxiety" condition). Prior to the shocks, subjects are allowed to wait alone, with other people who are about to be shocked, or with other people who are not to be shocked. Results in the initial and subsequent studies have consistently shown that subjects in the high threat condition overwhelmingly wish to wait with others who are about to undergo the same dilemma (e.g., Darley, 1966; Schachter, 1959; or see Cottrell & Epley, 1977 for review; for exceptions to this consistent pattern, see studies by Firestone, Kaplan, & Russell, 1973; Sarnoff & Zimbardo, 1961; Teichman, 1973). Also, there is some evidence that the affiliation with fellow sufferers serves to decrease anxiety and physiological arousal (Amoroso & Walters, 1969; Kiesler, 1966; Zimbardo & Formica, 1963).

Thus if "everyone is doing it" and they can wait together, this consensus-raising anticipatory excuse may serve the actor well.

Nobody Could Do It: Task Difficulty

If a forthcoming situation is a tough one, the anticipatory excuse-maker can implicitly or explicitly argue that most anyone in the same situation would do poorly. Very difficult tasks, therefore, have built-in consensus-raising excuse properties. The actor, going into a difficult performance situation, may assert to self and others, "I'll give it my best shot, but this looks like a sure-fire failure situation." In terms of subsequent motivational set, this is a no-loss circumstance for the excuse-maker. If the expected failure results, it can be discounted because the task difficulty will neatly take the responsibility; if a more positive outcome results, the actor can engage in an augmentation process because the success was attained in spite of the hard circumstances (see Kelley, 1971, for a discussion of the discounting and augmentation principles in forming attributions).

Upcoming difficult tasks should, based on the foregoing excuse logic, generate greater motivation than easier tasks because to try hard on difficult tasks has no negative implications for the actor's self-image. Research appears to especially support this conclusion for people who are either chronically (e.g., Feather, 1961; Karabenick & Youseff, 1968; Sarason, 1961) or situationally concerned about failure (Frankel & Snyder, 1978; Sigall & Gould, 1977).

Consistency Lowering

If a person behaves inconsistently, it is difficult to assess the "real" cause of the behavior. Thus it is to the person's benefit, in anticipation of a potential "bad" performance, to create ambiguity (see Snyder & Wicklund, 1981) as to the cause of his or her behavior. For example, if a person foresees a negative outcome, then one anticipatory excuse strategy is to suggest that the performance is not typical of him or her in the particular situation.

I'll Only Do It Here

One version of the consistency-lowering type of anticipatory excuse is the idea that "I'll only do it this time." Take, for example, a chronic dieter named George. George is on another diet and is doing very well until he finds an unopened sack of cookies in his cupboard. He argues to himself that the "new" George can "just this once" have a cookie or two. He rationalizes that this will be just a slight transgression in his otherwise laudably consistent dieting. With this anticipatory excuse in hand, George proceeds to grab "just one more" cookie with those same hands. To date, there does not appear to be any empirical research that has specifically addressed the "I'll only do it here" type of anticipatory excuse.

Drawing by Harris; © 1982 The Register and Tribune Syndicate, Inc.

I'm Not Even Going to Try

Another consistency-lowering approach is to suggest that "I'm not going to try." Through the reduction of effort in anticipation of a potentially bad performance, people maintain a positive self-image by reasoning that they would have done well had they tried. Research related to this reduced effort excuse does reveal that people will employ it in anticipation of a less than normal performance (Frankel & Snyder, 1978; Sigall & Gould, 1977; Smith, Snyder, & Handelsman, 1982). Reduced effort also may take the form of procrastination, as shown in the case study depicted at the beginning of this chapter; or the reduced effort may be embedded in the line "I'm very busy on several different things and can thus expend only a little effort on any one thing."* Snyder, Kleck, Strenta, and Mentzer (1979) pose it this way:

> We can also ask whether procrastination is sometimes a means of providing an excuse of lack of time for possible failure. Does the involvement in multiple and diverse achievement activities that characterize the Type A or coronary-prone behavior pattern allow such a person to lay failure on a single activity to having spread himself too thin? (p. 2306)

---

* One of the reasons that the reduced effort excuse may be employed before an anticipated bad performance is that actors know observers may be sympathetic to this excuse. Relevant research demonstrates that observers, after seeing others' bad performances, seek to have the actor who has ability prove that his or her bad performance wasn't due to lack of effort (Rest, Nierenberg, Weiner, & Heckhausen, 1973; Weiner & Kukla, 1970).

Distinctiveness Raising

Closely related to the consistency-lowering excuse maneuver is distinctiveness raising. Here the refrain is "I've been good in other ways." Thus the bad performer is constrained to just this situation, and the potential transgressor reasons that he or she has been "good" in other arenas. Take our dieter, George. Another tack that he may take upon finding the cookies in the cupboard is to assert that in other areas of his life he has been doing very well. He has worked hard at the office, and recently got a raise; he is a respected member of the church and a good father. Against the backdrop of these virtues, he decides that a temporary detour from his diet is permissible. Although this type of distinctiveness-raising anticipatory excuse appears to be intuitively accurate, to date it has not been tested empirically.

Self-Handicapping: Double and Triple Play Techniques

The term *self-handicapping* was introduced into the literature in 1978 by the social psychologists Edward Jones and Steven Berglas (1978; Berglas & Jones, 1978). Definitionally, it appears to have its roots in such previous concepts as defense mechanisms (see Freud, 1946), safeguarding (Adler, 1913, 1929, 1931, 1936), and impression management (Braginsky, Braginsky, & Ring, 1969; Goffman, 1959). Jones and Berglas (1978, p. 202) write, "The self-handicapper, we are suggesting, reaches out for impediments, exaggerates handicaps, and embraces any factor reducing personal responsibility for mediocrity and enhancing personal responsibility for success."

After a review of the developing self-handicapping area, Snyder and Smith (1982, p. 107) offered the following expanded definition of self-handicapping:

> Self-handicapping may be understood as a process wherein a person, in response to an anticipated loss of self-esteem resulting from the possibility of inadequate performance in a domain where performance clearly implicates ability or competence, adopts characteristics or behaviors that superficially constitute admission of a problem, weaknesses or deficit, but assist the individual in (1) controlling attributions (made by oneself or others) concerning performance so as to discount the self-relevant implications of poor performance and augment the self-relevant implications of success, (2) avoiding the threatening evaluative situation entirely, or (3) maintaining existing environmental conditions that maximize positive self-relevant feedback and minimize negative self-relevant feedback.

In this definition, it should be emphasized that the person does admit to a problem or weakness, but presumably this self-handicap is not as highly valued as is the self-esteem that is protected. That is to say, by emphasizing the negative and peripheral aspect of the self-handicap, the person avoids the implications of performance for more highly valued, central characteristics. Recall, for example, our procrastinator case example described earlier in this chapter. It was better for Susan Lindley to think of herself as a procrastinator (the self-handicap) than intellectually inferior or average.

Kelley's (1967) consensus, consistency, and distinctiveness information components may operate simultaneously in self-handicapping. (Recall that we introduced the double and triple play terms in Chapter 4 as a means of describing excuses that may simultaneously employ two or perhaps all three of the consensus, consistency, and distinctiveness components.) The following example illustrates how all three components are simultaneously operative.

> Consider the business executive who has become a chronic abuser of alcohol. Simultaneously unsure of his ability to continue advancing within the corporate structure (or even fearful of being replaced by younger, better trained employees) and placing much importance on such achievements, the individual faces a significant threat to self-esteem . . . The abuse of alcohol provides a ready explanation for marginal performance. Thereby the individual may discount his ability as a cause for failure (i.e., not being promoted, given a raise, etc.) by making an attribution to his drinking problem. Because of the alcohol problem, the executive may be excluded from competing among his peers for new higher positions, thus avoiding future evaluative situations. (Snyder & Smith, 1982, p. 108)

Here we see our business executive implicitly (or perhaps explicitly) employing consensus raising ("Anyone with a drinking problem would not do well!"), consistency lowering ("The alcohol makes me so damn unpredictable!"), and distinctiveness raising ("When I drink I'm not my normal competent self.") In terms of the dimensions along which we characterize excuses throughout this book, this drinking problem can be observed by others (self-evident); it may not be within the awareness of the problem drinker because it has insidiously grown as an excuse over time; and it is effective in excusing the "drinker" in his job and other settings as well (high pervasiveness).

In the drinking problem example, the consensus, consistency, and distinctiveness components all generate greater ambiguity as to the "real" underlying cause of a potential failure. That is, is it the alcohol or the lack of interpersonal or intellectual skills that is driving our executive's poor job performance? This example illustrates an inherent principle of self-handicapping excuses: people at times avoid accurate information when their self-esteem is threatened. Snyder and Wicklund (1981) call this state attribute ambiguity and suggest that self-handicapping is one phenomenon that reflects this motivational process. The self-handicapping symptoms thus help to generate a veil of ambiguity behind which the person may nurture a fantasy of self-esteem.

Although the particular type of anticipatory excuse known as self-handicapping is a relatively new construct, there are already several studies that support it. We review these at this point.

In one of the first articles on this topic, Jones and Berglas (1978) make the theoretical argument that alcohol may provide a rigorous self-handicap (recall the alcoholic business executive portrayed in the previous example). Two studies provide indirect support for the idea that alcohol consumption increases when it can serve as an alternative explanation for an impending poor performance in an ego-involving situation. Threat of shock did not serve to elevate the alcohol consumption of heavy social drinkers (Higgins & Marlatt, 1973), but the threat of being evaluated on social desirability by members of the opposite sex did serve to elevate alcohol consumption (Higgins & Marlatt, 1975). These two studies, taken together, suggest that increased alcohol consumption may be expected principally in anticipation of an evaluative threat situation where it can serve to diffuse responsibility for one's poor performance. In a recent test of this assertion within a self-handicapping mode, Tucker, Vuchinich, and Sobell (1981) found supporting evidence for the role of alcohol consumption as a self-protective strategy. When denied access to performance-enhancing options, college students who were social drinkers were found to increase their alcohol consumption in anticipation of an uncertain success situation.

Berglas and Jones (1978) performed two experiments to test the hypothesis that people may use drugs as a self-handicap. In a first study, research participants were placed in an anticipatory set in which they were either certain or uncertain about how they would perform on a forthcoming evaluative test. Prior to taking the test, participants were allowed to select a drug that would interfere with their performance on the subsequent test ("Pandocrin"), or a drug that would facilitate their performance on the subsequent test ("Activil"). The predicted self-handicapping resulted: 60% of the people in the uncertain anticipatory set selected the handicapping drug "Pandocrin" and only 19% did so in the certain anticipatory set. These results were replicated in a second study by Berglas and Jones (1978), as well as a subsequent study by Kolditz and Arkin (1982; note that self-handicapping occurred only in a public rather than in a private condition). Finally, another study reveals that coronary-prone individuals (i.e., Type A; see Freidman & Rosenman, 1959) are especially likely to select the handicapping drug Pandocrin rather than Activil in the face of an important and uncertain performance on an evaluative task (Weidner, 1980). (It should be emphasized that research participants never really had to ingest the bogus drugs Pandocrin or Activil in these studies.)

Self-handicapping has also been demonstrated in studies examining three anxiety-related symptoms. First, test-anxious people have been shown to strategically employ their anxiety symptoms in a pattern that suggests the protection of their self-esteem in an anticipated evaluative intelligence test (Smith et al., 1982). This study suggests that test anxiety is in part an "academic wooden leg" that protects the student's image.* Second, people with a history of

---

* The "academic wooden leg" is a play on the "wooden leg" game described in Eric Berne's *Games People Play* (1964). In Berne's framework, the person asking "What do you expect of a person with a wooden leg?" externalizes the blame for his or her problems and thereby preserves a sense of self-esteem.

undocumented physical complaints (hypochondriacs) appear to strategically report their physical symptoms in a pattern that reflects self-esteem protection in anticipation of a "social intelligence" evaluative test (Smith, Snyder, & Perkins, 1983). In a similar vein, it has been reported that pain may be used purposefully to avoid situations that generate doubts about one's ability to cope with life's demands (Elton, Stanley, & Burrows, 1978). Third, shy males appear to strategically use their shyness as a means of potentially preserving their self-esteem prior to a "social intelligence" evaluative test (Snyder, Augelli, & Smith, 1983).

The theoretical analysis and empirical evidence to date suggests that self-handicapping may be an image-protection device for people. Thus it does appear to be somewhat effective. Depending on the particular self-handicap, it may have low pervasiveness in that it pertains only to a given situation (e.g., test anxiety), or it may have relatively high pervasiveness in that it applies to several situations (e.g., alcoholism). In some cases self-handicapping is avowed through verbalizations (e.g., test anxiety, shyness, hypochondriasis); moreover, at times it may have self-evident physical manifestations (e.g., the drinking and behavioral correlates of alcoholism, the social reticence of shyness, etc.). In terms of awareness, there is at least one empirical study suggesting that people do not report an awareness of their self-handicapping behavior (Smith et al., 1982); moreover, it has been argued that the self-handicapping pattern may have to remain beyond awareness in order to fully serve the hypothesized self-protective function (Snyder & Smith, 1982). This hypothesized motivated lack of awareness deserves further scrutiny in subsequent studies on the self-handicapping phenomenon.

REFLECTIONS ON ANTICIPATORY EXCUSES

Most of us have a love–hate relationship with many of the evaluative arenas that we know we will face in our lives. The context of these upcoming important performances will vary from individual to individual, but it would be the rare person who did not have some performance arena that is important to him or her. The love–hate relationship with these impending arenas stems from the fact that they are risky—we often just do not know to what extent we will succeed in them.

Since we know that we are responsible for our performances in these risky arenas, to some extent the responsibility connection constrains the actor's behavior. As we saw earlier in this chapter (see "Lessening Apparent Responsibility"), the simplest solution is to engage in avoidance ploys. Sometimes it is the better part of valor to avoid, or make it appear that you have avoided, any connection with a risky performance situation. Much of what psychologists have previously called avoidance behavior may in part be anticipatory excuses.

Frequently, however, people do *not* opt for the simple avoidance resolution to their love–hate relationship with anticipated risky evaluative performance arenas. Rather, we decide to take the plunge into the risky evaluative arena. Poised at decision thresholds, our anticipatory excuses (see previous discussions "Reframing Performances" and "Lessening Transformed Responsibility") facilitate the process by which we knowingly undertake activities that may threaten our image. Thus clothed in our excuse masquerade, we venture into one risky arena after another. Given this role of anticipatory excuses as lessening the constraints against taking future risks, one might be prompted to ask whether such excuses are good or bad. Probably both. On the one hand, anticipatory excuses may have unleashed people to perform horrible acts; on the other hand, anticipatory excuses also may have helped people to undertake difficult tasks that are beneficial to themselves and society.

REFERENCES

Adler, A. Individual psychologische behandlung der neurosen. In D. Sarason (Ed.), *Jahreskurse für arztliche fortbilding.* Munich: Lehman, 1913.

Adler, A. *Problems of neuroses: A book of case-histories.* London: Kegan Paul, Trench, Truebner, & Co., 1929.

Adler, A. *What life should mean to you.* Boston: Little, Brown, & Co., 1931.

Adler, A. The neurotic's picture of the world. *International Journal of Individual Psychology,* 1936, **2**, 3–13.

Altman, I. *The environment and social behavior.* Monterey, Calif.: Brooks/Cole, 1975.

Amoroso, D. M., & Walters, R. H. Effects of anxiety and socially mediated anxiety reduction in paired-associate learning. *Journal of Personality and Social Psychology,* 1969, **11**, 388–396.

Atkinson, J. W. Motivational determinants of risk taking behavior. *Psychological Review,* 1957, **65**, 259–273.

Atkinson, J. W., & Feather, N. T. (Eds.), *A theory of achievement motivation.* New York: Wiley, 1966.

Bartlett, J. *Familiar questions.* Boston: Little, Brown, 1968.

Berglas, S., & Jones, E. E. Drug choice as a self-handicapping strategy in response to noncontingent success. *Journal of Personality and Social Psychology,* 1978, **36**, 405–417.

Berne, E. *Games people play.* New York: Grove Press, 1964.

Birney, R. C., Burdick, H., & Teevan, R. C. *Fear of failure.* New York: Van Nostrand-Reinhold, 1969.

Bok, S. *Lying: Moral choice in public and private life.* New York: Vintage Books, 1979.

Braginsky, B., Braginsky, D., & Ring, K. *Methods of madness: The mental hospital as a last resort.* New York: Holt, Rinehart & Winston, 1969.

Bramel, D. A. Selection of a target for defensive projection. *Journal of Abnormal and Social Psychology,* 1963, **66**, 318–324.

Conelley, E. S., Gerard, H. B., & Kline, T. Competitive behavior: A manifestation of motivation for ability comparison. *Journal of Experimental Social Psychology,* 1978, **14,** 123–131.

Cottrell, N. B., & Epley, S. W. Affiliation, social comparison, and socially mediated stress reduction. In J. M. Suls & R. L. Miller (Eds.), *Social comparison processes: Theoretical and empirical perspectives.* Washington, D.C.: Hemisphere, 1977.

Darley, J. M. Fear and social comparison as determinants of conformity behavior. *Journal of Personality and Social Psychology,* 1966, **4,** 73–78.

Elton, D., Stanley, G. V., & Burrows, G. D. Self-esteem and chronic pain, *Journal of Psychosomatic Research,* 1978, **22,** 25–30.

Feather, N. T. The relationship of persistence at a task to expectation of success and achievement-related motives. *Journal of Abnormal and Social Psychology,* 1961, **63,** 552–561.

Feldman-Summers, S. Implications of the buck-passing phenomenon for reactance theory. *Journal of Personality,* 1977, **45,** 543–553.

Firestone, I. J., Kaplan, K. J., & Russell, J. C. Anxiety, fear, and affiliation with similar-state versus dissimilar-state others: Misery sometimes loves nonmiserable company. *Journal of Personality and Social Psychology,* 1973, **26,** 409–414.

Frankel, A., & Snyder, M. L. Poor performance following unsolvable problems: Learned helplessness or egotism? *Journal of Personality and Social Psychology,* 1978, **36,** 1415–1423.

Freidman, M., & Rosenman, R. Association of specific overt pattern with blood and cardiovascular findings: Blood clotting time, incidence of arcus sinilis, and clinical coronary artery disease. *Journal of the American Medical Association,* 1959, **169,** 286.

Freud, A. *The ego and the mechanisms of defense.* New York: International Universities Press, 1946. (Originally published in 1936.)

Goffman, E. *The presentation of self in everyday life.* New York: Doubleday, 1959.

Greenberg, J. An interview with David Rosenhan. *APA Monitor,* 1981, **12**(6–7), 4–5, 35.

Harding, J., Proshansky, N., Kutner, B., & Chein, I. Prejudice and ethnic relations. In G. Lindzey & E. Aronson, (Eds.), *Handbook of social psychology* (Vol. 5). Reading, Mass.: Addison-Wesley, 1969.

Heider, F. *The psychology of interpersonal relations.* New York: Wiley, 1958.

Higgins, R. L., & Marlatt, A. Effects of anxiety arousal on the consumption of alcohol by alcoholics and social drinkers. *Journal of Consulting and Clinical Psychology,* 1973, **41,** 426–433.

Higgins, R. L., & Marlatt, A. Fear of interpersonal evaluation as a determinant of alcohol consumption in male social drinkers. *Journal of Abnormal Psychology,* 1975, **84,** 644–651.

Holmes, D. S. Dimensions of projection. *Psychological Bulletin,* 1968, **69,** 248–268.

Holmes, D. S. Projection as a defense mechanism. *Psychological Bulletin,* 1978, **85,** 677–688.

Jamous, H., & Lemaine, G. Compétition entre group d'inéglae resources: Experience dans un cadre naturel. *French Psychologie,* 1962, **7,** 216–222.

Jones, E. E., & Berglas, S. Control of attributions about the self through self-handicapping strategies: The appeal of alcohol and the role of underachievement. *Personality and Social Psychological Bulletin,* 1978, **4,** 200–206.

The Kansas City Star, August 3, 1975.

Karabenick, S. A., & Youseff, Z. I. Performance as a function of achievement motive level and perceived difficulty. *Journal of Personality and Social Psychology,* 1968, **10,** 414–419.

Kelley, H. H. Attribution theory in social psychology. In D. Levine (Ed.), *Nebraska Symposium on Motivation* (Vol. 15). Lincoln: University of Nebraska Press, 1967.

Kelley, H. H. *Attributions in social interaction.* Morristown, N.J.: General Learning Press, 1971.

Kelman, H. C. Violence without moral restraint: Reflections on the dehumanization of victims and victimizers. *Journal of Social Issues,* 1973, **29,** 25–61.

Kiesler, S. B. Stress, affiliation and performance. *Journal of Experimental Research in Personality,* 1966, **1,** 227–235.

Kolditz, T. A., & Arkin, R. M. An impression management interpretation of self-handicapping. *Journal of Personality and Social Psychology,* 1982, **43,** 492–502.

Lemaine, G. Inégalité, comparaison et incomparabilité: Esquise d'une théorie de l'originalité sociale. *Bulletin Psychologie,* 1966, **20,** 24–32.

Lerner, M. J. *The belief in a just world: A fundamental delusion.* New York: Plenum, 1980.

Milgram, S. Issues in the study of obedience: A reply to Baumrind. *American Psychologist,* 1964, **19,** 848–852.

New Republic, May 19, 1982, p. 43.

Rest, S., Nierenberg, B., Weiner, B., & Heckhausen, H. Further evidence concerning the effects of perceptions of effort and ability on achievement evaluation. *Journal of Personality and Social Psychology,* 1973, **28,** 187–191.

Ross, L., Greene, D., & House, P. The "false consensus effect": An egocentric bias in social perception and attribution processes. *Journal of Experimental Social Psychology,* 1977, **13,** 279–301.

Sarason, I. G. The effects of anxiety and threat on the solution of a difficult task. *Journal of Abnormal and Social Psychology,* 1961, **62,** 165–168.

Sarnoff, I., & Zimbardo, P. G. Anxiety, fear, and social affiliation. *Journal of Abnormal and Social Psychology,* 1961, **62,** 356–363.

Schachter, S. *The psychology of affiliation.* Palo Alto, Calif.: Stanford University Press, 1959.

Schlenker, B. R. Translating actions into attitudes: An identity-analytic approach to the explanation of social conduct. In L. Berkowitz (Ed.), *Advances in experimental social psychology* (Vol. 15). New York: Academic Press, in press.

Scott, M. B., & Lyman, S. Accounts. *American Sociological Review,* 1968, **33,** 46–62.

Sigall, H., & Gould, R. The effects of self-esteem and evaluator demandingness on effort expenditure. *Journal of Personality and Social Psychology,* 1977, **35,** 12–20.

Smith, T. W., Snyder, C. R., & Handelsman, M. M. On the self-serving function of an academic wooden leg: Test anxiety as a self-handicapping strategy. *Journal of Personality and Social Psychology,* 1982, **42,** 314–321.

Smith, T. W., Snyder, C. R., & Perkins, S. The self-serving function of hypochondria: Physical symptoms as self-handicapping strategies. *Journal of Personality and Social Psychology,* 1983, **44,** 787–797.

Snyder, C. R., Augelli, R., & Smith, T. W. Shyness as a self-handicapping strategy. Paper presented at the American Psychological Association Convention, Anaheim, Calif., August, 1983

Snyder, C. R., & Shenkel, R. J. Astrologers, handwriting analysts and sometimes psychologists use the P. T. Barnum effect. *Psychology Today,* 1975, **8**(10), 52–54.

Snyder, C. R., & Smith, T. W. Symptoms as self-handicapping strategies: The virtues of old wine in a new bottle. In G. Weary and H. L. Mirels (Eds.). *Integrations of clinical and social psychology.* New York: Oxford University Press, 1982.

Snyder, M. L., Kleck, R. E., Strenta, A., & Mentzer, S. J. Avoidance of the handicapped: An attributional ambiguity analysis. *Journal of Personality and Social Psychology,* 1979, **37,** 2297–2306.

Snyder, M. L., Wicklund, R. A. Attribute ambiguity. In J. H. Harvey, W. J. Ickes, & R. F. Kidd (Eds.), *New directions in attribution research* (Vol. 3). Hillsdale, N.J.: Lawrence Earlbaum Associates, 1981.

Steiner, I. D. Reactions to adverse and favorable evaluations of oneself. *Journal of Personality,* 1968, **36,** 553–564.

Teichman, Y. Emotional arousal and affiliation. *Journal of Experimental Social Psychology,* 1973, **9,** 591–605.

Tucker, J. A., Vuchinich, R. E., & Sobell, M. B. Alcohol consumption as a self-handicapping strategy. *Journal of Abnormal Psychology,* 1981, **90,** 220–230.

Weidner, G. Self-handicapping following learned helplessness treatment and the Type A coronary-prone behavior pattern. *Journal of Psychosomatic Research,* 1980, **24,** 319–325.

Weiner, B., & Kukla, A. An attributional analysis of achievement motivation. *Journal of Personality and Social Psychology,* 1970, **15,** 1–20.

Westin, A. F. *Privacy and freedom.* New York: Atheneum, 1970.

Wills, T. A. Downward comparison principles in social psychology. *Psychological Bulletin,* 1981, **90,** 245–271.

Zimbardo, P. G., & Formica, R. Emotional comparison and self-esteem as determinants of affiliation. *Journal of Personality,* 1963, **31,** 141–162.

CHAPTER 6

The Excuse-Making Actors: Individual Differences in Locus of Control

". . . your play needs no excuse. Never excuse."

WILLIAM SHAKESPEARE, *A Midsummer-Nights Dream*

"Excuse my dust."

DOROTHY PARKER (epitaph suggested for herself)

We have all made excuses at one or more points in our lives, and certain bad performance situations are likely to elicit excuse-making in almost everyone. The theoretical model depicted in Chapter 3, and elaborated in Chapters 4 and 5, attempts to outline when, where, and how a typical person engages in excuse-making. As with any psychological dimension (from intelligence to personality), however, people vary among themselves in excuse-making. The human variations on any given characteristic are known as individual differences (for recent reviews see Minton & Schneider, 1980; Willerman, 1979), and this chapter develops the hypothesis that there are individual differences in the tendency to make excuses.

The philosophical roots (see Chapter 2) and the theoretical model (see Chapter 3) of excuse-making center around one concept—*personal responsibility for one's actions.* Since there presently are no fully validated individual differences measures on excuse-making per se, a logical beginning point was to search for individual differences scales that are based on the concept of responsibility. This proved to be easy detective work since one of the most popular individual differences measures now in use—*locus of control*—is based on the responsibility concept.* Locus of control represents the extent to which a per-

---

* In addition to the locus of control individual differences measure, personal responsibility is assessed by the Inner Directedness dimension of Shostrum's (1972) Personal Orientation Inventory (POI). The POI, which is conceptualized as an index of self-actualization, is derived

son internalizes or externalizes the responsibility for his or her actions. As such, the external locus of control person may reflect the prototypic excuse-maker who is prone to readily dismiss any personal responsibility for "bad performances" in a variety of situations.

In the subsequent exposition of the locus of control individual difference variable, it should be emphasized that the researchers have not operated out of an "excuse-making" framework. It appears, however, that the empirical findings related to locus of control are very consistent with the excuse-making model proffered in this book. Thus although the locus of control individual differences variable described in this chapter springs from another theoretical model, it provides a reasonable index of variability in the propensity to make externalizing excuses in a variety of situations.

A LOOK AT AN EXTERNALIZER: THE CASE OF WILLIE B.

For some, the process of excuse-making is second nature. They constantly externalize the responsibility for their "bad" actions, reporting that they are controlled by luck, chance, or powerful others. These individuals are said to have an *external locus of control*. The following example provides a glimpse of such a person.

In 1971, a 36-year-old single white male named Willie B. (a pseudonym) came for outpatient psychotherapy at an urban mental health facility, where he was seen by one of the authors for a period of seven months. He was a small, soft-spoken man, who dressed very conservatively, usually with a white shirt and black slacks. Since Willie often missed weekly scheduled sessions, on the average he was seen once every two weeks. Initially, he was vague regarding his reasons for coming to the mental health facility, merely noting that he had repeatedly met with "a string of bad luck." Over several sessions, Willie recounted a series of jobs that he had held, some where he had quit and some where he was fired. In all of these work arenas, he appeared to feel a keen sense of evaluation on the part of his employers. After being fired from a dry cleaning job, for example, Willie described his boss as being very mean, ill-tempered, and out to get everyone. When Willie was dismissed from a job as a waiter, he described himself as not really trying very hard at it. Whether he quit or was fired, a recurring theme was that Willie either didn't try or something about the job (the boss, the work, the other employees) caused his problems. Generally, Willie showed a curious mixture of anxiety and calmness in regard to his jobs. He was apprehensive about work and his inability to find and keep a satisfying job, but his seemingly endless supply of excuses appeared to mask this anxiety.

---

from humanistic ideas of psychological growth. Although there is a moderate amount of research utilizing this scale, the studies are not particularly germane to the present excuse-making model.

Willie's "bad luck" also extended to his relationships with women. He reported being very attracted to women but uncertain about himself when he was with them. For several years Willie resolved this dilemma by avoiding women entirely. In the year prior to his seeking therapy, however, Willie had struck up a relationship with a woman he found to be very frustrating. Willie described her as being poor at expressing what she wanted out of the relationship, and he therefore never seemed to know where he stood with her. Further, he expressed the view that she was becoming more "bitchy," demanding, and critical of him over time. When asked whether it might help the relationship if Willie brought his girlfriend for a few sessions, he decided that this would be "like hitting your head against a brick wall" because she wouldn't talk much. Also, Willie wasn't sure he wanted to invest any more energy in the relationship and he asserted that he was thinking seriously about dumping her.

After describing this "string of bad luck," including jobs and relationships, an attempt was made to help Willie better understand his recurring "failures" and to see how he could change this pattern. Strategies for effecting improvement in either work settings or relationships were met with Willie's counterpoint that the other person or persons involved in the situation wouldn't allow him to behave in the suggested fashion. Implicity and explicitly, Willie reasoned that he had little responsibility for his problems. In fact, at this point Willie began to suggest that it was his parents' fault that he was the way he was. They were described as not preparing him for the harsh realities of work and interpersonal relationships. (It should be noted that Willie still lived at home with his mother and an older sister.) After a session of berating his parents, Willie B. missed several appointments. When contacted by phone, he told the therapist that he "hadn't asked the right questions that would cure him." He reported that he still didn't have a good job and, to make matters worse, his girlfriend had left him. Willie B. speculated that he might move to another city and get a fresh start. When asked about continuing therapy, Willie said he would think it over and call within a week. He never called.

THE INTRODUCTION AND EXPLOSION OF THE LOCUS OF CONTROL CONCEPT

Although the case of Willie B. was employed merely to illustrate an external locus of control, such examples relate to theory and research. In fact, it appears that the locus of control concept has its origins in another psychotherapy case (Phares, 1976). In 1954, E. Jerry Phares, under the clinical supervision of Julian Rotter, was seeing a young psychotherapy patient named Karl S. In attempting to understand the patient, it became evident that Karl S. lacked any major sense of control over his life. This case was initially viewed within the framework of the then newly emerging social learning theory (see Rotter, 1954; Rotter, Chance, & Phares, 1972), which eventually led to the development of the individual difference concept of locus of control (Phares, 1976). This set of circumstances illustrates the potentially rich and meaningful relationships among clinical practice, theory, and research.

Willie B. apparently believed that he had little control over his existence. For Willie B. and others like him, the locus of control seemingly rests *externally* rather than internally. In this vein, consider the words of Julian Rotter, who introduced the individual difference locus of control dimension in his 1966 article:

> When a reinforcement is perceived by the subject as following some action of his own but not being entirely contingent upon his action, then in our culture, it is typically perceived as the result of luck, chance, fate, as under the control of powerful others, or as unpredictable because of the great complexity of the forces surrounding him. When the event is interpreted in this way by an individual, we have labeled this a belief in *external control.* If the person perceives that the event is contingent upon his own behavior or his own relativity permanent characteristics, we have termed this belief in *internal control.* (p. 1)

In other words, there are measurable individual differences in the degree to which people report themselves (internal locus of control) or outside forces (external locus of control) as exerting the control in their lives.

In this same 1966 article, Rotter unveiled the Internal–External Control Scale (I–E Scale). The I–E Scale has 29 items (23 keyed items and 6 filler items), with a forced-choice format in which an external belief is juxtaposed against an internal belief. The items sample a variety of situations in order to derive a measure of generalized expectancies. Two example items, keyed in the external direction, follow:

a. The idea that teachers are unfair to students is nonsense.
*b. Most students don't realize the extent to which grades are influenced by accidental happenings.

*a. Many of the unhappy things in peoples' lives are partly due to bad luck.
b. People's misfortunes result from the mistakes they make.

Since the initial development of Rotter's I–E Scale, other researchers have criticized it on the grounds that it is not a unidimensional measure (e.g., Collins, 1974; Gurin, Gurin, Lao, & Beattie, 1969; Mirels, 1970). Moreover, a variety of other general adult locus of control scales have been developed (e.g., Collins, 1974; Gregory, Steiner, Brennan, & Detrick, 1978; Levenson, 1973a,b,c; Nowicki & Duke, 1974). The reader is directed to a recent volume edited by Lefcourt (1981) for an excellent review of the latest locus of control scales. Although the particular scales may in some cases have purer factor structures and have been employed by several researchers, Rotter's I–E Scale is the most widely employed scale. Also, the newer scales generally evidence moderate to high correlations with Rotter's original scale.

Individual differences in locus of control, as measured by the original I–E Scale and other related measures, have generated a vast amount of research. For example, by 1969, only three years after Rotter introduced the concept, over 300 studies were reported (Throop & MacDonald, 1971); by 1977 it was estimated that over 1000 studies were in existence (Phares, 1978). Indeed, the sheer amount of research on the locus of control notion has been phenomenal (Phares & Lamiell, 1977; Prociuk & Lussier, 1975; Thornhill, Thornhill, & Youngman, 1975).

What accounts for this remarkable proliferation of research? A plausible answer is that the locus of control construct has struck researchers as an extremely important issue in understanding human behavior (Phares, 1979). As Phares (1978) put it, "The enormous popularity of the I–E concept is not simply a function of its theoretical origins or the scale that was developed to measure it. I–E touches vibrant social phenomena that have been and still are very much alive in society" (p. 265). Our particular interest in the I–E dimension is its relevance to the concept of excuse-making. In subsequent sections we relate research on the I–E dimension to the responsibility evasion strategies that constitute excuse-making.

EXTERNALS' SENSITIVITY TO NEGATIVE FEEDBACK

As noted in the theory chapter, everyone gets a "bad review" now and then. Some people are likely to be more susceptible to the threat that is inherent in negative feedback situations. External as compared to internal locus of control individuals appear to be such people, as they are especially sensitive to bad reviews. For example, in an early study bearing on this topic, Efran (1963) reported that external as compared to internal locus of control high school students, after a failure experience, remember the experience more completely. Rotter's (1966) rationale for such results is revealing:

> It is possible that the functional value of a defensive tendency towards externality is indicated by these findings. The results suggest that the external has less need to "repress" his failures since he has already accepted external factors as determining his success and failure to a greater extent than those subjects scoring as more internal on the I–E Control Scale. (p. 22)

Related research reveals that, among individuals who are physically disabled, externals as compared to internals evidenced lower thresholds of recognition for tachistoscopically presented threatening stimuli (Lipp, Kolstoe, James, & Randall, 1968). Finally, Phares, Ritchie, and Davis (1968) gave negative personality feedback to college students; results revealed that the external locus of control people recalled the negative feedback to a greater degree than did the internal locus of control people.

In reviewing the aforementioned literature, Phares (1978) suggests that an analogy with Byrne's (1964) repression–sensitization concept is appropriate. Like the sensitizing person who is especially responsive to threatening feedback, the external locus of control person is a "live wire" who is anxiously apprehensive about personal feedback in general. This speculation is borne out by research revealing that an external locus of control is correlated with a variety of anxieties (see Lefcourt, 1976, for review), both specific (e.g., test anxiety, Butterfield, 1964; Liberty, Burnstein, & Moulton, 1966; Ray & Katahn, 1968) and more general in nature (e.g., manifest anxiety, Ray & Katahn, 1968; Watson, 1967). The emerging picture, therefore, is that the external locus of control person anxiously awaits life's inevitable "bad reviews." In the next two sections we turn to a description of the excuse-making activities of externals who have encountered negative feedback.

EXCUSE-MAKING AMONG EXTERNALS

Although the concept of locus of control did not specifically develop from the social psychological attribution of responsibility literature (viz. Heider, Kelley), the intimate relationship has been acknowledged by researchers within (see Phares, 1976) and without the locus of control paradigm (see Weiner, 1974). For those who emphasize the distinctions between the locus of control and attribution perspectives (e.g., Fontaine, 1972; Gregory, 1981), locus of control is treated as an expectancy variable that influences subsequent behaviors in situations that vary in controllability, while attribution is conceptualized as reflecting beliefs about causation after the person has acted and knows the outcome. If one grants this temporally based distinction between the locus of control and attributional causality notions, it is obvious that this distinction is a minor one. Further, in the context of the present book, as well as other attribution-oriented sources, attribution is conceived as forming beliefs about causation both before and after an outcome. The view of attributional causation as only a backward-looking causal analysis, therefore, is neither consistent with the present or previous attribution-based theory, nor is it consistent with the commonsense notion that we often analyze causality before an event. Overall, if there is a similarity between the locus of control and attribution of causality perceptives, then the I–E Scale should predict causal attribution patterns. Indeed, the subsequent sections reveal that an external locus of control person appears to attribute responsibility for his or her actions to external causes such as someone or something else. Further, in the subsequently described studies external locus of control people are shown to place causal responsibility outside of themselves before and after they fail. This is the essence of all excuse-making.

Attribution of Responsibility

In the previous chapters on retrospective and anticipatory excuses, we see that most people are prone to the excuse-making strategy of externalizing responsibility for their "bad reviews" (failure experiences). To demonstrate that the individual difference measure of locus of control mediates this typical excuse-making pattern, it would be necessary to show that external locus of control people especially externalize responsibility for their actions either before or after failure. Phares, Wilson, and Klyver (1971) provided the first test of this hypothesis. In their study, internal or external locus of control people were failed on tasks that were described as valid measures of "intellectual ability." Under circumstances where there were actually no distractions, external locus of control people blamed forces "outside of themselves" more than did internal locus of control people. Some of the blame attribution items are, upon inspection, classic excuses. For example, the external locus of control person could resort to such excuses as (1) "The instructions weren't clear," (2) "The test wasn't any good," (3) "Other people distracted me," (4) "This physical environment wasn't adequate," and (5) "I had other things on my mind" (see Phares et al., 1971, p. 287). Thus after failure external locus of control individuals may especially externalize their responsibility.

To further document the motivated excuse-making character of external relative to internal locus of control individuals, it is necessary to demonstrate that externals especially externalize responsibility after failure feedback *and do not do so after success feedback*. Several investigators have pursued this question. The work of Davis and Davis (1972) is exemplary. In a first study, external and internal people were provided with either success or failure feedback on an intelligence test. After the success feedback, both externals and internals equally attributed their performance to ability rather than luck; after failure feedback, however, the externals attributed their performance more to luck while the internals attributed their performance to ability. Likewise, in a second study of "social sensitivity," similar findings emerged. These results, and others like them, suggest that internals accept responsibility for success and failure, but that externals only accept responsibility for success (see Levine & Uleman, 1979). After reviewing the existent studies on this specific issue, Zuckerman (1979) concludes, "Since the findings indicate that externality on the I–E dimension is more often related to external attribution for failure than to external attribution for success, the interpretation of externality as a defense receives support" (p. 260). Indeed, if one reads the attribution questions utilized in this regard, it becomes apparent that they could as easily be labeled "excuses."

Preference for Chance versus Skill Activities

As shown earlier in the chapter on anticipatory excuses, people sometimes utilize their excuses before a potential failure situation. By selecting chance-rather than skill-determined tasks, for example, people may have a ready excuse for a subsequent poor performance. As a first step in testing this hypothesis, it is necessary to show that externals are more prone than internals to choose chance-determined tasks. The relevant research supports this reasoning, as externals do appear to manifest a preference for chance-related activities (Julian & Katz, 1968; Rotter & Mulry, 1965; Schneider, 1968, 1972). The next step in this analysis involves documenting the fact that externals' chance activity preferences reflect a fear of failure on ability-related activities. A study by Lamiell and Phares (1975) is particularly noteworthy in regard to this question. Initially, external and internal locus of control people are given a description of either a chance-determined test or a "pure" ability-determined skill test. Further, people were informed that the probability of success on the pure skill test was either .15, .50, or .80 (results revealed that this probability of success manipulation was effective). Next, the research participants were asked how important it was for them to do well on the task. When the probability of success on the skill test was low, the externals exhibited their usual preference for the chance as compared to the skill test; however, when the probability of success on the skill test was high, the externals tended to decrease their preference for the chance as compared to the skill test. The internals were relatively unaffected by the probability of success factor. If externals actually prefer the external reinforcement that seemingly accompanies success on chance as compared to skill tasks, then it follows that their motivation should not be influenced by the success probability on skill tasks. The Lamiell and Phares data reveal, however, that externals do increase their preference for a skill task if they believe they will succeed. These results thus suggest that the chance activity preferences of externals may reflect their "defensive" way of handling a low expectancy of success on anticipated skill tasks (see Phares, 1978, 1979).

Rationalization

Externals should find activities that have inherent excuses to be very appealing. This is similar to the logic in the previous section on externals' preference for chance-determined tasks. Phares (1979) called this the "give me an out" phenomenon. In a test of this proposition, Phares and Lamiell (1974) gave internal and external locus of control people the choice of selecting what type of intellectual test they would like to take. Four tests were described, with two tests having built-in rationalizations and two other tests having no such rationalizations. For example, in one test (level of aspiration board) the following rationalization was added: "I should probably tell you that we've been having trouble with this board lately. Either the table or the floor is not exactly level, and it usually creates problems ... At any rate, if you do poorly, there may be the possibility that we did not have it set up just right" (p. 874). Or the rationalization inherent in another task (symbol substitution) was as follows: "Unfortunately, some of the symbols or characters on this sheet did not print out very well—they are rather dim . . . I hope that it won't affect your performance too much, but there is always that possibility" (p. 874). Results revealed that external locus of control persons had a greater preference for the tests with built-in rationalizations than did internal locus of control research participants.

Sour Grapes

Sour grapes represents a reframing excuse strategy wherein the actor lessens the negativity of a bad performance by asserting that the performance wasn't an important one. Theoretically, external locus of control people should be more prone to sour grapes than internal locus of control people. In a test of this proposition, Phares (1971) recruited internal and external locus of control people to work on four subtests of intellegence. Research participants were given a brief description of each of the four tests. Next, people were failed on their two most important subtests. Finally, the research participants were instructed that they could change their preferences for the subtests because "we get more reliable answers after some real-life experience." As predicted, the external locus of control persons devalued the two tests more than did the internal locus of control persons. Thus external locus of control persons may especially invoke the sour grapes excuse as a way of handling the threat inherent in a failure.

Reduced Effort

Another excuse strategy outlined in previous chapters pertains to the ploy of "not trying." By verbalizing the fact that one won't try, or by actually not expending effort at a potentially threatening task, the actor has a potent transformed responsibility excuse. As with the previous excuse strategies, it follows that external as compared to internal locus of control people should especially utilize the reduced effort tactic. At least two reported studies address this issue. Ducette and Wolk (1972), for example, asked freshman girls in high school to estimate the amount of time that they would work to solve several puzzles. External relative to internal locus of control girls said they would persist for a shorter period of time in trying to solve the puzzles. In another study, college students were asked to work on an angle-matching task under instructions that emphasized reward or punishment related to performance. Under the reward set, externals and internals persisted for an *equal* amount of time at the task. More relevant to the present discussion, however, under the failure-related punishment set, the externals worked for a significantly *shorter* period at the task than did the internal locus of control research participants.

In summary, it appears that external locus of control people consistently place the responsibility for bad outcomes outside of themselves. This is reminiscent of the DIRTEing (Directing Internal Responsibility To External) process that we suggested, in a previous chapter, epitomizes excuse-makers. Further, it appears that externals engage in both anticipatory and restrospective excuse-making. For example, research reveals that before a potential failure situation, externals especially (1) prefer chance over skill tasks, (2) prefer tasks with built-in rationalizations, and (3) lower their reported effort expenditure. Additionally, the relevant research suggests that after a failure, the externals especially (1) attribute the responsibility to outside factors and (2) engage in sour grapes verbalizations.

EXCUSE-MAKING AMONG "DEFENSIVE" EXTERNALS

The previous section described excuse-making for the overall class of external locus of control individuals. From the very beginning of the locus of control concept, however, it has been suggested that there is a subset of externals who are especially likely to employ their external beliefs in a defensive fashion (Phares, 1973, 1976; Rotter, 1966). Since external locus of control people appear to be a more heterogeneous group than internal locus of control persons (see Hersch & Scheibe, 1967), it is possible that some subset of externals may be highly likely to employ "defensive" excuse-making tactics.

Measurement of "Defensive" Externality

Several methods have been employed to measure defensive externality. For example, Davis (1970) defined defensive externals (DEs) as people who verbalize external beliefs but otherwise behave like internals in that they take action; moreover, congruent externals (CEs) were defined as people who verbalize external beliefs and are also behaviorally passive. (Locus of control was measured by Rotter's I–E Scale, and willingness to act to improve academic skills was tapped through a modified version of Gore and Rotter's [1963] action-taking questionnaire.) By expressing external beliefs and behaviorally remaining active, Davis reasoned that defensive externals could readily protect themselves against potential failures.

Another approach utilized to identify defensive externals involves the interpersonal trust variable. Noting that externality correlates positively with a lack trust ($r = .53$; Hamsher, Geller, & Rotter, 1968), Hochreich (1968) reasoned that those externals who are also very lacking in interpersonal trust (Interpersonal Trust Scale; Rotter, 1967) may especially blame others for their failures. These defensive externals purportedly express a blaming and distrustful attitude toward others (see also Gregory et al., 1978), while the passive or congruent externals with high externality and high trust do not hold such attitudes.

Scales tapping processes similar to defensive externality also have been developed for use with children. In the Intellectual Achievement Responsibility

(IAR) Questionnaire by Crandall, Katkovsky, and Crandall (1965), an overall locus of control score is derivable for children. More important, subscores are available for estimating the child's externalization of responsibility for success and for failures. Examples, keyed in the direction of defensive externality for failure, are as follows:

If you can't work a puzzle, it is more likely to happen
- a. because you are not especially good at working puzzles, or
- *b. because the instructions weren't written clearly enough?

If your parents tell you you're acting silly and not thinking clearly, it is more likely to be
- a. because of something you did, or
- *b. because they happen to be feeling cranky?

If a teacher didn't pass you to the next grade, would it probably be
- *a. because she "had it in for you," or
- b. because your school work wasn't good enough?

In a similar vein, Mischel, Zeiss, and Zeiss (1974) introduced a preschool version of locus of control, which contained subscales reflecting externalization of positive and negative outcomes. This scale is known as the Stanford Preschool I–E Scale. Stephens and Delys (1973) developed the Stephens–Delys Reinforcement Contingency Interview as a verbally presented locus of control scale. Like the IAR, this scale has the capability of generating subscores reflecting the externalization of responsibility for success and for failure. Phares (1979) suggested that defensive externality in children may be defined by profiles that reflect an externalization of responsibility on the failure subscale and an internalization of responsibility on the success subscale of these various tests.

The Empirical Evidence

Generally, the aforementioned methods of distinguishing defensive externals reveal that the members of this subgroup of externals are adroit excuse-makers (Phares, 1974, 1976, 1978, 1979). For example, using the Davis (1970) technique for identifying defensive (DE) and congruent externals (CE), Lloyd and Chang (1977, reported in Phares, 1979) gave research participants positive or negative feedback about their performance on a social sensitivity test. The DEs accepted less responsibility following failure than did the CEs or the internals; moreover, the DEs accepted less responsibility for failure and more responsibility for success than did the CEs.

In studies employing the Hochreich (1968) technique, DEs generally evidence elevated excuselike responses. In one study, for example, research participants read Thematic Apperception Test stories and then made attributions for the protagonists' successes or failures (Hochreich, 1974). Results showed that male DEs attributed less responsibility to the story heroes after failures than did CEs or internals; moreover, this effect was amplified when the stories had achievement themes (the females did not evidence this pattern of results). In another study, after failure on an anagrams test, DEs blamed external factors more than did CEs or internals (Hochreich, 1975). Further, the DEs as compared to CEs evidenced the consensus-raising "everyone is doing it" excuse to a greater degree, that is, they reported that a greater percentage of fellow students would also fail the test. In a third study, DEs assumed credit for success and externalized blame for failure more than CEs or internals (Evans, 1973, reported in Phares, 1979). Finally, in an unpublished part of the 1974 Phares and Lamiell study, DEs were shown to have a significantly higher preference for tests with built-in rationalizations than did CEs or internals (Phares & Lamiell, 1973, reported in Phares, 1979).

CONCLUDING COMMENTS

Although the role of the locus of control variable has been explored in some detail in this chapter, there are obviously other individual differences dimensions that are worthy of further consideration in future work on the general topic of excuse-making. For example, the closest scales specific to excuse-making are still in the initial development stages. First, Jones (1981) developed a scale measuring the propensity to self-handicap (see Chapters 3 and 5). This 20-item scale includes factors tapping excuses ("I tend to make excuses when I do something wrong"), and health ("I sometimes enjoy being mildly ill for a day or two"). Second, Snyder and Stucky (1983) developed a 20-item scale that purportedly reflects the excuse-potential inherent in boredom-related statements. Items on this Kansas Boredom Scale allow persons to report boredom as a means of protecting their self-esteem (e.g., "People are dull," or "I feel nothing attracts my attention"). Third, researchers have begun the initial psychometric and validational work on locus of causality scales (see Barké, 1983, for a description of the Task Attribution Scale; and Ickes, in press, Ickes & Layden, 1978, for a description of the Attributional Styles Scale). These new scales have the capability of pinpointing persons who internalize causality for success and externalize causality for failure situations, and as such may tap an excuselike externalizing attributional process. In future research with these scales, it will be important to examine their correlations with the I–E scale in order to demonstrate their discriminate validity as well as to conduct the appropriate construct validational tests.

Because of the positive correlations between locus of control and anxiety, it is also interesting to speculate about the excuse-making potential that may be inherent in various individual differences measures of situation-specific anxieties. Generally, anxiety may occur in interpersonal or cognitive situations. The former anxieties often are called social anxieties, and the latter are called test anxieties. In regard to social anxieties, it has recently been suggested that socially anxious people may in part employ their anxiety as an excuse-related strategy for protecting self-esteem (see Leary & Schlenker, 1981; Schlenker & Leary, 1982). Although high as compared to low socially anxious people internalize rather than externalize responsibility after a failure experience (Arkin, Appelman, & Burger, 1980), they do appear to exhibit greater physical and psychological withdrawal from social settings (Pilkonis, 1977; Zimbardo, 1977) and self-handicapping behaviors (for males only; Snyder, Augelli, & Smith, 1983). In regard to test anxiety, writers have portrayed the test-anxious person as being very concerned with avoiding failure and disapproval (e.g., Phillips, Pitcher, Worsham, & Miller, 1980); this set suggests that test-anxious people may be primed for excuse-making responses. The results are inconsistent, however. For example, high as compared to low test-anxious people do not appear to blame external factors (such as a cognitive evaluative task) for their failures (Weiner & Sierad, 1975); on the other hand, high test-anxious individuals do evidence a strategic self-handicapping pattern of reporting their symptoms (Smith, Snyder, & Handelsman, 1982). Considering the present status of research related to the individual differences measures generating situation specific anxiety scores for social and cognitive arenas, therefore, it is most appropriate to consider these measures as reflecting promising possibilities for predicting excuse-related behaviors (especially self-handicapping maneuvers).

It should also be emphasized that there may be individuals whose excuse-making is elicited in response to reference group situations (Snyder & Smith, 1982). In this vein, the individual differences group variables of sex and age may represent fruitful dimensions for future work that is aimed at predicting persons who may be prone to excuse-making in particular contexts. For example, a fairly new body of research suggests that females should be likely to make excuses (i.e., defensive attributions after failure) on "female" tasks (Ayers-Nachamkin, 1982; Rosenfield & Stephan, 1978).

Given the many potentially new individual differences measures that may tap excuselike propensities, it is very possible that subsequent research will provide a clear picture of the type of person who should be especially prone to excuse-making. At present, however, the locus of control individual differences dimension offers the best available measure of persons who should be predisposed to excuse-making strategies. In particular, those individuals who report themselves at the external end of the scale have all the classic earmarks of people who are prone to excuse-making across a wide variety of situations. Not only are the external locus of control persons especially sensitive to the threat inherent in bad reviews, but they handle this sensitivity by actively resorting to the full range of responsibility-evasion excuse-making responses. Additionally, over the years, theoretical and empirical work has progressively moved toward conceptualizing the external locus of control person as manifesting a purposefully motivated defensive style. Indeed, when one examines the research on the broad category of individuals subsumed under the external label, or research on the subset of externals described as "defensives," the overriding conclusion is the same: external locus of control individuals are prone to excuse-making.

REFERENCES

Arkin, R. M., Appelman, A. J., & Burger, J. M. Social anxiety, self-presentation, and the self-serving bias in causal attribution. *Journal of Personality and Social Psychology,* 1980, **38,** 23–25.

Ayers-Nachamkin, B. Sex differences in self-serving biases: Success expectancies or role expectation? Unpublished doctoral dissertation, University of Kansas, 1982.

Barké, C. Development of the Task Attribution Scale. Unpublished Doctoral Dissertation, University of Kansas, 1983.

Butterfield, E. C. Locus of control, test anxiety, reaction to frustration, and achievement attitudes. *Journal of Personality,* 1964, **32,** 298–311.

Byrne, D. The Repression–Sensitization Scale: Rationale, reliability and validity. In B. A. Maher (Ed.), *Progress in experimental personality research.* New York: Academic Press, 1964.

Collins, B. E. Four separate components of the Rotter I–E Scale: Belief in a difficult world, a just world, a predictable world and a politically responsive world. *Journal of Personality and Social Psychology,* 1974, **29,** 381–391.

Crandall, V. C., Katkovsky, W., & Crandall, V. J. Children's beliefs in their own control of reinforcement in intellectual-academic situations. *Child Development,* 1965, **36,** 91–109.

Davis, D. E. Internal–external control and defensiveness. Unpublished doctoral dissertation, Kansas State University, 1970.

Davis, W. L., & Davis, D. E. Internal and external control and attribution of responsibility for success and failure. *Journal of Personality,* 1972, **40,** 123–126.

Ducette, J., & Wolk, S. Locus of control and extreme behavior. *Journal of Consulting and Clinical Psychology,* 1972, **39,** 253–258.

Efran, J. Some personality determinants of memory for success and failure. Unpublished doctoral dissertation, Ohio State University, 1963.

Evans, R. G. Defensive externality as an extension of the I–E construct. Unpublished master's thesis, Southern Illinois University, 1973.

Fontaine, G. Some situational determinants of causal attribution. Unpublished doctoral dissertation, University of Western Australia, 1972.

Gore, P. M., & Rotter, J. B. A personality correlate of social action. *Journal of Personality,* 1963, **31,** 58–64.

Gregory, W. L. Expectancies for controllability, performance attributions, and behavior. In H. M. Lefcourt (Ed.), *Research with the locus of control construct* (Vol. 1). New York: Academic Press, 1981.

Gregory, W. L., Steiner, I. D., Brennan, G., & Detrick, A. A scale to measure benevolent versus malevolent perceptions of the environment. *Journal Supplement Abstract Service,* 1978, **8,** No. 1679.

Gurin, P., Gurin, G., Lao, R. C., & Beattie, M. Internal–external control in the motivational dynamics of Negro youth. *Journal of Social Issues,* 1969, **25,** 29–53.

Hamsher, J. H., Geller, J. D., & Rotter, J. B. Interpersonal trust, internal–external control, and the Warren Commission Report. *Journal of Personality and Social Psychology,* 1968, **9,** 210–215.

Hersch, P. D., & Scheibe, K. E. On the reliability and validity of internal–external control as a personality dimension. *Journal of Consulting Psychology,* 1967, **31,** 609–613.

Hochreich, D. J. Refined analysis of internal–external control and behavior in a laboratory situation. Unpublished doctoral dissertation, University of Connecticut, 1968.

Hochreich, D. J. Defensive externality and attribution of responsibility. *Journal of Personality,* 1974, **42,** 543–557.

Hochreich, D. J. Defensive externality and blame projection following failure. *Journal of Personality and Social Psychology,* 1975, **32,** 540–546.

Ickes, W. Attributional styles and the self-concept. In L. V. Abramson (Ed.), *Attributional processes and clinical psychology.* New York: Guilford Press, in press.

Ickes, W., & Layden, M. A. Attributionl styles. In J. H. Harvey, W. Ickes, & R. Kidd (Eds.), *New directions in attribution research* (Vol. 2). Hillsdale, N.J.: Lawrence Erlbaum Associates, 1978.

Jones, E. E. Personal communication, August 1981.

Julian, J. W., & Katz, S. B. Internal versus external control and the value of reinforcement. *Journal of Personality and Social Psychology,* 1968, **8,** 89–94.

Lamiell, J. T., & Phares, E. J. Locus of control, probability of success, and defensiveness. Paper presented at the Midwestern Psychological Association, Chicago, May 1975.

Leary, M. R., & Schlenker, B. R. The social psychology of shyness: A self-presentational model. In J. T. Tedeschi (Ed.), *Impression management theory and social psychological research.* New York: Academic Press, 1981.

Lefcourt, H. M. *Locus of control: Current trends in theory and research.* Hillsdale, N.J.: Lawrence Erlbaum Associates, 1976.

Lefcourt, H. M. *Research with the locus of control construct* (Vol. 1, *Assessment methods*). New York: Academic Press, 1981.

Levenson, H. Multidimensional locus of control in psychiatric patients. *Journal of Consulting and Clinical Psychology,* 1973, **41,** 397–404. (a)

Levenson, H. Perceived parental antecedents of internal, powerful others, and chance locus of control orientations. *Developmental Psychology,* 1973, **9,** 268–274. (b)

Levenson, H. Reliability and validity of the I, P, and C scales: A multidimensional view of locus of control. Paper presented at the American Psychological Association, Montreal, August 1973. (c)

Levine, R., & Uleman, J. S. Perceived locus of control, chronic self-esteem, and attribution for success and failure. *Personality and Social Psychology Bulletin,* 1979, **5,** 69–72.

Liberty, P. G., Burnstein, E., & Moulton, R. W. Concern with mastery and occupational attraction. *Journal of Personality,* 1966, **34,** 105–117.

Lipp, L., Kolstoe, R., James, W., & Randall, H. Denial of disability and internal control of reinforcement: A study using a perceptual defense paradigm. *Journal of Consulting and Clinical Psychology,* 1968, **32,** 72–75.

Lloyd, C., & Chang, A. F. The usefulness of distinguishing between a defensive and a nondefensive external locus of control. Unpublished paper, University of Texas Health Center at Houston Medical School, 1977.

Minton, H. L., & Schneider, F. W. *Differential psychology.* Monterey, Calif.: Brooks/Cole, 1980.

Mirels, H. L. Dimensions of internal versus external control. *Journal of Consulting and Clinical Psychology,* 1970, **34,** 226–228.

Mischel, W., Zeiss, R., & Zeiss, A. Internal–external control and persistence: Validation and implications of the Stanford Preschool Internal–External scale. *Journal of Personality and Social Psychology,* 1974, **29,** 265–278.

Nowicki, S., & Duke, M. P. A locus of control scale for non-college as well as college students. *Journal of Personality Assessment,* 1974, **38,** 136–137.

Phares, E. J. Internal–external control and the reduction of reinforcement value after failure. *Journal of Consulting and Clinical Psychology,* 1971, **37,** 386–390.

Phares, E. J. *Locus of control: A personality determinant of behavior.* Morristown, N.J.: General Learning Press, 1973.

Phares, E. J. Social learning theory, locus of control, and defensiveness. Paper presented at the XV Interamerican Congress of Psychology, Bogotá, Colombia, December 1974.

Phares, E. J. *Locus of control in personality.* Morristown, N.J.: General Learning Press, 1976.

Phares, E. J. Locus of control. In H. London & J. Exner, Jr. (Eds.), *Dimensions of personality.* New York: Wiley, 1978.

Phares, E. J. Defensiveness and perceived control. In L. C. Perlmuter & R. A. Monty (Eds.), *Choice and perceived control.* Hillsdale, N.J.: Lawrence Erlbaum Associates, 1979.

Phares, E. J., & Lamiell, J. T. Internal–external control, interpersonal trust, and defensive behavior. Unpublished manuscript, Kansas State University, 1973.

Phares, E. J., & Lamiell, J. T. Relationship of internal–external control to defensive preferences. *Journal of Consulting and Clinical Psychology,* 1974, **42,** 872–878.

Phares, E. J., & Lamiell, J. T. Personality. In M. R. Rozenweig & L. W. Porter (Eds.), *Annual review of psychology.* Palo Alto, Calif.: Annual Reviews, 1977.

Phares, E. J., Ritchie, D. E., & Davis, W. L. Internal–external control and reaction to threat. *Journal of Personality and Social Psychology,* 1968, **10,** 402–405.

Phares, E. J., Wilson, K. G., & Klyver, N. W. Internal–external control and the attribution of blame under neutral and distractive conditions. *Journal of Personality and Social Psychology,* 1971, **18,** 285–288.

Phillips, B. N., Pitcher, G. D., Worsham, M. E., & Miller, S. C. Test anxiety and the school environment. In I. G. Sarason (Ed.), *Test anxiety: Theory, research, and applications.* Hillsdale, N.J.: Lawrence Erlbaum Associates, 1980.

Pilkonis, P. A. The behavioral consequences of shyness. *Journal of Personality,* 1977, **45,** 596–611.

Prociuk, T. J., & Lussier, R. J. Internal–external locus of control: An analysis and bibliography of two years research (1973–1974). *Psychological Reports,* 1975, **37,** 1323–1337.

Ray, W. J., & Katahn, M. Relation of anxiety to locus of control. *Psychological Reports,* 1968, **23,** 1196.

Rosenfield, D., & Stephan, W. G. Sex differences in attributions for sex-typed tasks. *Journal of Personality,* 1978, **45,** 244–259.

Rotter, J. B. *Social learning and clinical psychology.* Englewood Cliffs, N.J.: Prentice-Hall, 1954.

Rotter, J. B. Generalized expectancies for internal versus external control of reinforcement. *Psychological Monographs,* 1966, **80** (Whole No. 609).

Rotter, J. B. A new scale for the measurement of interpersonal trust. *Journal of Personality,* 1967, **35,** 651–665.

Rotter, J. B., Chance, J., & Phares, E. J. *Applications of a social learning theory of personality.* New York: Holt, Rinehart & Winston, 1972.

Rotter, J. B., & Mulry, R. C. Internal versus external control of reinforcement and decision time. *Journal of Personality and Social Psychology,* 1965, **2,** 598–604.

Schlenker, B. R., & Leary, M. Social anxiety and self-presentation: A conceptualization and model. *Psychological Bulletin,* 1982, **92,** 641–689.

Schneider, J. M. Skill versus chance activity preferences and locus of control. *Journal of Consulting and Clinical Psychology,* 1968, **32,** 333–337.

Schneider, J. M. Relationship between locus of control and activity preferences: Effects of masculinity, activity, and skill. *Journal of Consulting and Clinical Psychology,* 1972, **38,** 225–230.

Shostrum, E. L. *Personal Orientation Inventory Manual.* San Diego: Educational and Industrial Testing Service, 1972.

Smith, T. W., Snyder, C. R., & Handelsman, M. M. On the self-serving function of a wooden leg: Test anxiety as a self-handicapping strategy. *Journal of Personality and Social Psychology,* 1982, **42,** 314–321.

Snyder, C. R., Augelli, R., & Smith, T. W. Shyness as a self-handicapping strategy. Paper presented at the American Psychological Association Convention, Anaheim, Calif., 1983.

Snyder, C. R., & Smith, T. W. Symptoms as self-handicapping strategies: The virtues of old wine in a new bottle. In G. Weary & H. Mirels (Eds.), *Integrations of clinical and social psychology.* New York: Oxford University Press, 1982.

Snyder, C. R., & Stucky, R. J. Development of the Kansas Boredom Scale: An individual differences measure of excuse-making with boredom-related statements. Unpublished manuscript, University of Kansas, 1983.

Stephens, M. W., & Delys, P. A locus of control measure for preschool children. *Developmental Psychology,* 1973, **9,** 55–65.

Thornhill, M. A., Thornhill, G. T., & Youngman, M. B. A computerized and categorized bibliography on locus of control. *Psychological Reports,* 1975, **36,** 505–506.

Throop, W. F., & MacDonald, A. P. Internal–external locus of control: A bibliography. *Psychological Reports,* 1971, **28,** 175–190 (Monograph Supplement 1-V28).

Watson, D. Relationship between locus of control and anxiety. *Journal of Personality and Social Psychology,* 1967, **6,** 91–92.

Weiner, B. *Achievement motivation and attribution theory.* Morristown, N.J.: General Learning Press, 1974.

Weiner, B., & Sierad, J. Misattribution for failure and enhancement of achievement strivings. *Journal of Personality and Social Psychology,* 1975, **31,** 415–421.

Willerman, L. *The psychology of individual and group differences.* San Francisco: Freeman, 1979.

Zimbardo, P. G. *Shyness: What it is and what to do about it.* New York: Jove, 1977.

Zuckerman, M. Attribution of success and failure revisited, or: The motivational bias is alive and well in attribution theory. *Journal of Personality,* 1979, **27,** 245–287.

CHAPTER 7

The Development
of Excuse-Making

MARGARET SCHADLER AND BEVERLY AYERS-NACHAMKIN

It comes as no surprise to anyone who spends time with children that they make up excuses. In fact they become incredibly facile in their ability to justify a wide variety of behavior. Less constrained by experience and concern with credibility than adults, children draw on miracles and mirages. Preschool children's thin line between reality and fantasy enables them to evoke imaginary friends and magic on occasion. The legalistic workings of the young adolescent mind push truth to its limits.

In this chapter we draw on a wide variety of research as we describe some of our ideas about the development of excuse-making. These tentative and preliminary ideas are being formulated and revised as we observe children, review the literature, discuss our insights, and begin formal research on the problem. The speculative nature of this chapter will be evident, but we still feel obligated to state the obvious at the outset, if only to protect our own self-esteem (the anticipatory excuse is so effective). To borrow from the French, "Nous nous excusons"; that is, we excuse ourselves for the shortcomings of this work by making sure that our readers know, and by reminding ourselves, that the purpose of this chapter is to guide our search for understanding rather than to summarize our past efforts.

Excuses offered, we turn to an overview of this chapter. We briefly describe the development of the major precursors to excuse-making. These include concept of self and others, self-esteem, understanding of causality, responsibility and culpability, and knowlege of what constitutes acceptable acts. Language and logic are obvious components, but we deal with them only indirectly. After these preliminaries, we suggest a developmental sequence, framed in terms of

We thank Ellen Godfrey, Kathryn Minick, and C. R. Snyder for their comments on earlier versions. We also appreciate the children, particularly Jason, Jen, Mary Barbara, and Katy, whose excuse-making provided many insights into the developmental process. Beverly Ayers-Nachamkin is now at Wilson College, Chambersburg, Pennsylvania.

159

social and contextual interactions. We then describe some of the major arenas for children's excuses, the forms that their excuses take, and some of the factors that affect children's excuse-making.

PRECURSORS TO EXCUSE-MAKING

A Concept of Self and Others

William James (1890) suggested that the world must seem "one great blooming buzzing confusion" (p. 488) to the infant. From his view, the task of the developing infant and child is to make sense of the confusion by learning what is in the world and to identify and categorize things. Such a view suggests that the infant has some concept of world as distinct from self. Current notions, including ours, are more in line with Piaget's (1952) thesis that the neonate is totally egocentric in that there is no distinction between world and self. The first tasks of infancy, then, are differentiation between self and world and construction of a concept of self as it relates to and lives in the world. Simultaneously, one begins constructing knowledge of the world. Since numerous papers and books have been written on this enterprise, we touch only a few highlights that seem particularly relevant.

Conceptualization of self and others is a dynamic process, changing as children's thinking and activities change. Children develop a concept of self in the course of interacting with and learning about others. In looking at some of the known landmarks and the accomplishments that they represent, progress seems rapid. By age 2 children can recognize themselves in the mirror and in slides (Bertenthal & Fischer, 1978; Lewis & Brooks-Gunn, 1979). Many know their names. During the second year they expand their concept of self to include possessions, for example, "That my blanket/mommy/baby." They also begin to categorize themselves and others: "I a girl. You a boy." Gender, of course, is a major category; learning what being a boy or girl means involves years of work (see Huston, 1983). Gender labeling is usually accomplished in the second or third year (Slaby & Frey, 1975; Thompson, 1975). By the time they are 3, they are well aware of their gender, and distinguishing others on that dimension appears to be very important to them (e.g., Maccoby, 1966). Furthermore, children actively organize their experiences and behaviors around their sexual identity; they learn to behave in ways they see as appropriate to their sex. They become critical of cross-sex behaviors on the part of others. Rosenberg and Rosenberg (1981) found that school-aged children tend to sex-type occupations as part of learning sex roles. Turiel (1978a) found similar attitudes in his research on the development of social conventions. There are other categories such as age, size, family membership, ethnicity, neighborhood, and school that will be added as they become relevant (e.g., Harter, 1983). The particular self-images that children construct depend in part on their environment, but their insistence on classifying themselves and others, establishing identities and their bases, appears to be universal.

Paralleling the development of the self-concept, and intimately bound to it, is the development of empathy and perspective taking—the capacity to feel and see things from another's view. Children as young as 2 years can empathize with strong emotions; they will, for example, bring an upset friend or parent a favorite toy or security blanket (e.g., Hoffman, 1981). Children at this age will also turn a picture so that another person can see it (Lempers, Flavell, & Flavell, 1977), implicitly acknowledging that another's view is different from theirs. Further, 4- and 5-year-olds evidence perspective taking in simple tasks (e.g., Schachter & Gollin, 1979) and 7- and 8-year-olds demonstrate it in a variety of ways (e.g., Fishbein, Lewis, & Keiffer, 1972; Selman, 1980).

By the time children reach school age, they have identified themselves and others on a number of dimensions (Rosenberg, 1979). They know and can verbalize whether or not they like themselves (Bee, 1981). School-age children also render positive and negative evaluations about some of their capabilities and attributes as well as those of others. Awareness of self and others develops gradually, undergoing a number of changes (e.g., Harter, 1983; Selman, 1980). As they enter school, children are becoming self-aware; they are beginning to realize that they can think about themselves and about others. It's another step to realize that others can think about them; later they will discover that they can think about others thinking about them thinking about others and so on. Some of us may remember playing some variation of the game of "I thought that you'd think that I'd think that you'd think that . . ." Such recursive thinking seems to be an important component of self–other knowledge and esteem; it enables the individual to construct a concept of self that incorporates perception of self and perceptions of others' view of her or him (Harter, 1983; Rosenberg, 1979; Selman, 1980).

The self–other descriptions of younger children tend to be concrete, including physical categories, activities, and abilities (e.g., Montemayor & Eisen, 1977); their conceptualizations of self and others are neither well organized nor stable (Harter, 1983). Older children and adolescents focus on more abstract qualities such as beliefs, traits, and dispositions (Montemayor & Eisen, 1977; Rosenberg, 1979). Their views of self and others are relatively stable and integrated (Harter, 1983). Concept of self continues to develop throughout childhood, adolescence, and probably adulthood (e.g., Rosenberg, 1979). It also changes with the situation; for example, image of self as althlete is appropriate on the tennis court but not in the classroom. Those images or qualities of self that seem most important or essential at any time are those that get protected most carefully, perhaps at the expense of other roles (e.g., Ayers-Nachamkin, 1982; Scott & Lyman, 1968).

In summary, knowledge and valuation of self and others are constructed rapidly as children participate in a variety of social interactions and experience the consequences of their actions and those of others.

Self-Esteem

We will finesse the question of when (at what age) true excuse-making first occurs. Any answer to that question is highly variable, depending on the criteria used, the particular situation, and the characteristics of the children involved. However, a major prerequisite, and perhaps the last to develop, is the need to protect one's self-image.

The Self-Image Disparity

From where or what, then, does this need to psychologically self-protect come? As children grow, their activities and experiences broaden. Their physical, social, and cognitive skills increase as they encounter and deal with more and a greater variety of situations. They become more competent, knowledgeable, and aware of their own capacities. There is an inherent cost in this developing capability; more is expected of them, and they make increasing demands on themselves. Expectations, in fact, seem to exceed capacity, and the discrepancy increases with development. Zigler and his colleagues (e.g., Katz & Zigler, 1967; Phillips & Zigler, 1980) proposed that an increasing disparity between children's image of (real) self and ideal self is a natural concomitant of development. Their complex explanation of this increase involves two major factors. First, children incorporate social values, mores, and expectations as they mature. As a result they frequently make greater demands on themselves than they are able to fulfill; consequently, they experience guilt. The second factor is that, with increasing cognitive development, children can make finer distinctions, thus there is a greater range for discrepancies to occur. Research on real–ideal image disparity has shown that it generally increases with age, intelligence, and socioeconomic status (e.g., Katz & Zigler, 1967; Phillips & Zigler, 1980) and with measures of role-taking ability (Leahy & Huard, 1976).

Most of the research on self-image disparity has been conducted with children in the middle (second to sixth) grades. Lynch (1981) suggested that the idealized image of self develops between the ages of 6 and 9 with the real–ideal disparity emerging subsequently. It is interesting to note that preschool children make unreasonably high predictions about their performance on both physical and cognitive tasks, which they do not revise in light of subsequent failures to meet them. They also seem to evidence neither dismay nor frustration when they do not succeed (e.g., Ruble, Parsons, & Ross, 1976). The research by Zigler and colleagues (Katz & Zigler, 1967; Phillips & Zigler, 1980) shows that the age-related increase in self-image disparity is caused by both a decline in valuation of the real self and an increase in standards for the ideal self. Here, then, is the emergence of the need to protect one's self-esteem from harsh evaluation by oneself.

Gesell and Ilg (1946) described changes in interpersonal relations during the early school years that seem pertinent to the development of self-esteem and thus to its protection. They found that 6-year-olds are concerned with and often critical of their friends' behavior while evincing little concern about themselves. Further, 7-year-olds have begun to worry about what others think of them, and 8-year-olds are even more self-aware and concerned, not only with others' opinion of them, but also with meeting their own standards. Finally, self-criticism emerges around age 9.* This sequence suggests that the concern with others' view of the self may develop prior to self-evaluation and criticism. Similarly, we might expect children to use excuses to protect their public image before they use them to protect their view of themselves.

Social Comparisons

Infants and young children face and master a series of ultimately attainable physical skills. It's not a question for most infants of whether or not they will walk or even how well, but when. The attainment of new skills brings unmitigated pride and delight to the child's parents. Viewed from this perspective, success is not only assured, it is positively rewarded.

The day inevitably arrives, however, when success becomes a relative matter: "That drum is too noisy, Heather; why don't you play something quieter, like your sister does?" Thus begins the process of social comparison, using other people as a means of determining the adequacy of one's performance (Festinger, 1954). Veroff (1969) maintained that the motivation to compare oneself with others does not develop until the early school years unless the child has been exposed to "considerable reinforcement, usually from siblings or parents" (p. 50). In other words, some environmental circumstances are more conducive than others to the early introduction of social comparison processes as a salient feature of a child's life. Such circumstances include the existence of siblings or formalized preschool experience (e.g., Tesser, 1980).

A familiar example is that of the 2-year-old firstborn confronted with a new sibling who is a rival for center stage. Listening to the enthusiastic remarks of her or his parents, the 2-year-old responds plaintively, "I a baby too." Social comparison has reared its scaly head in this child's Garden of Eden, and the parents may well find their 2-year-old (or even an older child) attempting to compete in the infant's arena for a while. From this point on, the child's ability to generate excuses, as well as the perceived need for excuses, is likely to develop rapidly. The later-born sibling, however, will not have a time in her or his life that is free of the influence of some social comparison with the older sibling.

Since research has indicated that firstborn children, at least in upper socio-

---

* Although we use Gesell and Ilg's age norms, we wish to emphasize the sequence of development of self–other concerns rather than the ages given, which may vary across situations.

economic level families, tend to be higher achievers than later-borns (e.g., Glass, Neulinger, & Brim, 1974), the comparisons are less likely to be favorable to the later-born. Though the research has yet to be done, we posit that later-born children, confronted with the head start of an ambitious sibling, will develop their excuse-making potential at an earlier age than the firstborn, especially in those cases when only two or three years separate their ages.

Exposure to day care, preschool, or kindergarten is also likely to enhance the development of excuse-making skills needed to maintain self-esteem. Picture the child accustomed to building her block towers in the privacy of her living room accompanied by the approving murmurs of mother. Introduced into the preschool situation, she happily builds her favorite tower only to discover that another child has built a tower that is apparently grander in every respect, and the teacher is praising that tower and not her own. Her initial response might well be to reach out a chubby hand and reduce the offending tower to rubble. Via the social consequences of such an action, it will not be long before the child learns more acceptable means to make herself feel better about her tower or to garner the approval of others. She may go through a phase of imitation, but that will win no bouquets. She may learn to build better towers or shift to finger painting. She may also learn about the protective mantle of a good excuse: "Yes, but he hogged the good blocks so I didn't have enough for my tower."

Not all social comparisons have negative outcomes, of course, nor is comparison necessarily odious. Rubin (1980) suggested that children compare and compete among themselves in order to assess their own capabilities and limits. Similarly, Harlow (1971) reasoned that play fosters skill development and competency through peer challenges, competition, and mutual bolstering of courage. Thus comparison appears inevitable, as children discover their limits, strengths, weaknesses, and those of others. Some outcomes of such social or peer comparisons may not bolster one's image, but they seem to contribute to its formation.

Causality and the Responsibility Link

If one is to see one's image threatened by an unacceptable performance, the actor must (1) have acquired a concept of causality, (2) realize that one can be a causal agent, and (3) understand that one exerts control over one's behavior.

Three- and four-year-old children honor the temporal order principle (that cause precedes effect) in simple event sequences (Kun, 1978). They can also identify the cause when they see simple sequences of physical events (Bullock & Gelman, 1979). In some instances, they will also ascribe intentions and motives to explain someone's behavior (Keasey, 1978).

Children rapidly become more sophisticated about causality. Four-year-olds readily make causal inferences. Bullock (1979, cited in Gelman & Spelke,

1981) found that 4-year-olds will "trouble-shoot" simple systems that fail to work as they have in the past; for example, they will look for a break in the string connecting two toys if the one in front moves and the second doesn't; 3-years-olds do not search and might respond, "Won't work." By kindergarten, children have become relatively adept at identifying causes of basic emotions such as fear, happiness, sadness, and anger (Green, 1977).

Complicating any event sequence will delay, often as much as two to three years, the age at which children can identify the cause of an event. Siegler (1975; Siegler & Liebert, 1974) found that introducing brief delays between the cause and effect or adding an irrelevant but distracting event greatly interfered wth 5-year-olds' ability to identify the cause of a problem; these factors had less effect for 8- and 9-year-olds.

Covariation of Events

In many instances, attributions about causality and responsibility in social situations are thought to be made on the basis of covariation among events. Despite the widespread impact of Kelley's propositions concerning people's use of consensus, distinctiveness, and consistency information to make causal attributions, little attention has been given to their acquisition and use by children (Kassin, 1981; Sedlak & Kurtz, 1981). DiVitto and McArthur (1978) found that first-grade children used distinctiveness and consistency information to make actor (in the sense of the one who is performing an action) attributions (e.g., Paul shares his candy with everyone; he always shares). They also found that third graders were the youngest group to use consensus information to make situational or target attributions (e.g., nearly everyone shares with Bob). One explanation for this order of emergence of information use is that distinctiveness information is about the actor, whom we tend to see as the active or causal agent, thus it can be applied directly to the problem. Consensus information focuses on the situation or target person; using it requires the inference that the situation, not the actor, is the controlling factor. DiVitto and McArthur (1978) found that sixth graders, but not younger children, employed (low) consensus information for making personal or actor attributions, and only college students used (low) distinctiveness information to make situational or target attributions. These latter situations are quite complex in that they require the observer to discount the role of the person or stimulus for whom the information is supplied and then infer that something or someone else must be the cause.

DeVitto and McArthur, however, may have overestimated the difficulty of using consensus information. There is some evidence that kindergarten children, and in some instances even preschool children, can use consensus information (see Sedlak & Kurtz, 1981, for a review). More important, research on development of the use of covariation information typically involves highly constrained situations in which the child is asked to respond to a situation described in picture-stories by making a forced choice for comparison. Research in which children define the causal problems or are allowed to generate their own explanations of event sequences is notably absent, particularly in the social domain. Fein (1972) did find that young children tended to identify all event sequences (displayed in pictures) as causal; by age 7 they accurately discriminated between causal and noncausal social sequences, whereas such discriminability was not found for physical event sequences until age 11.

Cause–effect relationships involving people rarely are simple, and it seems to take many experiences and several years to acquire an understanding of complex causal sequences. Wimmer, Wachter, and Perner (1982) found that preschool children can make appropriate causal inferences about the relationships among effort, ability, and outcome if the contributing factors, task (e.g., painting a fence) and information provided, are all highly concrete. Children's ability to recognize that a person's behavior in more abstract situations may have multiple determinants is not evidenced until the fourth to eighth grades (e.g., Erwin & Kuhn, 1979; see also Kassin, 1981; Sedlak & Kurtz, 1981).

The development of causality is complex and not well understood. Children begin to acquire rudimentary notions of causality in infancy (Piaget, 1954), but understanding continues to develop throughout childhood and probably beyond. Despite their egocentrism, young children believe that causes are external to them and largely beyond their control. Five-year-olds are more likely to make external or target attributions than are older children or adults (Ross, 1981; Ruble, Feldman, Higgins, & Karlovac, 1979). Piaget (1929) argued that children impute purpose and life to inanimate objects. Young children also tend to attribute a person's liking for an object to the object's intrinsically attractive qualities rather than to the person's internally held criteria of beauty or utility (see Shantz, 1975). Until children come to understand that they can be a causal agent and make things happen, they do not see themselves as responsible. Hence young children's concept of self should be essentially unthreatened and, in the model adopted in this book, their excuses have a hollow ring.

Note that there is a potential paradox involved in coming to know that causes can be internal. As children come to understand that they can make things happen, they gain a sense of power. As that sense grows, so presumably do their image and value of self. However, that same perception of power must also carry with it a sense of limits, the knowledge that one's capacity is limited, even insufficient in some instances (see Chapter 2 for related discussion). And falling short can be threatening unless, of course, there is an excuse for doing so.

"This Won't Do": Learning about Unacceptable Performances

We have argued that the child must develop some essential prerequisites for excuse-making. An obvious candidate for the list is the understanding that certain acts and classes of acts are not acceptable. Although this prerequisite sounds simple on the face of things, it seems less so in actuality. Some acts are always unacceptable; others are context dependent. Some are bad, not in and of themselves, but because they have unacceptable consequences. Construction of a set of guidelines for determining what will do and what won't is a major task of childhood.

Turiel (1975, 1978a,b) classifies prescriptions for socially acceptable behavior into two distinct conceptual domains: morality (justice) and social convention, which he sees as "behavioral uniformities that serve the function of coordinating the actions of individuals participating in social systems" (1978a, p. 26). Morality is structured by underlying concepts of justice. The moral breach remains constant across social situations. Whether the young child is at the beach, in a store, or playing in the yard, it is wrong to hurt other people or to steal. The initial difference between acceptable and unacceptable performances in the moral domain is clear-cut. Even the mitigating circumstances—such as self-defense—are relatively few in number and hence comparatively easy to learn. Social conventions are far more complex. Whether or not the act is acceptable depends on the situation to a far greater extent than on the act itself. Consider an example from the child's point of view. Learning to walk was highly rewarded by Mom and Dad as was learning to run—with smiles, hugs, laughter, praise. The messages are clear: walking is good; running is good. But wait. Time goes by, and the growing child must learn that running in the yard is allowed, unless it is a formal garden or too nervewracking for Grandma and Grandpa. Running in the school building is not permissible except in the gym. Running in the gym is not acceptable when it is being used for an assembly. What children must learn, of course, is not a list of places to run but a set of principles by which they can determine acceptable behavior in a variety of contexts and conditions (Turiel, 1978a).

As with much of social knowledge, children generally learn their first lessons about acceptable and unacceptable actions from parents, although peers become important contributors later on. Moral knowledge is probably one of the first domains of conduct to be addressed by parents. The moral rules relevant to children are relatively simple, few in number, and emotionally laden; parents are likely to be both consistent and insistent about their acquisition. The crawling infant does not typically incur much in the way of punishment, with the notable exception of doing harm to others and to self. The toddler about to insert a finger into an electrical outlet has a hand slapped, is removed from the immediate area and told, "No! You mustn't do that; that will hurt you." The infant who grabs a handful of brother's hair is greeted with screams of pain and outrage; the offending fingers may be slapped or forceably disentangled, and the babe is told, "That hurts brother. You mustn't hurt other people." The infant who bites the nursing mother soon has a choice of a cup or bottle. The examples are legion, but the point is that certain moral rules are learned early and well; some behaviors are always wrong.

Peers, even young children, also recognize and enforce these basic moral codes. Turiel asserts that children as young as 3 to 5 years are able to distinguish between moral laws and social conventions. The studies (e.g., Nucci & Nucci, 1982; Nucci & Turiel, 1978; Turiel, 1978b; Weston & Turiel, 1980) that are consistent with this position typically involve situations in which children demonstrate their recognition (or lack thereof) of violations of morals and conventions. Young children are especially likely to notice moral breaches (Much & Shweder, 1978; Nucci & Turiel 1978). As children grow older, they focus increasingly on violations of social conventions, at least in school settings (Nucci & Nucci, 1982).

Damon (1977) maintains that peers learn positive justice, such as sharing and fair distribution, from each other. Similarly, Youniss (1980) holds that cooperation is learned through peer activities. In short, both parents and peers supply information about the quality of children's performances and the acceptability of their actions. The basic lesson, that some acts are acceptable and some are not, is mastered in early childhood. As activities and relationships change throughout life, children and adults continue to incorporate new standards into their existing knowledge.

THE MAKING OF EXCUSE-MAKERS

In asking "Who did it?" or "Did you do it?" the questioners are providing children with the opportunity to deny or at least justify their role in the affair. In fact, parents, other authorities, and older siblings invite children to make excuses when and where they are appropriate. Our informal observations suggest that when children, particularly young children, make excuses they do so largely in response to questions or demands for explanations typically from a parent, teacher, or some other authority figure. Both adults and older children model excuse-making. They also seem to tutor and to volunteer an explanation when none is forthcoming. Parents often comfort the crying or scared child with excusing phrases, "There, there, Mommy knows you didn't mean to." Consider another familiar script: "M.B., I know you don't track mud into the kitchen on purpose; you just forget, but . . ." In short, parents teach the elements of excuse-making. Peers and teachers offer advanced training.

As children grow older, gain experience, and become capable of more sophisticated reasoning, the lessons continue. It is probable that people use and expect more sophisticated excuses from children as they grow older. Denney and Duffy (1974) found that as the age of the children (6-, 10-, and 14-year-olds) increased, both the level of moral reasoning (Kohlberg's three main categories) used by the children and the level of moral reasoning implied by the mothers' treatment of the children increased. Zanna and Darley (1981) found that 70% of parents of young first-grade children made distinctions in severity of punishment that depended on foreseeability of the consequence and the intentionality of the act, whereas over 90% of parents of older children made these distinctions. As children become more knowledgeable about responsibility and about causes of bad performances, they should also be better prepared to excuse their acts in terms of these same qualities (e.g., "How could I know he was going to pull right up into the driveway [and over my bike]?").

The classroom was where we really began to be aware of the demand quality from the authority in the excuse interaction. A familiar example is the situation in which a child fails to turn in an assignment. The teacher asks why, and the child responds with a "pro forma" excuse: "I left it at home" or "I didn't have enough time." The consequences of responding with one of these lame excuses is likely to be a comment or two about responsibility and often an extension of the deadline (e.g., "If you planned your time wisely, you wouldn't have this problem; finish it up during study period and turn it in at the end of the day"). Such interactions between student and teacher are common and occasionally humorous, as illustrated by nine of William R. Jackson's excuses from *The Book of Lists #2:*

1. My little sister ate it.
2. My dog or cat did his duty on it.
3. We ran out of toilet paper.
4. Our furnace broke down and we had to burn my homework to keep from freezing to death.
5. I had to use it to fill a hole in my shoe.
6. I gave it to a friend and his house burnt down.
7. My mother threw it away by mistake.
8. I got hungry and there was no food to eat.
9. I did it, I swear, but I left it next to my poor sick mother who I was helping and caring for all night. (Wallace, Wallechinsky, Wallace, & Wallace, 1980, p. 494)

What would happen if the youngster had responded, perhaps more truthfully, with "I had better things to do"? It is highly likely that the teacher would respond in a very different fashion, possibly delivering a stern and lengthy lecture to the entire class on responsibility and moral degradation. The teacher might send the child to the principal for discipline or make an extra assignment. Consider the tenth excuse on the list:

10. Because I didn't feel like it! (Very often the last words ever spoken by a student.)

They may not be the last words, but they will earn failing grades whereas any of the others may buy time and a second chance for the offender. Why is the last so offensive? It appears that telling the truth in such a situation amounts to confrontation. Not only has the student failed to protect his or her own image, but the teacher's image is threatened by the implication that the assignment was unimportant. Further, the teacher's image as the authority in the classroom is threatened. Rather than risk such damage to his or her image, the teacher invokes strong measures. Of course, this kind of interaction also occurs between parent and child. For want of an excuse, harmony is lost. Making excuses pays off; sometimes the payoff is protection of the recipient's self-image as well as that of the excuse-maker.

Excuses may serve multiple functions in social interactions. If a person does not behave in the socially expected manner, a situation of accountability (Much & Shweder, 1978) is created. An excuse is then virtually demanded if smooth social functioning is to be maintained or restored. The social actor is expected to explain the unexpected behavior in order to bridge the gap between what was expected and what was actually done (Scott & Lyman, 1968). This is the sense, then, in which excuses appear to grease the wheels of social interaction and help maintain social structure. It is also in this sense that there is a demand quality to excuse-making.

Adults seem to play the major role in fostering excuse-making, particularly with young children. As we have hypothesized and illustrated, adults demand, suggest, coach, and model excuse-making; they often supply excuses when children fail to provide them. Excuse-making is a concomitant of moral education and a vital component of socialization, so adults inadvertently teach children to make excuses as they teach them to be polite, considerate, and socially adept.

It is not our intention to suggest that adults are consciously nurturing master excuse-makers. Rather, excuse-making seems to be a natural by-product of the socialization process. Furthermore, in encouraging more subtle and sophisticated judgmental abilities on the part of children, adults are also providing the fodder for potential excuses. An interesting speculation is that stricter, more fundamentally religious families may raise children who are not as skilled as their more liberal peers in the artful use of excuses. If life's choices, judgments, and behaviors are always presented as good or bad, right or wrong, and without ambiguity, "good" excuses may be difficult to come by (see Chapter 10, "Two Worlds without Excuses" section, for a related discussion).

THE MAKING OF EXCUSES

The Emergence of Excuses

It does not appear that children initially assemble all the prerequisite concepts and skills and then learn to make excuses. Rather, as these prerequisites emerge and interrelate, we also begin to see approximations to excuses in young children.

The Big Bang Theory

Part of the generic vocabulary in toddlerhood is the phrase "Oh, Oh," uttered when a disaster occurs in the vicinity. The prototypical scene is the vase splintering into pieces as it hits the floor. The nearby 2-year-old says, "Oh, Oh" and then begins to cry. This response can be highly effective. The adult, hearing the crash, arrives at the scene ready to focus on the damage done. Instead, she or he is distracted by the toddler's response and often turns to comforting the babe and excusing the misdeed.

We are not implying either awareness or intentionality on the part of toddlers. There is no evidence to suggest that children use "Oh, Oh" to forestall trouble. Rather, the response is effective in blunting the edge of the adult's anger and engendering sympathy. Our point is that children's behavior does influence adult responses, and they, in turn, may affect the responses of children in subsequent occurrences of similar events.

Opening Off-Broadway: Pre-Excuses

In the development of excuse-making, there is a phase that we label "pre-excuses." Like the Off-Broadway opening, the pre-excuse phase enables children to get their act together, add new scenes, and fine-tune their roles. Superficially the pre-excuse looks convincingly like the real thing. There is an antagonist, usually a parent, and a protagonist, typically a preschooler, a plot such as preparation for bed, and a dialogue:

> "I can't go to bed yet."
> "Why not?"
> "Because I haven't kissed Daddy goodnight."
> "He'll come in when he gets home."
> "I'm not wearing my nightgown."
> "It's in the laundry; has to be pajamas tonight."
> "I need another story."
> "Tomorrow night."
> "I can't find Bear."
> "He's already in your bed."
> "My room's too far away."
> "Enough. Let's go."
> "Mom . . ."

Although this scene certainly has the form of an excuse-making session, it is missing some essential features. There is no bad performance (even her exasperated mother enjoyed it), and thus there is no threat to her self-image. Rather, there is a child who is intent on attaining her positive goal of delaying her bedtime. She is using the form of an excuse in an attempt to influence her environment (parents).

Shifting to potentially bad performances, a familiar form of pre-excuse is the "not-me" syndrome. Here we have the situation where Mom finds the kitchen and 3-year-old Johnny's face freshly decorated with peanut butter.

"Have you been into the peanut butter?!"
"Not me!"

Another common scene is:

"Who's been tracking mud through the house?!"

There stands Mary with mud to her knees promptly responding,

"Not me."

These sound more like excuses. There is an unacceptable performance involved, and both children use simple denial of responsibility. However, as in many instances of pre-excuses, self-esteem just doesn't seem to be threatened.

Plays open Off-Broadway to allow producers and cast to preview their act and gauge audience response before the opening that really counts. During the pre-excuse phase, children do not seem to be protecting their self-image. All other elements of the drama seem to be present, but, in the final analysis, the price of an unsuccessful explanation is not a blow to the image (although it may be to the seat of the pants).

Rehearsals

Pre-excuses may serve a number of vital functions, one of these being the development of an excuse repertoire, another being the skill of improvising them on the spot.

It is well established that situational factors such as familiarity affect children's processing capacity (e.g., Shatz, 1978). We suspect that emotional and motivational factors do also, with intense levels reducing their effectiveness in dealing with the available information. Relative to excuses, children use a variety of creative justifications when they are left to their own devices with little or no pressure to produce. Here is an example with the adult side of the dialogue omitted but obvious.

"I don't need a bath this morning."
"My bed took all the dirt off."
"It's a magic bed."

The 5-year-old speaker enjoys a bath once in the tub, so there's little cost if she loses. On the other hand, she does have something better to do with her time so she'll try to avoid taking one. Again, we are not implying conscious intent (or lack of it for that matter) but simply noting that the low pressure situation is optimal for the construction of an imaginative dodge.

Consider another situation with a precocious 2½-year-old whose mother is exploring a mysterious disappearance with a question reflecting curiosity rather than accusation: "I can't find the spring that goes on your (toy) bird." The child looks interested but makes no response to this opening gambit so Mom continues: "Do you know what happened to the bird's spring?"

"The Easter Bunny (a large stuffed toy) picked it up and threw it in the drawer."

However, responding under pressure seems to be a skill that requires additional practice to develop. Thus, when confronted with an irritated parent demanding an explanation for a playmate's tears, the 2½-year-old child says nothing; the 5-year-old reverts to well-worn protests: "It was an accident."

Given this early experience, we would expect to see advanced skills demonstrated in later childhood, and indeed they are. An 11-year-old recently went to somewhat elaborate lengths to obtain permission to attend a party while "grounded." During the three weeks prior to the party, she employed an amazing repertoire of anticipatory excuses. From her mother's perspective, the high point of this endeavor occurred when two of her friends appeared at the door to offer her the excuse that the party was really a surprise going-away party for the daughter (who was moving in three months). However, even the experts may not be immune to pressure. When it came right down to the wire and time had run out, the 11-year-old reverted to the simple routines that she'd developed years ago: "Everyone else is going." "They won't like me anymore." "I'll be left out." Not all progress was lost, however; she delivered these old saws with the staging of an experienced excuse-maker complete with quavering voice and a hint of tears.

In short, the luxury of time and low-demand situations enable young children to develop and elaborate their repertoires. Parental demands for explanations, however, do provide opportunities for children to learn to generate excuses under pressure.

The Repertoire

In the model of excuse-making developed in this book, the actor is linked to a performance by apparent and transformed responsibility links. An excuse is an attempt to manipulate perception of either the quality of the performance or one of these links. For children, "not me" and other simple denials are efforts to sever the apparent responsibility link. Bowerman (1981) recounts a magnificent example of severing the apparent responsibility link to a bad event:

A 3½-year-old steps onto a wooden floor, whereupon a distinctly cracking sound is heard. Her 6-year-old sister says, "(younger sister) broke the floor." The younger sister immediately denies responsibility, "No, I didn't." She then elaborates, "I stepped on it . . . and it broke." (pp. 28–29)

The child knows that she did not do anything out of the ordinary, and floors do not ordinarily break, thus she disclaims responsibility.

Young children also learn to reframe performances. Taking the toys of younger siblings frequently is explained with reframing techniques: "She gave it to me"; "I was just showing him how"; "She didn't want it anymore"; "I was just holding it for him"; "He wanted me to have it." The message is clear; the child has discovered that things are not always the way they appear to be.

Perhaps the last component in the responsibility chain to be manipulated and understood by children is the transformed responsibility link. This link seems to be the most complex and removed part of the chain. The performance is bad, and the performer has been identified with it. The only option remaining is to try to establish extenuating circumstances that reduce the perpetrator's responsibility for the outcome. Such efforts to transform responsibility appear to develop later than denying and reframing bad acts. Simple transformation efforts, particularly through consensus raising, do appear in the repertoire of kindergarten and first-grade children ("Jose and Alma were already doing it when I got there. I just wanted to play, too."). In short, we suggest that children master simple instances of the basic forms of excuses early in their young lives. In fact, they seem to be acquiring expertise in the art of image protection before they have any real need for it. Their motivation, when evidenced, seems much more immediate and external: avoidance of punishment and attainment of positive goals.

By the time children are ready for school, they are well-versed excuse-makers. A number of additional changes occur during the later years of childhood and early adolescence. The number of arenas in which excuses are used will increase dramatically as will the categories of recipients and, most important, the images of self that will have to be protected.

Onstage: Self-Protective Excuses

It is often proposed that initially children learn what constitutes unacceptable behavior in order to avoid punishment (e.g., Kohlberg, 1963). Furthermore, Darley and Zanna (1982) suggested that children learn from their parents' behavior that excuses can mitigate their punishments. We now suggest that children first learn these lessons in the context of moral behavior.

Logically, if rules within the moral domain are learned earliest, children are also likely to make their earliest bona-fide excuses within this domain. Much and Shweder (1978) recorded and analyzed "situations of accountability," which they defined as situations in which an account of an unacceptable behavior is demanded or offered. These researchers found that kindergarten chil-

dren recognize moral breaches in behavior and that they will be held accountable for them. The children most often tried to explain these breaches through
lessening apparent responsibility (e.g., denying that they committed the act).
They also tried to reframe the act to make it appear justifiable under the circumstances. Note the following example from Much and Shweder in which
Tammy and Nina are washing a table, and Agnes comes to help.

Tammy: "I'm sorry but you can't help."
Alice comes over from her painting and intervenes, "She can help. You don't
have to be just rude."
(Tammy begins to cry.)
Teacher (approaching): "What's the matter?"
Tammy: "She pinches me."
Teacher (to Alice): "Why?"
Alice: *"She wouldn't let Agnes help."* (p. 28)

When unacceptable behavior is in the moral domain, resultant discussions and
excuses appear to revolve around the consequential factors intrinsic to the action itself. Hence, "it almost appears as though a person who breaches a moral
principle must deny the breach through redefinition, in order to avoid blame"
(Much & Shweder, 1978, p. 37).

Social conventions are typically highly situation dependent and less clearly
defined than moral rules, thus children seem to require broader exposure to a
variety of social arenas and higher levels of cognitive development in order to
master them. Adults are concerned with the transmission of these rules and
regulations, and they respond to violations of them in such a way as to point
out the reasons for the particular rules as well as advertise the negative sanctions that would be incurred by offenders (Nucci & Turiel, 1978). When misbe-
havior within the social conventional domain is called to account, both the resultant discussions and children's excuses seem to focus on the social context;
for instance, one may deny that the breached rule pertains in the given situation. In explaining their behavior in these situations, children make use of "a
legalistic orientation rich in references to conditions, consequences, and rule
formulations" (Much & Shweder, p. 38). These results suggest that children
learn how to explain and excuse their breaches as they learn the rules and
practices of morality and social interaction. Young children rarely respond to
violations of social conventions by other children, but with age, they learn to
call each other to task. Nucci and Nucci (1982) found that children's use of rule
statements and reminders decreased between the second and seventh grades; at
the same time, their use of ridicule in response to breaches of social conventions increased. Nucci and Nucci's interpretation of these findings is that older
children are likely to assume that the transgressor knows the governing conventions and thus they "use personal attacks on the transgressor to achieve social conformity" (p. 411). Such attacks should threaten the self-image, thus necessitating the use of well-developed excuse-making capabilities.

Elaborating the Repertoire

There are important aspects of an action that qualify its nature and thus affect excuse-making. One factor is that of intentionality. Researchers in the Piagetian tradition have established that young children, reasoning at the preoperational level, focus on the consequence of an action rather than intentionality of the perpetrator when assessing the seriousness of the action. However, even young children can use intention in making moral judgments and do so when it is not overshadowed by highly salient effects of consequence (see Grueneich, 1982; Karniol, 1978; Keasey, 1978, for reviews).

Preschool children appear to regard others' behavior as intentional; thus they typically fail to distinguish between accidental and purposive acts (e.g., Smith, 1978). At least in terms of "harm-doing" actions, Karniol (1978; see also Shantz, 1983) concluded that by age 5 or 6 children are able to distinguish between outcomes that are accidental and those that have been deliberately caused. For instance, children assign less punishment to a person who has accidentally injured another person than to one who has intentionally hurt another (e.g., Farnhill, 1974). This distinction clearly is vital to advanced excuse-making. The child who possesses less advanced cognitive processing skills is essentially reduced to basic denial of actions ("I didn't do it"), which is probably tantamount to wishful thinking in many cases. However, the child who understands that it is far less serious to have accidentally caused harm and who can articulate this notion has a powerful tool at his or her disposal for transforming the responsibility for the performance ("I didn't mean to"). Darby and Schlenker (1982) reported that children recognize that apologies reduce the negative effects of a transgression. They also found that children believe that more elaborate apologies are needed when the transgressor is viewed as responsible because he or she wasn't paying attention for an accident (bumping into a person) and when damage resulted (dishes were broken). Fourth and seventh graders, but not kindergarten and first-grade children, thought that more elaborate apologies reflected greater remorse.

Even more sophisticated excuses may be forthcoming once the child learns that intentional harm-doing acts may be justified on other grounds, such as prior provocation or a worthy goal (end justifies means). Darley, Klosson, and Zanna (1978) found that 5-year-olds were able to distinguish among contextual conditions that mitigated intentionally committed harmful acts. However, their procedures reduced the cognitive demands of the task considerably compared to "in vivo" events and involved recognition rather than use. It is not clear that 5-year-old children's information processing skills are adequate to handle the complexity of these problems in everyday occurrences, particularly where both situational analyses and relevant explanations must be self-generated. Such endeavors seem destined to be relegated to later years.

In addition to the distinction between accidentally and intentionally unacceptable performances, researchers have investigated the development of children's ability to differentiate foreseeable from unforeseeable accidental consequences. Here the question is when children begin to see that the accident that might have been prevented is less acceptable than the utterly unpredictable accident. Zanna and Darley (1981) found that children seem to acquire the concept of foreseeability about the time they are in the first grade. Apparently children come to understand that acts causing unforeseeable harm are more excusable than those whose consequences could have been anticipated. Here, then, is another means of modifying one's responsibility for an event. However, we again suspect that fully understanding the concept of foreseeability and using it as an excuse in, and only in, appropriate situations is a slow development. Mastery of such complex concepts and the underlying logic requires experience using them and watching others use them. As we might expect, such opportunities abound with both adult and peer audiences.

CHILDREN'S THEATERS

Peers and Play

To this point, we have concentrated on adult–child relationships in the development of excuse-making. The child–adult relationship is unilateral and authoritative (Youniss, 1980), thus adults can demand excuses from children and get them. What then of peers? What role, if any, do they have in this long, intricate process?

Peer relationships are equilateral and reversible (Youniss, 1980). Peers may assume unilateral relationships (e.g., leader–follower) for a time, but this unilateral state will hold only as long as all participants consent to it. If one chooses to exit, the imbalance is destroyed; thus the underlying relationship among peers, as the term implies, is one of equality.

Children learn from peers; the lessons are mutual and learned through discovery. Youniss (1980) holds that cooperation is necessarily learned from peers because the freedom to engage in or withdraw from the relationship is a necessary condition for cooperation to emerge. Similarly, children learn the skills needed to deal with equals and to form and maintain friendships in peer arenas. Note that adults may help by sharing their knowledge, by modeling, and by conveying the relevant principles. However, the adult's role is that of coaching from the sidelines. The adult may give examples or even briefly role-play to show the child how it might be done, but the children must work out the system among themselves.

Children learn to use explanatory statements with their peers at an early age. Preschoolers consistently use justificatory statement forms (we hesitate to call them excuses or explanations), probably because they have learned that such forms are more effective than unadorned demands or commands. In the example below, B. tries to join L. and J., who are playing. They don't want him and make up a rule (about bare feet) to keep him out of their play.

    B. "What is this? a city? a train?"
    L. "You can't play with bare feet."
    J. "Yeah, go away!" (Corsaro, 1981, p. 217)

Very young children bluntly state their position then add a reason that is typically arbitrary and self-serving. They tend to give themselves preferential treatment and assume that others will conform to their position (Damon, 1977). The reasoning of somewhat older children appears to be more objective, and the reasons appear to be logically connected to the statement; however, their thinking is still inflexible and unilateral (e.g., Damon, 1977).

    The language and style of peers, while honest, is often unnecessarily harsh or even cruel, at least in the eyes of adults. Consider this interchange:

    "Do you want to play house with me?"
    "No, I like Morgan better than you."

We also heard the following conversation between two 10-year-olds:

    "Do you want to come over and play at my house?"
    "No. I don't like to go there; your mother always gets mad and yells at us."

Children seem to accept such explanations. The 10-year-old above simply agreed with the assessment of his mother's temper, and the two of them went to the park. A child may or may not be hurt by another child's honest statement, but they don't seem to regard such statements as bad performances that require excuses until they are well into preadolescence.

    Older children show increasing responses to transgressions involving social convention (Nucci & Nucci, 1982). Fine (1981) described peer taunting among a group of preadolescents that continued until one boy threw another's hat out the window of their school bus. That act exceeded the legitimate range of behavior and terminated the activity. The thrower had "sullied his social self. Although he was not sanctioned by his friends, he apologized to the victim, claiming he really didn't mean to get rid of the hat" (Fine, 1981, p. 46). The social conventions of children often are not those of adults, nor are some even acceptable to adults, but they exist and are honored. Breaches must be excused.

    Rituals may be used as excuses particularly among preadolescents. Children, especially boys, use game rules, rituals, and chants to settle disputes and to terminate arguments (Fine, 1981; Piaget, 1965). Opie and Opie (1959, cited by Fine, 1981) used the example of "finders keepers, losers weepers" as a ritualistic declaration to settle an ownership dispute. As Fine (1981) pointed out, children say that rules are absolute but they are in fact negotiated. By holding the concept of a rule as absolute and therefore outside themselves, children can argue and negotiate among themselves as to what rule applies to the problem at hand and then invoke the agreed-upon rule to dispose of the issues without destroying the social group. This procedure saves face for all those involved. Citation of such a law may settle a dispute instantly; more likely it will permit those involved to argue the applicability of the rule rather than the moral integrity of the principals.

Our conversations with preadolescents suggest that peers use other forms of excuses that protect the image of the maker and facilitate continued peer social interaction. For example, some ninth-grade boys were playing volleyball. Jay attempted to play a ball that would obviously have landed out of bounds. He muffed the play, costing his team a point. Jay said, "I thought I could get it." Players on both teams snorted and jeered with good-natured disbelief. According to our insightful and verbal young cohorts, Jay's absurd excuse was obligatory; it acknowledged his error and gave the others permission to tease him. Silence or self-castigation, on the other hand, would have made his peers uncomfortable, thus constituting a social breach.

Schofield (1981) suggests that preadolescents use playful teasing as a means of testing romantic waters. Similarly, pushing and other forms of playful touching allow the preadolescent to explore physical contact with the other sex in minimally threatening contexts. Her point is that preadolescents and early adolescents are greatly concerned with rejection and failure in cross-sex relations, and their early contacts can be written off as play if their target responds in a genuinely negative fashion. The system may be awkward, but it affords effective protection of an important image. The peer teasing, particularly among males, that greets many such overtures may also be part of the elaborate protection scheme. It is evident from Fine's (1981) and Schofield's (1981) work that preadolescent males, while vehemently denying their interest in the other sex, tease each other about girls as a matter of course; denials are expected. Such routines are protective in that they contribute to the cover story of lack of interest and enable the participants to become accustomed to being teased about girlfriends before such relationships develop. Such patterns of behavior suggest interesting if not obvious forms of anticipatory excuse-making among preadolescents.

School

It would be difficult to overestimate the impact that school has on the developing child. Kagan (1974) notes,

> Competence in academic subjects is a *sine qua non* for the American child. It is difficult, if not impossible, to fail this requirement completely and still retain a sense of dignity and worth in childhood. (p. 89)

The concept of failure as reflecting an inadequacy may be acquired in the early school years as standards are imposed on children and the degree of success in meeting those standards is made clear. It does take some time for children to learn how important it is not to fail in the academic domain. For instance, there appear to be age-related differences in the affective response to failure. Ruble et al. (1976) found that when children actually failed at a matching familiar figures test, 6-year-olds did not feel as badly about their poor performance as 10-year-olds did. Furthermore, when these children were given social comparison information (e.g., "Almost all children your age get this answer correct," implying an easy task), the older children felt even worse. The younger children seemed to be unaffected by the comparative information.

Barden, Zelko, Duncan, and Masters (1980) found that 12- to 13-year-olds anticipated that they would feel "Just OK" rather than sad or mad if they were to fail to give correct answers to math problems. The authors suggest that older children, having had greater experience of failure, have become affectively tolerant of such experiences. Alternatively, they may have become sufficiently skilled in generating excuses for themselves and others that the emotional impact of failure is mitigated. In fact, the denial of affective involvement may itself be an excuse: "Big deal—I wasn't really trying."

Sex Differences

Boys and girls use different explanations in accounting for their successes and failures in academic arenas. Nicholls (1975) found that fourth-grade boys who failed on a stimulus matching task attributed their failure to bad luck. Fourth-grade girls who failed on the same task said they were no good at the task. Similarly, Hess, Holloway, and King (1981) found that girls cited lack of ability to explain their performance in their worst subjects. This sex difference in achievement situations is well documented, especially for college-age students (Bar-Tal, 1978; Deaux, 1976; Frieze, Parsons, Johnson, Ruble, & Zellman, 1978; Ickes & Layden, 1978; Zuckerman, 1979). Particularly in the mathematical domain, which is where the bulk of this research has been conducted (e.g., Dornbusch, 1974; Fennema, 1981; Parsons, Meece, Adler, & Kaczala, 1982; Parsons, Ruble, Hodges, & Small, 1976), males typically place more blame for failure on external circumstances (e.g., bad luck, difficulty of the task) than females do. Females tend to blame themselves for failure (e.g., lack of ability). In the arena of academic achievement, males appear to use self-protective excuses whereas females do not.

Dweck and her colleagues (see Dweck & Goetz, 1978) have conducted extensive research on the attributions for performance in achievement situations. They contend that girls and boys receive different feedback regarding their classroom performance; this difference is reflected, in turn, in the explanations they give for their own performances. Dweck, Davidson, Nelson, and Enna (1978) observed fourth- and fifth-grade classrooms extensively over a period of five weeks, coding every occurrence of evaluative feedback given by teachers to students in academic settings. They found that the vast majority of negative feedback given to girls regarding their work referred specifically to its intellectual aspects. When girls performed poorly, their teachers often indicated that they lacked intellectual skill; for example, "I don't think you quite understand the difference between nouns and pronouns, Marie." Since both girls and teachers agree that girls try to do well in school (Coopersmith, 1967; Digman, 1963; Dweck, Goetz, & Strauss, 1980; Stevenson, Hale, Klein, & Miller, 1968), it is unlikely girls would use the excuse that they didn't try hard enough. Teachers praise girls more than boys (Dweck et al., 1980), hence girls are unlikely to excuse their failure in terms of teacher discrimination, another possible excuse. Dweck suggests that girls may have little choice but to view themselves as personally responsible for their failures, a type of learned helplessness. In contrast, boys are not seen as trying to do well in school. When they succeed, praise is enthusiastic and personal (e.g., "See what you can do when you put your mind to it"), presumably to reinforce and encourage such activity. When boys fail, teachers more often criticize their academic performance in terms of lack of effort or in a nonspecific manner (e.g., "This work is sloppy, Tom"). Feedback of this nature leaves the male free to engage in excuse-making and may even encourage it.

Since the expectations for appropriate sex-role performance are so different for males and females (e.g., Broverman, Vogel, Broverman, Clarkson, & Rosenkrantz, 1972), it seems logical to speculate that their excuse-making will also differ. First, different behaviors will be seen as unacceptable and therefore necessitating excuses. Second, the kinds of excuses that they make in similar situations may differ. For instance, a girl can excuse many behaviors with personal attributions such as "I was afraid" or "I'm too shy to do that." Such excuses would be regarded as inappropriate for boys who are expected to be brave and forthright. Scott and Lyman (1968) make the point that a normative structure governs the nature and types of communication between the persons in roles, including the kinds of accounts that may be required and given and the manner in which they are given. Sex is an ascribed role (Sarbin & Allen, 1968) that consistently influences our social interactions. Children are in the business of learning expectancies and behaviors, many of which are correlated with their gender indentity. Boys receive more criticism from teachers in the classroom than girls (cf. Brophy & Good, 1974; Feshback, 1969), thus they may have more opportunity to practice their excuse-making skills and to have such behavior more frequently modeled for them by same-sex peers. Boys also may offer more excuses than girls.

Parental Images

Even parents may feel their images are invested in their children's academic performances. Hess et al. (1981) found that mothers explained their child's performances in school in ways that protected or enhanced their own self-esteem.*

---

* The children gave different excuses that were more consistent with the research on academic performances cited earlier.

Given choices of ability, effort, training, and personality, the mothers of fifth- and sixth-grade children rated ability most heavily in explaining their children's success. In considering explanations for their daughters' performance in their poorest subject, mothers blamed lack of effort, although giving some weight to personality characteristics. Mothers of boys divided the blame for low performance almost equally among effort, training, and personality. Hess et al. interpreted these results as being self-protective attributions (excuses). Parental images are enhanced by having a bright child, whereas having a lazy child is not as bad as having a dull one since poor effort may be attributed to the child. Furthermore, the authors claimed that many mothers seemed surprised by the request to explain the low performance and said they had not thought about it. Such a strategy is also self-protective; one does not have to account for things that one does not consider.

Good and Bad Lines

The question arises as to the kinds of excuses children at various levels of development understand and find acceptable. Parallel to the explanations they offer, preschool and kindergarten children, who reason intuitively, accept almost any cover story even if it is misleading or irrelevant (Chandler, Paget, & Koch, 1978). Their major requisite seems to be that the form, statement plus reason, be employed. Chandler et al. (1978) also found that young children linked a defensive response to the immediate situation; they failed to realize that events occurring much earlier could cause a particular response.

Understanding of various psychological defense mechanisms as they are used as excuses increases with age and level of cognitive development (Chandler et al., 1978; Dollinger & McGuire, 1981). Dollinger and McGuire found that displacement was the best understood and projection the most poorly understood of the defense mechanisms. Chandler et al. also found that projection was a difficult concept to understand. Somatization, rationalization, denial, and self-blame are intermediate in difficulty of understanding according to Dollinger and McGuire.

As we might expect from our general hypothesis that excuses facilitate social interactions as well as maintain esteem, older children find some types of excuses and their makers more acceptable than others. Dollinger, Staley, and McGuire (1981) presented fifth- and sixth-grade children with a story in which a team lost an important softball game although the players had tried hard, wanted to win, and had played pretty well. The reactions of four members of the losing team were described, then each participant was asked to rate those players on likability, happiness, smartness, and goodness. The player who acknowledged the loss but offered no excuse was rated the smartest, the "most good," and the most likable. The player who projected the blame on the other team by saying that they cheated was given the lowest rating on these qualities.

The other two players who used denial ("Doesn't matter to me if we lose") and self-blame ("It's all my fault") were given intermediate ratings. All players were rated as feeling sad, although the players using self-blame and projection were considered the saddest.

Dollinger and McGuire (1981) found similar results in a study of 4- to 12-year olds. They concluded that the children in their study evidenced greater attraction to story characters who internalized (e.g., self-blame and somatization) than to those who used externalizing excuses (e.g., projection, displacement).

These results are evidence that excuses may detract from their maker if used when they aren't warranted or if they make the recipient uncomfortable. Furthermore, those who shifted blame to others were viewed in the most negative light, suggesting that excuses that protect oneself at the expense of one's peers may be costly in the long run. Clearly, children evaluate the excuses of others, and they evaluate others in light of their excuses. These evaluations reflect the interactive nature of excuse-making.

SUMMARY

We close as we opened, with the obvious statement that children make excuses. Children make them because excuses are expected and demanded from them. As children are taught the moral and social rules of their society and subcultures, they are also taught to explain their violations of them. Excuses are an integral part of the social system. The basic form of the excuse is mastered early, apparently during the preschool years. During these early years, excuses seem to be used largely as a matter of form—to prolong conversation or maintain the social interaction. With use, excuses become a habit. The first self-protective function of excuses, also emerging during the preschool years, seems to be avoidance of punishment. During the early school years esteem-protection appears to emerge, first to protect the self from critical appraisal by others and then from self-criticism.

Children make excuses at home, in school, and on the playground. Excuses are used with peers and adults, with members of the same and the other sex, for the self and for others, and across the age range. All of these factors appear to affect the nature of the excuse and what must be excused. Viewed analytically, the domain of excuse-making seems highly complex, yet children seem to master the necessary elements as or even before they are needed. Their excuses range from being shopworn and flimsy to creative and leakproof. Rarely are children caught without an excuse, although someone else may supply it for them. Such is the importance of this social lubricant and psychological cover.

REFERENCES

Ayers-Nachamkin, B. J. Sex differences in self-serving biases: Success expectancies or role expectations. Unpublished doctoral dissertation. University of Kansas, 1982.

Barden, R. C., Zelko, F. A., Duncan, S. W., & Masters, J. C. Children's consensual knowledge about the experiential determinants of emotion. *Journal of Personality and Social Psychology,* 1980, **39,** 968–976.

Bar-Tal, D. Attributional analysis of achievement related behavior. *Review of Educational Research,* 1978, **48,** 259–271.

Bee, H. *The developing child* (3rd ed.). New York: Harper & Row, 1981.

Bertenthal, B. I., & Fischer, K. W. Development of self-recognition in the infant. *Developmental Psychology,* 1978, **14,** 44–50.

Bowerman, W. R. Applications of a social psychological theory of motivation to the language of defensiveness and self-justification. In M. M. T. Henderson (Ed.), *1980 Mid-America linguistics conference papers.* Lawrence: University of Kansas Linguistics Department, 1981.

Brophy, J., & Good, T. *Teacher-student relationships: Causes and consequences.* New York: Holt, Rinehart & Winston, 1974.

Broverman, I. K., Vogel, S. R., Broverman, D. M., Clarkson, F. E., & Rosenkrantz, P. S. Sex role stereotypes: A current appraisal. *Journal of Social Issues,* 1972, **28,** 59–78.

Bullock, M., & Gelman, R. Preschool children's assumptions about cause and effect: Temporal ordering. *Child Development,* 1979, **50,** 89–96.

Chandler, M. J., Paget, K. F., & Koch, D. A. The child's demystification of psychological defense mechanisms: A structural and developmental analysis. *Developmental Psychology,* 1978, **14,** 197–205.

Coopersmith, S. *The antecedents of self-esteem.* San Francisco: Freeman, 1967.

Corsaro, W. A. Friendship in the nursery school: Social organization in a peer environment. In S. R. Asher & J. M. Gottman (Eds.), *The development of children's friendships.* Cambridge: Cambridge University Press, 1981.

Damon, W. *The social world of the child.* San Francisco: Jossey-Bass, 1977.

Darby, B. W., & Schlenker, B. R. Children's reactions to apologies. *Journal of Personality and Social Psychology,* 1982, **43,** 742–753.

Darley, J. M., Klosson, E. C., & Zanna, M. P. Intentions and their contexts in the moral judgments of children and adults. *Child Development,* 1978, **49,** 66–74.

Darley, J. M., & Zanna, M. P. Making moral judgments. *American Scientist,* 1982, **70,** 515–521.

Deaux, K. Sex: A perspective on the attribution process. In J. H. Harvey, W. J. Ickes, & R. F. Kidd (Eds.), *New directions in attribution research* (Vol. 1). Hillsdale, N.J.: Lawrence Erlbaum Associates, 1976.

Denney, N. W., & Duffy, D. M. Possible environment causes of stages in moral reasoning. *The Journal of Genetic Psychology,* 1974, **125,** 277–283.

Digman, J. M. Principal dimensions of child personality as inferred from teachers' judgments. *Child Development,* 1963, **34,** 43–60.

DiVitto, B., & McArthur, L. Z. Developmental differences in the use of distinctiveness, consensus, and consistency information for making causal inferences. *Developmental Psychology,* 1978, **14,** 474–482.

Dollinger, S. J., & McGuire, B. The development of psychological-mindedness: Children's understanding of defense mechanisms. *Journal of Clinical Child Psychology,* 1981, **10,** 117–121.

Dollinger, S. J., Staley, H., & McGuire, B. The child as psychologist: Attributions and evaluations of defensive strategies. *Child Development,* 1981, **52,** 1084–1086.

Dornbusch, S. M. To try or not to try. *Stanford Magazine,* 1974, **2,** 51–54.

Dweck, C. S., Davidson, W., Nelson, S., & Enna, B. Sex differences in learned helplessness: II. The contingencies of evaluative feedback in the classroom; III. An experimental analysis. *Developmental Psychology,* 1978, **14,** 268–276.

Dweck, C. S., & Goetz, T. E. Attributions and learned helplessness. In J. H. Harvey, W. Ickes, & R. F. Kidd (Eds.), *New directions in attribution research* (Vol. 2). Hillsdale, N.J.: Lawrence Erlbaum Associates, 1978.

Dweck, C. S., Goetz, T. E., & Strauss, N. L. Sex differences in learned helplessness: IV. An experimental and naturalistic study of failure generalization and its mediators. *Journal of Personality and Social Psychology,* 1980, **38,** 441–452.

Erwin, J., & Kuhn, D. Development of children's understanding of the multiple determination underlying human behavior. *Developmental Psychology,* 1979, **15,** 352–353.

Farnhill, D. The effects of social judgment set on children's use of intention information. *Journal of Personality,* 1974, **42,** 276–289.

Fein, D. A. Judgment of causality to physical and social picture sequences. *Developmental Psychology,* 1972, **8,** 147.

Fennema, E. Attribution theory and achievement in mathematics. In S. R. Yussen (Ed.), *The development of reflection.* New York: Academic Press, 1981.

Feshback, N. Student teacher preferences for elementary school pupils varying in personality characteristics. *Journal of Educational Psychology,* 1969, **60,** 126–132.

Festinger, L. A. A theory of social comparison processes. *Human Relations,* 1954, **7,** 117–140.

Fine, G. A. Friends, impression management, and preadolescent behavior. In S. R. Asher & J. M. Gottman (Eds.), *The development of children's friendships.* Cambridge: Cambridge University Press, 1981.

Fishbein, H. D., Lewis, S., & Keiffer, K. Children's understanding of spatial relations. *Developmental Psychology,* 1972, **7,** 21–33.

Frieze, I. H., Parsons, J. E., Johnson, P., Ruble, D., & Zellman, G. *Women and sex roles.* New York: Norton, 1978.

Gelman, R., & Spelke, F. The development of thoughts about animate and inanimate objects: Implications for research on social cognition. In J. H. Flavell & L. Ross (Eds.), *Social cognitive development: Frontiers and possible futures.* Cambridge: Cambridge University Press, 1981.

Gesell, A., & Ilg, F. *The child from five to ten.* New York: Harper & Row, 1946.

Glass, D. E., Neulinger, J., & Brim, O. G. Birth orders, verbal intelligence and educational aspirations. *Child Development,* 1974, **45,** 807–811.

Green, S. K. Causal attribution of emotion in kindergarten children. *Developmental Psychology,* 1977, **13,** 533–534.

Grueneich, R. Issues in the developmental study of how children use intention and consequence information to make moral evaluations. *Child Development,* 1982, **53,** 29–43.

Harlow, H. F. *Learning to love.* San Francisco: Albion, 1971.

Harter, S. Developmental perspectives on the self-esteem. In P. H. Mussen (Ed.), *Manual of child psychology* (Vol. 4): *Social and personality development,* E. M. Hetherington (Ed.). New York: Wiley, 1983.

Hess, R. D., Holloway, S. D., & King, D. R. Causal explanations for high and low performances in school: Some contrasts between parents and children. Paper presented at the Society for Research in Child Development, Boston, April 1981.

Hoffman, M. L. Perspectives on the difference between understanding people and understanding things: The role of affect. In J. H. Flavell & L. Ross (Eds.), *Social cognitive development: Frontiers and possible futures.* Cambridge: Cambridge University Press, 1981.

Huston, A. Sex-typing. In P. H. Mussen (Ed.), *Manual of Child Psychology* (Vol. 4): *Social and personality development,* E. M. Hetherington (Ed.). New York: Wiley, in press.

Ickes, W., & Layden, M. A. Attributional styles. In J. H. Harvey, W. J. Ickes, & R. F. Kidd (Eds.), *New directions in attribution research* (Vol. 2). Hillsdale, N.J.: Lawrence Erlbaum Associates, 1978.

James, W. *Principles of psychology* (Vol. 1). New York: Henry Holt, 1890.

Kagan, J. The psychological requirements for human development. In N. B. Talbot (Ed.), *Raising children in modern America: Problems and prospective solutions.* Boston: Little, Brown, 1974.

Karniol, R. Children's use of intention cues in evaluating behavior. *Psychological Bulletin,* 1978, **85,** 76–85.

Kassin, S. M. From laychild to "layman": Developmental causal attribution. In S. S. Brehm, S. M. Kassin, & F. X. Gibbons (Eds.), *Developmental social psychology.* New York: Oxford University Press, 1981.

Katz, P., & Zigler, E. Self-image disparity: A developmental approach. *Journal of Personality and Social Psychology,* 1967, **5,** 186–195.

Keasey, C. B. Children's developing awareness and usage of intentionality and motives. In C. B. Keasey (Ed.), *Nebraska symposium on motivation* (Vol. 25). Lincoln: University of Nebraska Press, 1978.

Kohlberg, L. The development of children's orientations toward a moral order: 1. Sequence in the development of moral thought. *Vita Humana,* 1963, **6,** 11–33.

Kun, A. Evidence for preschoolers' understanding of causal direction in extended causal sequences. *Child Development,* 1978, **49,** 218–222.

Leahy, R. L., & Huard, C. Role-taking and self-image disparity in children. *Developmental Psychology,* 1976, **12,** 504–508.

Lempers, J. D., Flavell, E. R., & Flavell, J. H. The development in very young children of tacit knowledge concerning visual perception. *Genetic Psychology Monographs,* 1977, **95,** 3–53.

Lewis, M., & Brooks-Gunn, J. Toward a theory of social cognition: The development of self. In I. C. Uzgiris (Ed.), *Social interaction and communication during infancy.* San Francisco: Jossey-Bass, 1979.

Lynch, M. Self-concept development in children. In M. D. Lynch, A. A. Norem-Hebeisen, & K. Gergen (Eds.), *Self-concept: Advances in theory and research.* Cambridge, Mass.: Ballinger, 1981.

Maccoby, E. (Ed.) *The development of sex differences.* Stanford, Calif.: Stanford University Press, 1966.

Montemayor, R., & Eisen, M. The development of self-conceptions from childhood to adolescence. *Developmental Psychology,* 1977, **13,** 314–319.

Much, N. C., & Shweder, R. A. Speaking of rules: The analysis of culture in breach. In W. Damon (Ed.), *New directions for child development: Moral development* (Vol. 2). San Francisco: Jossey-Bass, 1978.

Nicholls, J. G. Causal attributions and other achievement-related cognitions: Effects of task outcome, attainment value, and sex. *Journal of Personality and Social Psychology,* 1975, **31,** 379–389.

Nucci, L. P., & Nucci, M. S. Children's social interactions in the context of moral and conventional transgressions. *Child Development,* 1982, **53,** 403–412.

Nucci, L. P., & Turiel, E. Social interactions and the development of social concepts in preschool children. *Child Development,* 1978, **49,** 400–407.

Parsons, J. E., Meece, J. L., Adler, T. F., & Kaczala, C. M. Sex differences in attributions and learned helplessness? *Sex Roles,* 1982, **8,** 421–432.

Parsons, J. E., Ruble, D. N., Hodges, K. L., & Small, A. W. Cognitive-developmental factors in emerging sex differences in achievement-related expectancies. *Journal of Social Issues,* 1976, **32,** 47–62.

Phillips, D.A., & Zigler, E. Children's self-image disparity: Effects of age, socioeconomic status, ethnicity and gender. *Journal of Personality and Social Psychology,* 1980, **39,** 689–700.

Piaget, J. *The child's conception of the world.* New York: Harcourt, Brace, 1929.

Piaget, J. *The origins of intelligence.* New York: International Universities Press, 1952.

Piaget, J. *The construction of reality in the child.* New York: Basic Books, 1954.

Piaget, J. *The moral judgment of the child.* New York: Free Press, 1965.

Rosenberg, M. *Conceiving the self.* New York: Basic Books, 1979.

Rosenberg, M., & Rosenberg, F. The occupational self: A developmental study. In M. D. Lynch, A. A. Norem-Hebeisen, & K. Gergan (Eds.), *Self-concept: Advances in theory and research.* Cambridge, Mass.: Ballinger, 1981.

Ross, L. The "intuitive scientist" formulation and its developmental implications. In J. H. Flavell & L. Ross (Eds.), *Social cognitive development: Frontiers and possible futures.* Cambridge: Cambridge University Press, 1981.

Rubin, Z. *Children's friendships.* Cambridge, Mass.: Harvard University Press, 1980.

Ruble, D. N., Feldman, N. S., Higgins, E. T., & Karlovac, M. Locus of causality and the use of information in the development of causal attributions. *Journal of Personality,* 1979, **47,** 595–614.

Ruble, D. N., Parsons, J. E., & Ross, J. Self-evaluative responses of children in an achievement setting. *Child Development,* 1976, **47,** 990–997.

Sarbin, T. R., & Allen, V. L. Role theory. In G. Lindzey & E. Aronson (Eds.), *Handbook of social psychology* (Vol. 1). Reading, Mass.: Addison-Wesley, 1968.

Schachter, D., & Gollin, E. S. Spatial perspective taking in young children. *Journal of Experimental Child Psychology*, 1979, **27**, 467–478.

Schofield, J. W. Complementary and conflicting identities: Images and interaction in an interracial school. In S. R. Asher & J. M. Gottman (Eds.), *The development of children's friendships*. Cambridge: Cambridge University Press. 1981.

Scott, M. B., & Lyman, S. M. Accounts. *American Sociological Review*, 1968, **33**, 46–62.

Sedlak, A. J. & Kurtz, S. T. A review of children's use of causal inference principles. *Child Development*, 1981, **52**, 759–784.

Selman, R. L. *The growth of interpersonal understanding: Developmental and clinical analyses*. New York: Academic Press, 1980.

Shantz, C. U. Social Cognition. In P. H. Mussen (Ed.), *Manual of child psychology*, (Vol. 2): *Cognitive development*, J. H. Flavell & E. M. Markman (Eds.). New York: Wiley, 1983.

Shantz, C. U. The development of social cognition. In E. M. Hetherington (Ed.), *Review of child development research* (Vol. 5). Chicago: University of Chicago Press, 1975.

Shatz, M. The relationship between cognitive processes and the development of communication skills. In C. B. Keasey (Ed.), *Nebraska symposium on motivation* (Vol. 25). Lincoln: University of Nebraska Press, 1978.

Siegler, R. S. Defining the locus of developmental differences in children's causal reasoning. *Journal of Experimental Child Psychology*, 1975, **20**, 512–525.

Siegler, R. S., & Liebert, R. M. Effects of continuity, regularity, and age on children's inferences. *Developmental Psychology*, 1974, **10**, 574–579.

Slaby, R. G., & Frey, K. S. Development of gender constancy and selective attention to same-sex models. *Child Development*, 1975, **46**, 849–856.

Smith, M. C. Cognizing the behavior stream: The recognition of intentional actions. *Child Development*, 1978, **49**, 736–743.

Stevenson, H. W., Hale, G. A., Klein, R. E., & Miller, L. K. Interrelations and correlates in children's learning and problem solving. *Monographs of Society for Research in Child Development*, 1968, **33** (7, Serial No. 123).

Tesser, A. Self-esteem maintenance in family dynamics. *Journal of Personality and Social Psychology*, 1980, **39**, 77–91.

Thompson, S. K. Gender labels and early sex role development. *Child Development*, 1975, **46**, 339–347.

Turiel, E. The development of social concepts: Mores, customs, and conventions. In D. J. DePalma & J. M. Foley (Eds.), *Moral development: Current theory and research*. Hillsdale, N.J.: Lawrence Erlbaum Associates, 1975.

Turiel, E. The development of concepts of social structure: Social convention. In J. Glick & K. A. Clarke-Stewart (Eds.), *The development of social understanding*. New York: Gardner Press, 1978(a).

Turiel, E. Distinct conceptual and developmental domains: Social convention and morality. In C. B. Keasey (Ed.), *Nebraska Symposium on Motivation* (Vol. 25). Lincoln: University of Nebraska Press, 1978(b).

Veroff, J. Social comparison and the development of achievement motivation. In C. P. Smith (Ed.) *Achievement-related motives in children.* New York: Russell Sage, 1969.

Wallace, I., Wallechinsky, D., Wallace, A., & Wallace, S. *The book of lists #2.* New York: Bantam Books, 1980.

Weston, D. R., & Turiel, E. Act-rule relations: Children's concepts of social rules. *Developmental Psychology,* 1980, **16,** 417–424.

Wimmer, H., Wachter, J., & Perner, J. Cognitive autonomy of the development of moral evaluation of achievement. *Child Development,* 1982, **53,** 668–676.

Youniss, J. *Parents and peers in social development.* Chicago: University of Chicago Press, 1980.

Zanna, M. P., & Darley, J. M. Judgments of responsibility for foreseeable and unforeseeable accidents. Paper presented at the Society for Research in Child Development Biennial Meeting, Boston, April 1981.

Zuckerman, M. Attribution of success and failure revisited, or: The motivational bias is alive and well in attribution theory. *Journal of Personality,* 1979, **47,** 245–287.

CHAPTER 8

Excuses Gone Awry

Once I was crazy and my ace in the hole
Was that I knew that I was crazy
So I never lost my self-control
I'd just walk in the middle of the road
I'd sleep in the middle of the bed
I'd stop in the middle of a sentence
And the voice in the middle of my head said
Hey, Junior, where you been so long
Don't you know me
I'm your ace in the hole ...

Ace in the hole
Lean on me
Don't you know me
I'm your guarantee

PAUL SIMON, *"Ace in the Hole"*

As the preceding chapters make clear, excuses are a normal part of everyday life. They serve a useful, even essential role in our efforts to maintain an affirmative sense of ourselves and are occasionally indispensable aids in promoting positive social relationships. An effective excuse enables us to transit through our shortcomings in work, love, and play, and to emerge with intact optimism about ourselves and our lives. By the same token, an effective excuse enables others to endure our shortcomings and to reaffirm their faith in us. Yet the suspicion persists that there is a darker, more malignant side to the excuse masquerade. The focus of this chapter is the role that excuses play in psychopathology and the problems of living.

We begin by examining a number of clinical examples that illustrate how the use of excuses may play both adaptive and maladaptive roles in peoples' lives. Subsequently, our focus shifts to an examination of several contrasting "schools" of thought about the nature and etiology of psychopathology. In our review of these theories, our primary concern is to illustrate the role they ascribe to the use of excuses in the development and maintenance of deviant behavior. Finally, we turn to a consideration of the idea that deviant behavior itself may serve important excuse-making functions. This thesis is developed through a discussion of the excuse-making value of illness behavior in general and alcohol use and depression specifically.

THE ADAPTIVE-MALADAPTIVE CONTINUUM OF EXCUSE-MAKING

The purpose of this section is not to detail an exhaustive catalogue of excuses that may be typified as either adaptive or maladaptive. It is, rather, to use clinical examples to illustrate some of their major constructive and destructive aspects. We first propose that excuses and excuse-making may be thought of as varying along certain characteristic dimensions with regard to their maladaption potential. Second, we suggest that the manner in which excuses are "used" also influences whether or not they are beneficial. In focusing on these aspects of excuse-making, we do not exclude the possibility that there are other fruitful schemes for thinking about the problems associated with excuses. Our choice is based on our belief that these dimensions provide *at least* two meaningful ways of thinking about how and why excuses "go awry."

Issues Relating to Characteristic Dimensions of Excuses

Although there are a variety of dimensions along which the characteristics of excuses may vary (see Chapter 3 for a discussion of the awareness, avowal/self-evident, effectiveness/pervasiveness, and anticipatory/retrospective dimensions), there are three that strike us as being particularly relevant because of their relationship to problems in living. The first is the intensity or extremeness of the excuse. In general, we feel that the more extreme excuses are, the more likely they are to be associated with serious problems and to have unfavorable consequences. A second important dimension is the extensiveness of the excuse-making. Excuse-making that pertains to a broad range of situations and experiences in a person's life has a greater potential for adversely affecting normal development and adjustment. Third, we believe that the reversibility or stability of excuses is an important determinant of their impact. Excuses that tend to perpetuate themselves or that set in motion related chains of events would appear to have particularly high risk value. The following paragraphs provide some clinical examples of how these dimensions may relate to maladaption.

Extremity

The first characteristic of excuses that we examine is their extremity. Some excuses (e.g., "white lies") are relatively "mild," are socially approved, are widely seen as "humane," and are nearly *de rigueur* in certain contexts. Such excuses may be justified effectively through exonerative moral reasoning (see Chapter 4) and even transformed into virtues. Telling a "white lie" to avoid a dreaded party, for example, can be regarded as serving a greater good—saving the hostess' feelings. Telling the hostess the truth would, in most circles, be considered an unconscionable social *faux pas.* While such benign and moderate excuse-making may cement the fabric of polite society, more extreme instances can threaten the very foundations of civilization. In discussing the heinous crimes of the Charles Manson "family," for example, Ernest Becker (1975) observed that the family members excused their murderous acts on the grounds that they were simply following Manson's orders. This, in turn, was followed by a perverse act of exonerative moral reasoning. In Becker's words, "They seemed to feel that they were doing their victims 'a favor,' which seems to mean that they sanctified them by including them in their own 'holy mission' " (p. 138).

The hazards of extreme excuses can also be seen in a psychotherapy case once seen by one of the authors. Lewis W. requested psychotherapy because of problems adjusting to college. Socially and academically, Lewis was functioning at a marginal level. He reported being suspicious and distrustful of others and "used" his distrust in a remarkable way in therapy. He informed the therapist that he could never trust a therapist who didn't look him "squarely" in the eyes at all times. The therapist quickly trained himself to do this, but was "rewarded" by Lewis' next excuse for not working in therapy—he couldn't trust a therapist who wouldn't sit touching and holding his hand throughout the session.

Over a two-month period therapy with Lewis consisted almost entirely of working through a sequence of increasingly extreme excuses for unwillingness to accept therapy. His last excuse was that he couldn't trust a therapist who wouldn't conduct therapy in the dark, in the nude! This final excuse was encountered just before the college's Thanksgiving break and Lewis never returned from home. We include this example here because it illustrates the point that extreme excuses make it difficult for others to relate to us. In Lewis' case, they also precluded his being able to profit from therapy beyond what he gained from the process of working through some of the initial barricades he erected against looking at himself. Obviously, Lewis' extreme excuse-making was associated with serious problems.

Extensiveness

The second characteristic of excuses that we identified was their extensiveness. Extensive excuse-making can frequently result in far-reaching failures to profit from important life experiences. One self-evident principle of effective coping with life is that an individual must have sufficient contact with "the facts" to make realistic and adaptive adjustments in behavior and thinking patterns. The pervasive use of excuses to distort the meaning of experiences or to avoid important developmental tasks can result in serious debilities. As Zimbardo and Radl (1981) observe, for example, there is a cyclical nature in such problems as shyness. Shyness breeds avoidance, which results in lost opportunities to develop self-esteem, which begets increased shyness, and so on. This perspective is consistent with Bandura's (1977) theory of self-efficacy. In Bandura's view, one's beliefs about his or her ability to achieve desired outcomes in life derive from experiences of being able to deal effectively with situations. Avoidance of opportunities to develop effective coping skills can only lead to lowered feelings of self-efficacy and increased avoidance. Such a pattern can be seen in the case of Ben M.

Ben M., a 23-year-old client of one of the authors, sought treatment for a debilitating social phobia. It all began, he reported, when he was in the second grade. While reading aloud in class, he started to visibly tremble and was subsequently teased by his classmates. Dating from that time, he had successfully avoided each and every opportunity to engage in public speaking by using a variety of excuses and ploys, including avoiding classes that involved student presentations. This strategy was now failing because he was enrolled in a college curriculum that made classroom presentations and critiques mandatory. He began to have anxiety attacks in *any* situation where he might be watched (e.g., on the golf course, playing tennis, and talking with friends in a bar).

Ben M.'s case is interesting because it illustrates both the worst and best sides of excuses. His excuse-based avoidance had clearly damaged his ability to succeed in his chosen career, but his successful treatment was effected, in part, by training him to become a more effective excuse-maker! After several months of behaviorally and cognitively oriented treatment, he was able to make appropriate use of several facilitating excuse strategies. In the face of disappointing performances, he was able to raise consensus (directed homework assignments had confirmed for him that nearly all of his peers became visibly nervous during presentations), he was able to heighten distinctiveness (following a program of graduated in vivo assignments he had to admit that he did do most other things well), and he was able to lower consistency (one especially threatening homework assignment had gone so spectacularly well that he knew he could, at times, do things as well as any of his peers). He was able to excuse his more feeble efforts on the grounds that he had a lot to make up for after so many years. Follow-up contacts with Ben M. indicate that he now has a reputation for being one of the best speakers in his classes.

Stability

The final dimension of excuses that we discuss in terms of the adaptive–maladaptive continuum is their stability or reversibility. Whereas some excuses are very temporary or limited in their implications, others may have long-lasting or far-reaching implications. Life is replete with excuses that are reversible in that they do not restrict the user's freedom of movement or choice in other arenas or on subsequent occasions: "Not tonight, Honey, I have a headache." "I'm sorry I was so abrupt with you yesterday, but I was under a lot of stress and had a deadline to meet." "I would *love* to go with you, but I have to study tonight." Excuses may begin to lose some of their reversibility when they strain the receiver's credibility. For example, one of the authors (Higgins) will never forget one excuse that he received after asking a college acquaintance for a date: "I would really like to go, but several weeks ago some of us girls were talking about the possibility of having a slumber party. I don't know if we will have one but, if we do, it *might* be on that night!" This excuse was not reversible because Higgins got the unintended message. To be honest though, it probably did not adversely restrict the girl's freedom of movement.

The really serious problems associated with irreversible excuses are seen in those instances where the excuse-maker alienates important individuals in his or her life or somehow feels compelled to "live up" to some of the more self-destructive implications of the excuse. Yalom (1980), for example, describes a case that illustrates the idea that the use of an excuse to avoid responsibility for a failing may serve to lock an individual into a nonproductive or self-defeating manner of living. Yalom's client was a woman who, in order to diminish her culpability for the break-up of her marriage, used the excuse that she "couldn't" stop smoking. Her husband left her, ostensibly because he couldn't stand to see her ruining her health, after giving her the ultimatum to give up either smoking or the marriage. In subsequent therapy, Yalom explored this client's reluctance to quit smoking despite the fact that she suffered from Buerger's disease, which was complicated by nicotine. According to Yalom, "One of the important themes that arose was her realization that, if she stopped smoking now, then that would mean that *she could have stopped smoking before*" (p. 320).

A similar process may be seen at work in instances where "boredom" has been used as an excuse for the failure of students to perform well in their classes. Once an individual has proclaimed a class to be boring and has disclosed this to peers, it becomes more difficult to make a serious investment in profiting from the course without "losing face."

It may be that those excuses that are the least reversible are those that require the individual to accept some form of "label" (e.g., addicted smoker, bored student). As discussed later in this chapter, labels tend to be self-perpetuating, not least of all because the individual (especially if self-labeled) takes on the burden of having to live up to that label. In some instances, this may be so trivial as having to stay in bed all day because the excuse of being "sick" was used to get out of school or work. In more extreme instances, this may require accepting "treatment" and the adoption of a new life style. Recall, for example, the case of Senator Wilbur Mills, the former chairman of the U.S. Senate Ways and Means Committee, who was discovered one night cavorting around in the Washington tidal basin with a nearly nude prostitute. Mills blamed his behavior on his being an alcoholic and shortly thereafter entered a treatment program. He later made the rounds as a speaker denouncing the evils of alcohol.

The previous examples have been offered to briefly highlight some of the ways in which excuses may be seen to lie along an adaptive–maladaptive continuum. We next suggest that the way excuses are used can also determine whether they are constructive or destructive influences in an individual's life.

Issues Relating to the Use of Excuses

It appears to us that there are important differences among people in the way they incorporate excuses into their lives. Any given individual also uses excuses differently as a function of the different situations he or she encounters as well as his or her particular vulnerabilities. Here we are interested not so much in the matter of individual differences in excuse-making as in whether excuses are used "responsibly." This may seem to be an unusual notion insofar as we have argued throughout this book that excuse-making is specifically designed to cut off or delimit responsibility. Nevertheless, there are many instances in which making excuses implies a responsibility to take steps to eliminate the need for subsequent excuses. We believe that excuses that are not followed by "corrective" actions are far more likely to lead to maladaption than are those that are followed by remedial measures.

© United Feature Syndicate, Inc.

The theoretical orientation of the preceding chapters has been that excuses are employed in the service of maintaining self-esteem in the face of "bad acts." However, excuses themselves are regarded as bad acts more often than not (e.g., Wahlroos, 1981). One has only to accuse someone of making an excuse to experience the truth of this. The artless use of excuses, then, may elicit negative social reactions. The intentional use of excuses may also be counterproductive because the individual then has one more negative performance for which to account. For these and other reasons (e.g., see our foregoing discussion of the consequences of extensive excuse-making), excuses are best used in moderation.

One adaptive aspect of a well-used excuse is that a certain degree of psychological liberty accrues to the individual who uses it. As suggested earlier, a critical issue then becomes what use is made of that liberty. An example of constructive use was described to us following a faculty symposium in which the basic outline of excuse theory (see Chapter 3) was presented. A colleague approached us arguing that a distinction needed to be made between excuses and "reasons." He then related a personal story. He had been accustomed to teaching two 1½-hour sections per week for his three-credit courses, but he was receiving unsatisfactory feedback from students regarding his performance. He decided that his ineffectiveness was the result of becoming fatigued in such long classes and subsequently changed to teaching three 50-minute classes. He argued that, since his teacher evaluations improved following this, his "fatigue" was a "reason" and not an excuse. The merits of his argument are incidental to the present point, which is that this individual used the liberty he gained from making an untested attribution to fatigue to effect constructive changes in his behavior. Constructive use is not always made of such opportunities, as can be seen in the case of Mrs. X.

Mrs. X. was engaged in an extramarital affair of nearly three years duration at the time she entered therapy with the stated goal of wanting to improve her marriage. Her "justification" for her affair was that her husband was so uncommunicative that she was powerless to resist the opportunity to receive affection from her lover. Having directed her internal responsibility to an external source (DIRTEing; see Chapter 4), she was in a position simultaneously to feel "OK" about her behavior and to take constructive steps to improve her marital relationship—her stated intention. However, as in much of life, things are rarely so simple. When the therapist suggested that the marital relationship might be best addressed in couples therapy, Mrs. X. declined, saying that her *husband* would never consent. When the therapist attempted to explore ways in which Mrs. X. might improve communications with her husband, she declined on the grounds that, if she did so, it would fail because *he* would never change his behavior. Homework assignments designed to decrease the couple's pattern of mutual avoidance were accepted but never implemented because she claimed that *he* would only demand sex from her before she was ready. Eventually it became clear that Mrs. X. was unwilling to do *anything* constructive about her role in the marriage, including separation or divorce. As she finally put it, if she were to get better, the *therapist* would refuse to see her anymore! Mrs. X.'s insistence on bolstering her excuses with even more excuses effectively guaranteed her continued unhappiness in her marriage.

To function effectively (or even minimally) in this social world, interpersonal problems and conflicts must be faced and resolved. Just as with adjusting to personal problems, adjusting to interpersonal problems requires the ability to recognize at least the bare outlines of reality and to accept some personal responsibility for change. To the extent that excuse-making is so pervasive that this process is thwarted, the ability to function in social contexts suffers. Wahlroos (1981) and Bach and Wyden (1969), among others, have developed guidelines designed to facilitate interpersonal conflict resolution. The ability to accept a modicum of personal responsibility and to avoid excessive excuse-making (especially blaming) are minimal preconditions. In doing therapy with couples, one is regularly reminded of how quickly accusations and blaming can cascade into the dim recesses of the past as each spouse seeks to excuse his or her behavior on the grounds of the other's prior actions: "Yes, but you . . . !"

Mr. and Mrs. P. illustrate vividly how excuse-based failures to accept responsibility for constructive change can lead to the dissolution of a marriage. They contracted for couples therapy in order to resolve a difficult dispute. The couple had grown up in the same rural midwestern city and had been child-hood sweethearts. Following their marriage, Mrs. P. had agreed to follow Mr. P. to a large city where he had secured an administrative position with an ad-vertising firm if, at the end of five years, he would follow her to a location of her choice. The five years were soon to expire and they were locked in combat over whether or not Mr. P. would comply with their agreement.

Mrs. P. insisted on returning to their home town. Mr. P., however, was rap-idly advancing in the advertising firm and, recognizing that he could never get a similar administrative position in his small home town, considered such a move to be professional suicide. He wanted to renegotiate their contract. They *insisted* that the co-therapists take sides in the dispute and, by arguing the re-spective positions, attempt to resolve the conflict while they sat passively by as observers. When the therapists suggested they would be more comfortable in the role of helping Mr. and Mrs. P. work through their conflict, both declined. As Mr. P. put it, "If I were to acknowledge that her position has merit by seriously attempting to understand it, my own position would be weakened. I didn't come here for that—I came here to get my way." Incredibly (so the therapists thought) Mrs. P. supported her husband's stand on this, but the rea-son soon became clear: by supporting his excuse for avoiding serious work in therapy, she was absolved from taking *his* position seriously! This put them in a position to dissolve the marriage and go their separate ways knowing that they had "tried" to salvage their relationship. Both were bitter toward the therapists for having failed to solve their problem.

The foregoing examples support our contention that excuses are least likely to eventuate in unfortunate consequences when they are followed by construc-tive efforts at behavior change. Although excuses can buy a bit of "grace," they do not, in themselves, correct any underlying problems. Indeed, they may exac-erbate them. Having said this, however, we would now like to suggest that there are times when the only real underlying problem is the lack of a good ex-cuse and that making one available can dramatically alter maladaptive behav-ior patterns.

For the Lack of a Good Excuse

Whereas most of the previous examples address the notion that a variety of maladjustments may result from the use of excuses, the lack of an excuse may also lead to difficulties. The case of Ben M., discussed earlier, speaks to this point. A case described by Marvin Rosen (1975) is also illustrative. A 12-year-old boy was referred to treatment for a severe problem involving compulsive speech rituals. The ritualistic behavior began following a doctor-prescribed re-gime of limited activity and the avoidance of strenuous activity for a knee ail-ment. This presented several problems for the boy since he continued to be pressured by friends to engage in play activities. Ultimately, psychotherapy was sought. Following a period of behavioral treatment for some aspects of the problem, the therapist contacted the boy's physician and requested that the boy's leg be immobilized in a cast. Among other things, the therapist felt this "would provide a visible sign of his leg problem to peers who disbelieved he had a medical problem" (p. 458). According to Rosen, "The introduction of this measure resulted in a dramatic cessation of speech repetition" (p. 458). It could be argued that the cast provided the boy with a credible (and social esteem-raising) excuse for his need to avoid certain activities and relieved him of the need to develop alternate means of dealing with the resultant anxiety.

A second example involves a case that was seen by one of the authors. Although the case raised a variety of issues, one important concern was the sexual relationship between the client and his wife. The client had a history from boyhood of being extremely sensitive about his physical attractiveness. He had been born with one leg shorter than the other and never felt a part of normal peer activities, including heterosexual relationships. He described his sexual relationship with his wife as being virtually nonexistent. Their pattern was for him to tentatively caress her in bed and, when she didn't immediately respond by turning over and reciprocating, he would almost literally bounce several inches off the surface of the bed, do a 180-degree flip, land on his other side facing away from his wife, and sulk until he fell asleep. He was positive that she found him physically unattractive. At the therapist's suggestion, the client agreed to bring his wife in for couples therapy. She, it turned out, was very eager to discuss their sexual difficulties. She had been feeling for a long time that he was uninterested in her because he never seemed to persist very long in his lovemaking attempts. In fact, she had adopted a policy of waiting to see if he was "really" interested by deliberately not responding to his advances immediately. His lack of persistence was interpreted to mean that he really didn't care for her. The revelation that the client hadn't been trying hard enough and that his wife really did long for his affection was all it took to produce a dramatic turn-around in their love life. We would submit that affording the client with the excuse that his difficulties had resulted from his not trying hard enough gave him the courage he needed to reapply himself and to discontinue his self-esteem deflating attributions concerning the source of his sexual difficulties.

Summary of Adaptive–Maladaptive Excuse Continuum

This section provides several suggestions concerning the ways that excuse-making may relate to problems of maladaption. As indicated, many characteristics of excuse-making heighten the likelihood that adverse consequences will accrue. We also discuss the idea that excuses imply opportunities for constructive action and that, when such opportunities are ignored, the risk of maladaption is increased. Finally, we argue that there are occasions when serious problems may result from the lack of adaptive excuse-making. In the following section, we turn our attention to a consideration of what the theoretical literature relating to the problem of individual psychopathology has to say about the role of excuse-making and responsibility avoidance in the etiology of deviant behavior.

MODELS OF ADJUSTMENT AND MALADJUSTMENT

The idea of using excuses runs throughout many theoretical formulations of individual psychopathology whether or not it is stated explicitly. Despite the pervasiveness of the notion, however, no single systematic treatment of excuses has been presented. Nearly always, excuses are there, but often only in the form of "symptoms." Furthermore, excuses (if they are even called that) usually are presented as only one symptom among many that may serve similar functions. In this section we review a number of theoretical perspectives on psychopathology with the goal of illuminating the roles they ascribe to excuse-making.

The Psychoanalytic Model—Freud

Several of the classical ego-defensive mechanisms described by Freud and his followers bear strong resemblance to the notion of excuses as outlined in this book. Denial, projection, rationalization, and reaction formation all fit easily into one or more of the excuse categories discussed previously. From the perspective of classical psychoanalysis, however, such defense mechanisms are seen as operating exclusively on an *unconscious* level. In the face of threats to the ego, anxiety is generated and ego-defensive maneuvers engaged—all automatically and beyond the individual's conscious awareness or control. Rather than being a voluntary actor, the individual is a passive pawn who is pushed and pulled by psychic forces that, by definition, are beyond his or her understanding. There is little if any room for the notion of individual responsibility within the orthodox psychoanalytic system since any action, be it larceny, incest, or sloppy housekeeping, is determined by unconscious conflicts and pregenital fixations.

The psychic apparatus, as elaborated by Freud, consists essentially of the id, the ego, and the superego. The id, which is the biological component of personality, embodies our basic animal and instinctual natures. Ruled by the pleasure principle, its goal is the elimination of all tension and the gratification of all instinctual needs. It is insistent in its demand for immediate gratification, it is illogical, and it operates beyond the individual's conscious awareness.

The ego is the psychological component of the personality. It evolves out of and becomes differentiated from the id over time as the individual matures physically, gains the capacity to differentiate himself or herself from the rest of the world, and encounters the frustrations inherent in having to meet basic needs through others over which he or she has no direct control. The ego operates according to the "reality principle" and serves as a buffer between the id

and the outside world. Through the exercise of rationality and realistic thinking, the ego is charged with the task of formulating plans of action for meeting
the individual's basic needs within the constraints imposed by external reality.
The ego is also charged with the responsibility of meeting the individual's
needs in ways that do not invite the wrath of the superego.

The superego, which evolves out of the child's efforts to extricate himself or
herself from the dilemma posed by the Oedipus (or Electra) complex, represents the introjected values, morals, and ideals of society as they are expressed
in the parents. It is the superego that sits in judgment of the individual's acts
and thoughts and that dispenses psychological rewards and punishments. It is
here where the notion of excuse-making in the defense of self-esteem is most
clearly represented in Freudian theory. If an individual's conduct (both external and internal) is consistent with the standards of "good" embodied in the superego, he or she is rewarded with feelings of self-love and acceptance. If the
conduct is "judged' to be "bad" by the superego, the individual is punished
with feelings of guilt and self-hate. Defensive excuse-making is most likely to
be employed by the ego when it experiences moral anxiety in anticipation of
impending guilt and self-condemnation. Such defensive excuse-making may
take the form of denial, projection, rationalization, displacement, reaction formation, and so on, and to the extent that it serves to lessen the condemnation of
the superego, the individual's "self-esteem" is preserved or safeguarded. In our
terminology, the individual's censurable behavior has been "excused."

In summary, Freudian ego-defensive operations can be seen to serve excuse-making functions as defined in this book. This is apparent in relatively
isolated or circumscribed instances in which the ego must struggle to maintain
its integrity in the face of threats from the superego. In a broader sense, however, orthodox Freudian theory, with its dual assumptions of psychic determinism and unconscious processes, affords all of humanity a blanket excuse for
its conduct. As Rank (1945) observed,

> The unconscious, just as the original meaning of the word shows, is a purely neg-
> ative concept, which designates something momentarily not conscious, while
> Freud's theory has lifted it to the most powerful factor in psychic life. The basis
> for this, however, is not given in any psychological experience but in a moral ne-
> cessity, that is, to find an acceptable substitute for the concept of God, who frees
> the individual from responsibility. (p. 28)

Acceptance of the theory nicely severs the apparent responsibility link to one's
behavior, including the responsibility for making excuses.

Social-Analytic Models

A variety of competing models of human mental life and psychopathology
have been proposed since Freud's groundbreaking work. In many of these

models, the concepts of self-esteem and individual responsibility play central roles. They therefore provide fertile ground for the excuse masquerade.

Karen Horney

In her major work, *Neurosis and Human Growth* (1950), Horney details a theory of neurosis that is astonishingly rich in examples of how excuse-making not only serves the neurotic's needs, but also of how the neurosis, itself, is the excuse *par excellence* for failing to realize one's potentials. Fundamental to Horney's theory are the assumptions that human nature involves a striving toward "self-realization" and that this can be accomplished only when people assume responsibility for themselves. Horney believed that neurosis develops when the individual's self-realization is derailed by the intervention of adverse circumstances.

When faced with adverse circumstances that thwart the natural movement toward self-realization, the individual experiences "basic anxiety." To cope with the resulting feelings of isolation and helplessness, the individual develops strategies for minimizing them. This inevitably leads to a growing alienation from self as the individual increasingly sacrifices the goal of self-realization in favor of the goal of security and safety. According to Horney, "Not only is his real self prevented from a straight growth, but in addition his need to evolve artificial, strategic ways to cope with others has forced him to override his genuine feelings, wishes, and thoughts" (p. 21). Finally, the individual becomes confused, not knowing "where he stands or 'who' he is" (p. 21).

But the individual needs some sense of identity and thus manufactures one—through an act of imagination an *idealized image* of the self is created. "In this process he endows himself with unlimited powers and with exalted faculties; he becomes a hero, a genius, a supreme lover, a saint, a god" (p. 22). Because the idealized image promises fulfillment and gives the individual a sense of worth, it is maintained tenaciously. Furthermore, *"The energies driving toward self-realization are shifted to the aim of actualizing the idealized self"* (p. 24). Striving for an idealized self means nothing less than striving for perfection, what Horney refers to as *"the search for glory"* (p. 24).

Being subject to mortal limitations is a constant, painful, and unwelcome reminder to the neurotic of the discrepancy between the reality of existence and the idealized fantasy. The neurotic responds, not by revising the fantasy, but by issuing "neurotic claims":

> And so, instead of tackling his illusions, he presents a claim to the outside world. He is entitled to be treated by others, or by fate, in accord with his grandiose notions about himself. Everyone ought to cater to his illusions. Everything short of this is unfair. He is entitled to a better deal. (p. 41)

The discerning reader may already see that the groundwork is laid for an excuse-based existence. In Horney's words, "By raising his needs to the dignity of claims, he denies his own troubles and places the responsibility for himself on other people, on circumstances, or on fate" (p. 63).

The problem of self-esteem is a special one for the neurotic. Horney felt that there is a "strict cause-and-effect relation between existing personal assets and the feeling of self-confidence" (p. 88). In that the neurotic's self-esteem is based on insubstantial, if not fictitious, assets it is exquisitely susceptible to threats. Rather than being founded on what one *is,* the neurotic's self-esteem is founded on the unobtained and unobtainable, idealized *goal.* A variety of excuse strategies are employed in the service of bolstering the neurotic's self-esteem (neurotic pride) in the face of threats. Neurotics may assuage humiliation by vindictively turning the tables on their tormentors (i.e., derogating the source). They may lose interest in those things where their pride has been hurt (i.e., "sour grapes"). They may deny or reinterpret. They may also begin to avoid all situations where their pride might be hurt in the future. Perhaps most important, "since all these measures are more a camouflage than a remedy for his pride, he may start to cultivate his neuroses because the neurosis with a capital N then becomes a precious alibi for the lack of accomplishment" (p. 107).

The self-esteem or pride of neurotics is not only assailed by external threats. They also come to hate and despise their "real" selves since they are constantly reminded of the vast discrepancy between who they really are and their idealized, impossible goal of perfection. Most of this self-hate is unconscious and is dealt with through a process of externalization: It is directed "outward, against life, fate, institutions, or people," or it "remains directed against the self but is perceived or experienced as coming from the outside" (p. 116). This excuse-based inability to experience honest self-criticism further cements the alienation from self and makes it impossible for the neurotic to engage in a process of constructive change. What always suffers in the process of self-alienation is the *"faculty of assuming responsibility for self"* (p. 168).

Viewing Horney's theory of neurosis from the perspective of excuse theory, it is clear that a variety of excuse strategies are integral to the neurotic process. Furthermore, there is an integrated quality to them—they serve the central goal of allowing the neurotic individual to maintain the illusion that the idealized self-image is an attainable goal. The "bad act" that must be excused is not an isolated or peripheral event or behavior, it is the fundamental failure to achieve the idealized goal of personal perfection. Also noteworthy is the idea that the neurosis may come to serve as an alibi or justification for the neurotic's failure to achieve that goal.

Alfred Adler

In several important ways, Adler's "individual psychology" was the antithesis of Freud's psychoanalytic theory (Hall & Lindzey, 1957). Whereas Freud emphasized the motivating function of inborn biological instincts, Adler emphasized the dominance of inborn social urges, as illustrated by his concept of "social interest." In essence, Adler believed that people are biologically predisposed to act in accord with the broader interests of mankind. However, this predisposition is subject to derailment by the intervention of adverse circumstances or thwarting influences.

Adler also rejected Freud's "hard determinism." He believed that people are endowed with a "creative self" which operates in a highly subjective manner to interpret and make sense of the world as well as to forge an individualized approach to achieving life's central goal—superiority. The nature of this individualized approach to dealing with life, the "style of life," is largely a function of the nature of the obstacles (inferiorities) encountered by the child on the road to superiority and is specifically shaped by the characteristic methods the child selects to overcome (compensate for) those obstacles or inferiorities.

A few words are in order with regard to the concepts "inferiority" and "superiority." For Adler, striving for superiority meant striving for a greater state of personal completion. He regarded the struggle to attain superiority as the universal and central motivation for humankind.

> The impetus from minus to plus never ceases. Whatever premises all our philosophers and psychologists dream of—self-preservation, pleasure principle, equalization—all these are but vague representations, attempts to express the great upward drive. (Adler, quoted in Hall & Lindzey, 1957, p. 120)

Feelings of inferiority are also universally experienced according to Adler. They arise from a "sense of incompletion or imperfection in any sphere of life" (Hall & Lindzey, 1957, p. 121). Such feelings serve the struggle for superiority because they alert the individual to any deficiencies that must be overcome or compensated for in its pursuit. Although feelings of inferiority are a normal and healthy aspect of psychic life, the individual who, for whatever reason, feels himself or herself to be highly inadequate and unable to squarely face life's challenges and tasks may develop an "inferiority complex."

The inferiority complex is at the core of neurosis. The state of discouragement that accompanies the inferiority complex leads the neurotic to seek superiority in ways that run counter to the social interest—primarily in ways that are selfish and self-aggrandizing. In an effort to conceal their felt inferiority from themselves and others, neurotics seek power, prestige, interpersonal dominance, and influence. They come to view the world in a black and white fashion, dividing the world into winners and losers, weak and strong. This bifurcated view of reality becomes the guiding fiction around which they construct their styles of life. They endeavor to cultivate those characteristics which are regarded as strong and eschew those that are weak. Having lost courage, they use excuses and tricks to avoid defeat and to gain advantages. They behave as if they actually were inferior in an effort to safeguard their fiction of superiority.

> The safeguarding tendency which originates in the feeling of insecurity forces us all, especially the child and the neurotic, to leave the more obvious ways of in-

duction and deduction to use such devises as the schematic fiction. Through the safeguarding tendency the individual aims at getting rid of the feeling of inferiority in order to raise himself to the full height of the self-esteem, toward complete manliness, toward the idea of being above. (Adler, in Ansbacher & Ansbacher, 1967, pp. 109–110)

According to Adler, neurotic symptoms safeguard the individual's self-esteem by serving as excuses. The individual unknowingly selects and develops symptoms until they seem to be "real obstacles. Behind his barricade of symptoms the patient feels hidden and secure. To the question, 'What use are you making of your talents?' he answers, 'This thing stops me; I cannot go ahead,' and points to his self-erected barricade" (Adler, in Ansbacher & Ansbacher, 1967, p. 265). The price the neurotic pays for this protection is suffering. In relative terms, however, it is a good buy— the suffering would be much greater were the sense of worthlessness to be openly confronted. Furthermore, the suffering serves to justify the excuse.

Ansbacher and Ansbacher (1967), in their edited version of Adler's writings, suggest that there are two main varieties of neurotic safeguarding strategies: aggression and withdrawal. Two types of aggression are depreciation and accusation. Through depreciation of others, neurotics enhance their own self-esteem and sense of superiority, excusing their own failures by making them appear insubstantial in comparison. Aggression through accusation allows neurotics to fix the "blame" for their failures on someone or something external— on "fate."

It is the fault of my parents, my fate; because I am the youngest, was born too late; because I am a Cinderella; because I am perhaps not the child of these parents, of this father, of this mother; because I am too small, too weak, have too small a head, am too homely; because I have a speech defect, a hearing defect, am cross-eyed, nearsighted; because I have misshaped genitals, because I am not manly, because I am a girl; because I am by nature bad, stupid, awkward; because I have masturbated; because I am too sensuous, too covetous, and naturally perverted; because I submit easily, am too dependent and obedient; because I cry easily, am easily moved; because I am a criminal, a thief, an incendiary, and could murder someone; my ancestry, my education, my circumcision are to blame; because I have a long nose, too much hair, too little hair; because I am a cripple; because I have been pampered, and because I have been discriminated against. (Adler, in Ansbacher & Ansbacher, 1967, p. 270)

As mentioned above, safeguarding strategies may also involve withdrawal:

He sees everything with the eyes of his vanity. He approaches every situation and problem of life with fearful anticipation as to whether his prestige will be assured, seldom finds this to be the case, and therefore feels compelled to withdraw from the problems of life. His retreat is effected by means of his symptoms; and the symptoms are the results of shock effects. These shock effects he has found useful in obtaining relief from a difficult situation. There is then no incentive for him to give up the shock effects which have served a purpose for him; so he holds on to them. (Adler, in Ansbacher & Ansbacher, 1967, p. 278)

The withdrawal may be effected through "moving backward" (e.g., suicide attempts, agoraphobia, fainting, hysterical paralysis). By using such dramatic symptoms, neurotics simultaneously avoid challenges and enforce their wills over others. Strategies for "standing still" (e.g., insomnia and resultant inability to work, impotence, asthma) also serve neurotics by allowing them to avoid moving forward to face life's tasks.

Strategies of "hesitation and back-and-forth" are designed to waste time. According to Adler, "Usually the following mechanism can be found: first a difficulty is created and sanctioned, and then its conquest is attempted, in vain" (Adler, in Ansbacher & Ansbacher, 1967, p. 275). Withdrawal is also effected through the "construction of obstacles" (e.g., fatigue, constipation, stomach disorders):

> If the decision falls against him, he can refer to his difficulties and to the proof of his illness which he has himself constructed. If he remains victorious, what could he not have done if he were well, when, as a sick man, he achieved so much— one-handed, so to speak! (Adler, in Ansbacher & Ansbacher, 1967, p. 276)

Finally, anxiety may serve as a powerful ally for the individual who has adopted a pattern of withdrawing from life's tasks in order to safeguard his self-esteem. "In the anxious person we ... meet ... the well-known type who feels himself forced by necessity to think more of himself and consequently has little left over for his fellow man" (Adler, in Ansbacher & Ansbacher, 1967, p. 277).

In summary, Adler held that neurotic symptoms serve several important functions for the individual: (1) they serve as excuses if life denies longed-for triumphs; (2) they allow important and threatening decisions to be postponed or avoided; and (3) they enhance the impressiveness of those goals that are attained since they have been achieved *despite suffering*. As with Horney, these excuse strategies (symptoms) are not consciously employed although the related suffering is consciously experienced. To consciously use excuses or symptoms to safeguard one's self-esteem would undermine their very purpose—allowing the individual to maintain the fiction of superiority while traversing the "socially useless" side of life.

The Moral Model—O. H. Mowrer

In his 1961 book, *Crisis in Psychiatry and Religion*, Mowrer detailed a "guilt theory" of neurosis. He contrasted his theory of neurosis to Freud's in the following terms:

According to Freud and his followers, the neurotic is in trouble, not because of anything actually wrong which he has *done*, but merely because of things he would *like* to do but, quite unrealistically, is *afraid* to. By contrast, the other view is that in neurosis (and functional psychosis), the individual has committed tangible misdeeds, which have remained unacknowledged and unredeemed and that his anxieties thus have a realistic social basis and justification. (p. 84)

The central thesis of Mowrer's theory, then, is that neurosis results not from repression of instincts and impulses but from repression of *conscience*. In contrast to Freud, Mowrer believed that the person is "preeminently a *social being*" (p. 126), and that the neurotic's suffering derives from the rupturing of social ties that results from hidden "sins." For Mowrer, a central feature of this suffering is the resulting erosion of the individual's "self-respect."

In simplified form, Mowrer's "guilt theory" may be roughly summarized in the following propositions: (1) the individual commits "tangible misdeeds" that "outrage" his or her conscience by violating moral standards and values; (2) the individual who is destined for neurosis attempts to deal with the resulting guilt by "repressing" his or her conscience; and (3) the price of this repression is loss of self-respect, alienation from social ties, and suffering. The relevance of this model to excuse theory is most evident at step 2, the repression of conscience.

According to Mowrer, one of the more prevalent means of repressing conscience is the primitive defense of denial: "If our thesis be correct, the essence of psychopathology is systematic *denial* of who one is; and if we misrepresent ourselves to others, it is not surprising that we soon begin to appear alien, strange, and 'unfamiliar' even to ourselves" (p. 217). Although Mowrer regarded denial as the "essence" of psychopathology, other excuse stragegies are employed: "Those persons who react to personality crisis by becoming resentful and bitter and who blame *others* rather than themselves are well on the way to a permanently paranoid adjustment, and with a poor prognosis" (p. 101). In another section of his book, Mowrer offers a quote from Wilhelm Stekel which makes the point that symptoms of organic disease may serve the neurotic's flight from responsibility:

But there are stereotyped ways by which we can be aided in exposing the wiles of conscience, and in discovering when parapaths are play-acting—for they often persuade themselves that they have no conscience, and take refuge in an ostensibly organic disease in order to escape the torment of self-reproach. (Wilhelm Stekel, in Mowrer, 1961, p. 23)

Although Mowrer makes few explicit references to excuse strategies, it is clear that he believed accepting responsibility for one's actions is essential for mental health: "But when the individual can blame *himself* and see his predicament as one for which *he* is largely responsible and which *he* can do something toward changing, the prospects of recovery—and personal transformation—are much brighter" (p. 101). Elsewhere, Mowrer makes a similar point: "It is surely unrepented and unredeemed evil actions that destroy our self-respect and moral credit; and one can hardly escape the conclusion that these cannot be recaptured by any means other than compensating good actions and deeds" (p. 232).

Mowrer felt so strongly about the importance of accepting one's responsibility for one's actions and of atoning for their consequences that he took a very critical stand toward Freudian psychoanalysis. He felt that psychoanalysis, "by championing the rights of the body in opposition to a society and moral order which were presumed to be unduly harsh and arbitrary" (p. 82), was counterproductive on at least three counts. First, the analytic goal of unrepressing locked-up "evil" instincts and impulses tended to encourage the commission of tangible misdeeds rather than just imaginary ones. He therefore characterized psychoanalytic therapy as "the Devil's work" (p. 125) and believed that successful analysis tended to create psychopaths. Second, he believed that psychoanalytic theory removed the responsibility for one's conduct from the shoulders of the analysand and placed the burden on parents and society:

> It follows, ineluctably, that the individual is not "to blame" for his so-called neurotic difficulties. It is rather his father, mother, siblings, teachers, minister—*anyone* but himself. And soon the analysand, under his pernicious tutelage, is luxuriating in self-pity and smoldering resentment. (p. 238)

In other words, Mowrer felt that psychoanalytic theory—and the therapeutic technology based on it—encouraged the very repression of conscience and avoidance of responsibility that he believed was at the heart of neurosis.

A third criticism of psychoanalysis grew out of Mowrer's conviction that neurotic individuals, to be "cured," must not only acknowledge or confess their "sins," but they must also redeem themselves through compensating actions and deeds. He felt that psychoanalysis, like certain churches, was involved in promoting a doctrine of "cheap grace": "Despite its exorbitant fees, psychoanalysis also preaches a doctrine of cheap, easy grace. If you can only pay for it, buy it, someone else will do the real work of curing you, while you lie comfortably on a couch" (p. 149). In another place, Mowrer writes:

> Perhaps one of the reasons why classical psychoanalysis, with its cardinal emphasis upon "free association," so often makes a painful and productive start and then tails off into years of dull and unprofitable talk is that it does not help the analysand move from free association (confession) on to atonement, except to the extent that the financial sacrifice which analysis usually entails provides it in at least temporary or "symptomatic" form. (pp. 101–102)

In summary, although Mowrer makes few explicit references to "excuses" per se, it is clear that his theory of psychopathology is firmly based on the idea that it derives from failure to acknowledge and accept responsibility for actions and misdeeds. Running from responsibility merely compounds moral guilt and deepens psychic distress and self-alienation.

Humanistic Models

Carl Rogers

In his book *Client-Centered Therapy*, Carl Rogers (1965) outlined a theory of psychotherapy and personality that has been extremely influential, especially in the fields of psychology, counseling, and social work. His theory of personality, which was presented in the form of 19 "propositions," is what interests us here.

One of the most basic propositions in Rogers' theory is that "the organism has one basic tendency and striving—to actualize, maintain, and enhance the experiencing organism" (proposition 4, p. 487). As part of the self-actualizing process, the individual gradually comes to differentiate between those aspects of the experiential field that are "self" and those that are "non-self." This differentiation results in a self-concept, "an organized, fluid, but consistent conceptual pattern of perceptions of characteristics and relationships of the 'I' or the 'me,' together with values attached to these concepts" (proposition 9, p. 498). The values attached to the various aspects of the self concept are derived, primarily, from two sources. First, experiences are valued positively or negatively based on whether or not they are organismically experienced as maintaining or enhancing the self-actualization process. Second, the individual may adopt or "introject" the values of others. This avenue sets the stage for the development of "conditions of worth."

As the individual's awareness of "self" develops, he or she develops a parallel need for positive regard from others. As Patterson (1980) observes, the satisfaction of the need for positive regard is reciprocal in that "the individual's positive regard is satisfied when the individual perceives himself or herself as satisfying another's need" (p. 481). Furthermore, the values associated with certain aspects of the "self" structure are more likely to be derived from the regard of others than from the individual's own internal valuing process when the two sources of values are in conflict. If certain aspects of the self are positively regarded by others and different aspects are negatively regarded, the individual will tend to integrate only those that are positively valued into the self-concept. In this manner, an incongruence between the actual self and the self-concept evolves.

Once the individual has incorporated conditions of worth into his or her self-concept, the psychic stage is set for the excuse masquerade. The reason for this is that self-experiences that are inconsistent with the self-concept are threatening and cannot be accurately perceived and symbolized. The resulting state of incongruence inevitably results in a measure of maladjustment and psychological vulnerability due to the perceptual rigidity and distortion of reality that are inherent in the individual's defensive posture.

Despite the effects of a state of incongruence, most of the individual's perceptions and behaviors will continue to be consistent with the self-concept. Occasionally, however, important experiences or behaviors will occur which the individual is unable to deny or distort enough to avoid becoming aware of the state of incongruence. Such experiences are perceived as threats and the individual will respond defensively by organizing the self-structure even more rigidly in order to maintain it. This defensive behavior will frequently involve excuse-making. As Rogers puts it, when behavior is inconsistent with the self-concept, "the behavior is not 'owned' by the individual" (proposition 13, p. 509). Rogers illustrates the psychological dialectic involved with a case example in which the main actor's self-concept includes the central notion that she is a "good and loving mother":

> With this concept of self she can accept and assimilate those organic sensations of affection which she feels toward her child. But the organic experience of dislike, distaste, or hatred toward her child is something which is denied to her conscious self. The experience exists, but it is not permitted accurate symbolization. The organic need is for aggressive acts which would fulfill these attitudes and satisfy the tension which exists. The organism strives for the achievement of this satisfaction, but it can do so for the most part only through those channels which are consistent with the self-concept of a good mother. Since the good mother could be aggressive toward her child only if he merited punishment, she perceives much of his behavior as being bad, deserving punishment, and therefore the aggressive acts can be carried through, without being contrary to the values organized in her picture of self. If under great stress, she at some time should shout at her child, "I hate you," she would be quick to explain that "I was not myself," that this behavior occurred but was out of her control. "I don't know what made me say that, because of course I don't mean it." (1965, pp. 511–512)

It is clear that excuses play a role in Rogers' system. In the case described above, for instance, both conscious and unconscious excuses are utilized. Unconscious excuses to the effect that her child "deserves" punishment justify the woman's aggression against him. Conscious excuses in the form of "I wasn't myself" (i.e., it wasn't *really me*) are brought into play when the mother has experiences that cannot be defended against unconsciously. Excuses, for Rogers, may be best regarded as "symptoms" of an underlying state of incongruence between the organic "self" and the self-concept. In a larger sense, however, they also contribute to the developing psychopathology. The extensive use of denial, for example, only serves to further erode the individual's ability to make life adjustments on a realistic basis. Furthermore, Rogers regarded the drive toward self-actualization as the "one basic tendency and striving" of people. While such excuse strategies as denial and distortion may provide the individual with temporary victories over threats to the regnant self-concept, they merely set the stage for a more prolonged and difficult struggle in the future. Recall the dilemma of the "good and loving mother." Having impulsively given expression to the negative side of her ambivalence toward her child and having disowned her behavior, she must guard vigilantly against future recurrences if she is to avoid even more disconcerting clashes between her "true" self seeking actualization and her conditions of worth-based self-concept.

Abraham Maslow

Like Rogers, Maslow (1968) held that a basic drive or growth force impels us toward self-actualization, the full realization of our inherent potentials. However, Maslow believed that such "basic" needs as safety, love, and self-esteem must be met before the individual may move freely from one level of self-actualization to the next. This led to his making a fundamental distinction between "deficit-motivated" and "growth-motivated" behavior. Growth-motivated behavior emerges only when, with the safety that comes from having the basic needs satisfied, the individual is free to confidently experience the delights of growth and development. When the needs for safety and growth are in conflict, the need for safety will win out. The tragedy is that what is mortgaged in this psychic "economy" is the individual's "true self."

In addition to sacrificing the "true self" by submitting to the need for safety, the neurotic, to some extent, sacrifices his or her self-esteem. Mowrer, in proposing his "guilt theory" of neurosis (see above), spoke of the psychic corrosion that results from "tangible misdeeds." Within Maslow's system, the fundamental misdeed of individuals who exchange growth for security is that they deny or turn away from their true calling and nature. According to Maslow, "all these people perceive in a deep way that they have done wrong to themselves and despise themselves for it" (p. 7).

Perhaps the most effective way to examine the role of excuses in Maslow's system is to reproduce and comment on a graphic illustration that he presented in his book *Toward a Psychology of Being* (1968, p. 47). Recall that, according to Maslow, the individual is faced throughout life with fundamental choices between safety and growth. This existential dilemma is illustrated in Figure 8.1. In addition, however, Maslow included four sets of "valences" that serve to illuminate the psychological operations involved in making the choices. The valences on the "safety" side of the illustration may be thought of as "defensive" operations. As such, they bear a strong resemblance to some of the excuse strategies addressed earlier in this book. Enhancing the dangers, for example, may serve to raise consensus ("Anyone faced with such a difficult/dangerous choice would have done or would do the same."). By the same token, enhancing the dangers may serve to raise distinctiveness ("It's only in this particularly dangerous situation that I fall short of the mark."). On the surface of it, minimizing the attractions would appear to have elements of the fabled "sour

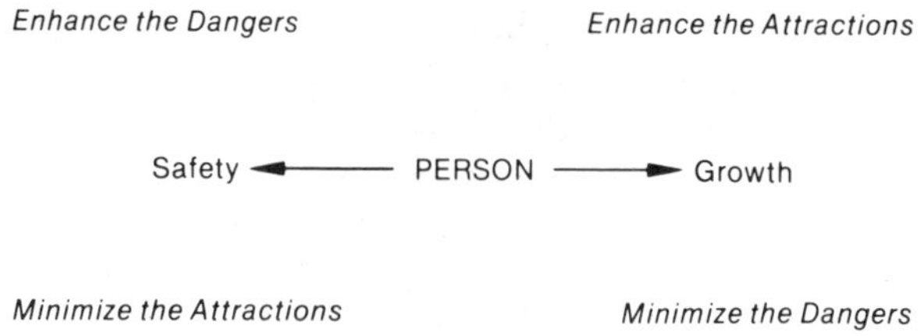

Enhance the Dangers   *Enhance the Attractions*

Safety ◄———— PERSON ————► Growth

Minimize the Attractions   *Minimize the Dangers*

Figure 8.1.   The choice between safety and growth. (From *Toward a Psychology of Being*, by A. H. Maslow. New York: Van Nostrand-Reinhold, 1968, p. 47.)

grapes" excuse as a retrospective rationalization. As an anticipatory excuse-making operation, minimizing the attractions appears to have much in common with the reframing strategy referred to previously as derogating the setting (see Chapter 5).

In his book *Motivation and Personality* (1954), Maslow outlined six degrees of need priority. Presented in their descending order of priority for the individual, they are (1) physiological needs, (2) safety needs, (3) belongingness needs, (4) love needs, (5) self-esteem needs, (6) self-actualization needs. As indicated, the more basic need priorities must be met or satisfied before self-actualization needs may ascend to the first order of business. This general schema provides another means of understanding the role of excuses within Maslow's system. Needs for belongingness and love, for example, may be best met if individuals can preserve their images in the eyes of others (the external audience). By the same token, the need for self-esteem may be best preserved by viewing failures and shortcomings from a relatively benign vantage point. Although making excuses may register at some deep level to the individual's discredit (in the sense that they involve turning away from the higher call to self-actualization and growth), an excuse-based avoidance of growth should continue so long as basic needs remain unmet.

One additional topic that Maslow (1968) addresses is worth mentioning here. Although he gives relatively little direct attention to the issues of responsibility and responsibility avoidance, he does address the problem of avoidance of knowledge and regards this as an avoidance of responsibility.

> In general this kind of fear is defensive, in the sense that it is a protection of our self-esteem, of our love and respect for ourselves. We tend to be afraid of any knowledge that could cause us to despise ourselves or to make us feel inferior, weak, worthless, evil, shameful. We protect ourselves and our ideal image of ourselves by repression and similar defenses, which are essentially techniques by which we avoid becoming conscious of unpleasant or dangerous truths. (p. 60)

According to Maslow, the avoidance of knowledge operates on at least two levels. On one level, we may avoid knowledge about our environment or those around us because of a fear of the "consequences that flow from knowing, a fear of its dangerous responsibilities" (p. 66). At another level, we may avoid knowledge of ourselves. In particular, Maslow focuses on "a denying of our best side, of our talents, of our finest impulses, of our highest potentialities, of our creativeness" (p. 61). Here, again, the point is that acknowledging or recognizing our "best" side brings with it a challenge to accept the responsibility and burden of living up to it. From the perspective of this book, one way of thinking about the avoidance of knowledge is that, by denying or repressing our awareness (knowledge) of the truth, we excuse our failures to act.

Maslow's theory can be construed as "endorsing" excuse-making and other regressive or deficit-motivated behaviors. As Maslow put it:

> Part of the paradox in this situation is that in a very real way, even the "bad" choice is "good for" the neurotic chooser, or at least understandable and even necessary in terms of his own dynamics. We know that tearing away a functional neurotic symptom by force, or by too direct a confrontation or interpretation, or by a stress situation which cracks the person's defenses against too painful an insight, can shatter the person altogether. (Maslow, 1968, p. 53)

Ultimately, *"all* choices are in fact wise, if we grant two kinds of wisdom, defensive-wisdom and growth-wisdom" (p. 54).

The Existential Model

One cannot read the existential literature for long without discovering that there is no integrated existential theory of personality and psychopathology. However, there do appear to be several persistent themes or common elements. From the perspective of this book, probably the most important of those themes is the emphasis placed on the notion of individual responsibility.

Individual responsibility is, indeed, at the heart of the existential attitude. The concept of *Umwelt* or "being-in-the-world" (Binswanger, 1963; Boss, 1963) conveys this clearly. For us, the important feature of this concept is that the world does not exist apart from the individual: the world is the construction of (and therefore the responsibility of) the being who exists within it. As May (1958, pp. 59–60) explains it:

> *World is the structure of meaningful relationships in which a person exists and in the design of which he participates.* Thus world includes the past events which condition my existence and all the vast variety of deterministic influences which operate upon me. But it is these *as I relate to them,* am aware of them, carry them with me, molding, inevitably forming, building them in every minute of relating. For to be aware of one's world means at the same time to be designing it.

Another concept that is central to the existential emphasis on individual responsibility is *Dasein*, "the being who is there, who has a there in that the being knows he or she is there and can take a stand with reference to that fact" (Patterson, 1980, p. 525). Being capable of self-awareness and awareness of events and influences brings the inevitable responsibility of making choices and decisions. Frankl (1971) describes this existential fact as follows:

> There is nothing conceivable that would condition a man wholly, i.e., without leaving to him the slightest freedom. Man is never fully conditioned in the sense of being determined by any facts or forces. Rather *man is ultimately self-determining*—determining not only his fate but even his own self for man is not only forming and shaping the course of his life but also his very self. To this extent man is not only responsible for what he does but also for what he is, inasmuch as *man does not only behave according to what he is but also becomes according to how he behaves.* In the last analysis, man has become what he has made out of himself. (p. 473)

In this process, we all shoulder an awesome responsibility. We are ultimately accountable for ourselves and our lives but we must discharge our responsibility in the context of an existence that has a number of important "givens" or boundary conditions. First, we all have to confront and deal with the fact of our mortality. Second, we must confront our basic freedom since we are, ultimately, the authors of our own existence. This is both liberating and terrifying since there is no preordained, structurally determined outcome for our choices and actions. Third, we must deal with the fact of our existential isolation. No matter how much we strive for contact and fusion with others, we are doomed to be solitary sojourners in this universe. Finally, we are faced with the ultimate meaninglessness of the universe into which we enter. As Frankl has observed, we are meaning-seeking creatures awash in a universe without inherent meaning. We are, individually, responsible for finding and creating meaning in our lives. This, too, is a fearful prospect.

To be aware of the foregoing "ultimate concerns" (Yalom, 1980) is to experience "existential anxiety." Consequently, we are tempted to run away from or to avoid too much awareness of our true condition in life (Tillich, 1952). Yalom (1980) has graphically depicted this dynamic in his book *Existential Psychotherapy* (p. 10) (see Figure 8.2). Although painful, existential anxiety is the *sine qua non* of the "authentic" existence that is characterized by "an openness to nature, to others, and to ourselves, because we have decided to meet the world straight on without hiding it from us or us from it" (Prochaska, 1979, p. 72). To use defense mechanisms such as denial or repression to avoid awareness and existential anxiety is to sacrifice our self-esteem and to deviate from the path of achieving authentic being. As Tillich (1952) pointed out, the only real solution to the problem of existential anxiety (and self-esteem) is to accept it as one of the costs we must incur if we are to achieve our uniquely human potential.

While the price of authentic existence is existential anxiety, the price of an inauthentic existence is "existential guilt," the guilt that comes from failing to live up to our potentials. At long last, we have arrived at the domain of the ex-

Figure 8.2.   The relationship of ultimate concerns, existential anxiety, and defense mechanisms. (From *Existential Psychotherapy*, by I. D. Yalom. New York: Basic Books, 1980, p. 10.)

cuse-maker, the individual who attempts to avoid the anxiety of authentic existence and simultaneously attempts to fend off existential guilt and the resulting self-condemnation (low self-esteem) by living a life of lies. According to Prochaska (1979),

> Lying is the foundation of psychopathology. Lying is the only way we can flee from nonbeing, to not allow existential anxiety into our experience. When confronted with nonbeing, . . . we have two choices: to be anxious or to lie. (p. 75)

The lies we tell ourselves take many forms, many of which serve an excuse-making function. Compulsivity, for example, may serve as an excuse for failing to accept responsibility for our behavior. By creating "a psychic world in which one does not experience freedom but exists under the sway of some irresistible ego-alien ('not-me') force," the individual promotes the lie that he is excused from being responsible (Yalom, 1980, p. 225). We may slavishly adhere to rules and guidelines in order to lie about our responsibility for the decisions we make. By the same token, we may excuse the responsibility for our decisions and actions by pointing the finger at some "authority." Fromm (1964) addresses this and similar problems extensively in his book *Escape from Freedom*.

Although specific acts and decisions confront us with the problem of existential anxiety and threaten our self-esteem, perhaps the greatest threat is our mortality. Ernest Becker (1975) argues that we have a fundamental need to achieve heroic stature, to "earn a feeling of primary value, of cosmic specialness, of ultimate usefulness to creation, of unshakable meaning" (p. 5). The central obstacle encountered, and the greatest threat to our self-esteem, is the inevitability of our death. According to Becker, our need to excuse ourselves of this fatal flaw is the central driving force in the human psyche. Excuses, then, can be seen as a means of maintaining the "lie" that we are not ultimately helpless in the face of the void. As Becker pointedly expresses it, "we might well say that mental illness represents styles of bogging-down in the denial of creatureliness" (p. 210).

Psychiatric symptoms are one means of avoiding responsibility for the failure of our struggle for heroism. Hypochondriacs promote, through their behavior, the lie that death and illness can be avoided if only they can seek enough medical attention. Phobics promote the lie that the real issues in life are not death and meaninglessness by narrowing the scope of their existential struggle to the arena of picayune fears that distract them from the real challenge and allow them to cultivate the illusion that heroic stature can be achieved by wrestling with the minutiae on the sidelines of life. The individual who engages in hero worship promotes the lie that immortality can be achieved by immortalizing others. Those who cling to a belief in some "ultimate rescuer" promote the lie that they don't have to accept the responsibility for acting and choosing, for the nature of their existence.

Examples of how various forms of psychopathology "fit" into the existential model abound, but the present point has been sufficiently made. To briefly summarize, the existentialists hold that we are the authors of our own existence. This authorship, though not of our own choosing, confronts us with the awesome responsibility of squarely facing our dilemma if we are to achieve an authentic existence. The price of accepting the challenge is a life filled with existential anxiety. The price of failing to accept the challenge is guilt. Excuses, including the various forms of psychopathology, are the methods employed by those who have lost courage in the face of the challenge to avoid both the responsibility of striving for authentic existence and the anxiety that accompanies the struggle. For the existentialist, then, excuses are the very fabric from which psychopathology is constructed.

The Behavioral Model

The fundamental assumption of learning theories of behavior and personality is that all complex human behavior is learned. From this perspective, excuses would be best thought of as "operant" behaviors, meaning that they are used because their use is reinforced by either positive outcomes or the avoidance of negative outcomes. In this sense, excuse-making behavior is subject to the same learning principles that are held to govern other operant behaviors.

A second assumption of behaviorism is that "abnormal" behavior is not qualitatively different from "normal" behavior. The defining characteristic of abnormal behavior is not that it is inherently pathological, it is that it is "maladaptive" *within the social context in which it occurs.* Accordingly, abnormal or maladaptive behavior is defined by its social consequences. In general, behaviorists would regard a behavior as maladaptive if (1) it is regarded as inappropriate by significant others in the individual's environment and (2) it results in a reduction in the amount of positive reinforcement the individual receives from that environment (Ullmann & Krasner, 1969). Once learned, excuse-making may become maladaptive when (1) the environment changes in such a way that excuses are no longer rewarded, (2) the excuse-maker enters a new environment in which excuses are not rewarded or are punished, or (3) the making of excuses interferes with the individual's ability to learn new, more adaptive behaviors.

From this "straightforward" perspective, excuse-making might persist as a maladaptive behavior for one or more of several reasons. For example, an important body of research indicates that behavior that has been reinforced on an intermittent basis may persist for long periods despite the removal of all rein-forcement. Skinner (1950), in fact, suggested that it is possible, using intermit-tent reinforcement, to condition responses that will never extinguish or be un-learned!

A second possible reason that excuse-making behavior may persist despite its no longer being adaptive is that, if such behavior has been learned as a re-sponse to avoid punishment, it is probable that the occasions associated with the punishment have come to elicit conditioned anxiety (Mowrer, 1960). Con-sequently, even though the acts which the individual attempts to excuse may no longer elicit punishment from the environment, he or she may continue using excuses in response to the conditioned anxiety. Generalization of the conditioned fear response may also occur so that the anxiety and excuse-mak-ing will be elicited by situations that pose no realistic danger but which are sim-ilar to the original fear-learning conditions.

Ullmann and Krasner (1965, 1969) offer an additional perspective on how excuse-making behavior may be learned and maintained through operant con-ditioning. They suggest that individuals may be reinforced for adopting the "role" of being sick. So-called sick-role behavior may be reinforcing because it elicits attention and forgiveness and allows the individual to be excused from responsibility and from facing aversive situations. As an excuse-making strat-egy, sick-role behavior bears a strong resemblance to the "self-handicapping" strategy discussed in Chapter 5.

Although this discussion makes it clear that the use of excuses can be un-derstood readily from a behavioral perspective, no attention has been paid to the problem of how self-esteem maintenance can be integrated into the behav-ioral model. To this point, our discussion has focused exclusively on the exter-nal audience (environment) and on relief from classically conditioned anxiety as the sources of reinforcement for excuse-making behavior. To get a perspec-tive on how the internal audience comes into play within the learning theory model, we turn to a consideration of the social learning theory of Albert Ban-dura.

Relative to other schools of behavior theory, social learning theory places great emphasis on the role of self-regulatory processes in psychological func-tioning. Inherent in the idea that excuses preserve or maintain self-esteem is the assumption that there are "internal" standards of conduct, the violation of which threatens our regard for ourselves. Bandura (1977) addresses the manner in which internal standards of conduct come to be established and influence behavior. Primarily, standards of performance are learned through observation and modeling as well as through extrinsic reinforcement for performances that meet or exceed a given level of proficiency. Once learned, the standards, which may be based on moral or esthetic values as well as on levels of proficiency, are internalized.

The acquisition of internal standards for performance forms the basis for the development of self-concepts, which are defined by Bandura (1977) in terms of the tendency to judge oneself either positively or negatively. Overly harsh or demanding internal standards may lead to various kinds of psychic distress: "Dysfunctional self-evaluative systems figure prominently in some forms of psychopathology by activating excessive self-punishment or creating self-produced distress that motivates various defensive reactions" (p. 140). This clearly suggests that self-criticism is aversive and that its alleviation may serve as a reinforcer for behaviors that alleviate it.

According to Bandura (1977), the anticipation of self-criticism usually is sufficient to deter the individual from engaging in acts that violate or fall short of those standards. However, when, for any of a variety of reasons, individuals have engaged in censurable behavior, they may learn to "disengage" themselves from self-evaluative consequences. The various disengagement strategies Bandura describes resemble many of the excuse-making strategies addressed throughout this book. The schematic seen in Figure 8.3, which is reproduced from page 156 of Bandura's book, illustrates the point. As the schematic suggests, censurable conduct may be rendered acceptable through a process of exonerative moral reasoning, through diminishing its negativity by contrasting it with even more reprehensible acts by others or by relabeling it in a more benign or euphemistic fashion. Bandura regards these strategies as particularly effective "because they not only eliminate self-generated deterrents, but engage self-reward in the service of inhumane conduct" (p. 156).

The second category of disengagement strategies is aimed at "obscuring or distorting the relationship between actions and the effects they cause" (p. 156). An individual may, for example, displace the responsibility for the act onto some authority or diffuse the responsibility among a number of individuals.

A third category of disengagement strategies operates essentially by distorting or minimizing the harm done. As Bandura observes, "As long as they disre-

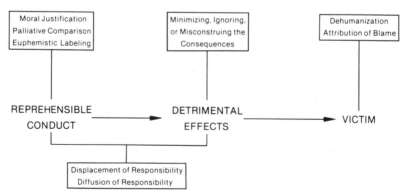

Figure 8.3. Disengagement strategies from censurable behavior. (From *Social Learning Theory,* by A. Bandura. Englewood Cliffs, N.J.: Prentice-Hall, 1977, p. 156.)

gard the detrimental effects of their conduct, there is little likelihood that self-censuring reactions will be activated" (p. 157). Finally, Bandura suggests that self-critical tendencies may be disengaged by demeaning the victim (if any) of the censurable conduct: "Maltreatment of individuals who are regarded as subhuman or debased is less apt to arouse self-reproof than if they are seen as human beings with dignifying qualities" (p. 157). The victim also may be blamed: "One can always select from the chain of causes an instance of defensive behavior by the adversary and view it as the original instigation" (p. 158).

In summary, excuse-making is relatively easy to integrate into learning theory conceptualizations of behavior. From the point of view that has been traditionally most comfortable for learning theory advocates (i.e., that behavior is environmentally determined), excuse-making can be viewed as operantly conditioned behavior which serves to obtain positive reinforcement or to avoid punishment. As we saw, this point of view is compatible with the possibility that excuse-making may become maladaptive by persisting despite changing reinforcement contingencies. However, Bandura's social learning theory is most directly relevant to our view that excuse-making serves self-esteem protecting functions.

Summary of Models of Adjustment and Maladjustment

The preceding selective survey of theories of personality has addressed the manner in which excuses and responsibility evasion *theoretically* figure into psychopathology. In some instances (e.g., psychoanalytic theory) we have seen that excuses are regarded primarily as symptoms of underlying psychic conflicts. In other instances (e.g., existential theory), the problem of responsibility evasion forms the very basis for psychological difficulties; in still others (e.g., learning theory), excuses are neither symptoms nor causes of psychopathology—they are simply learned behaviors that may come to be maladaptive in certain contexts. The orientation of the following section shifts from a theoretical consideration of the role that excuses play in psychopathology to a consideration of some of the ways that excuses may actually be involved in deviant behavior.

ABNORMAL BEHAVIOR AND THE EXCUSE

To our knowledge, there is no focused body of empirical literature on the relationship between responsibility evasion and mental health. However, some authors have described the use of excuses in various psychopathological conditions and there is some evidence that certain deviant or maladaptive behaviors may function to absolve people of responsibility. It is to a selective overview of some of this literature that we now turn.

Illness Behavior as a General Category

Generally speaking, illness behavior (and here we are primarily interested in "deviant," "maladaptive," or "psychopathological" behavior) derives its power to serve as an excuse from notions that it is somehow involuntary—that the individual is not accountable for his or her behavior. American psychiatry has long been impressed with the idea that psychological disturbances are analogous to physical disturbances in that both derive from some presumably identifiable disease process. The implications of this analogy are far-reaching. From our perspective, one of the more interesting implications is that notions of individual accountability for behavior are diluted to the point that the individual is regarded more as a victim than as an actor. For example, whereas some individuals experience progressive loss of vision because they suffer from the identifiable disease of diabetes, others are thought to drink alcohol to excess because they suffer from the hypothetical "disease" of alcoholism.

Insanity as a defense against legal culpability has excellent credentials. The recent trial of John Hinckley, Jr. is a case in point. In his trial for the shooting of President Reagan and several other individuals, Hinckley's defense was that he was legally "insane" (i.e., incapable of appreciating the wrongness of his act). It was interesting to see that whether or not Hinckley performed the alleged act was irrelevant to the case. The vast majority of testimony revolved around a debate over whether Hinckley was "mentally ill." In the end, the jury decided that the prosecution had failed to meet the challenge of proving that Hinckley was sane beyond a reasonable doubt and the verdict was innocent by reason of insanity. In effect, Hinckley was excused from being held responsible for his act because it hadn't been proved that he wasn't sick at the time of the shooting.

We could labor long over a discussion of the application of psychiatry to law and the myriad issues involved. Let us, instead, refer the interested reader to Thomas Szasz' provocative *Law, Liberty, and Psychiatry* (1963). The central point we wish to establish at this juncture is that even the legal system of justice has formally sanctioned the view that "mental illness" renders an individual not responsible for his conduct. Taking a lesson from the learning theory view of deviant behavior outlined above, we might wish to ask a simple, yet important question: Might not the fact that "crazy" behavior is rewarded in such a manner encourage individuals to adopt a "sick role" as a means of dealing with their problems?

In posing this question, we are not only referring to crazy behavior that is rewarded through release from criminal accountability. There are many less drastic, though effective rewards for emotionally disturbed conduct. An acquaintance of one of the authors, for example, escaped the military draft during the Viet Nam conflict because he successfully convinced the military doctors that he suffered from schizophrenia. He had carefully planned and rehearsed his "symptoms" so as to be convincing but "subtle." More in keeping with the theme of the current book, it has been suggested by a number of authors that deviant behavior may be motivated by the goal of self-esteem maintenance. Kaplan (1980), for example, argued that deviant behavior serves "self-enhancing functions" through three primary avenues:

1. Intrapsychic or interpersonal avoidance of those aspects of the normative structure that are subjectively associated with the genesis of negative self-attitudes
2. Symbolic or physical attacks upon the normative structure, its representations, or its representatives
3. Substitution of new experiences with self-enhancing potential for experiences within the normative structure. (pp. 175-176)

For purposes of the present discussion, we focus primarily on the first of the three avenues suggested by Kaplan.

The Strategic Use of Psychiatric Symptoms

It has long been recognized that patients within mental hospitals (Goffman, 1961) become "institutionalized" and difficult to dislodge. Anyone who has worked in a psychiatric hospital is aware that, almost with each passing day, the prospect of returning to the outside world can become increasingly frightening to the inpatient, posing many esteem-threatening possibilities for failure. One implication of this is that psychiatric patients may *deliberately* use their symptoms ("sickness") to avoid release from hospitals (i.e., to avoid "those aspects of the normative structure that are subjectively associated with the genesis of negative self-attitudes" [Kaplan, 1980, p. 175]). This, in fact, was the contention of Ludwig and Farrelly (1967) in their article "The Weapons of Insanity." In their words, "Professionals seem to have overlooked the rather naive possibility that schizophrenic patients become 'chronic' simply because they choose to do so" (p. 737). Ludwig and Farrelly describe a variety of clinically observed strategies and techniques (weapons) that psychiatric patients employ in their struggle against hospital staff to remain institutionalized. Braginsky, Braginsky, and Ring (1969), however, offer some empirical evidence for the strategic use of emotional disturbance in the battle to remain hospitalized.

Braginsky et al. (1969) reported two studies designed to examine the possibility that psychiatric inpatients strategically use their "symptoms" to control their hospital fate. In the first study (originally reported by Braginsky, Grosse, & Ring, 1966), it was hypothesized that psychiatric newcomers (first admissions hospitalized for less than three months) would be motivated to gain release while psychiatric oldtimers (patients hospitalized for over three months) would show more motivation to stay in the hospital. The authors constructed a questionnaire and then generated two versions of it by simply changing the title. One version was called the "Mental Illness Test" and the other was called the "Self-Insight Test."

Subjects in the Mental Illness Test condition were told that people who answered "true" to many items were still ill and could expect to remain hospitalized for a long period of time. Subjects in the Self-Insight Test condition were told that "true" answers were indicative of self-awareness and that people who answered "true" to many items could expect brief hospitalizations. The results indicated that oldtimers gave more "true" answers to the "Mental Illness" version of the test than to the Self-Insight version. Newcomers, however, did just the opposite, giving fewer "true" responses to the Mental Illness version than to the Self-Insight version. These findings were interpreted as indicating that the patients systematically altered their responding in order to enhance their odds of achieving their goals (i.e., release for the newcomers and continued hospitalization for the oldtimers).

A second study described by Braginsky et al. (1969) was originally reported by Braginsky and Braginsky (1967). This study was designed to see whether psychiatric inpatients could successfully manage the impressions that psychiatrists formed of their mental status. The subjects were 30 schizophrenics who had been continuously hospitalized for more than two years and who were residing on an open ward. They were individually interviewed by a staff psychologist who was unaware of the nature of the information subjects had been given about the purpose of the interview. In point of fact, there were three different conditions. Subjects in the "Discharge" condition were led to believe that they were being interviewed to determine if they were ready to be discharged. Subjects in the "Open Ward" condition were told they were being interviewed to determine if they should remain on the open ward or should be placed on a closed ward. Subjects in the "Mental Status" condition were told the interview was simply to find out how they were getting along.

The interviews were tape-recorded and subsequently rated by three staff psychiatrists who were unaware of the nature of the study and who were unfamiliar with the subjects. It was hypothesized that the patients would try to create a greater impression of illness in the Discharge condition than in the Open Ward condition because of their presumed desire to remain in the hospital and yet to retain their open-ward status. It was also expected that the patients' self-presentation in the Discharge and Mental Status conditions would be similar because it was anticipated that the patients would regard the mental status interviews as evaluations of their suitability for discharge. The psychiatrists' ratings confirmed that the patients in the Open Ward condition were seen as suffering from less psychopathology and as needing less hospital control than subjects in both the Discharge and Mental Status conditions. The patients in the latter two conditions did not differ significantly.

The foregoing studies provide empirical support for the notion that even psychiatric patients suffering from what is presumably the most debilitating form of psychopathology, schizophrenia, are capable of presenting their symptoms in a planful, strategic fashion (see also Fontana, Klein, Lewis, & Levine, 1968; Sarbin & Mancuso, 1980). While it is possible to regard such impression management (Goffman, 1959) as primarily oriented toward the pursuit of hedonic goals, a closer look suggests that self-esteem maintenance is also at issue (Snyder & Smith, 1982). In line with Kaplan's (1980) classification of the avenues through which deviant behavior may be self-enhancing, it is evident that avoiding discharge from a psychiatric hospital may serve to avoid esteem-threatening circumstances. It is also the case that the hospital environment, for an oldtimer, represents a predictable, manipulable life setting that can provide numerous opportunities to have self-enhancing experiences (Ludwig & Farrelly, 1966, 1967).

Goffman (1959) observed that, in interpersonal encounters, it serves the interests of individuals to control the reactions that others have toward them. According to Goffman, "This control is achieved largely by influencing the definition of the situation" (p. 4). The strategic presentation of "symptoms" is one way that psychiatric patients may manipulate the definitions of relationships. Artiss (1959), Belknap (1956), Haley (1963), and Schlenker (1980) made similar observations. Haley (1963), for example, observed that "a symptom may represent considerable distress to a patient subjectively, but such distress is preferred by some people to living in an unpredictable world of social relationships" (p. 15). As Haley points out, the psychiatric symptom is doubly effective as a means of defining and controlling relationships because, owing to contemporary views concerning the nature of psychopathology, the symptomatic individual is excused from owning responsibility for the symptoms.

We alluded to the possibility that contemporary views of psychopathology may play a powerful role in promoting the strategic use of psychiatric symptoms. One important feature of contemporary psychiatry is that there is an elaborate system of diagnostic labeling.

The Role of Labeling in Encouraging Sick-Role Behavior

As presently codified in the *Diagnostic and Statistical Manual of Mental Disorders* (American Psychiatric Association, 1980), the system of diagnoses presents an impressive array of "official-sounding" labels for a wide variety of "syndromes." Thomas Scheff (1971) and others have commented on the manner in which the practice of psychiatric diagnosis encourages and mantains deviant behavior patterns.

Once an individual has entered the mental health system, either for help with problems in living or in order to avoid stresses in the outside world, powerful social forces can operate to reinforce and consolidate the individual's adoption of a sick role (Scheff, 1971). Central to this process is the practice of diagnositc labeling. First of all, evidence suggests that people in "helping" roles are inclined to view clients' emotional problems as arising more from personal factors than from situational factors (e.g., Batson, 1975; Snyder, 1977; Snyder, Shenkel, & Schmidt, 1976). Second, once a label has been attached, the search is on for evidence to confirm it. Scheff (1971) argued that evidence that supports the label is sought and focused on while disconfirming evidence is ignored or given less weight. Langer and Abelson (1974), for example, found that analytically oriented clinicians regarded an individual as more disturbed when he was presented as a "patient" than when he was presented as a "job applicant." Rosenhan (1973) made a similar point when he observed that psychiatric diagnosis is largely influenced by contextual variables—if an individual is in a psychiatric hospital, there must be something wrong with him.

According to Scheff (1971), when the people around a labeled individual begin to respond "uniformly in terms of the traditional stereotypes of insanity, his amorphous and unstructured rule-breaking tends to crystallize in conformity to those expectations, thus becoming similar to the behavior of other deviants classified as mentally ill and stable over time"(p. 82). The destructive possibilities associated with the process of labeling, according to Scheff, are potentiated by the medical bias toward finding illness when there is reason to suspect that there may be some present: "Most physicians learn early in their training that it is far more culpable to dismiss a sick patient than to retain a well one" (p. 110). If a label *can be* attached, it is likely that one *will be* attached.

Also promoting the adoption and maintenance of a deviant or sick role, according to Scheff (1971), is the fact that patients are rewarded for conforming to the role prescribed by their label: "That is, patients who manage to find evidence of 'their illness' in their past and present behavior, confirming the medical and societal diagnosis, receive benefits" (p. 84). Physicians and other mental health personnel (also other patients) may actually instruct patients on proper sick-role behavior. Whereas appropriate sick-role behavior may be reinforced, Scheff suggests that when labeled "deviants" attempt to return to conventional roles, they are punished for doing so or are denied access to conventional roles. This may take such forms as job discrimination as well as disapproving reactions from physicians or peers. Not to be overlooked in the social instigation of sick-role behavior is the likelihood that the individual in question may be in a state of confusion, stress, and, according to Scheff (1971), heightened suggestibility:

> When gross rule-breaking is publicly recognized and made an issue, the rule-breaker may be profoundly confused, anxious, and ashamed. In this crisis it seems reasonable to assume that the rule-breaker will be suggestible to the cues that he gets from the reactions of others toward him. But those around him are also in a crisis; the incomprehensible nature of the rule-breaking, and the seeming need for immediate action lead them to take collective action against the rule-breaker on the basis of the attitude which all share—the traditional stereotypes of insanity. (p. 88)

Summary of Illness Behavior as a General Category

In summary, the central point of this section is that psychopathology generally is regarded by society as involuntary in nature and, consequently, provides an officially sanctioned excuse for behavior that might otherwise be esteem-threatening if responsibility had to be accepted. Given this, it is no major surprise to find that psychiatric "symptoms" may be used, at least on occasion, as excuses for unacceptable behavior. Indeed, as the above discussion has indicated, contemporary psychiatric practice and views are such that the adoption of sick-role behavior is frequently facilitated and encouraged.

Whereas the preceding comments have been focused on general illness behavior as a possible excuse strategy, the following, more specific, sections on alcohol use and depression are intended to serve as more detailed examples of behaviors or forms of maladaption that have implications for excuse theory.

Alcohol Use as an Excuse Strategy

Theories of alcohol use or abuse typically posit that alcohol use serves some instrumental function related to alcohol's drug properties. Among the possible instrumental functions that have been suggested are tension reduction (Higgins, 1976 for review), relief from conflict (Conger, 1956), heightened sense of power or control (McClelland, Davis, Kalin, & Wanner, 1972), relief from social inhibitions (Nathan & O'Brien, 1971), and facilitation of "ego-syntonic" behaviors and affects (Mendelson, La Dou, & Solomon, 1964). Although the pharmacology of alcohol may be an important determinant of the motivations for drinking, it is also possible that its value, in many situations, derives less from its pharmacology than from societal expectations and attitudes regarding the consequences of drinking.

Expectancies Associated with Drinking

There is a growing body of evidence suggesting that the mere expectation of having consumed alcohol can have a substantial influence on postdrinking behavior. Lang, Goeckner, Adesso, and Marlatt (1975) instructed alternate halves of their subjects that they would be consuming either alcohol or a nonalcoholic beverage but then actually administered a beverage that either did or did not correspond with subjects' expectations (i.e., some subjects who were told they would receive alcohol actually received a placebo and vice versa). Following the beverage consumption, subjects were either provoked to anger by an experimental confederate or experienced a neutral interaction. Later, when subjects were supposedly delivering electrical shocks to the confederate, it was found that those who *believed* they had consumed alcohol behaved more aggressively than subjects who did not believe they had consumed alcohol even if they had.

Wilson and Abrams (1977), in a similar study, led male subjects to believe that they were receiving either alcohol or no alcohol and then delivered a beverage that either did or did not meet their expectations. In the context of a subsequent brief social interaction with a female confederate, the male subjects who *believed* they had consumed alcohol showed significantly less increase in heart rates than subjects who *believed* they had not consumed alcohol. Whether subjects actually did or did not consume alcohol had no significant effect on heart rates.

Wilson and Lawson (1976) examined the effects of alcohol and expectancy on sexual arousal. Alcohol had no effect on penile tumescence during exposure to films with sexual content, but the *belief* of having consumed alcohol resulted in increased sexual arousal. Lang, Searles, Lauerman, and Adesso (1980) found that subjects rated erotic slides as more sexually stimulating after drinking beverages they believed to contain alcohol than after drinking beverages they believed not to contain alcohol. Interestingly, subjects who scored high on a measure of sex guilt also viewed the slides for a longer period of time when they believed they had consumed alcohol. This was not true for the low and moderate sex-guilt subjects. In an informal review of this study, Marlatt and Rohsenow (1981) make the following comment about the Lang et al. (1980) finding:

> Lang's findings suggest that men whose normal sexual response is inhibited by sexual guilt or social restraints will show the greatest disinhibition effect when they believe they are drinking alcohol. *There is an important personal payoff in this process, since the men can absolve themselves of responsibility for their actions by blaming alcohol for their disinhibited behavior.* (p. 68, emphasis added)

In their interesting book, *Drunken Comportment*, MacAndrew and Edgerton (1969) make many compelling observations regarding the use of alcohol to excuse disinhibited behavior and specifically note the role that social sanctions play in furthering the use of alcohol as a "time-out" from responsible action. They also propose a theory of drunken behavior that is of interest here: "Over the course of socialization, people learn about drunkenness what their society 'knows' about drunkenness; and, accepting and acting upon the understandings thus imparted to them, they become the living confirmation of their society's teachings" (p. 88).

The prevailing wisdom about the effects of alcohol on behavior in contemporary America is that it paralyzes the higher cortical control centers in the brain, disinhibiting primitive behaviors, emotions, and urges that are normally held in check. Because the general societal attitude toward alcohol is heavily weighted toward the notion that its effects are debilitative, *there are many instances in which the strategic use of alcohol can provide important personal advantages.* One type of possible advantage is that alcohol intoxication might serve as a prior excuse for censurable behaviors.

Self-Handicapping and Alcohol Use

In a review of the tension-reduction theory of alcohol consumption and related research, Higgins (1976) proposed a general model of tension-motivated drinking:

> Alcohol consumption may reduce the stress associated with life circumstances in which an individual experiences a need to act effectively or to exercise control but experiences uncertainty regarding his ability to do so. An inability to exercise control or to act effectively might result from either behavioral deficits or constraints (environmental or psychological) on behavior. The reinforcing properties of such stress reduction might lead to increased alcohol consumption (a) when alcohol is available, (b) when the individual feels a need to act effectively but is uncertain or doubtful about his ability to do so, (c) when the outcome of the individual's behavior or circumstance is highly valued, (d) when the resulting stress is sufficiently arousing, and (e) when there is a basis in the individual's experience to expect that the consumption of alcohol in that specific situation will serve a useful function (i.e., tension reduction). (pp. 64–65)

We would now suggest that an important tension-reducing function of alcohol is based on the apparent fact that, for both internal and external audiences, alcohol intoxication is seen as an extenuating and mitigating circumstance that lessens accountability for esteem-threatening performances. This view is essentially identical to the recently expressed views of Jones and Berglas (1978).

In a theoretical article, Jones and Berglas (1978) elaborated on more traditional Adlerian notions of drug and alcohol use in the service of self-esteem maintenance (see Steffenhagen, 1974) to suggest that drug or alcohol use may be particularly functional for individuals who are faced with challenges to their self-esteem. Specifically, Jones and Berglas suggest that when individuals are faced with an evaluation experience over which they have uncertain control, the strategic use of intoxicants may protect their threatened self-esteem by creating attributional confusion as to the possible source of any less-than-adequate performance. In other words, if an individual has consumed alcohol before a negatively evaluated performance, it is unclear whether the appropriate attribution to make regarding the act is to the effects of the alcohol or to the personal characteristics and abilities of the actor. Independent of the actual effects of alcohol, then, the individual who "self-handicaps" by drinking prior to an evaluated performance gains important leverage over the outcome of the evaluation.

To date, the self-handicapping theory of alcohol and drug use has received direct support in several empirical studies. Berglas and Jones (1978) reported two studies that found that college students who were led to anticipate a threatening evaluation over which they had uncertain control tended to increase their selection of a bogus performance-inhibiting drug (Pandocrin) over a bogus performance-enhancing drug (Activil) when given the choice. By the same token,

Tucker, Vuchinich, and Sobell (1981) found that college student social drinkers increased their consumption of alcohol when led to anticipate a threatening evaluation over which they had uncertain control.

These studies suggest that alcohol (or drug) consumption may serve a strategic function for individuals who are faced with theatening evaluations. Although alcohol use as a "self-handicapping" strategy theoretically serves to assuage potential threats to self-esteem, there is no empirical evidence that self-esteem is, indeed, preserved or maintained by such use. There is some evidence, however, that the esteem in which *others* hold an individual following censurable behavior is positively influenced by prior alcohol consumption.

Gelles (1972) observed that the majority of wife-beating incidents are preceded by alcohol use by the husband, but that the abused wives typically attribute their husbands' actions to their drinking—essentially, the wives report that if it weren't for the booze, everything would be OK. The offending husbands, naturally enough, tend to agree. Gelles goes so far as to suggest that some abusing husbands "drink in order to provide an excuse for becoming violent" (p. 116). Snell, Rosenwald, and Robey (1964) make a similar point. They go further, however, in suggesting that periodic attacks following drinking may serve an important role in preserving marital equilibrium and, as such, are functional for some marriages. Supposedly, if pent-up hostilities couldn't be occasionally discharged and blamed on alcohol, consequences would be more dire for marriages than wife-beating!

Two recent empirical studies have specifically addressed the question of how alcohol intoxication on the part of an abusing husband influences impartial judges' ratings as to his level of responsibility and accountability. Richardson and Campbell (1980) presented college undergraduate judges with a description of an incident of wife abuse. To determine the influence of alcohol intoxication on the judges' ratings of accountability for the incident, different groups of judges were told that the husband, the wife, or both were intoxicated at the time of the incident. The results indicated that the abusing husband was held *less* accountable when he was presented as intoxicated.

More recently, Carducci and McNeely (1981) reported a replication and extension of the Richardson and Campbell study. Carducci and McNeely used both alcoholics and college undergraduates as judges in their study. As with the Richardson and Campbell study, the judges were presented with a description of an incident of wife abuse in which the husband, the wife, or both were presented as intoxicated. The pattern of results for the college undergraduate judges was similar to that in the Richardson and Campbell study—the husband was seen as less responsible for the incident when he was presented as intoxicated. The result for the alcoholic judges was just the opposite. They tended to hold the husband *most* accountable when he was presented as intoxicated. The reason for the contrasting findings for college undergraduates and alcoholics is unclear. It is possible, however, that the more negative bias the alcoholic subjects expressed toward the intoxicated wife beater was related to the fact that they were recruited from among participants in an alcohol treatment program.

Both of these studies suggest that, at least for undergraduate college student judges, an intoxicated wife beater tends to be excused for his behavior. The undergraduates appeared to believe that the intoxicated husband's behavior was, to some extent, caused by the alcohol. Right or wrong, this belief appears to have translated into a more accepting attitude toward the wife beater who was "fortunate" enough to be drunk.

So far as the present authors are aware, there are *no* reported studies that experimentally examined how offenders' evaluations of their own accountability are influenced by intoxication. There is one suggestive study, however. McCaghy (1968) reported a study in which men who had been convicted of child molestation were asked to rate their attitudes toward other child molesters. Three groups of child molesters were studied. One group claimed to have been intoxicated at the time of their offense. The second and third groups did not claim intoxication. One, however, denied that they had committed the offense they were convicted of, whereas the other group acknowledged their crime. McCaghy found that those child molesters who claimed to have been intoxicated at the time of their offense expressed significantly more derogatory attitudes toward other child molesters than did those who did not claim to have been intoxicated. We would suggest that those subjects who claimed intoxication may have held more derogatory attitudes because, *having the excuse of intoxication, they could deny their personal membership in the reviled fellowship of child molesters.* In effect, they could disparge child molesters without disparging themselves. By admitting a relatively minor problem (alcohol abuse), they were enabled to simultaneously admit their crime and deny personal responsibility for it. A selection of quotes from the subjects in McCaghy's study illustrates the point:

> "If I were sober it never would have happened."
> "My trouble is strictly drinking."
> "I have an alcohol drinking problem, not a sex problem."
> "Drinking is the reason. I could always get a woman. I can't figure it out. A man's mind doesn't function right when he's got liquor on it." (p. 48)

Summary of Alcohol Use as an Excuse Strategy

In our preceding discussion of alcohol use, we have attempted to point out that it may serve a variety of excuse functions. We indicated that the mere belief of having consumed alcohol appears to allow people to behave in ways that they typically would not. As MacAndrew and Edgerton (1969) suggest, societal attitudes toward alcohol further the use of alcohol as a means of gaining an official "time-out" from responsible (or at least ordinary) conduct. We also reviewed evidence that alcohol intoxication can play an exonerative role in situations in which behavior falls short of socially or self-approved standards. Although it appears that people can and do use alcohol in an apparently strategic fashion in order to "soften" potentially negative evaluations, it remains to be determined what role such "excuse-motivated" drinking plays in the development or maintenance of problem drinking patterns. In the following section we examine the relationship between excuse-making and a very different type of problem—depression.

Depression and Excuses

This discussion refers primarily to what has been traditionally known as "neurotic depression." Our comments may be much less applicable to depressive disorders that have a heavy biological component (e.g., bipolar disorder) than to depressive disturbances that appear to be more "functional" in nature (e.g., unipolar disorder, dysthymic disorder) (American Psychiatric Association, 1980). Nevertheless, for ease of presentation, we use the "generic" term of depression throughout the discussion.

Probably to a greater extent than with any other psychopathology, depression has been theoretically and empirically linked with low self-esteem. Bibring (1953) was among the earliest theorists to observe directly that depression was a disorder of self-esteem. Since then, numerous researchers have noted that low self-esteem is part of the symptomatic picture presented by depressives, and others (e.g., Becker, 1979; Brown, 1979) have directly implicated *vulnerable* self-esteem as a factor predisposing to the development of depressions. In point of fact, the literature is replete with studies suggesting that depressed individuals are their own "worst enemies" in that they behave and think in ways that further injure their self-regard.

Self-Defeating Cognitions and Perceptions in Depression

Beck (1967) theorized that depression is the consequence of a pattern of dysfunctional cognitions. In essence, he proposed that people cause their depression because of their distorted way of construing the world. Central to this manner of construing is a "triad" of negative and pessimistic views of the world, the self, and the future. Among the consequences of this negative cognitive triad are tendencies to highlight and overemphasize negatives while ignoring and underemphasizing positives. According to Beck, this pattern of subjective distortion contributes to the development of a negative self-concept and depressed mood: "I concluded that the way an individual structures his experiences determines his mood. Since the depressed person consistently makes negative conceptualizations, he is prone to have a consistently negative mood" (p. 261).

There is considerable support for Beck's (1967) views. Hammen and Krantz (1976), for example, studied groups of depressed and nondepressed women.

Following a "therapeutic talent test," the subjects were given either success feedback, failure feedback, or no feedback. Although the depressed and non-depressed women made similar predictions of how well they would do on the test, the depressed women evaluated themselves more negatively following the feedback. They also then reported lower expectancies of success on an antici-pated test of their "empathic ability." These tendencies were most pronounced for the depressed women in the failure feedback condition. Hammen and Krantz suggested that their findings "may represent dysfunctional informa-tion-processing strategies that may serve to perpetuate if not enhance the feel-ings of depression and hopelessness" (p. 584).

Nelson and Craighead (1977) tested the prediction that, relative to nonde-pressed individuals, depressed individuals would overestimate the amount of punishment they received in the context of a study. When subjects received punishment on 70% of their experimental trials, the depressed subjects did overestimate the amount of punishment they received. When subjects received 30% punishment, however, the depressed subjects recalled accurately while the nondepressed subjects *underestimated* the amount of punishment. Nelson and Craighead suggested that "while nondepressed individuals may filter out a cer-tain amount of low-frequency negative feedback in order to maintain a positive self-image, depressed persons may remain particularly sensitive to all instances of aversive stimulation" (p. 386).

Lewinsohn, Mischel, Chaplin, and Barton (1980) reported a related finding that depressed psychiatric inpatients were rated as less socially competent than nonpsychiatric controls. Of interest here, however, was their finding that the depressed patients' self-perceptions were more accurate than were those of the nonpsychiatric controls, who tended to see themselves more positively than did the observers. Furthermore, as the depressed patients' treatment progressed, their self-perceptions increasingly evidenced the positive bias that character-ized the nonpsychiatric controls. The authors conclude their article with the statement, "To feel good about ourselves we may have to judge ourselves more kindly than we are judged" (p. 212).

Oliver and Williams (1979) examined the attributions that depressed and nondepressed subjects made with regard to their failure or success on what was presented as a test of perception. Success and failure were manipulated via feedback that the subjects had either placed at the 85th percentile of subjects (success) or at the 20th percentile (failure). They found that nondepressed sub-jects tended to make "internal" attributions (i.e., to skill or ability) following success and "external" attributions (i.e., to luck or task difficulty) following failure. Depressed subjects, in contrast, tended to make internal attributions following both success and failure. The authors suggested that the effect of making internal attributions for failure would be to diminish self-esteem.

The foregoing studies do not exhaust the literature pertaining to the manner in which depressed and nondepressed individuals differ in how they cognitively process information or view themselves (see, for example, Krantz & Hammen, 1979; Lobitz & Post, 1979; Peterson, 1979). They do, however, strongly suggest that depressed individuals are more likely than nondepressed individuals to report viewing themselves in ways that might serve to diminish their self-esteem. An important question arises as to why depressed individuals behave in this apparently self-defeating way.

Depression as an Interpersonal Strategy

As our earlier review of Bandura's social learning theory of personality illustrates, the concept of self-efficacy is closely linked to the concept of self-esteem. According to Bandura (1977), when individuals have a low sense of self-efficacy (i.e., they feel they are unlikely to be able to effect desired outcomes), they are unlikely to engage in or persist in activities related to those outcomes. To the extent that depression and low self-efficacy are linked, this would imply that depression tends to be characterized by behavioral sluggishness, loss of interest in the environment, and low tolerance for frustration, all of which have been described as common symptoms of depression (Hamilton, 1982; Seligman, 1975). Such "symptoms" would tend to result in the avoidance of esteem-threatening performance arenas and therefore could be construed as having "strategic" excuse value. Other common depressive symptoms may have strategic value in esteem-threatening situations that cannot be avoided.

Warren (1976) tested the hypothesis that individuals who are low in self-esteem have greater discrepancies between their achieved levels of performance and their internal standards for performance than do individuals with high self-esteem. She found that the high and low self-esteem males performed equally well on a cognitive problem-solving task, but that the low self-esteem subjects had "greater discrepancies in the expected direction between their standards for successful achievement and their perceived performance levels" (p. 973). Although these findings seem plausible and straightforward, let us suggest that an experimental situation in which an investigator asks individuals to make attributions and judgments regarding their performances is an *interpersonal* context.

Insofar as people commonly attempt to manage the impressions others have of them (Goffman, 1959; Haley, 1963; Schlenker, 1980), it seems reasonable to examine the possibility that, when they are asked to report their attributions and judgments about their behavior, they do so in a way that is designed to define and control the nature of the interpersonal relationship. In the study by Warren, for example, it is possible that the low self-esteem subjects reported that their performances fell short of their standards in order to create a particular impression in the eyes of the experimenter. This may also be true of the studies reviewed above that documented depressed individuals' tendencies to predict failure following negative feedback (e.g., Hammen & Krantz, 1976), to be relatively sensitive to instances of punishment (e.g., Nelson & Craighead,

1977), and to make internal attributions for failure (e.g., Oliver & Williams, 1979). What type of impression might these behaviors be designed to create? One possibility was suggested by Shaw (1982). In discussing the differences in cognitive style displayed by depressed and nondepressed individuals, Shaw speculated that depressed individuals may attempt to "maintain high internal standards while trying to lower the expectations of others by predicting failure" (p. 135). In general, we would suggest that the type of impression an individual attempts to create in another's eyes is a function of the particular needs of the individual. We elaborate on this notion in the following section by examining some common interpersonal needs of depressives.

Personality "Styles" and Depression

Although people with a wide variety of personality "styles" experience depression, it is often stated that depression is a relatively common problem for individuals with "dependent" or "compulsive" personality patterns (e.g., American Psychiatric Association, 1980; Chodoff, 1972; Fenichel, 1945; Millon, 1981). According to Millon (1981), the experiential backgrounds of individuals with dependent personalities are characterized by pampering and overprotection, whereas those of individuals with compulsive personalities are characterized by overcontrol and harsh punishment for "bad" behavior. In the instance of the dependent personality, according to Millon, the consequence is the failure to forge an independent sense of competence and ability to function. In the instance of the compulsive personality, the consequence is a rigid style of self-control designed to avoid transgressions against harsh internalized standards. In either instance, negative or "bad" performances represent serious threats to the individual's psychological stability.

For dependent individuals, censurable behavior threatens the continuation of the dependent relationships upon which they rely so heavily. According to Millon (1981), dependent individuals' feelings of inadequacy and insecurity lead them to "downgrade themselves, claiming to lack abilities, virtues, and attractiveness. They are disposed to magnify their failures and defects" (p. 113). Furthermore, such self-abasement is regarded as having strategic value: "Clinically, this pattern of self-depreciation may best be conceived as a strategy by which dependents elicit assurances that they are not unworthy and unloved. Hence, it serves as an instrument for evoking praise and commendation" (p. 113). Millon further asserts that "by claiming weakness and inferiority, dependents effectively absolve themselves of the responsibilities they know they should assume but would rather not" (p. 113). This sounds very much like self-handicapping.

According to Millon, censurable behavior threatens the security of individuals with compulsive personalities because, "having opted for a strategy in which rewards and security are granted to those in power, they must, at all costs, prevent losing the powerful's respect and protection" (p. 227). When faced with situations that call for decisions or actions for which there are no clear-cut guidelines, the compulsive individual is subject to depressions. Unable to direct resentment or anger toward those who control the reinforcements in their lives, compulsive individuals are likely to suffer from depressions that are characterized "primarily by diffuse apprehension, marked feelings of guilt, and a tendency to complain about personal sin and unworthiness" (p. 234).

Depressive Symptoms as Strategies

There are two things about this discussion of depression in dependent and compulsive individuals that we would like to emphasize. First, depression in both groups is described as involving self-demeaning behavior. Second, the depressive behavior in both groups is, paradoxically, described as having adaptive value. For both the dependent and the compulsive individual, depression is seen as functioning to avoid losing the support and approval they so badly need. This suggests that depression, at least for some individuals, may be the "price" they pay to avoid even greater threats to their security and self-esteem. It's as if the approval and support of the "external audience" is so critical to the sense of well-being of these individuals that they are willing to sacrifice some of their personal self-regard in order to retain it. This theme emerges clearly in some psychodynamic formulations of the development of depression.

A number of psychodynamically oriented writers (e.g., Gero, 1936; Nemiah, 1961; Rado, 1928) focused on the intense "narcissistic" needs of depressed individuals. According to Nemiah (1961), for example, our ability to feel secure is based on our ability to keep open our narcissistic supply lines (i.e., to avoid alienating or losing those whose approval, love, support, and encouragement we need). When the sources of our narcissistic supplies are lost or disappoint us, we are likely to feel hate, rage, bitterness, and the like. However, since these emotions only serve to further threaten our continued ability to derive nurturance from the object of our conflict, the negative feelings are turned inward. The anger, hate, disappointment, and bitterness we feel are transformed into guilt, self-castigation, and self-punishment in order to avoid further alienating the threatened love object and suffering the consequent more severe loss to security.

Alfred Adler directly construed the use of self-punishment and depressive symptoms as efforts to control others and hence to preserve security:

> Melancholia develops in individuals whose method of living has from early childhood on been dependent upon the achievements and the support of others. Such individuals will always try to lean on others and will not scorn the use of exaggerated hints at their own inadequacy to force the support, adjustment, and submissiveness of others. When a difficulty arises, they will evade the main issue, the continuation of their development, or even the adherence to their own sphere of action. According to the melancholic perspective, life resembles a difficult and enormous hazard, the preponderant majority of men are hostile, and the world

consists of uncomfortable obstacles. By concretizing their subjective inferiority feeling, melancholiacs openly or implicitly raise the claim to a higher "disability compensation." (Adler, in Ansbacher & Ansbacher, 1967, p. 319)

More recently, Coyne (1976) proposed an interactional description of depressive behavior, focusing on the mutual shaping that takes place between the behavior of the depressed individual and the behavior of others in the depressed individual's environment. Coyne suggested that the depressed individual "finds that by displaying symptoms he can manipulate his environment so that it will provide sympathy and reassurance" (pp. 34–35). Such manipulative use of depressive symptoms, however, can lead to the growing irritation of those individuals being manipulated and to an even more defensive use of depressive symptoms:

> Members of the social environment who have been repeatedly provoked and made to feel guilty may retaliate by withholding the responses for which the depressed person depends on them. The depressed person may become aware of the inhibiting influence his symptoms have on the direct expression of negative feelings, and may use these symptoms aggressively, while limiting the forms that counteraggression can take. (Coyne, 1976, pp. 35–36)

The aforementioned theories clearly suggest that depressive symptoms have instrumental value in that they may serve to control the responses of others. Their value would appear to be related to their self-handicapping qualities. As Shaw (1982) suggested, depressed individuals may focus on their inadequacies and weaknesses as a way of lowering others' expectations of them. Accordingly, they may be held to lower standards of performance and, indeed, may be excused altogether from entering threatening life arenas (e.g., having to take independent action or to make independent decisions) where their sense of personal efficacy is low. By using their symptoms to claim a "disability compensation," to use Adler's term, depressives may also induce others to protect and take care of them, further insulating them from threats to their security. There is even some experimental evidence that self-punitive behavior may be adopted as a means of forestalling (being excused from) aversive input from others in situations where criticism or punishment might be forthcoming.

Stone and Hokanson (1969) tested the hypothesis that people would engage in self-punitive behavior if they could thus avoid aversive stimulation from another person. Their subjects could avoid an aversive shock from an experimental partner if they self-shocked with a milder electrical shock. Not only did the subjects increase the frequency of their self-shocking over time, but also, as time passed, the self-administered shocks became increasingly associated with autonomic arousal reduction. The finding was interpreted as indicating that masochistic behaviors may be adopted if they have arousal-reducing consequences.

In a subsequent study, Forrest and Hokanson (1975) tested the hypothesis that "one component of depression may be related to the instrumental value that depressive, self-demeaning displays have in controlling aversiveness and threat from others" (p. 347). In their study, depressed and nondepressed subjects interacted with a confederate on a task in which they could either punish (shock) or reward each other for their performances. In addition, the subjects were able to punish (shock) themselves if they felt they had been at fault. There were two levels of self-administered shock, moderately high and low. The results indicate that the depressed subjects shocked themselves more frequently than did the nondepressed subjects. Moreover, it was the more painful level of shock that was associated with the increased self-punitiveness by depressed subjects, and there was a difference between the depressed and nondepressed groups in terms of which form of punishment (self-administered or confederate-administered) was most effective in reducing physiological arousal. For the nondepressed subjects, physiological arousal decreased the most following a confederate-administered shock. For depressed subjects, the greatest reduction in physiological arousal occurred following self-administered shock. According to the authors,

> Depressed patients have learned to cope with environmental and interpersonal stresses with self-punitive and/or nonassertive behaviors and these behaviors have been successful in dealing with their normal day-to-day existence. At times when situational stresses become great, this limited behavioral repertoire may be invoked to a degree that may seriously impair adequate functioning and these people may manifest a clinical depressive or masochistic episode. (p. 356)

The studies by Hokanson and his colleagues suggest that self-punitive behaviors may be learned and employed by depressed individuals as a means of terminating and/or forestalling aversive input from others. At present, however, there is only tentative evidence that self-punitiveness or depressive symptoms actually do curtail potentially critical or aversive behavior by others. Platt (1977; cited by Strack & Coyne, 1983) found that subjects formed negative private reactions to a self-derogating confederate while expressing positive public reactions. Strack and Coyne (1983) tested the hypothesis that subjects who interacted with a depressed individual would emerge from the interaction with negative feelings about their depressed partner, but that they would express positive reactions when they believed their reactions would be shared with the depressed person. The subjects interacted with either a depressed or nondepressed individual and then completed questionnaires regarding their perceptions of their partner. Equal halves of the subjects completed the questionnaires believing that their perceptions either would or would not be shared with their partner. The authors found that subjects who interacted with a depressed partner were more likely to form negative impressions of the partner and that, when subjects believed their responses would be confidential, they were more likely to express negative reactions. Although this effect did not differ significantly for subjects who had interacted with the depressed and nondepressed partners, those who had interacted with a depressed partner were more likely to report that their responses were less honest when they believed that they would be shared.

Summary of Depression and Excuses

To summarize, there is mounting evidence that depressed individuals are more likely than others to report attributing failures to themselves, to exaggerate their failures, and to be particularly sensitive to potential criticism. The prevailing attitude in the literature toward such findings is to regard them as reflecting a style of cognitive processing that serves to undermine the depressed individual's self-esteem. Although this may be the case, it is also possible that such behaviors advance the interpersonal goals of depressed individuals by warding off even greater threats to their security.

Several authors have suggested that depressed individuals may "use" self-punishment and/or depressive symptoms to forestall aversive interpersonal input (i.e., in order to exercise preemptive control over a threatening environment). It may be that emphasizing one's failings and criticizing one's abilities in the interpersonal context of a research investigation has an analogous function. Whether or not potential criticism is preempted, such a "strategy" might be reinforced because of the diminished subjective negativity of any actual criticism. To the present authors' knowledge, this possibility has yet to be empirically investigated. We can, however, think of many instances in which individuals have elicited support from their social environment by "playing up" their faults: "Boy, I really blew that one!" "Oh, you didn't do *that* bad."

CONCLUDING COMMENTS

In this chapter we attempted to illustrate, from a clinical perspective, the importance of motives to safeguard self-esteem and to examine, both theoretically and empirically, some of the ways that the devices employed in service of the motives may go awry. The primary focus, of course, has been on the ways in which psychological "symptoms" and deviant behaviors may counterproductively support and maintain self-defeating patterns of responsibility evasion. In some instances, the excuse value of deviant behavior or emotional incapacitation is apparent (e.g., blaming alcohol intoxication for one's indiscretions). In other instances, one has to look considerably below the surface in order to perceive the excuse value of particular behaviors. As the preceding section on depression illustrated, for example, the self-castigation and self-punitiveness characteristic of many depressives appear, on the surface, to make no sense as excuse strategies. Upon closer examination of the interpersonal contexts in which depression frequently occurs, however, even self-blame and masochism may be seen to serve important self-protective functions.

One of the more self-defeating aspects of "using" psychological symptoms or deviant behaviors as excuses is the heavy price one pays for the luxury. Entering the role of "psychiatric invalid" may excuse one from many onerous responsibilities, but it also entails being stripped of one's dignity, self-determination, and freedom of movement. How can one account for the paradoxical willingness of many individuals to pay this heavy price?

Accounting for the Paradoxical Use of Symptoms as Excuses

As noted, the use of "symptoms" as excuses entails a willingness to accept the self-defeating consequences of such behavior. In this section, we present three possible explanations for this paradox. First, it has commonly been observed that immediate reinforcement is a more potent determiner of behavior than long-range punishment. In many instances the immediate benefits of using psychological symptoms to excuse one from responsibility or to avoid threatening situations may be more salient than the long-term negative consequences of so doing. One of the present authors, for example, worked with an adolescent boy who justified his repeated avoidance of certain classes at school on the grounds that if he went, he would become so nervous that he would lose control of his bowels and be extremely embarrassed. He clearly recognized the long-range self-defeating aspects of his school avoidance and was greatly concerned about its negative impact on the remainder of his life. Nevertheless, the immediate relief he gained each time he left school prior to his feared classes was strong enough to support the avoidance over a protracted period of time. It is noteworthy that he had never experienced the loss of bowel control that he feared.

Second, in thinking about why some individuals are willing to pay the heavy price of using "psychiatric" excuses, it is also helpful to consider the severity of the threat associated with the failure to have an "out." Although it is unlikely that individuals do a formal "cost–benefit" analysis prior to excusing themselves from threatening life arenas, there are certainly various degrees of threat associated with failing to do so. In the preceding discussion of depression, for example, it was noted that individuals with dependent and compulsive personalities are relatively susceptible to serious depressions. These are individuals for whom the prospects associated with independent and self-directed actions are particularly terrifying—either because of their especially low sense of personal efficacy (e.g., dependents) or because of their more than usually strong fear of making mistakes and being out of control (e.g., compulsives). In this context, it might be helpful to recall our earlier discussion of Maslow's (1954) hierarchy of needs. Maslow suggested that more basic needs for safety and security must be met before an individual can make growth-motivated as opposed to deficit-motivated decisions. It seems reasonable to suppose that those individuals who suffer from serious or pervasive failures to have their basic security needs met will be relatively likely to resort to "drastic" measures to avoid growth challenges.

Third, let us suggest that it is unlikely that all (or even many) forms of psychological deviance are the direct *result* of excuse-making or are initially motivated by excuse-making needs. It seems more likely that the excuse value of psychological symptoms and/or behavioral deviance are "discovered," either vicariously or through personal experience. A depressed individual, for example, may learn that friends and relatives rally around with support and concern when he or she acts depressed. Another individual may discover that having an alcoholic "blackout" effectively frustrates others' efforts to blame him or her for actions that took place during the "lost" time. By the same token, a woman may discover that she can literally get away with murder when she acts out her aggressive impulses during the time she is experiencing premenstrual tension (New York Times News Service, December 29, 1981). In this sense, the excuse value of psychological symptoms may be best thought of as a side benefit, albeit one that may help to maintain the symptoms or to increase the likelihood of their recurrence.

Overall Perspective and Conclusions

At this point in our discussion of "excuses gone awry," the reader has patiently followed us through a sometimes convoluted web of examples, theories, findings, and speculations. It seems appropriate, here at the end, to step back a bit and draw out some general notions regarding the role of excuses in psychological problems. The central organizing principle, of course, remains our conviction that motives to preserve, maintain, or safeguard self-esteem are pervasive mediators of behavior. It seems, however, that the purpose or function of any given behavior within an excuse-making context can be fully understood only by appreciating the individual's special vulnerabilities and concerns.

We believe that psychological problems are usually associated with difficulties in maintaining a sense that we can exert meaningful control over our lives and destinies. To feel awash in an ebb and flow of events that is beyond influence can be profoundly disturbing. If failures to succeed on specific tasks and performances threaten us, how much more will failures on the major life projects of work, love, and meaning injure our self-regard? It is no wonder that excuses become an important part of the lives of those who have lost their faith in themselves. Skillfully used, excuses allow them to avoid confronting the possibility of "ultimate" failure and to win reprieves from apparent defeats. Excuses in the context of serious psychopathology or problems in living, we submit, are ways of holding life "at bay" until the possibilities of real victory seem tangible enough to risk engaging in direct battle with the demons of fear and self-doubt.

Helping to bring this state of "tangible possibilities" about is the topic of our next chapter.

REFERENCES

American Psychiatric Association. *Diagnostic and statistical manual of mental disorders.* American Psychiatric Association, 1980.

Ansbacher, H. L., & Ansbacher, R. R. *The individual psychology of Alfred Adler.* New York: Harper & Row, 1967. (Originally published by Basic Books, New York, 1956.)

Artiss, K. *The symptom as communication in schizophrenia.* New York: Grune and Stratton, 1959.

Bach, G. R., & Wyden, P. *The intimate enemy: How to fight fair in love and marriage.* New York: Morrow, 1969.

Bandura, A. *Social learning theory.* Englewood Cliffs, N.J.: Prentice-Hall, 1977.

Batson, C. D. Attribution as a mediator of bias in helping. *Journal of Personality and Social Psychology,* 1975, **32,** 455–466.

Beck, A. T. *Depression: Causes and treatment.* Philadelphia: University of Pennsylvania Press, 1967.

Becker, E. *The denial of death.* New York: Free Press, 1975. (Originally published by the Free Press, New York, 1973.)

Becker, J. Vulnerable self-esteem as a predisposing factor in depressive disorders. In R. A. Depue (Ed.), *The psychobiology of the depressive disorders: Implications for the effects of stress.* New York: Academic Press, 1979.

Belknap, I. *Human problems of a state mental hospital.* New York: McGraw-Hill, 1956.

Berglas, S., & Jones, E. E. Drug choice as a self-handicapping strategy in response to noncontingent success. *Journal of Personality and Social Psychology,* 1978, **36,** 405–417.

Bibring, E. The mechanism of depression. In P. Greenacre (Ed.), *Affective disorders.* New York: International University Press, 1953.

Binswanger, L. *Being-in-the-world: Selected papers of Ludwig Binswanger.* New York: Basic Books, 1963.

Boss, M. *Psychoanalysis and daseinanalysis.* New York: Basic Books, 1963.

Braginsky, B. M., & Braginsky, D. D. Schizophrenic patients in the psychiatric interview: An experimental study of their effectiveness at manipulation. *Journal of Consulting Psychology,* 1967, **21,** 543–547.

Braginsky, B. M., Braginsky, D. D., & Ring, K. *Methods of madness: The mental hospital as a last resort.* New York: Holt, Rinehart & Winston, 1969.

Braginsky, B. M., Grosse, M., & Ring, K. Controlling outcomes through impression-management: An experimental study of the manipulative tactics of mental patients. *Journal of Consulting Psychology,* 1966, **30,** 295–300.

Brown, G. W. The social etiology of depression—London studies. In R. A. Depue (Ed.), *The psychobiology of the depressive disorders: Implications for the effects of stress.* New York: Academic Press, 1979.

Carducci, B. J., & McNeely, J. A. Alcohol and attributions don't mix: The effect of alcohol on alcoholics' and nonalcoholics' attributions of blame for wife abuse. Paper presented at the American Psychological Association Convention, Los Angeles, 1981.

Chodoff, P. The depressive personality. *Archives of General Psychiatry*, 1972, **27**, 666–673.

Conger, J. J. Alcoholism: Theory, problem and challenge. II. Reinforcement theory and the dynamics of alcoholism. *Quarterly Journal of Studies on Alcohol*, 1956, **17**, 296–305.

Coyne, J. C. Toward an interactional description of depression. *Psychiatry*, 1976, **39**, 28–40.

Fenichel, O. *The psychoanalytic theory of neurosis.* New York: Norton, 1945.

Fontana, A. F., Klein, E. B., Lewis, E., & Levine, L. Presentation of self in mental illness. *Journal of Consulting and Clinical Psychology*, 1968, **32**, 110–119.

Forrest, M. S., & Hokanson, J. E. Depression and autonomic arousal reduction accompanying self-punitive behavior. *Journal of Abnormal Psychology*, 1975, **84**, 346–357.

Frankl, V. E. Dynamics, existence and values. In H. J. Vetter & B. D. Smith (Eds.), *Personality theory: A source book.* New York: Appleton-Century-Crofts, 1971.

Fromm, E. *Escape from freedom.* New York: Avon Books, 1964. (Originally published by Holt, Rinehart & Winston, 1941.)

Gelles, R. J. *The violent home.* Beverly Hills, Calif.: Sage Publications, 1972.

Gero, G. The construction of depression. *International Journal of Psycho-Analysis*, 1936, **17**, 423–461.

Goffman, E. *The presentation of self in everyday life.* New York: Doubleday, 1959.

Goffman, E. *Asylums.* Garden City, N.Y.: Anchor Books, 1961.

Haley, J. *Strategies of psychotherapy.* New York: Grune and Stratton, 1963.

Hall, C. S., & Lindzey, G. *Theories of personality.* New York: Wiley, 1957.

Hamilton, M. Symptoms and assessment of depression. In E. S. Paykel (Ed.), *Handbook of affective disorders.* New York: Guilford Press, 1982.

Hammen, C. L., & Krantz, S. Effect of success and failure on depressive cognitions. *Journal of Abnormal Psychology*, 1976, **85**, 577–586.

Higgins, R. L. Experimental investigations of tension reduction models of alcoholism. In G. Goldstein & C. Neuringer (Eds.), *Empirical studies of alcoholism.* Cambridge, Mass.: Ballinger, 1976.

Horney, K. *Neurosis and human growth.* New York: Norton, 1950.

Jones, E. E., & Berglas, S. Control of attributions about the self through self-handicapping strategies: The appeal of alcohol and the role of underachievement. *Personality and Social Psychology Bulletin*, 1978, **4**, 200–206.

Kaplan, H. B. *Deviant behavior in defense of self.* New York: Academic Press, 1980.

Krantz, S., & Hammen, C. L. Assessment of cognitive bias in depression. *Journal of Abnormal Psychology*, 1979, **88**, 611–619.

Lang, A. R., Goeckner, D. J., Adesso, V. J., & Marlatt, G. A. Effects of alcohol on aggression in male social drinkers. *Journal of Abnormal Psychology*, 1975, **84**, 509–518.

Lang, A. R., Searles, J., Lauerman, R., & Adesso, V. Expectancy, alcohol, and sex guilt as determinants of interest in and reaction to sexual stimuli. *Journal of Abnormal Psychology*, 1980, **89**, 644–653.

Langer, E. J., & Abelson, R. P. A patient by any other name . . . : Clinician group differences and labeling bias. *Journal of Consulting and Clinical Psychology*, 1974, **42**, 4–9.

Lewinsohn, P. M., Mischel, W., Chaplin, W., & Barton, R. Social competence and depression: The role of illusory self-perceptions. *Journal of Abnormal Psychology*, 1980, **89**, 203–212.

Lobitz, W. C., & Post, R. D. Parameters of self-reinforcement and depression. *Journal of Abnormal Psychology*, 1979, **88**, 33–41.

Ludwig, A. M., & Farrelly, F. The code of chronicity. *Archives of General Psychiatry*, 1966, **15**, 562–568.

Ludwig, A. M., & Farrelly, F. The weapons of insanity. *American Journal of Psychotherapy*, 1967, **21**, 737–749.

MacAndrew, E., & Edgerton, R. B. *Drunken comportment*. Chicago: Aldine, 1969.

Marlatt, G. A., & Rohsenow, D. J. The think-drink effect. *Psychology Today*, 1981, **15**, 61–64ff.

Maslow, A. H. *Motivation and personality*. New York: Harper & Row, 1954.

Maslow, A. H. *Toward a psychology of being*. New York: Van Nostrand-Reinhold, 1968.

May, R. Contributions of existential psychotherapy. In R. May, E. Angel, & H. F. Ellenberger (Eds.), *Existence: A new dimension in psychiatry and psychology*. New York: Basic Books, 1958.

McCaghy, C. H. Drinking and deviance disavowal: The case of child molesters. *Social Problems*, 1968, **16**, 43–49.

McClelland, D. C., Davis, W. N., Kalin, R., & Wanner, E. *The drinking man*. New York: Free press, 1972.

Mendelson, J. H., La Dou, J., & Solomon, P. Experimentally induced chronic intoxication and withdrawal in alcoholics. Part 3. Psychiatric findings. *Quarterly Journal of Studies on Alcohol*, 1964, Supplement No. 2, 40–52.

Millon, T. *Disorders of personality: DSM-III: Axis II*. New York: Wiley, 1981.

Mowrer, O. H. *Learning theory and behavior*. New York: Wiley, 1960.

Mowrer, O. H. *The crisis in psychiatry and religion*. Princeton, N.J.: Van Nostrand, 1961.

Nathan, P. E., & O'Brien, J. S. An experimental analysis of the behavior of alcoholics and nonalcoholics during prolonged experimental drinking: A necessary precursor of behavior therapy? *Behavior Therapy*, 1971, **2**, 455–476.

Nelson, R. E., & Craighead, W. E. Selective recall of positive and negative feedback, self-control behaviors, and depression. *Journal of Abnormal Psychology*, 1977, **86**, 379–388.

Nemiah, J. C. *Foundations of psychopathology*. New York: Oxford University Press, 1961.

New York Times News Service. PTM hormonal problems used as defense. *Lawrence (Kansas) Journal-World*, 1981, December 29, p. 6.

Oliver, J. M., & Williams, G. The psychology of depression as revealed by attribution of causality in college students. *Cognitive Therapy and Research,* 1979, **3,** 355–360.

Patterson, C. H. *Theories of counseling and psychotherapy.* New York: Harper & Row, 1980.

Peterson, C. Uncontrollability and self-blame in depression: Investigation of the paradox in a college population. *Journal of Abnormal Psychology,* 1979, **88,** 620–624.

Platt, B. Perceived adjustment and positivity of self-presentation as determinants of others' public and private evaluations. Unpublished doctoral dissertation, Miami University, 1977.

Prochaska, J. O. *Systems of psychotherapy: A transtheoretical analysis.* Homewood, Ill: Dorsey, 1979.

Rado, S. The problem of melancholia. *International Journal of Psycho-Analysis,* 1928, **9,** 420–438.

Rank, O. *Will therapy and truth and reality.* New York: Knopf, 1945.

Richardson, D. C., & Campbell, J. L. Alcohol and wife abuse: The effect of alcohol on attributions of blame for wife abuse. *Personality and Social Psychology Bulletin,* 1980, **6,** 51–56.

Rogers, C. R. *Client-centered therapy.* Boston: Houghton Mifflin, 1965. (Originally published by the Riverside Press, Cambridge, Mass., 1951.)

Rosen, M. A dual model of obsessional neurosis. *Journal of Consulting and Clinical Psychology,* 1975, **43,** 453–459.

Rosenhan, D. L. On being sane in insane places. *Science,* 1973, **179,** 250–258.

Sarbin, T. R., & Mancuso, J. C. *Schizophrenia: Medical diagnosis or moral verdict?* New York: Pergamon Press, 1980.

Scheff, T. J. *Being mentally ill: A sociological theory.* Chicago: Aldine, 1971.(Originally published by Aldine, Publishing Company, Chicago, 1966.)

Schlenker, B. R. *Impression management: The self-concept, social identity, and interpersonal relations.* Monterey, Calif.: Brooks/ Cole, 1980.

Seligman, M. E. P. *Helplessness: On depression, development, and death.* San Francisco: Freeman, 1975.

Shaw, B. Stress and depression: A cognitive perspective. In R. W. J. Neufeld (Ed.), *Psychological stress and psychopathology.* New York: McGraw-Hill, 1982.

Skinner, B. F. Are theories of learning necessary? *Psychological Bulletin,* 1950, **57,** 193–216.

Snell, J. E., Rosenwald, R. J., & Robey, A. The wifebeater's wife: A study of family interaction. *Archives of General Psychiatry,* 1964, **11,** 107–113.

Snyder, C. R. "A patient by any other name" revisited: Maladjustment or attributional locus of problem. *Journal of Consulting and Clinical Psychology,* 1977, **45,** 101–103.

Snyder, C. R., Shenkel, R. J., & Schmidt, A. Effects of role perspective and psychiatric history on diagnostic locus of problem. *Journal of Consulting and Clinical Psychology,* 1976, **44,** 467–472.

Snyder, C. R., & Smith, T. W. Symptoms as self-handicapping strategies: The virtues of old wine in a new bottle. In G. Weary & H. L. Mirels (Eds.), *Integrations of clinical and social psychology.* New York: Oxford University Press, 1982.

Steffenhagen, R. A. Drug use and related phenomena: An Adlerian approach. *Journal of Individual Psychology,* 1974, **30,** 238–250.

Stone, L. J., & Hokanson, J. E. Arousal reduction via self-punitive behavior. *Journal of Personality and Social Psychology,* 1969, **12,** 72–79.

Strack, S., & Coyne, J. C. Social confirmation of dysphoria: Shared and private reactions to depression. *Journal of Personality and Social Psychology,* 1983, **44,** 798–806.

Szasz, T. S. *Law, liberty, and psychiatry.* New York: Macmillan, 1963.

Tillich, P. *The courage to be.* New Haven, Conn.: Yale University Press, 1952.

Tucker, J. A., Vuchinich, R. E., & Sobell, M. B. Alcohol consumption as a self-handicapping strategy. *Journal of Abnormal Psychology,* 1981, **90,** 220–230.

Ullmann, L. P., & Krasner, L. *Case studies in behavior modification.* New York: Holt, Rinehart & Winston, 1965.

Ullmann, L. P., & Krasner, L. *A psychological approach to abnormal behavior.* Englewood Cliffs, N.J.: Prentice-Hall, 1969.

Wahlroos, S. *Excuses: How to spot them, deal with them, and stop using them.* New York: Macmillan, 1981.

Warren, N. T. Self-esteem and sources of cognitive bias in the evaluation of past performance. *Journal of Consulting and Clinical Psychology,* 1976, **44,** 966–975.

Wilson, G. T., & Abrams, D. Effects of alcohol on social anxiety and physiological arousal: Cognitive versus pharmacological processes. *Cognitive Therapy and Research,* 1977, **1,** 195–210.

Wilson, G. T., & Lawson, D. M. Expectancies, alcohol, and sexual arousal in male social drinkers. *Journal of Abnormal Psychology,* 1976, **85,** 587–594.

Yalom, I. D. *Existential psychotherapy.* New York: Basic Books, 1980.

Zimbardo, P. G., & Radl, S. *The shy child.* New York: McGraw-Hill, 1981.

CHAPTER 9

Interventions for Excuses

Neurosis and psychosis are modes of expression for human beings who have lost courage. Any-one who has acquired this much insight . . . will thenceforth refrain from undertaking with per-sons in this state of discouragement tedious excursions into mysterious regions of the psyche.

ALFRED ADLER *(in Ansbacher & Ansbacher, 1967, p. 343)*

Excuses as Real Problems

The previous chapter developed the thesis that excuse-making and psycho-pathology are intimately intertwined. Similarly, a variety of clinical examples were presented in support of the notion that excuses also contribute to and complicate more ordinary problems in living. We saw that excuses may be re-garded as problems in and of themselves (e.g., the learning model) when their use results in negative consequences, that they may be regarded as "symptoms" of more fundamental psychological problems (e.g., the psychoanalytic model), and that they may be regarded as basic attempts to deal with the uniquely human dilemmas that are inherent in our existence (e.g., the existential model). Given the myriad forms that excuse-making takes and the diversity of roles that excuse-making plays in our lives, it is no surprise that the bounds of mod-eration occasionally are trespassed and that excuses become a cause for con-cern—and a focus for therapeutic intervention. The goal of this chapter is to examine some of the therapeutic issues posed by excuses and to outline a vari-ety of therapeutic intervention strategies for dealing with those that have "gone awry."

Orientation of the Present Chapter

This chapter is written primarily with a professional audience in mind, al-though individuals without a professional stake in dealing therapeutically with excuse-making may find certain suggestions and ideas helpful in their personal lives. The orientation throughout the discussion of interventions for excuses is eclectic; techniques and strategies that have been derived from a variety of the-oretical perspectives are surveyed. In this sense, there is little that is unique or "new" about the suggestions presented here. Perhaps the most innovative aspect of the following discussion is that the unifying and organizing themes are the nature of excuse-making, as it is conceptualized in this book, and the forms of maladaption that excuse-making may take.

Ends Before Beginnings

Interventions designed to effect behavior change serve best when they are derived from a theoretical framework that provides a basis for understanding the function of the targeted behavior in the individual's life and for specifying the types of changes that are desirable and maintainable. One doesn't have to take the position that all emotional and behavioral problems are "symptoms" of underlying and deep-seated psychic conflicts to appreciate that there are reasons for most of the things we do and feel. Similarly, one doesn't have to invoke the principle of "symptom substitution" to understand that simply eliminating a problem behavior may be folly—either because it is counterproductive or because it is nearly impossible to do so without taking into account its role in the individual's life.

It is naive to believe that excuse-related problems can be treated by simply eliminating excuse-making. In this chapter we suggest that approaches to the effective treatment of excuse-related difficulties must, of necessity, be highly individualized and based on a conceptual understanding of the issues involved in each case. The first section develops this thesis through a brief review of the therapeutic *goals* (ends) deemed appropriate by each of the theoretical perspectives on excuses addressed in the previous chapter. In subsequent sections our attention turns first to the business of making some suggestions designed to help the interested clinician *assess* the excuse-making behavior of his or her clients. Next we turn to the matter of presenting a variety of intervention *strategies* (means) by which to achieve the goals of treatment deemed to be appropriate once a client's excuse-making behavior has been sufficiently understood. Finally, we devote some time to a discussion of the problem of excuse-bolstered resistance to therapeutic change and to some ways of dealing with it.

THE QUESTION OF "ENDS"

The Psychoanalytic Model

At a general level, the central goal of orthodox Freudian psychoanalysis is to make the unconscious conscious. This goal is a direct derivative of the central tenets of Freudian theory with its fundamental assumptions of psychic causality and unconscious processes. As pointed out in Chapter 8, psychoanalytic theory holds that each individual's behavior is determined by a complex interplay of unconscious, intrapsychic dynamics. Libidinal and aggressive instincts from the id constantly seek expression and gratification but are opposed by societal strictures and prohibitions as embodied in the superego. The ego is left to mediate this conflict and engages in ego-defensive operations as it attempts to gratify the id's needs in ways which do not invite the punitive wrath of the superego. The ego's utilization of defensive operations is so pervasive and extensive that Maddi (1972) observed that literally *all* behavior can be properly regarded as defensive from the Freudian perspective.

The central importance of raising unconscious processes to consciousness can be readily appreciated by understanding that, to the extent that psychic energy is bound up in keeping unconscious contents from becoming conscious, the individual is functioning inefficiently and is hindered from meeting his or her needs in a reality-oriented fashion. When, through the process of psychoanalysis, the individual achieves insight into the nature of the (formerly) unconscious forces determining his or her behavior, the energy that was bound up in repressing those unconscious contents becomes available for more productive use. This leads us to a second important goal of Freudian psychoanalysis—the substitution of more sophisticated and enabling ego defenses for more primitive and disabling ones.

Although the goal of making the unconscious conscious is never fully realizable, even in the most ideal of circumstances, the individual who has achieved insight into the nature of some of his or her basic intrapsychic conflicts is in a far stronger position to love and work productively. Insight allows such primitive ego defenses as repression to be eschewed in favor of more enabling defenses such as sublimation wherein the individual expresses and seeks gratification for his or her instinctual needs in ways that promote self-love, social regard, and cultural achievement (Freud, 1930). Rather than repressing and denying gratification for primitive sexual and aggressive urges, the individual channels those urges into socially productive avenues such as work, love, art, and play. The difference between the "normal" and"neurotic" individual is not that the former is less defensive than the latter, but rather that the former uses "better" defenses.

Finally, in line with our primary focus on excuse-making as a means of avoiding painful injuries to self-esteem, an important goal in the treatment of excuse-making from the psychoanalytic perspective is that of reducing the "severity" of the superego. To the extent that the individual has introjected overly harsh or restrictive standards of conduct, ego-defensive excuse-making becomes more likely. When the individual's behavior, thoughts, or fantasies violate the introjected values and standards of parents, as embodied in the superego, the ego is "punished" with feelings of guilt and self-hate and is likely to respond with such defenses as rationalization, projection, and denial (see Chapter 8). Consequently, treatment of the individual who engages in extensive ego-defensive excuse-making will probably need to focus on achieving insight into the libidinal and aggressive conflicts that characterized the phallic developmental period when the superego was formed. Ideally, this would enable the individual to reevaluate the neurotic and childlike strictures that characterize overly harsh superegos and, through an act of choice, to replace them with more mature and functional guidelines for conduct.

The Social-Analytic Models

Karen Horney

Although Horney rejected Freud's mechanistic and biological view of human personality in favor of a more humanistic and interpersonal attitude, she agreed that insight and self-understanding were the fundamental goals of treatment on the path to "self-realization." As she put it, "The road of analytic therapy is an old one, advocated time and again throughout human history. In the terms of Socrates and the Hindu philosophy, among others, it is the *road to reorientation through self-knowledge*" (1950, p. 341).

In contrast to Freud's pessimistic determinism, Horney advocated the optimistic (and humanistic) view "that curative forces are inherent in the mind as they are in the body, and that in cases of disorders of body or mind the physician merely gives a helping hand to remove the harmful and to support the healing forces" (1950, p. 248). This led her to view psychotherapy as consisting of both "disillusioning" and constructive processes. The early goal of therapy is to promote the undermining of the client's neurotic pride system (see Chapter 8) so that he or she becomes increasingly disillusioned with and aware of the futility and limitations associated with the vain striving to realize the "idealized" self. With this process of disillusionment comes a weakening of the client's resistance to change: "The therapeutic value of the disillusioning process lies in the possibility that, with the weakening of the obstructive forces, the constructive forces of the real self have a chance to grow" (p. 348).

In simplified form, then, Horney viewed the goals of therapy as (1) aiding the client in overcoming the obstacles preventing the self-healing process by encouraging disillusionment with the "search for glory," and (2) assisting and strengthening the developing self-healing process by providing direction, focus, and encouragement as the client struggles with the conflicts along the road to health.

An inevitable part of any successful struggle for self-realization is a growing ability to accept responsibility for what one is rather than to externalize responsibility (i.e., make excuses) for what one has failed to become. Successive steps along the road to assuming this responsibility are occasioned by "repercussions" in the form of renewed feelings of self-hate and self-contempt as the individual confronts the discrepancies between his or her real and idealized selves and chooses to affirm the former. However, the therapist can offer support through encouragement that such repercussions are sure signs that the individual is on the right track and that the distressed feelings are "growing pains."

> Each time the meaning of a repercussion is understood by the patient he comes out of it stronger than before. The repercussions gradually become shorter and less intense. Conversely the good periods become more definitely constructive. The prospect of his changing and growing becomes a tangible possibility within his reach. (1950, pp. 362–363)

Alfred Adler

Ansbacher and Ansbacher (1967) divide the general goals of Adler's approach to therapy into three parts: understanding the specific lifestyle of the client, explaining the client to himself or herself, and strengthening the client's social interest. The first two parts relate to a general goal shared by most forms of psychological treatment—that of consciousness raising or increasing insight. The last part, increasing the client's social interest, derives specifically from Adler's unique philosophy of the nature of people. We address the three goals of Adler's approach to treatment sequentially.

Adler believed that each individual's approach to dealing with the problems of living (the lifestyle) was unique and the product of a creative "self." As a consequence, he espoused what we would now call a phenomenological approach to understanding people. He believed that therapists could fully appreciate clients' problems only by intuitively understanding their idiosyncratic ways of viewing the world and themselves and by having an individualized awareness of their superiority goals and guiding beliefs (fictions) about how to attain those goals:

> The partially unconscious course of the neurosis, which contradicts reality, is explained primarily by the unswerving tendency of the patient to arrive at his goal. The contradiction to reality, that is, to the logical demands of society, is related to the limited experiences and the peculiar human relationships which were effective at the time of the construction of the life-plan in early childhood. Insight into the meaning of this plan is best acquired through artistic and intuitive empathy with the essential nature of the patient. (Adler, in Ansbacher & Ansbacher, 1967, p. 328)

Once the therapist has achieved and verified an understanding of the client, the second major goal of treatment is explaining the client to himself or herself. First, this involves aiding clients in becoming aware of and understanding their goals of superiority (see Chapter 8):

> There must be uncovered, step by step, the unattainable goal of superiority over all; the purposeful concealment of this goal; the all-dominating, direction-giving power of the goal; the patient's lack of freedom and hostility toward mankind,

which are determined by the goal. (Adler, in Ansbacher & Ansbacher, 1967, p. 333)

Second, clients are led to understand how their specific "styles of life" operate in service of their superiority goals. Adler felt that this was "the most important component in therapy. The reason for this is that the life-plan in its entirely can be kept intact only if the patient succeeds in withdrawing it from his own criticism and understanding" (Adler, in Ansbacher & Ansbacher, 1967, p. 334).

The final goal of Adler's approach to treatment is reawakening and strengthening the client's "social interest." Adler believed that the best approach to giving his clients the courage necessary to eschew their goal of attaining individual superiority and to return to the "useful side of life" was to establish a truly human relationship with them and to inspire them through his own display of social interest. First of all, therapists must frustrate their clients' efforts to place them in a superior position because to fail to do so would only stimulate the clients' neurotic needs to bring down or defeat them. Second, therapists must establish their benign and unselfish interest in the clients' welfare: "For the psychologist the first rule is to win the patient; the second is never to worry about his own success; if he does so, he forfeits it. The psychotherapist must lose all thought of himself and all sensitiveness about his ascendency, and must never demand anything of the patient" (Adler, in Ansbacher & Ansbacher, 1967, p. 341). Third, Adler believed that it was important to bolster clients' courage and social interest through the continued use of encouragement:

Altogether, in every step of treatment, we must not deviate from the path of encouragement. This is in accordance with the conviction of Individual Psychology, by which so much untenable vanity feels offended, that "everybody can do everything" with the exception of amazingly high achievement, about the structure of which we cannot say very much anyway. (Adler, in Ansbacher & Ansbacher, 1967, p. 342)

As Ansbacher and Ansbacher (1967) point out, Adler believed that once a client has gained in courage and social interest and has come to understand his or her basic mistakes in striving for individual superiority, he or she will choose to no longer make those mistakes.

Mowrer's Moral Model

Although Mowrer did not develop a system of psychotherapy based on his moral model of neurosis, what he regarded as important goals of psychotherapy is clear. Based on his belief that neurosis and "functional psychosis" result from the moral erosion and psychic self-alienation that (he believed) accompany the commission of unacknowledged misdeeds, Mowrer (1961) focused on the importance of "confession" as the first step in redeeming oneself. The acceptance of personal responsibility and accountability that is implicit in the concept of "confession" forms the foundation for repairing the individual's relationship to himself or herself as well as to others. For Mowrer, however, mere confession would not suffice.

As we pointed out in Chapter 8, Mowrer believed that one of the reasons psychoanalytic treatment was unproductive is that it failed to help the analysand to move beyond free association (confession) to atonement. Mowrer (1961) speculated that some types of psychopathology (e.g., depression) may even be regarded as forms of self-punishment—in effect, self-imposed "sentences" designed to help the individual "pay" for his or her guilty deeds. Indeed, Mowrer drew a clear analogy between moral and criminal codes in terms of the importance of restitution:

> Now is the moral law less demanding than the civil and criminal codes? Does conscience have less rectitude than a court? Unless we can answer the question affirmatively, it follows that in the moral realm, no less than in law, confession is not enough and must be accompanied by restitution. This possibility has been generally neglected in our time and may account for widespread confusion and misdirected therapeutic and redemptive effort. (p. 100)

In summary, Mowrer's (1961) guilt theory of neurosis directly implies that successful therapy should be directed toward eliciting "confessions" (acceptance and acknowledgment of personal responsibility for transgressions) and toward assisting and encouraging individuals to atone for or make reparations for the negative consequences of their acts. Only in this way, he believed, can people unburden themselves of the moral guilt that severs their connectedness to others and repair the moral corrosion that alienates them from themselves.

Humanistic Models

Carl Rogers and Client-Centered Therapy

In contrast to most systems of psychotherapy, the goal of client-centered therapy is not to change the client in any particular way. Indeed, Rogers' system of client-centered therapy often is referred to as "nondirective" therapy. Probably the only true goal of orthodox client-centered therapy is for the therapist to establish a therapeutic climate that doesn't obstruct the client's own inherent tendency to self-actualize.

As described in Chapter 8, Rogers (1965) held that each individual has "one basic tendency and striving—to actualize, maintain, and enhance" itself (p. 487). Rogers advocated the view that the mind, just as the body, has self-healing tendencies that must only be unleashed to express themselves. In addition,

Rogers believed that the self-actualizing force in each individual is capable of directing its own growth. Indeed, it is essential that it do so.

Since Rogers held that the individual's internal growth force will automatically exert itself when external obstacles to such self-healing are absent, the focus of the client-centered therapist is on removing obstacles to growth: "Under certain conditions, involving primarily complete absence of any threat to the self-structure, experiences which are inconsistent with it may be perceived, and examined, and the structure of self revised to assimilate and include such experiences" (p. 517).

Since Rogers' theory of psychopathology implicates the destructive role of introjected "conditions of worth" in the individual's self-structure (see Chapter 8), the therapist's main task (goal) is to avoid imposing any conditions of worth on the client within the therapeutic relationship. Three fundamental therapist attitudes or therapeutic conditions are essential to the therapy process: (1) the therapist must experience unconditional positive regard for the client, (2) the therapist must experience an accurate empathic understanding of the client's experiences and communicate this understanding, and (3) the therapist must be "genuine" in the relationship. Rogers held that if these three facilitating conditions are established in a therapy relationship, therapeutic change and growth in the client are *inevitable* within the relationship. Central to such change is the client's growing ability to be aware of and to integrate all aspects of his or her self-experience into the self-structure and to turn from an external locus of self-evaluation to an internal locus of self-evaluation. From the perspective of excuse theory, an important aspect of this process of self-actualization is the individual's growing ability to "own" responsibility for his or her behaviors and feelings.

Abraham Maslow

In most fundamental regards, the views of Rogers and Maslow are similar. Some significant, though perhaps peripheral, differences do exist, however. Whereas Rogers held that the urge toward self-actualization was the one core tendency and striving in the human organism, Maslow (1968) held that there were *two* core tendencies: the urge toward self-actualization, and the urge to satisfy physical and psychological survival (safety) needs. Both theorists were in essential agreement on the characteristics of the self-actualized individual, on the idea that the basic nature of humankind is not essentially "evil," and on the idea that the individual's natural movement toward growth and self-actualization falls on hard times through the imposition of obstacles and impediments by the physical and social environment. Because of these similarities in theory and orientation, we will dispense with a more detailed and separate rendering of the goals of psychotherapy from the perspective of Maslow's theory. Suffice it to say for our purposes that, for Maslow, the road to personal fulfillment lies in the direction of removing impediments from the path of the individual's inherent actualizing tendencies (Maddi, 1972).

The Existential Model

As we discussed in Chapter 8, the avoidance of the anxiety that inevitably confronts those who remain open to living an authentic existence takes many forms. This avoidance expresses itself in many instances as psychopathology and, in the sense that it is a retreat from responsibility, manifests itself in a variety of excuse-making strategies. Given that the avoidance of authenticity is at the core of psychopathology from the existential perspective, it follows directly that the achievement of authenticity is the "central concern of psychotherapy" (Bugental, 1965, p. 45).

One of the cardinal features of inauthenticity is lying about ourselves and the nature of our existence. The lies we tell ourselves (excuses we make for ourselves) promote the myth that we are "objects" with limited choices and therefore limited responsibility. An antidote for psychopathology and inauthenticity, then, is honesty—an openness to being *fully* aware of the present moment, to seeing ourselves as "subjects" with the ability to choose how to live in the moment, and to taking the responsibility for our choices, for the direction of our lives, and for "constituting" the very world in which we live.

Achieving an honest self-awareness involves facing directly our mortality, our isolation, our freedom, our need to act, our choices, and our responsibility for creating our lives and meaning. Since acknowledging these things leads to the experience of existential anxiety, achieving an authentic existence also means learning to accept this anxiety and to transform it into a creative and affirmative force in our lives. There is no Pollyanna-like optimism here. The choice between authenticity and inauthenticity is a choice between existential anxiety and existential guilt. Though the choice may seem harsh, the goal of existential psychotherapists is to help their clients confront (become aware of) the reality of it and to help them find the strength and courage to choose anxiety—and the growth and richness of experience that such a choice makes possible. As Ernest Becker (1975) observed, "In some way one must pay with life and consent daily to die, to give oneself up to the risks and dangers of the world, allow oneself to be engulfed and used up. Otherwise one ends up *as though dead* in trying to avoid life and death" (p. 210).

The Behavioral Model

Since the general learning theory view is that all complex behavior is learned, it can be safely said that the general goal of learning-based approaches to the treatment of maladaptive behavior is to help the individual learn more adaptive ways of behaving. How this general goal is approached within the context of any given case, however, is highly variable and dependent on the nature of the specific behavior(s) and environment(s) involved.

As we noted in Chapter 8, excuse-making behavior would not be regarded as either inherently adaptive or maladaptive by classical learning theory advocates. Rather, the desirability of excuse-making would be evaluated on the basis of its social consequences. Any behavior that evokes negative reactions (punishment) from the environment or results in a decrease in the amount of positive reinforcement received would be regarded as more or less maladaptive (Ullmann & Krasner, 1969). Conversely, any behavior that evokes positive reactions (reinforcement) or results in a decrease in the amount of punishment received would be regarded as more or less adaptive. Consequently, a classical behavioral therapist would not be inclined to regard excuse-making as a problem behavior unless the individual could receive more positive reinforcement (or less punishment) by engaging in alternative behaviors. In any event, the behavior therapist's primary concern would be helping the individual learn the most effective ways available to cope with his or her particular circumstances. This could very well include teaching excuse-making (or more effective excuse-making) if it seemed likely that doing so would enhance the individual's adaptation.

The issue of excuse-making becomes a little more complicated when viewed from the perspective of contemporary social learning theory. Social learning theory, in contrast with classical learning theory, is concerned with self-regulatory processes in addition to environmental contingencies (e.g., Bandura, 1977b). The notion that individuals have internal standards for performance and generate self-reinforcements and punishments for their conduct has some important implications for the behavioral treatment of excuse-making. The idea that individuals actively construe their environments (i.e., interpret and "make sense" of them from their own idiosyncratic vantage points) and interact with them in a reciprocally determining fashion also has important implications. Behavior therapists who operate out of a social learning framework not only have to be concerned with the reinforcement contingencies that characterize the individual's environment, but they also have to be concerned with the individual's personal interpretation of that environment as well as with the individual's reactions to his or her own behavior.

As a result of the emphasis placed on cognitive mediating processes by social learning theory, therapeutic interventions derived from the theory frequently are aimed at altering the individual's thoughts (cognitions) about things. For example, an individual who makes excuses in order to avoid situations that are *objectively* benign but *subjectively* threatening may need only to have his or her beliefs about the situations altered to relinquish excuse-making. By the same token, individuals who engage in excuse-bolstered avoidance of situations in which they feel a low sense of self-efficacy due to unrealistically high internal standards of performance may need only to reappraise or modify their personal standards to be able to relinquish their excuse-making. Of course, it may also be important for such individuals to learn to improve their behavioral skills in such situations.

The variety of situations in which excuse-making may be a focus of behavioral intervention and the number of possible specific goals of such interventions is too great to enable us to elaborate all of them. The essential point we would like to make about the goals of behavioral interventions for excuse-making is that such goals will virtually always be oriented toward helping individuals to learn more effective skills for dealing with their life circumstances. Such skills may be overtly behavioral (e.g., improved communication skills) or they may be covert and "cognitive" (e.g., improved ability to establish reasonable internal standards for performance or to discriminate threatening from nonthreatening situations). In many, if not most, interventions for excuse-making, the most effective form of treatment will aim at improving both overt behavioral and covert cognitive coping skills.

Conclusions Regarding Therapy Goals

Despite the obviously selective and cursory nature of the preceding review of therapy goals, we hope that we have succeeded in representing at least the major themes that are important to the viewpoints surveyed. Moreover, we would like to suggest that there is a compelling commonality among the various "schools" of thought when one looks beyond the differences in language and terminology to "grasp" the underlying concepts. After all, the different systems of psychotherapy have evolved from the study of the same subject matter—the human "critter" with all its foibles, peculiarities, and unique potentials. It is no wonder, then, that we have theorists struggling to understand the same phenomena and arriving at idiosyncratic but complementary views. There are, undoubtedly, many who will take exception to our characterizations of the various schools of thought and to our selection of ideas to emphasize. Fault may also be found with our following selection of those therapy goals that we believe are "generic" in the sense that they are shared by most, if not all, of the theories reviewed.

In keeping with our eclectic stance, we propose that the broadest goal that characterizes all therapy approaches is that they aim to help people overcome the obstacles they encounter on their individual roads to growth, fulfillment, and happiness. Within this general context, several more specific common aims may be elaborated: raising consciousness; learning new, more adaptive, ways of behaving; and revising counterproductive self-referential schemes. We believe that these three aims of treatment provide a meaningful framework for thinking about interventions for excuses. Furthermore, we hold that other possible common aims of therapy systems (e.g., enhancing responsibility assumption, increasing choice potentials, fostering the courage needed to risk the hazards of change) may be realizable in full or in part as a function of effecting those aims listed above. Consequently, in our subsequent discussion of specific therapeutic strategies and techniques for dealing with excuse-making, our presentation will be organized around those three therapy goals that we feel are most central to the issues at hand.

Before diving into a discussion of how to go about intervening in cases of problematic excuse-making, we would first like to spend some time on the matter of assessing excuse-making. As we pointed out at the beginning of this chapter, effective interventions must be based on an understanding of the issues and dynamics involved in the *individual* case. We have just completed a review of several theoretical perspectives on how therapeutic interventions would address cases *in general.* What follows now is a section designed to give the interested clinician some ideas on how he or she may go about understanding the use of excuses by particular clients.

THE QUESTION OF ASSESSMENT

When setting out to change something, it helps to know what it is! Most problem-solving efforts are preceded by a period of "sizing up" the situation. In the psychotherapeutic enterprise, this "sizing up" process is more commonly referred to as "assessment." Ideally, an assessment should lead to an understanding of the client's particular strengths and weaknesses as well as an appreciation of the relevant characteristics of his or her environment. Clinicians typically have a variety of strategies available to them to aid in the assessment process: interviews, demographic information questionnaires, personality tests (e.g., MMPI, Rorschach, TAT), specific self-report measures (e.g., depression scales, anxiety scales, personal interest scales), behavioral observation, and skills tests (e.g., intelligence tests). When it comes to assessing excuse-making, however, the formal options are limited. As we discussed in Chapter 6, there currently are no standard or published assessment *instruments* that have been developed specifically to aid in the assessment of excuse-making. There are, nevertheless, some suggestions we can make to help the interested clinician improvise. First we turn our attention to identifying a number of diagnostic signs of excuse-making that can be observed within the context of a therapeutic relationship.

Signs of Strategic Excusing

Informal assessment of clients' problems, strengths, changes, and the process of therapy itself is an ongoing feature of any therapeutic intervention. The clinician monitors the client's verbalizations and behaviors to detect clues regarding the status and progress of treatment. Clinicians also monitor their own feelings and reactions to clients in order to gain an understanding of the dynamics of the therapeutic relationship. Moreover, clinicians frequently "test" their hunches and ideas by observing their clients' reactions to interpretations, confrontations, feedback, and reflections. These preexisting features of the therapeutic enterprise are superbly amenable to the assessment of much excuse-making behavior.

In the context of discussing the problem of identifying self-handicapping behavior (see Chapter 5), Snyder and Smith (1982) suggest three specific things for which to look. First, they suggest that "clients who emphasize the importance of evaluative arenas on their sense of self-esteem" (pp. 118–119) may be inclined to employ defensive excuse-making strategies in those arenas. Second, they suggest that clients who evidence symptoms in specific situations *may* be employing those symptoms strategically. Such symptoms may be physical, emotional, or behavioral in nature. Third, they point out that clients who self-handicap will admit to weaknesses or deficits. Presumably such deficits would be offered to account for more esteem-threatening problems in other areas. Snyder and Smith also suggest that the clinician may wish "to routinely consider the self-handicapping properties for most all maladaptive behavior patterns" (p. 119). Although the reporting of "symptoms" and the admission of defects may be specific hallmarks of self-handicapping forms of excuses, we would suggest that pronounced concern with esteem-related evaluative arenas will signal the potential involvement of a variety of excuse-making strategies.

In the context of outlining a typical pattern for how "unconsciously manufactured" excuses come about, Sven Wahlroos (1981) also describes some useful clues to the presence of excuse-making. Without detailing all eight of the stages Wahlroos identified, we will attempt to summarize what he reported as important characteristics of "unconscious" excuses. First, excuses are likely to involve faulty reasoning or exonerating motives. The excuse-maker will not recognize the logical flaws and will minimize or overlook contradictions and inconsistencies. Second, the behavior or belief being excused or explained will reflect negatively on the excuse-maker or someone he or she is trying to protect. Third, if the excuse or explanation contains elements of truth, they are likely to be overemphasized. Fourth, if the excuse-maker's logic is challenged, he is likely to "defend it with an emotional intensity that suggests that his feelings of self-worth are at stake, or he may simply become indignant or switch to another explanation" (p. 13). Finally, if the recipient of the excuse asserts that the excuse-maker *is* responsible to some extent, the excuse-maker "is likely to become upset and react with either indignation or denial of responsibility or both" (p. 13).

The above suggestions for detecting excuses are relatively straightforward. However, there are even more basic signs that are common features of psychotherapy. Therapists are routinely confronted with clients who stubbornly resist their best efforts to be helpful. This resistance frequently takes the form of simple, repetitive communications. Amazingly, though, it is often only recognized when we discover our growing sense of frustration. Most clinicians, at some point in their careers, have been reduced to helpless submission by the "yes ... but" of an impassive (and persistent!) client. How many therapists, even after learning their lesson "the hard way," are occasionally tempted to "fly" *just one more* suggestion by a client who has defeated previous ones with a simple "I would but . . ."? Only a few hours prior to drafting these very words, one of the present authors was seeing an adolescent client who *insisted* that he really wanted to talk to his dad about a problem . . . *but* . . . dad was in a bad mood and wouldn't listen. Without belaboring the point further, these are patented, forged-in-fire excuses. Any therapist who encounters them can safely presume that the client is avoiding some threatening action or arena.

"I would like to . . . but I *can't!*" "I want to tell (my husband) how I feel . . . but when I do, it always comes out wrong!" These variations on the "yes . . . but" theme point to some personal deficit in order to avoid doing something. As Adler remarked about the excuse-making client, "To the question, 'What use are you making of your talents?' he answers, 'This thing stops me; I cannot go ahead,' and points to his self-erected barricade" (Adler, in Ansbacher & Ansbacher, 1967, p. 265). Just as commonly, however, clients point the finger at some external cause of their distress or failure. Recently, one of the present authors was supervising a couple therapy case by watching a videotape recording of a session. The wife was lamenting that she *couldn't* restrain herself from becoming hysterical and agitated when she encountered unexpected complications in her activities. Pausing for a moment, her face lit up like she had been struck with a profound realization. "I know what it is! It started back when I was a little girl and it's been the same way ever since. I don't have any trouble any other time, but when something unexpected comes up, I *always* get upset whenever it's hot, humid, and hazy!"

It would be possible to continue elaborating specific "signs" of excuse-making that can be detected through informal methods and through remaining sensitive to what is transpiring in the therapeutic relationship. In a sense, the following section on the use of psychometric approaches to the assessment of excuse-making does just that. In contrast to the preceding suggestions, however, the ones we present next frequently are amenable to being used in the context of employing specific assessment instruments.

The Psychometric Approach

In Chapter 6 we described a number of individual differences measures that may ultimately prove helpful in assessing proneness to excuse-making (e.g., the Locus of Control Scale by Rotter, 1966). We will not review these measures further here. Instead, we would like to address a few additional comments to the problem of identifying those arenas where clients are most likely to employ excuses.

As we pointed out above, Snyder and Smith (1982) suggested that clients who emphasize the importance of evaluative arenas for their self-esteem are likely candidates for excuse-making (self-handicapping). This implies that important clues to locating areas of high excuse-making activity may be obtained from measures of specific types of fear or concern. This is likely to be true of situations where performances may receive negative evaluations (e.g., test situations, interpersonal arenas) and excuses may be generated to lessen the potential impact on self-esteem. It is also likely to be true of situations that do not necessarily involve evaluated performances but may reveal unacceptable weaknesses or arouse excessive fears. People with specific phobias, for example, generate all kinds of "reasons" for avoiding potential encounters with their phobic object or situation. As an illustration, several years ago one of the present authors supervised a doctoral dissertation that examined the relative efficacy of two forms of behavioral treatment for acrophobia (fear of heights; see Pendleton, 1979; also see Pendleton & Higgins, in press). Many of the acrophobic subjects in this study related how they routinely found themselves concocting elaborate "reasons" for refusing attractive social engagements and other opportunities that might place them in situations where their fears would be aroused (e.g., rooftop restaurants, vacations to the Grand Canyon).

The use of psychological assessment instruments to identify specific fears or concerns may be valuable for more than simply pinpointing high excuse-potential arenas. These instruments may also be useful for discerning the types of excuse a client is most likely to employ. As mentioned in Chapter 6, Leary and Schlenker (1981) and Schlenker and Leary (1982) have suggested that people use their fears *as excuses.* Moreover, recent research by one of the present authors and his students indicates that individuals with specific fears are more likely than individuals without those specific fears to use them in a self-handicapping fashion. Snyder, Augelli, and Smith (1983), for example, found that self-reported high shyness males (but not females) were more likely than low shyness males to inflate their reporting of shyness symptoms when they believed that shyness would interfere with the accurate measurement of their social competence. By the same token, Smith, Snyder, and Handelsman (1982) found that high test-anxious females inflated their reporting of test-anxiety symptoms when they believed that test anxiety had been shown to hinder performance on an anticipated test of intelligence. Low text-anxious females did not show this pattern.

As a final example of how measures of specific concerns may serve as a "Geiger counter" for excuses, consider a study reported by Smith, Snyder, and Perkins (1983). These authors selected subjects scoring either "high" or "low" on a measure of hypochondriasis. When led to anticipate being evaluated on a "social intelligence" test which, it was alleged, discriminated against people with a history of physical problems, the high hypochondriasis subjects (but not the low hypochondriasis subjects) inflated their reporting of physical symptoms.

Thus far we have focused on possible ways to assess the use of excuses at a general level (e.g., how to identify that they are happening and where they are most likely to be found). In the following section, we shift our attention to the issue of how to gain a more complete understanding of the roles or functions that specific excuses (or types of excuses) may be serving in the lives of clients.

Assessing the Excuse Itself

Before formulating specific intervention strategies for excuse-making, it is important to determine some of the important parameters of the behavior. Upon close examination, a therapist might well decide that no intervention is necessary or appropriate. One of our frequently repeated views is that some excuses have legitimate uses. Unless one looks carefully before one leaps, one runs some (perhaps small) risk of creating an iatrogenic problem that outweighs the one being treated. Presuming that intervention is deemed to be appropriate, however, we have previously expressed the opinion that excuses (or any behaviors, for that matter) play a role in peoples' lives and that the nature and value of that role must be appreciated before an effective intervention can be accomplished. It is to the end of understanding the "nuts and bolts" of the individual's excuse-making that the specific assessment of excuses should be targeted.

Important questions to ask about any targeted excuse include the following:

1. What is being excused?
2. How central is the excused behavior to the person's self-esteem and how is it related?
3. When does the excuse-making occur and what are the important features of the excuse-making occasions?
4. Where does the excuse-making occur and who is the "critical" consumer of the excuse?
5. What role does the consumer of the excuse play in the excuse-maker's life?
6. How often does the excuse-making occur? Is it an infrequent or pervasive feature of the individual's life?
7. How drastic or extreme is the excuse and, if it is extreme, does the excuse-maker have any appreciation of the fact?
8. What effect does the excuse-making have on the person's interpersonal environment—that is, what are the interpersonal consequences?
9. Is the excuse-making interfering with the individual's ability to profit from important experiences and to adapt to changing conditions? If so, how much?
10. Is the excuse-making interfering with the individual's ability to accurately perceive his or her own behavior and feelings and/or the behavior and feelings of others? If so, how serious is the perceptual distortion?
11. Is there an appropriate or more adaptive alternative to the individual's excuse-making?

On occasion, a therapist may find it useful to enlist the help of the excuse-making client in gathering the data necessary to answer some of these questions. It may also be that this, in itself, is sufficient to have a substantial impact on the behavior. This is probably most likely to be the case when the excuse-making is relatively nonfunctional—that is, it is largely habitual and does not play an important role in helping the individual maintain his or her self-esteem. Therapists engaged in the practice of behavior modification, for example, have long observed that the mere practice of having a client monitor his or her problem behaviors will often have the effect of reducing them (e.g., Kazdin, 1974; McFall, 1970; Sundberg, 1977). Habitual behaviors, including excuses, are often "unconscious" in the sense that the individual does not actively decide to use them. The process of self-monitoring may make the individual sufficiently aware of what he or she is doing to allow active decisions about how to respond.

Engaging a client in some phases of the assessment process and raising his or her awareness of the excuse-making behavior may have benefits that extend beyond merely allowing active decisions about formerly habitual responses. For example, an individual may discover that he or she has been taking the "blame" (i.e., making internal attributions) for things that are more appropriately attributed to other factors or individuals. Consequently, excuses that may have been generated to soften the negative self-relevant implications of the internal attributions can be abandoned. As an illustration of this, an acquaintance of one of the present authors reported having disconcerting interactions with a teacher of hers over a period of several years. There was an awkward, painful quality to her meetings with him and she began finding "reasons" to avoid him. She felt the problem was caused by something about her but couldn't put her finger on what it was. After being prompted to pay close attention to what was happening when she was with the teacher and to observe his behavior with other students as well, she discovered that *he* was acting strangely. Furthermore, she found that other students also felt awkward around him, thereby getting consensual validation of her perceptions. With the increased awareness she derived from closely monitoring her interactions with the teacher, she was able to rid herself of her negative self-attributions and to feel more comfortable about her meetings with him.

As we have attempted to indicate, the goal of assessment with regard to excuse-making is to gain an understanding of the "what," "how," and "why" of any one individual's behavior. By its very nature, the process of assessment is oriented toward the generation of "diagnostic" impressions. Although this is undeniably the case, we argue in the next section that the use of assessments of either a formal or informal nature to generate diagnostic labels (dispositional diagnoses) is to be avoided in the case of excuse-making behavior.

The Importance of Avoiding "Dispositional Diagnosis" of Excuse-Making

A careful reader of the previous sections on assessing excuses will immediately recognize the wisdom of avoiding applying the label of "excuse-maker" to a client ("My therapist says I'm a chronic excuse-maker. How can I be expected to get ahead in life with a problem like that?"). Although there is no empirical evidence that being labeled an "excuse-maker" leads people to go "one up" by using the label itself as an excuse, we have just reviewed some evidence that people who have labeled themselves in certain ways (e.g., "shy," "test anxious") may indeed use that label—or at least the reporting of the behavior—in a defensive fashion (also see our discussion in Chapter 8 on the adverse effects of labeling). Furthermore, there is reason to believe from other sources that making dispositional attributions of dysfunctional behavior to the self may lead to counterproductive increases in the unwanted behavior.

Storms and McCaul (1976) suggested that when individuals interpret unwanted or disturbing behaviors as being caused by something inherent, it leads to an increase in anxiety or emotionality that may worsen the original condition. Furthermore, they suggest that an exacerbation cycle may be established whereby the worsening in the behavior may "confirm" and reinforce the dispositional attribution that leads to even more anxiety, and so on. Although this model seems most plausibly applicable to behaviors that are directly influenced by anxiety (Storms and McCaul focus primarily on insomnia and stuttering as examples), it is reasonable to hypothesize that some analogous process might exist for excuse-making. In fact, Storms and McCaul argue that "any behavior may be subject to an exacerbation cycle if it (a) can lead to negative self-attributions and (b) is further increased by the anxiety those self-attributions may cause" (p. 154). We would argue that making excuses often *is* regarded as "bad form" and that being labeled as an excuse-maker *can* lead to negative self-attributions.

Concluding Comments on Assessment

In this section on the assessment of excuse-making we elaborated on the view expressed throughout this chapter—effective interventions for excuses must be predicated on an understanding of the excuse(s) in the ecology of the individual's personal and interpersonal life. In the following section we take up the task implied by the title of this chapter and present a variety of intervention strategies and methods that may prove helpful in the treatment of individual excuse-makers. Although our primary emphasis is on excuse-making per se, we acknowledge that excuses typically occur as a feature of an individual's broader problems in living and, consequently, interventions designed to deal with them usually must be designed to fit within the context of a more comprehensively oriented treatment plan.

THE QUESTION OF "MEANS"

Following our review at the beginning of this chapter of the types of therapy goals associated with various schools of psychotherapy, we selected three goals that we deemed to be "generic" in the sense that they were shared, in some form, by all of the schools. Although we concluded that there were probably other generic goals, we selected the following three to be addressed more fully in relationship to our discussion of interventions for excuses: raising consciousness; learning new, more adaptive ways of behaving; and revising counterproductive self-referential schemes. Although intervention strategies and techniques designed to address each of these goals may well have implications for one or both of the others, we arrange them into the categories on the basis of where we feel they fit best.

In our presentation of intervention techniques and strategies, we do not attempt to provide a comprehensive cataloguing of all possibilities. Rather, we focus on those having the broadest applicability. Although our goal is to be eclectic in terms of the methods we survey, we must acknowledge that some psychotherapy schools (e.g., behaviorism) have defined a far wider and more diverse variety of intervention techniques than others (e.g., psychoanalysis). As a consequence, the reader will notice some unevenness in how various systems of psychotherapy are represented.

As we noted, our view is that interventions designed to deal with excuse-making will most frequently occur within the context of a broader treatment plan. Accordingly, it is important to be aware that the techniques reviewed below are likely to play an adjunctive role. There will be many instances, however, where a thorough excuse-oriented intervention plan might be sufficient to deal with a client's presenting problems. This seems most likely to be the case with problems stemming from avoidance of important life arenas. Despite the potential importance of a comprehensive discussion of the issues involved in integrating interventions for excuses into a more general treatment plan, space does not permit us to attempt this here. In the final section of this chapter, however, we have some things to say about an issue that eventually confronts clinicians in almost all of their cases—dealing with excuse-based resistance to change. First, though, let us turn to a sequential rendering of the three generic treatment goals that we identify as having special relevance to the treatment of excuse-making behavior.

Raising Consciousness in the Treatment of Excuses

Increasing awareness of excuse-making and the situational and personal issues that motivate it are important components of effective interventions. The clinician will find that raising a client's awareness of the parameters of his or her excuse-making will commonly be intertwined with and parallel to the process of assessment that we discussed earlier in this chapter. In this sense, the assessment of excuse-making is more than just a prelude to effective treatment: it is an integral component of the treatment. Consequently, the distinction we are drawing between assessment and intervention is somewhat arbitrary. Nevertheless, in the interests of facilitating our presentation of consciousness-raising techniques, we discuss them apart from the business of assessment. In doing so, we divide our discussion into the categories of increasing awareness of excuse-making and increasing awareness of factors that lead to excuse-making.

Increasing Awareness of Excuse-Making

Clients will rarely present themselves as having a problem with making excuses. It falls on the shoulders of the clinician to recognize the occurrence of excuses and to decide whether their use merits attention as a therapeutic issue. If the decision is in the affirmative, a variety of options are available. Most obviously, the clinician may elect to "confront" the client with his or her excuse-making and to inquire about it. It is not as important to "label" the behavior as excuse-making as it is to help the client realize that he or she is trying to disown some aspect of his or her behavior, thoughts, or feelings. Indeed, labeling the behavior is likely to arouse defensiveness in instances where it is "motivated" (i.e., it is not simply "habitual"). Consequently, the clinician should consider using forms of confrontation that vary from the relatively "oblique" to the more direct.

The oblique confrontation of excuses may be accomplished in a variety of ways. If the clinician is operating out of a "client-centered" framework, he or she may prefer to work into his or her reflective statements the notion of discomfort with whatever is being excused. For example, in working with a 36-year-old male client who "explained" his frustrating inability to refuse his older brother's frequent requests for money with the statement that the older brother was too upset over his recent divorce to feel up to getting a job, one of the present authors used the following reflective statement: "You seem to be saying that your brother's divorce makes it impossible for you to refuse him, but you're frustrated because you don't feel you should *have* to take care of him." This led to the client's saying that he didn't *have* to give his brother money all the time, but he was afraid that if he didn't, it might mean that he didn't love his brother. As it turned out, this client had a long history of feeling victimized by members of his family but always did as they wanted and rationalized doing so because of what he feared asserting himself would mean. Reflectively confronting his tendency to externalize responsibility for giving in to his brother led to his becoming aware of a pervasive pattern of defensively protecting himself from potential self-criticism.

Oblique confrontation of excuse-making may be more direct than simple reflective statements. In a case cited previously in this chapter (the couple where the woman blamed heat, humidity, and haze for her emotional outbursts), for example, the therapist pointed out that whenever it appeared that the couple was coming close to dealing with some of their conflicts, they became frightened and deflected the focus of therapy onto external reasons for their emotional distress. At this, the couple acknowledged that their problems seemed like "a huge pile of shit" between them and confessed that they were afraid they couldn't be resolved. The externalizing was their way of avoiding this possible "terrible truth" about their marriage. As of this writing, this couple is still in therapy. Although they continue to externalize the blame for their problems when things get difficult in therapy, they are increasingly aware of it and are starting to "catch" themselves doing it. Only minimal "prompts" are required from the therapist to get them back on track and looking at the way they relate to each other.

This example illustrates the importance of a second stage in the process of raising consciousness about excuse-making. Once an excuse has been confronted, and examined, it is usually necessary to continue giving "feedback" about subsequent occurrences. To the extent that making excuses has become habitual or "unconscious," continued feedback is useful in helping clients to solidify their awareness of the behavior and the motivations behind it.

A related group of consciousness-raising techniques is illustrated in the work of Fritz Perls, the founder of Gestalt therapy. Perls was firm in his belief that all forms of responsibility evasion must be recognized and discouraged, and he took an active stance in bringing this about. He was very aware, for example, of clients' avoidance of personal pronouns and directly coached them to "own themselves": "And so I ask that they find their way from 'It's a busy day' to 'I keep myself busy,' from 'It gets to be a long conversation' to 'I talk a lot.' And so on" (Perls & Baumgardner, 1975, pp. 45–46). Similarly, Perls frequently encouraged clients to follow their statements with the phrase, "and I take responsibility for it" (Levitsky & Perls, 1973). A variation on these techniques was to prompt clients to change statements such as "I can't" to "I won't" in order to heighten their awareness of their personal responsibility. While these techniques capitalize on the power of repetitively verbalizing ownership of responsibility, other techniques take the approach of increasing responsibility awareness by "prescribing" the symptom.

Viktor Frankl (1963) advocated the use of a technique called "paradoxical intention" to heighten responsibility awareness. In this technique, the client is coached to deliberately and willfully produce the "symptom" being focused on. A similar approach is employed by practitioners of brief, strategic psychotherapy (e.g., Ascher & Efran, 1978; Coyne & Segal, 1982; Haley, 1963). Techniques like symptom prescription may prove useful for more than raising awareness of excuse-making. Because they avoid arousing the clients' resistance to change (the therapist is telling them *not* to change!), clients are placed in the paradoxical position of having to change in order to resist the therapist's influence (see Haley, 1963). We will say more about this later in our discussion of dealing with excuse-bolstered resistance to change.

One relatively simple approach to increasing clients' awareness of their excuse-making behavior was briefly addressed in our earlier section on assessing excuses—having clients monitor and count their behavior outside the therapy context. This may be assisted by the use of wrist counters, daily diaries, shifting objects from one pocket to another, tally sheets, and so on. Using this strategy will entail defining the behavior of interest in such a way that the client can tell whether he or she has engaged in it. Such counting procedures commonly are employed by behavior therapists treating habit behaviors like nail biting and cigarette smoking, but they may also be helpful in monitoring feelings (e.g., depression, anxiety, shyness, anger) and self-perceptions (e.g., unassertive, unattractive, awkward, competent). As mentioned in the section on assessment, self-monitoring procedures often lead to "spontaneous" reductions in problem behaviors as the client becomes increasingly aware of them and, as a consequence, capable of making active decisions about them.

Before concluding the topic of raising awareness of excuse-making, we would like to say a few words about group therapy modalities. Because of their inherent advantages in dealing with issues concerning interpersonal relationships, therapy groups can be an especially useful forum for identifying and dealing with problems of responsibility evasion (Yalom, 1980). To the extent that an individual's excuse-making is activated by the interpersonal dynamics operating in a group, group treatment can be a powerful aid in the assessment of excuses. Moreover, groups can provide a continuing and meaningful source of feedback and support for change. Some forms of group therapy (e.g., transactional analysis; Berne, 1966) pointedly and systematically focus on the "transactions" among group members for the explicit purpose of discovering how the members relate to each other and what they are attempting to accomplish. Through becoming more aware of what they are doing and why they are doing it, group members are taught to achieve more "social control." In other words, they gain the ability to make new decisions about the kinds of transactions they wish to promote and/or undertake.

Thus far we have concentrated on ways of increasing clients' awareness of their excuse-making activities. In the following section, we shift our emphasis to ways of increasing clients' consciousness concerning the factors that motivate their excuse-making. In many instances, as we shall see, there is no clear separation between the two types of consciousness raising. Rather, the distinction is a useful convention that we have adopted to facilitate our presentation of these techniques.

Increasing Awareness of Factors That Lead to Excuse-Making

In a general sense, the factors that lead to excuse-making can be conceptualized as originating either within the individual or within the individual's environment. Although this assertion is appealing in its simplicity, the reality of the matter is probably more complex. As we pointed out in Chapter 3, for example, it is likely that internal and external "audiences" for excuses "fuse" in such a way that the individual develops internal representations of external audience concerns (e.g., external standards for performance become internalized through the developmental process). We suggested, therefore, that individuals are typically concerned with *revolving self-images* in which the clean separation between the internal and external audience is lost. Although our conceptual model of excuses holds that the "locus of audience" issue is complex at a theoretical level, our position here is that it is important to keep the "locus of audience" issue simple at a practical level. We believe that the typical excuse-making client is unlikely to appreciate the subtlety of the "revolving images" concept—especially in the early stages of treatment. Consequently, we advocate retaining the "simplistic" separation between internal and external factors (audiences) when working with clients, and we will organize our following discussion accordingly.

The primary concern in raising clients' awareness of external factors related to their excuse-making is to help them identify those circumstances that "prompt" or elicit their excuses. This will, in most instances, proceed apace with the process of increasing awareness of excuse-making per se. Indeed, we present no additional techniques here beyond those that we identified in the previous section. Instead, we suggest that the techniques and strategies designed to enhance awareness of excuse-making be modified and broadened in scope to include paying attention to those aspects of the excuse arena that seem most salient to the individual. These aspects might include the physical structure of the environment, the presence of specific individuals or types of individuals, specific activities being engaged in, and specific anticipated events or activities.

Increasing awareness of external factors can be very beneficial for treatment. First, it is likely that many clients will not have closely scrutinized the specific excuse-eliciting features of their environment and may be engaging in excuses in a broader variety of situations than is "necessary." Carefully defining the "critical" components of their experiential field may quickly and easily permit a greater range of flexibility and movement. For example, George T., an adolescent client who had a social phobia, used excuses to avoid situations where other people would be present. After closely observing those situations that caused him discomfort, however, he realized that he experienced strong anxiety only in situations where he had to remain seated and would have to walk in front of people in order to leave. Situations that did not have these features ceased to be a problem.

Second, close examination of eliciting circumstances may lead to the realization that they are not, after all, as threatening as had been thought. This happened to Mike F., who had a speech phobia and avoided engaging in activities where he might have to speak in front of people, either formally or informally.

His anxiety was reinforced by his belief that audiences were generally very critical of speakers and ready to "jump down their throats" at the slightest hint of dysfluency. After being assigned the task of sitting in audiences and closely observing reactions to speaker errors and discomfort, he discovered that audiences were largely empathic and tolerant rather than hard and critical. This insight was very helpful in getting him to change his avoidance pattern.

The third point we raise in support of the importance of helping clients become aware of the external features of their excuse-making arenas is that it provides direct access to the internal factors motivating their excuses. If a client can identify the salient aspects of his or her excuse-making environment, the clinician is in a position to explore more directly and efficiently the feelings and thoughts that are stimulated by those aspects. This point, then, leads us to our discussion of increasing clients' awareness of the internal or intrapersonal factors promoting excuse-making.

The primary technique we suggest for raising clients' consciousness concerning the internal factors motivating their excuse behavior is familiar to all clinicians—the exploratory interview. Some of the assessment aids we suggested earlier in this chapter may prove helpful in identifying general intrapersonal issues. Penetrating to the core of each individual client's idiosyncratic concerns, however, requires the flexibility of the clinical interview. In acknowledging this, we are also acknowledging an inherent limitation in the eclectic stance we have attempted to maintain throughout this chapter.

As we pointed out in Chapter 8 and reiterated at the beginning of this chapter, excuse-making may be viewed from a wide variety of theoretical perspectives. It is to be expected that clinicians holding different theoretical views will take widely differing approaches to understanding the intrapsychic dynamics of the individual excuse-maker. For example, where the Freudian psychoanalyst might choose to explore the psychosexual symbolism of the excused act(s) with the goal of understanding why they are unacceptable to the superego, the behavior therapist might choose to explore the manner in which anxiety became classically conditioned to the excused act(s). We take no stand with regard to which theoretical orientation has the better grip on the "truth." Our belief is that any theoretical perspective is capable of providing the individual excuse-maker with a meaningful and facilitating way of looking at himself or herself and understanding the whys and wherefores of his or her behavior. We only assert our often-stated view that it is important to understand excuse-making behavior from a view that lends itself to appreciating the self-esteem issues that, we hold, are at the heart of the problem.

In summary, this section has been directed at providing suggestions for improving the client's awareness and understanding of his or her self-defensive excuse-making. We have argued that the process of consciousness raising lays the foundation for effective interventions. In the following sections we take a closer look at some other techniques and strategies for building upon this foundation. Our attention turns next to the matter of teaching clients new and more adaptive ways of behaving.

Learning New, More Adaptive Ways of Behaving (Decreasing Evaluative Threats)

The theory of excuse-making that we have proffered throughout this book is that excuses are motivated by desires to cut off or lessen the self-esteem–threatening implications of "bad acts" or substandard performances. What could be more natural, then, than to consider the therapeutic implications of directly enhancing the ability of the excuse-maker to behave effectively? If an individual feels confident that his or her performances will be adequate, there is no reason to engage in anticipatory excuse-making. Moreover, adequate performances, viewed retrospectively, should not occasion exculpatory excuses. In line with this logic, the central thrust of the present section is to develop the idea that clinicians who deal with excuse-makers should *always* consider the possibility that their clients' behavior is being motivated by skill deficits and should explore the ways in which any such deficits can be remediated.

To facilitate our discussion of techniques and strategies designed to promote more adaptive ways of behaving, we have elected to take a somewhat unconventional view of skill deficits. Most clinicians would agree that such things as lack of assertiveness, poor writing ability, social awkwardness, and inefficient study habits would denote skill deficits. The notion that problems involving "surplus" emotionality (e.g., phobic behavior) or dysphoric affect (e.g., depression and shyness) denote skill deficits may be somewhat more unusual. Nevertheless, there is reasonable justification for viewing them in this way.

In the context of relating his concept of "self-efficacy" to the problem of phobic behavior, Bandura (1977a) writes the following:

> It is often the case that fears and deficits are interdependent. Avoidance of stressful activities impedes development of coping skills, and the resulting lack of competency provides a realistic basis for fear. Acquiring behavioral means for controlling potential threats attenuates or eliminates fear arousal. (p. 199)

By the same token, other authors have argued that depression often results from a lack of social skill: "Social skill, defined as the emission of behaviors which are positively reinforced by others, is seen as an area of deficit especially important in the development of depressive behaviors" (Lewinsohn & Shaffer, 1971, p. 87). Finally, in talking about shyness, Zimbardo and Radl (1981) point out the importance of social skill deficits:

> In addition to their awareness of being fearful and aroused, many shy people are all too aware that they suffer deficits in social skills. They lack adequate verbal

skills necessary to feel comfortable in conversations. They lack assertiveness skills to negotiate interpersonal conflicts and to initiate action in their best interest. Finally, they may be insensitive to the nuances of appropriate social behavior needed, for example, to get someone's attention, to interrupt effectively, to handle compliments, or to know when to strike before the iron gets too hot. (p. 14)

Although we acknowledge that there may be other productive ways of viewing disorders of surplus emotionality and dysphoric affect, we suggest here that treatments for such disorders can be conceptualized as relying on skill enhancement.

Our presentation of interventions for excuses that are related to skill deficits is in two parts. In the first part we examine treatments for excuses that are related to ineffective overt behavioral skills. In the second part we focus on treatments for excuses that derive from "covert" skill deficits that must be inferred from their "indirect" manifestations in overt behavior and/or emotionality.

Treating Excuses Motivated by Overt Behavioral Skill Deficits

For our purposes, overt behavioral skill deficits include those that can be easily verified by an external observer who has access to the relevant arenas. The techniques for treating excuses that derive from such deficits are among the most simple and straightforward ones that we discuss in that they rely on the didactic processes of instructing, demonstrating, and practicing. As a consequence, virtually any instructional method may be employed. Probably the most commonly used teaching methods in clinical practice, however, are behavioral rehearsal or role playing (e.g., Goldsmith & McFall, 1975; Schwartz & Higgins, 1979), coaching (e..g, McFall & Lillesand, 1971; McFall & Twentyman, 1973), modeling (e.g., Bandura & Barab, 1973; Bandura, Jeffery, & Gajdos, 1975; Bandura, Jeffery, & Wright, 1974), and contingency management (e.g., Tharp & Wetzel, 1969).

The manner in which behavioral deficits might relate to retrospective excuses is relatively clear: the self-esteem threat resulting from some substandard performance would motivate the individual to engage in face-saving defensive maneuvers. The manner in which skill deficits relate to anticipatory excuses is somewhat more involved. We feel that Bandura's (1977a,b) theory of self-efficacy provides a useful framework of thinking about this problem. Bandura (1977a, p. 193) defines an "efficacy expectation" as "the conviction that one can successfully execute the behavior required to produce the outcomes" that one desires. A person who suffers from low efficacy expectations is likely either to avoid the behavioral arena or to show a lack of persistence if the arena is entered. We suggest that either avoidance or lack of persistence is likely to result in esteem-saving excuse-making.

The number of possible instances in which overt behavioral deficits result in defensive excuse-making is nearly limitless. Also, the treatment of excuse-making, whether anticipatory or retrospective, is virtually the same if the excusing is based on performance inabilities. In the interest of brevity, and because this type of excuse-making is relatively easy to understand, we cite only two illustrations of cases in which skill-training methods have been successfully employed to treat excuses deriving from overt behavioral inadequacies.

The first illustration is the case of Debbie B. Debbie was a college undergraduate who, through a variety of complicated circumstances, found herself "dating" two homosexual men at the same time. At the time she began dating the men, she was not aware of their homosexual orientations. Debbie was in a quandary as to what to do with her relationships. On the one hand, she liked both men very much and valued their continued friendship. On the other hand, she "saw the handwriting on the wall" and realized that she would never have the kind of intimate heterosexual relationship she wanted if she continued to spend all her time with her homosexual friends. She knew that she wanted to place much greater limits on the time she spent with them but was afraid that she would alienate them and lose their friendship if she were to tell them how she felt. Consequently, she continued spending a great amount of time with them, rationalizing her behavior with such thoughts as "They would be very hurt if I told them how I felt" and "I'll be able to tell them how I feel when I find another guy I really enjoy."

By the time Debbie came in for therapy, she was torn with conflict. After satisfying himself that he understood what was happening in Debbie's life, the therapist began exploring ways that Debbie could express her feelings to her friends without "blowing them away." As Debbie thought about some of the possibilities, she became increasingly optimistic that there *were* ways to do it. Ultimately she chose an approach that she felt most comfortable with and decided to approach one of her friends who would be the least likely to take offense. After repeated role-played conversations and rehearsals, she finally was confident enough to take the risk of trying what she had learned. It worked! Her friend understood her position and was willing to remain friends. Within two days, she had approached her second friend with equally gratifying results.

The second example involves Howard M., a graduate student in cellular biology who was at the point in his degree program where he had to take his written comprehensive exams before he could begin working on his dissertation. This was the first time in his career that he had been faced with the kind of self-directed and self-organized studying that comprehensive exams require. He had scheduled his exams several times but, each time, had canceled them at the last minute because he was bewildered by the material and unprepared. This is not what he told his department, however. They heard all manner of excuses relating to unforeseen and obligatory commitments, family difficulties, and so on. When Howard finally sought therapy for his problem, he was asked to describe his studying habits.

Howard reported that he would begin reading an article that he thought was important. Shortly into the article, he would run across a reference that seemed to be vital background information. Setting aside the first article, he would secure the second and begin reading it only to discover that it, too, referred to articles he hadn't read. He would then set that article aside to begin reading the new source, etc., etc., etc. Unbelievably, Howard reported that in months of study he had completed only a handful of articles! His next scheduled exam date was coming up in three months and he was desperate. Howard was quickly taught a new approach to studying that focused on completing one article at a time and *then* deciding if he needed to search out further background information. However, he was to read completely all the articles he had accumulated on each topic before he could go to the library for more. The other details of the study program are unimportant. What is noteworthy is that Howard accomplished more in a few weeks than he had been able to in months of frantic scrambling. By the date of his exams, he was worried but felt he had a good chance of passing. He did.

These examples illustrate the importance of paying attention to concrete behavioral skill deficits when attempting successful interventions with patterns of excuse-bolstered avoidance. It is equally important to consider the potential involvement of skill deficits in cases of retrospective excuse-making. The reason for this, as we pointed out earlier, is that if an individual is sufficiently skilled to perform adequately in performance arenas, there is no reason or need to make excuses. In cases where the deficits are, indeed, overt, it is relatively easy to recognize the need to implement a remedial program of skill building. In the next section we examine approaches to dealing with excuse-making that results from skill deficits that are not externally apparent but seen through indirect manifestations.

Treating Excuses Motivated by "Hidden" Skill Deficits

Each of us has many talents and abilities (and inabilities) that remain at the level of covert mental events yet have important ramifications for our overt behavior. We speak, for example, of "problem-solving" ability, "conceptual" ability, "organizational" ability, and "intellectual" ability. We also speak of the ability to make "discriminations," to make "judgements," to "see things in perspective," and to "discern" relationships. None of these abilities is directly observable. We make inferences about them on the basis of overt behaviors. In this section we suggest that excuse-making is an overt behavior that is frequently related to a number of covert or "hidden" abilities (or inabilities) that can be modified and improved.

If the clinician is satisfied that his or her excuse-making client is not suffering from important deficits in overt performance ability, it is time to look for more subtle skill problems. One common "sign" of covert skill deficiencies is anxiety, and the clinician would be wise to consider the inhibiting role that anxiety may have on the expression of adaptive behavior. One possible manifestation might be that the individual has an adequate behavioral repertoire but the utilization and expression of the relevant behavior(s) are "tainted" by the interference of anxiety (e.g., Eisler, Frederiksen, & Peterson, 1978; Fiedler & Beach, 1978; Schwartz & Gottman, 1976). Another possible manifestation is that the individual may be behaviorally adept but may avoid performance arenas because of concerns about experiencing excessive anxiety. Earlier in this chapter, for example, we cited the effect that acrophobia (fear of heights) had on the social behavior of subjects in a research investigation. In either instance, enhancing the individual's ability to deal with his or her anxiety may have a salutary effect on the overt expression of behavior—and on excuse-making.

There are several effective strategies for training individuals to have better control over their anxiety. One way is to enhance the individual's overt behavioral skill and thereby lessen his or her anxiety about entering and/or being in certain performance arenas. This is the issue we addressed in the previous section. Another set of techniques focuses on teaching the individual more direct forms of control over anxiety. Examples include systematic desensitization (Wolpe, 1958), flooding (Malleson, 1959), implosive therapy (Stampfl & Levis, 1967), relaxation training (Jacobsen, 1938), anxiety management training (Suinn & Richardson, 1971), and stress inoculation training (Meichenbaum, 1977). Although the effectiveness of some of these techniques has traditionally been thought to trade on such "automatic" processes as "counterconditioning" (e.g., desensitization and relaxation training), some authors have pointed out the importance of conceptualizing them as engendering self-control skills (e.g., Denney, 1980; Goldfried, 1971) and modifying the procedures to capitalize on this feature. We would add that, at the very least, the effective application of these procedures results in the client's experiencing a greater degree of control over his or her anxiety.

The foregoing techniques are designed primarily to help clients learn to *control* their anxiety. Various other techniques have been developed to "correct" maladaptive cognitive processes that are thought to underlie the development of anxiety. Albert Ellis (1958, 1962), for example, proposed that people literally create their own anxiety and dysphoric emotions by continuously reindoctrinating themselves with irrational and self-defeating thoughts and philosophies. Rational Emotive Therapy (Ellis, 1958) is designed to help people critically reexamine these irrational beliefs and to substitute rational and facilitating ones. Variations on Ellis' idea that anxiety and related dysphoric emotions derive from maladaptive cognitions have been proposed by a number of subsequent authors. For example, negative self-referential thoughts and self-statements have been shown to be associated with test anxiety (Holroyd, Westbrook, Wolf, & Badhorn, 1978), low self-esteem (Vasta & Brockner, 1979), reduced assertiveness (Schwartz & Gottman, 1976), social anxiety (Cacioppo, Glass, & Merluzzi, 1979), and depression (Weintraub, Segal, & Beck, 1974). Furthermore, procedures designed to train people to engage in more positive self-referential speech and cognitions have been shown to be effective in the treatment of low assertiveness (Linehan, Goldfried, & Goldfried, 1979), fear of flying (Girodo & Roehl, 1978), and test anxiety (Hussian & Lawrence, 1978), among other things (see Kendall & Hollon, 1979, for reviews).

These findings imply that the clinician who is attempting to treat excuse-bolstered patterns of avoidance in the context of anxiety or related forms of dysphoria might do well to consider the possible benefits of teaching more adaptive forms of self-referential speech and cognitions. Also, the clinician may wish to consider that the excuse-making individuals are focusing excessively on the potentially negative consequences of their behavior to the exclusion of the potentially positive consequences (Fiedler & Beach, 1978). In such instances efforts aimed at bringing some "balance" into the anticipated consequences might disinhibit behavior. In other instances the clinician may find that the individual is underestimating his or her level of behavioral skill and avoiding performance arenas as a result. College students who score high on measures of social anxiety *and* social skill, for example, have been found to underestimate their level of skill (Clark & Arkowitz, 1975; Curran & Wallander, 1979). In such cases it may prove helpful to teach clients to more accurately appraise their abilities.

The final area we would like to address in this section on teaching clients more adaptive covert behaviors emerges from a growing interest in the importance of cognitive attributional processes in regulating behavior and emotional reactions. The importance of attributional processes to excuse-making should be clear to the reader who recalls our presentation of excuse theory in Chapter 3. Just as we suggested that the kinds of attributions people make about their behavior may lead them to make or not make excuses, we suggest here that training people to make different attributions about their behavior and environments may be an effective form of intervention for excuse-making.

To date, attempts to modify or remediate maladaptive behaviors and emotions through the application of "attribution therapy" have fallen into one of two major categories: attempts to teach clients to misattribute their arousal, and attempts to retrain clients' "attributional styles." The misattribution approach is based on the idea that dysfunctional emotional arousal is promoted or exacerbated when an individual attributes the arousal to internal sources (recall our earlier discussion of the ideas of Storms and McCaul, 1976). The goal of misattribution therapy, then, is to get the distressed individual to shift his or her attributions to external or nonemotional sources of arousal. Although a considerable body of literature has grown up around the idea of misattribution therapy, the current evidence suggests that, for a variety of reasons, this approach may not be very amenable to use in clinical practice (for review see Harvey & Weary, 1981). Consequently, we focus our attention on attribution therapies that are designed to retrain attributional styles.

For the most part, attempts to alleviate maladaptive behavior patterns through attribution retraining focus on getting people to shift their attributions of failure from internal and stable causes to internal and unstable causes. For example, Dweck (1975) found that children who were trained to attribute failures to lack of effort and successes to ability showed greater perseverance and maintained their level of performance following failure. Children who had only been exposed to success and who had been trained to attribute their success to ability, however, showed deterioration in performance following failure. In a recent study, Wilson and Linville (1982) argued that it may prove particularly beneficial in many instances to train people to "attribute their problems to temporary factors that are apt to change rather than to permanent, unchangeble causes" (p. 368). They exposed college freshmen who reported being concerned about their academic performance to survey information indicating that college freshman frequently have academic concerns and that grades typically improve over the course of a four-year college career. Furthermore, they had their subjects view videotaped interviews with advanced college students who reported consistent improvements in their grades throughout their stays in college. The authors found that this simple intervention led to significant increases in grade-point averages after one year and to significant reductions in dropout rates at the end of the freshman year.

Findings such as these strongly indicate that there are many instances in which altering the ways clients think about their problems can be a powerful influence in changing maladaptive behavior patterns. A recent experience of one of the present authors further illustrates this point. Gary T. is a high school sophomore who developed a social phobia during his freshman year in school. Between the fall and spring semesters he became seriously ill with a gastrointestinal disorder that resulted in flatulence and frequent and urgent defecation. He subsequently developed a strong anticipatory anxiety about returning to his school classes, fearing that he would be overwhelmed by a need to defecate. Although he had never been in a situation where he had lost control, he insisted that he would if he went to school. Gary's anxiety symptoms were his excuse for refusing to attend classes.

Initial therapy with Gary used a form of imaginal desensitization combined with graduated exposure to features of the school environment (in vivo desensitization). When this had progressed sufficiently, Gary agreed to attend church with his family. He experienced considerable anxiety in the church environment but, with support from his family, was able to endure it. Prior to the church attendance assignment, the therapist had been careful to *predict* that Gary's anxiety would show a consistent pattern of diminished severity each time he went. This was important because Gary bolstered his refusal to attend school classes with the excuse that he simply couldn't go to school day after day if he had to continually fight off his anxiety. After seeing that his anxiety in church *did* diminish over time, he began to more seriously entertain the possibility that it would do the same in school. We submit that Gary had been trained to reattribute his distress to a condition that would change for the better with time (cf. Wilson & Linville, 1982), and that it was this "improved prognosis" that was largely responsible for his growing willingness to face his fear.

Our final point with regard to the use of "attribution therapy" in the treatment of excuses relates to the importance of conducting therapy in such a way that clients attribute any improvements in their conditions to themselves rather than to the therapist. The importance of this has a long history. Adler commented, "One of the most important devices in psychotherapy is to ascribe the work and the success of the therapy to the patient at whose disposal one should place oneself in a friendly way, as a coworker" (in Ansbacher & Ansbacher, 1967, p. 338). A variety of recent studies attest to the wisdom of this notion (e.g., Colletti & Kopel, 1979; Davison, Tsujimoto, & Glaros, 1973; Davison & Valins, 1969). Colletti and Kopel (1979), for example, found that long-term reduction in cigarette smoking was significantly related to the degree to which individuals made self-attributions concerning their improvement. Such findings strongly suggest that clinicians would be well-advised to encourage clients to "own" their successes. To do otherwise is to encourage them to attribute their successes to external circumstances or supports that may or may not be present outside the context of therapy. Many clinicians have worked with clients who acknowledge that they are doing much better but avoid termination by using the excuse that they couldn't keep it up without continued therapy.

Concluding Comments on Building Adaptive Ways of Behaving

In this section we have attempted to develop the argument that excuse-making commonly derives from skill deficits. As we have indicated, such skill deficits may be overt in the sense that they involve inadequacies in the area of implementation, or they may be covert in the sense that they involve maladaptive and self-defeating patterns of cognitions and attributions. In both instances, we have suggested that related excuse-making can be effectively treated through techniques and strategies aimed at building a more adaptive repertoire of skills, and we have presented an array of approaches designed to accomplish this. In the following section we address the role of revising counterproductive self-referential schemes in the treatment of excuse-making.

Revising Counterproductive Self-Referential Schemes

In our survey of selected theories of psychopathology and psychotherapy in Chapter 8 and in our review of those theories in this chapter, we saw repeated instances in which individuals were thought to experience distress (and, from our perspective, to make excuses) because of the ways they evaluate themselves. For example, we noted the negative influence of harsh or critical super-egos (i.e., Freud), of idealized self-images (i.e., Horney), of inferiority complexes (i.e., Adler), of conditions of worth (i.e., Rogers), of excessively high internal standards (i.e., Bandura), of moral guilt (i.e., Mowrer), and so on. Our view is that each of these ways of looking at the dynamics of neurosis and defensive behavior connotes a lack of self-acceptance. Accordingly, our subsequent discussion of revising counterproductive self-referential schemes focuses on helping clients move to a greater degree of self-acceptance and positive self-regard.

Our first observation is that the problem of promoting self-acceptance is intimately connected to the topic of our last section—promoting adaptive behavior. As we pointed out in Chapter 8, it is widely held that self-esteem is directly related to the extent to which performances and aspirations coincide (Bandura, 1977b; Coopersmith, 1967; Horney, 1950; Warren, 1976). If performance adequacy can be enhanced, self-acceptance is likely to increase. As Yalom (1980) stated, "If one is to love oneself, one must behave in ways that one can admire" (p. 334). Nevertheless, the very notion of "counterproductive self-referential schemes" suggests that the problem of self-acceptance frequently goes beyond problems of objective performance attainment—it often relates to the way people subjectively *appraise* themselves and their performances.

That there are differences in the ways people with high and low self-esteem appraise themselves and their performances is apparent from some of the research previously reviewed. Recall in Chapter 8, for example, our discussion of evidence that low self-esteem individuals are more inclined to make internal attributions for failures (e.g., Oliver & Williams, 1979) and to be more adversely affected by negative feedback (e.g., Hammen & Krantz, 1976). Furthermore, we reviewed evidence suggesting that individuals low in self-esteem were relatively unlikely to express positive biases toward themselves and their behavior (e.g., Lewinsohn, Mischel, Chaplin, & Barton, 1980; Nelson & Craighead, 1977). Such findings strongly implicate negatively distorted self-perceptions (or the absence of positive self-biases) in individuals who suffer from low self-acceptance. In the remainder of our discussion of revising counterproductive self-referential schemes, we examine a variety of strategies for helping people change the ways they relate to themselves.

Therapist Acceptance and Positive Regard

One frequent strategy for improving self-acceptance derives from the humanistic philosophies advocated by such theorists as Rogers (1965) and Maslow (1968). As we discussed earlier in this chapter, these individuals (also see Horney, 1950) hold that there are inherent growth tendencies in human beings that need only be unshackled to exert themselves. Rogers (1965) argued that establishing the three therapist conditions of unconditional positive regard, accurate empathy, and genuineness would enable individuals' self-actualization tendencies to emerge and to lead the individuals to greater self-acceptance. Other authors such as Adler (Ansbacher & Ansbacher, 1967) also commented on the importance of therapists taking a benign and unselfish interest in the clients' welfare. We endorse the value of establishing an accepting, positive atmosphere in therapy to encourage the exploration and revision of negative self-percepts, but we also caution that such conditions are unlikely, in themselves, to promote therapeutic change. As Rachman and Wilson (1980) observed in their review of relevant psychotherapy outcome literature, such conditions should be supplemented by appropriate selection of therapeutic techniques and strategies to address clients' other problems.

Consensus Raising

Another strategy we find to be helpful in promoting self-acceptance and defeating counterproductive self-attitudes is related to the concept of consensus raising that we discussed in Chapter 3. Clients frequently hold the belief that they are alone or unique in their problems and reach many negative self-referent conclusions as a result. A dramatic example of this can be seen in the recent upsurge of women reporting to psychological clinics for help with problems of bulimia (binge–purge eating patterns). Within the last several years, there has been an increase in the amount of media attention paid to bulimia and, as more and more women have discovered that they are not alone in having this problem, a growing number have sought treatment. Our own experience with bulimic women in the University of Kansas Psychological Clinic is that most of them have closely guarded their "secret" (often for many years), and have managed to deceive even family members and roommates. By using the excuse that they could control the behavior if they wanted to, they also manage to deceive themselves. The growing public awareness of such eating disorders as bulimia and anorexia nervosa appears to have enabled many of them to acknowledge that they are, in fact, out of control. Whereas only five years ago bulimic clients were a rarity in our Psychological Clinic, they now represent 15–20 percent of our client population.

Some recent experimental evidence attests to the potential value of consensus-raising information for promoting self-acceptance and realistic help seeking. Snyder and Ingram (in press) studied high and normally test-anxious female subjects. The subjects first completed a self-report inventory and were told that their responses indicated that they suffered from test anxiety. They were then told that their problem was common or uncommon, or they were given no consensus information. The primary dependent measure of the study was the extent to which the subjects indicated intentions to seek help for their test anxiety. Among the high-anxious subjects, those who were told their problem was common (high consensus) were the most likely to report help-seeking intentions, while those who were told their problem was uncommon were the least likely to do so. High-anxious subjects who received high consensus information were also the most likely to rate their problem as serious and to report an inability to cope with it on their own. Although Snyder and Ingram did not include a measure of self-acceptance in their study, it seems reasonable to suggest that the test-anxious subjects who received high consensus information responded as they did at least partly because of a greater ability to accept themselves despite their problem.

There are many ways of promoting consensus-based improvements in self-acceptance. As an "authority" on mental health, for example, a therapist may convey information about the incidence of problems. When doing so, however, it is important that the seriousness of the clients' problems not be demeaned. Bibliotherapy can also be employed. By reading information about other people with similar problems, clients can gain a greater understanding and acceptance of themselves. In some instances, other forms of factual information may be available for therapeutic use. Earlier in this chapter, for example, we cited a study by Wilson and Linville (1982) in which college freshmen were exposed to survey information that demonstrated that the freshman year is difficult for many students.

Clients can often be given homework assignments that expose them to situations where consensus-raising information is likely to be encountered. As an illustration, earlier in this chapter we spoke of Mike F., an individual with a speech phobia. Mike had changed his attitudes about the reactions audiences have toward speakers after following through on assignments to sit in audiences and to observe their reactions. These assignments also allowed Mike to observe that other speakers experienced visible signs of anxiety in front of groups. Mike was subsequently encouraged to share his fears with friends and acquaintances and discovered that they, too, experienced anxiety. As the evidence accumulated that he was not unique, different, or somehow "defective," Mike was helped to see himself in a more positive light and to risk exposing himself to feared speaking arenas.

Distinctiveness Raising

To this point, we have presented two approaches to promoting self-acceptance and defeating counterproductive ways of looking at oneself—establishing an accepting and positive atmosphere in therapy and undermining negative self-perceptions through consensus raising. Another important means of building greater self-acceptance and defeating counterproductive self-referential schemas is the use of techniques designed to increase the distinctiveness of clients' areas of deficiency. In talking about the cognitive styles of depressed individuals, Beck and others (e.g., Beck, 1967; Hollon & Beck, 1979) cite the tendency of depressed people to overgeneralize or maximize the negative implications of undesirable events or aspects of themselves. Wright (1960), in talking about problems associated with the rehabilitation of individuals with physical disabilities, refers to a similar process using the concept of "spread."

In simplified form, the notion of spread refers to a process whereby individuals overgeneralize the negative implications of a focalized or specific disability in such a way that a negative halo effect results. Ideas such as these directly imply that efforts designed to help an individual delimit (raise the distinctiveness of) his or her negative self-perceptions may be helpful in narrowing the scope and intensity of defensive excuse-making. Techniques designed to accomplish this could include focusing therapy on building upon strengths rather than overcoming weaknesses, surveying areas of accomplishment and adequacy, and setting up self-monitoring procedures designed to provide empirical evidence to refute global negative self-evaluations.

The approaches to enhancing self-acceptance that we have discussed thus far may be thought of as working hand-in-hand with each other. The first step, of course, is to enable the individual to express his or her self-doubts and concerns by being accepting and nonjudgmental. Once these areas have been uncovered, consensus- and distinctiveness-raising strategies may be helpful. Although these techniques may be effective when employed in a one-on-one encounter between the therapist and client, we believe that such encounters work best when supplemented by other-oriented strategies. Clients can and do discount therapists' persuasive attempts by using such reasons for disbelieving as "You're a therapist. It's your job to make me feel better." and "You're paid to say those kinds of things." It is more difficult to discredit noninvolved sources of information. Other-oriented strategies may also have benefits in addition to providing corrective feedback and information about the "self."

Encouraging Involvement with Others

Clients with problems of self-acceptance frequently tend to isolate themselves from others in an emotional sense. This may take the form of physical avoidance, or it may take the form of avoidance of intimacy through enforced superficiality. However they do it, many clients learn to conceal what they feel are their unacceptable parts. Few therapists have not heard clients say something like, "But if they only knew what I'm *really* like, they would reject me!" The therapist's acceptance of the client's presumed deficiencies is an important first step in promoting self-acceptance, but it is often necessary to assist the client in becoming reintegrated into his or her social environment. This may be accomplished by persuading or encouraging clients to share their concerns with relatively "safe" people in their lives (perhaps in therapy groups) and then, if needed, to broaden the scope as they gain in confidence that their "true" selves are not abhorrent to others. This can open up many new sources of support and reinforcement—sometimes with spectacular success.

One of the present authors recently had the experience of working with a graduate student who felt that she was a "charlatan" despite the fact that she was objectively one of the more successful students in her doctoral program. Although her peers had elected her to serve as a student representative to faculty meetings and sought her advice on many academic matters, she doggedly held that she was, down deep, incompetent. The therapist, somewhat humorously, suggested that her efforts to conceal her "true charlatan self" were causing her so much distress that it might be best to get it out into the open "once and for all." He proposed that she construct a signboard that she could wear over her shoulders and write on it, in large letters, CHARLATAN. She could then wear it around her department for several days. The therapist argued that this would be an extremely efficient way of letting everyone in on her secret and would, in one bold stroke, relieve her of the burden of maintaining her illusion of competence.

For three weeks, the therapist inquired as to whether the client had completed her "assignment" yet and encouraged her to do so. After four weeks, she came to therapy reporting that she hadn't worn a signboard, but had confided her secret fears to a couple of friends. She was amazed at their response. They felt like charlatans, too! It wasn't long before a whole group of her graduate student friends had ordered buttons with the word "charlatan" on them and were proudly wearing them to school. Not only had her secret "defect" been accepted, but it opened up a whole sequence of positive and cooperative interactions with others. Shortly thereafter, this client terminated therapy. She reported feeling much better about herself and being confident that she would be able to "check out" her fears with others in the future. She wanted to know, though, if the therapist had *really* wanted her to carry a signboard around!

Although somewhat dramatic, this example illustrates the importance of checking out our beliefs about how others feel about us as a way of promoting self-acceptance. As often as not, we are our own worst critics. Having said this, however, we must acknowledge that there are times when great caution is warranted when encouraging clients to "confess" their flaws. On occasion, it may result in the feared rejection, or worse. This calls for judgment on the therapist's part, although most clients will resist taking risks until they feel they are ready. Nevertheless, a therapist can lose credibility with clients if he or she is insensitive to the true dimensions of their guilt. In instances where it is not advisable to encourage clients to "go public" with their self-doubts and/or misdeeds, the therapist may have to rely on efforts to help the client to leave the past behind and to forge a new basis for self-respect and self-acceptance.

Decreasing Objective Self-Awareness

Although we argued earlier in this chapter that a certain amount of self-awareness is important for the treatment of excuse-making, we suggest here that there are times when self-awareness may become counterproductive. Duval and Wicklund (1972) differentiated between two types of self-awareness: objective and subjective. In the state of objective self-awareness, the individual is thinking about himself or herself. In the state of subjective self-awareness, the individual's attention is oriented toward the environment.

According to Duval and Wicklund, the state of objective self-awareness typically is associated with negative feelings about the self because individuals are inclined to make invidious comparisons between their actual behavior and their idealized standards for performance. Indeed, Ickes, Wicklund, and Ferris (1973) report experimental evidence that states of objective self-awareness do lead to lowered feelings of self-esteem. Such findings lend empirical support to an idea that has long been based on clinical wisdom—that too much self-preoccupation is counterproductive. They also suggest that a potentially useful therapeutic strategy for dealing with problems of low self-acceptance is to focus the client's awareness and attention onto the environment or others in the environment. To the extent that efforts to promote states of subjective self-awareness are successful, Duval and Wicklund's (1972) theory predicts that the individual will experience fewer threats to self-esteem and, we would suggest, will have less motivation to engage in excuse-making. How does one go about promoting subjective self-awareness?

In earlier sections of this chapter, we cited examples of cases in which having clients focus their attention on their environments proved beneficial—because they learned some important things about the environment or revised some mistaken notions, for example. Objective self-awareness theory implies that such strategies may have also helped the clients to experience less negative affect about themselves. The present authors have commonly found that individuals who are anxious in social situations (and therefore find many "reasons" to avoid them) are preoccupied with how well they are doing when interacting with others. Frequently, they are so caught up with what they are going to say and how they are going to say it that they lose contact with the natural "flow" of conversation and *do* appear awkward when they finally participate. This, of course, leads to further self-recriminations, a consolidation of their negative self-images, and even more vigilant self-preoccupation (cf. Storms & McCaul, 1976). Homework assignments designed to get such clients to enter social interactions with the deliberate intention *not* to speak, but to simply observe others and to be interested in them, are often useful in breaking the self-preoccupation cycle. Moreover, clients in such situations commonly "discover" themselves participating in a spontaneous and gratifying fashion. These experiences have a beneficial effect on the way clients think about themselves in addition to teaching them a new way of approaching social interactions (i.e., to be attentive to and interested in others).

A related technique has been described by Adler (see Ansbacher & Ansbacher, 1967). Based on his philosophical belief in the importance of stimulating and fostering clients' "social interest," Adler frequently encouraged clients to focus their attention on how they might be of use to or helpful to others. Adler believed that neurotic individuals are constantly attempting to safeguard their self-esteem by focusing on themselves so that they might prevent any expression of their felt inferiority. In agreement with our preceding discussion, he believed that this self-focusing was inherently counterproductive and he advocated the importance of having clients work toward some positive goal that was external to themselves:

> It is a question of where their interest and attention is directed. If they are striving toward an object external to themselves, they will quite naturally train and equip themselves to achieve it. Difficulties will represent no more than positions which are to be conquered on their way to success. If, on the other hand, their interest lies in stressing their own drawbacks or in fighting these drawbacks with no purpose except to be free from them, they will be able to make no real progress. (Adler, in Ansbacher & Ansbacher, 1967, pp. 112–113)

Lowering Unrealistically High Standards

As a final topic in our discussion of revising counterproductive self-referential schemes, we would like to comment on the importance of lowering unrealistically high internal standards for performance. Individuals who hold themselves up to unreasonable standards are likely to experience many unnecesary threats to their self-esteem and to engage in defensive excuse-making as a result. When exploring clients' areas of concern, we have found it helpful to inquire how they feel they *should* be able to perform. Therapists who ask this question will be struck by how many clients demand perfection of themselves. Not infrequently, such perfectionism is used as an excuse for avoiding threatening performance arenas ("If I can't do it *right* I don't want to do it at all!"). Whether or not they are used as excuses, however, lofty standards are a definite impediment to healthy self-regard.

There are many ways of thinking about how people come to suffer from overly stringent standards or idealized goals. Some of the possible ways have been reviewed in previous sections of this book (e.g., Chapter 8). Regardless of how one chooses to think about such things, it is important for clinicians to consider their possible role in motivating excuse-making and to help clients to become aware of their perfectionistic tendencies. This forms the basis for the possibilty of making new decisions about standards and values that will be more facilitating of self-acceptance. The methods for accomplishing this will rely heavily on the individual therapist's theoretical beliefs about how maladaptive standards become internalized and function.

Concluding Comments on the Question of Means

In this section on techniques and strategies for treating excuse-making behavior, we divided our presentation into three major sections: increasing awareness, learning more adaptive behaviors, and revising counterproductive self-referential schemes. We attempted to provide a variety of suggestions and ideas for thinking about and devising interventions. In the following section, we briefly address one last issue that relates more to the process of therapy than to problems of excuse-making in the natural environment. Broadly stated, that issue is the use of excuses to resist therapeutic change.

DEALING WITH EXCUSE-BOLSTERED RESISTANCE TO THERAPEUTIC CHANGE

To this point, our main concern has been with interventions that are designed to deal with excuse-making in the natural environment, although we have occasionally alluded to the fact that clients also use excuses in the context of therapy. That this happens will come as no surprise to experienced therapists. Clinicians who are accustomed to thinking about therapy relationships in terms of transference phenomena or who simply regard therapy relationships as representing, in microcosm, the larger world of interpersonal relationships will immediately recognize that therapy is a rich source of instigations to make excuses. This makes perfect sense once you think about it. Therapy often involves clients' taking hard looks at those parts of themselves that are the least attractive or doing things that they are afraid to do. Little wonder, then, that they find many excuses for maintaining the status quo.

Our goal in discussing the issue of excuse-bolstered resistance is not to provide a comprehensive survey of the variety of techniques and strategies for dealing with it. We focus primarily on techniques that may be regarded as having a "paradoxical" quality about them. Even here, though, we make no attempt at a complete survey, since the number of therapeutic techniques that may be thought of as having paradoxical aspects is very large (for reviews see Newton, 1968a; 1968b; Raskin & Klein, 1976). Our intention is to use a few selected examples of paradoxical strategies to illustrate the general principles involved in using them to deal with resistance. Beyond this, we suggest that the social-psychological theory of "psychological reactance" (Brehm, 1966; Brehm & Brehm, 1981) may provide a useful way of thinking about some of the underlying mechanisms of paradoxical approaches to the management of resistant clients.

The very notion of "resistance" to change implies that it is a negative phenomenon. This is only partly true. A client's resistance can be a rich source of information about the nature of his or her problems and can open up many therapeutic possibilities. As Erickson noted:

> Such resistance should be openly accepted, in fact, graciously accepted, since it is a vitally important communication of a part of their problems and often can be used as an opening into their defenses. This is something that the patient does not realize; rather, he may be distressed emotionally since he often interprets his behavior as uncontrollable, unpleasant, and uncooperative rather than as an informative exposition of certain of his important needs. (Erickson, in Haley, 1967, p. 472)

Psychoanalytically oriented therapists are accustomed to thinking about resistance as an integral part of the therapeutic process—interpreting and working through successive "layers" of resistance is the *sine qua non* of many insight-oriented "depth psychologies." We do not argue against this approach to resistance since many important gains can undoubtedly be made by helping a client understand and work through his or her defensive behavior. Rather we take the position that resistance often can be prevented, bypassed, or even transformed into constructive change.

Turning Resistance Against Itself

Perhaps the most fundamental suggestion we can offer for minimizing the occurrence of excuse-bolstered resistance to treatment is the following: *never encourage clients to do anything they aren't ready and able to do.* Pressing clients to stretch beyond what they feel are "safe" limits will invariably generate resistance (excuses) and/or precipitate termination. The clinician who insists on engaging in a struggle over who will control the client's behavior will quickly discover that he or she has initiated a battle that can only lead to defeat for both parties. The therapist will lose because only the client can change his or her behavior. The client will lose because the client can assert his or her control only by *not* changing. The therapist who would be effective has no real choice other than to allow the client to have at least the *illusion* of being in control of his or her behavior.

Having made this point, we can now offer a revision of our advice for minimizing excuse-bolstered resistance to change: *never encourage clients to do anything they aren't ready and able to do* unless *you really don't want them to do it.* As an illustration of this principle, recall our previous discussion of the graduate student who was encouraged to wear the sign saying CHARLATAN around her neck. This was clearly something that she wasn't ready to do, *but* the therapist really didn't want her to. The real goal was to get her to do what she ultimately did and had been resisting doing for some time—to confide her fears to a close friend. This client had repeatedly balked at the idea of revealing her fears to anyone, claiming that she "just couldn't" because they would make fun of her, wouldn't understand, and so on. The signboard ploy was intended to distract her from the real goal by getting her to focus on a more extreme action. As intended, she resolved her dilemma (and asserted her control) by taking the relatively safe route of "going private" rather than "going public."

A related technique for minimizing resistance to change is giving clients several "options" from which to choose, with the option the therapist is really interested in being the least onerous one. Often, as in the case of the female graduate student, the real goal appears less objectionable by comparison and is selected. In a recent case, for example, one of the present authors was working with a client who steadfastly insisted that he "couldn't" make prior decisions about what he was going to do because, as soon as he did, he would be "overwhelmed by doubt" and wouldn't be able to follow through. This client routinely avoided certain situations. As he explained it, he "intended" to do the things he knew he should do, but he "just didn't." His passive way of avoiding was obviously a way of denying any clear-cut responsibility for his behavior. The therapist was interested in increasing this client's responsibility awareness and carefully explained that he *was* making decisions, he was only making them in a way that gave him the feeling that he wasn't. He agreed that there was some truth in this, but when encouraged to make a decision about the following day during the session, he insisted that he would like to but couldn't because then he would get too anxious and wouldn't follow through on it. Persisting, the therapist pointed out that, *if he chose to,* the client *could* decide what he was going to do the next day in the session, but that he might prefer to make a decision later that evening at home, in the morning, a few minutes before his avoided activity, or *3 seconds* before his avoided activity. Believing that the therapist really wanted a decision in the session, the client quickly agreed to the 3-second option and, furthermore, agreed to write his decision down on a piece of paper at the 3-second mark each day for the following week. The therapist had obtained what he wanted (a more active and responsible approach to decision making) and the client felt he had obtained what he wanted (the avoidance of making a decision in the session and the option of continuing to avoid his dreaded activity).

Accepting and Encouraging Resistance in Order to Minimize It

We believe that when dealing with resistance to change, it is important to recognize that almost all clients are ambivalent about therapy. There is a desire to feel better (or they wouldn't be in therapy), and yet there is a need to retain their defenses and their control over their destiny. If recognized, this truth can be put to use. Milton Erickson, one of the most influential hynotherapists, openly advocated that clients' resistance be accepted and even encouraged (see previous quote from Haley, 1976). This strategy immediately redefines the resistance as cooperation and places the client in a position of having to change in order to manifest resistance. As Haley (1973) explained it:

> This acceptance approach is typical of hypnosis and is also Erickson's fundamental approach to human problems whether or not he is using hypnosis. What happens when one "accepts" the resistance of a subject and even encourages it? The subject is thereby caught in a situation where his attempt to resist is defined as cooperative behavior. He finds himself following the hypnotist's directives no matter what he does, because what he does is defined as cooperation. Once he is cooperating, he can be diverted into new behavior. The analogy Erickson uses is that of a person who wants to change the course of a river. If he opposes the river by trying to block it, the river will merely go over and around him. But if he ac-

cepts the force of the river and diverts it in a new direction, the force of the river will cut a new channel. (p. 24).

There are many interesting variations on the strategy of accepting and encouraging resistance in order to transform it. The interested reader is encouraged to consult the writings of Jay Haley (1963, 1967, 1973) for more comprehensive discussions of this approach. For our purposes, two of the more common variations suffice. First, clients frequently generate excuses to avoid the threats associated with changing too fast. Consequently, one strategy is to encourage them to *go slowly,* to not change too fast. As Coyne and Segal (1982) suggest, "Treatment generally proceeds most quickly when the client is not under undue pressure to solve the problem immediately or facing some real or imagined deadlines" (p. 258). This also relieves the client of having to make excuses to the therapist (or himself or herself) for not making rapid progress.

A related strategy for dealing with resistance is symptom prescription. As mentioned earlier, this strategy has much in common with Frankl's (1963) method of "paradoxical intention." The basic approach in symptom prescription is to encourage the client to continue his or her symptomatic behavior for some plausible-sounding reason. Once they are relieved of having to try to stop their symptoms or to control them, clients often find that they are less problematic. Coyne and Segal (1982) suggest that symptom prescription may be most useful for problems that "are maintained by efforts to stave off their occurrence" (p. 259). One interesting aspect of symptom prescription is that the clients' resistance to the treatment will often shift in the direction of attempting to get the therapist to let them *stop* being symptomatic!

Haley (1963) describes a case of Milton Erickson's that illustrates the use of symptom prescription. Erickson's client was a woman who wanted to lose weight. However, she reported a previous pattern of losing weight and immediately gaining it back again. After eliciting the woman's agreement to lose weight "in a way that met her personality needs" (p. 53), Erickson instructed her to gain 15 to 25 pounds. As she gained weight, the woman became increasingly resistant to gaining more, but Erickson insisted. Finally, after the woman had gained 20 pounds, Erickson allowed her to stop. According to Haley, the woman "then went on a diet, lost the wieght she wanted to lose, and has continued to maintain a low weight" (p. 53).

An interesting illustration of the combined use of the "go slow" and symptom prescription techniques occurred recently in a case that is being supervised by one of the present authors. The client, a middle-aged female, had been complaining at length about her inability to clean her house, which was a veritable "pig stye." Her inability was blamed on her arthritic shoulder, her confusion about what to keep and what to throw away, the lack of any remaining storage room in which to put things, her husband's refusal to help her, and so on. The therapist, a graduate student, had been attempting to help the woman

make realistic plans and set reasonable goals for accomplishing the cleaning—
all to no avail. The excuses for failing to act just kept rolling.

Ultimately, the therapist was encouraged to instruct the woman to take no
steps to clean the house, but to simply sit and ponder the impossibility of ever
getting it done, paying due attention to all of the many difficult decisions she
would have to make, the large amount of time the cleaning would consume,
and all the hassles she would get from her family for disrupting their routines.
The therapist explained that the problem was so difficult that it would be best
for the client to learn to accept and live with it. The woman returned to therapy
the following week reporting that she had been on a housecleaning "binge,"
whereupon the therapist cautioned her that she was moving too fast, that she
was changing things too precipitously, that she might injure her shoulder, and
that she should slow down so that she could give herself a chance to decide if it
was really wise to change her lifestyle. After all, it was explained, she had been
living in a mess for years and it might be serving some important psychological
needs. The woman protested that she had many plans for things to clean and
had begun several projects that she wanted to finish. The therapist reluctantly
agreed to let her continue, but warned that there might be repercussions if she
didn't take it easier. The housecleaning persisted.

Usurping the Client's Resistance

In a sense, many paradoxical approaches to dealing with client resistance place
the therapist in a "devil's advocate" position. Playing the devil's advocate is a
skill that Frank Farrelly (Farrelly & Brandsma, 1974) raised to an art form.
Farrelly's basic strategy is to preempt clients' resistance to change by beating
them to the punch:

> The single most succinct label for the role of the provocative therapist is that of
> Devil's Advocate. The therapist sides with and (if successful) becomes the nega-
> tive half of the client's ambivalence toward himself, significant others, and his
> life's goals and values. The therapist plays the Satanic role by tempting and urg-
> ing the client to continue his "sinning," his deviant and pathological behavior
> patterns for "good" and plausible reasons. He takes the "crooked" portion of the
> script in the therapeutic interview, thereby provoking the client to take the more
> rational, "straight," and psychologically adaptive portion of the script. (p. 57)

The logic of Farrelly's provocative strategy is fairly direct. When faced with
a therapist who humorously, perceptively, and in an exaggerated fashion paro-
dies and encourages clients' self-defeating thoughts and behaviors, they have
little left to do but to "defend" themselves by asserting their strengths and abilities and to counter the therapist's characterizations by proving them to be
wrong. Of particular interest to us is Farrelly's approach to excuse-making and
responsibility assumption:

If the therapist excuses the client, the client will tend not to excuse himself and tend to adopt more responsibility for his behavior, his values, and his attitudes; if the therapist offers sufficiently inane rationalizations for the client's pathological behaviors, the client will tend to offer explanations of low level inference and to employ scientific principles of thought, especially the law of parsimony, Occam's razor. (p. 52)

Resistance and Psychological Reactance

At this point we draw back from any further elaboration of specific techniques or strategies for dealing with excuse-bolstered resistance and reflect briefly about the psychological processes that may underlie the effectiveness of the approaches we have focused on. It seems to us that one common characteristic underlies all of the strategies that we described: they reduce threats to the individual's freedom to continue behaving in the old ways, either because they directly encourage or accept its continuance or because the alternatives presented are so "extreme" that the individual has a wide range of choice. This suggests that one important component of approaches for dealing with resistance is the minimization of psychological "reactance."

As pointed out previously, Brehm (1966) and Brehm and Brehm (1981) introduced and elaborated a theory of psychological reactance. This theory says, in effect, that when individuals encounter threats to important freedoms (e.g., freedoms to act, choose, or think), they become motivationally aroused. This motivational state, termed reactance, leads to efforts to restore the threatened freedom or, this being impossible, to increased valuation of the freedom.

Sharon Brehm (1976) suggested that psychological reactance may be related to a variety of interesting clinical phenomena, including resistance to change. According to her, reactance may be aroused by the simple possibility of adopting new behaviors since to do so implicitly threatens the freedom to engage in old behaviors. The paradoxical approaches to resistance that we discussed above (e.g., "go slow," symptom prescription) could be seen as countering such reactance by accepting or encouraging the individual's continued symptomatic behavior. Furthermore, as Brehm points out, such approaches may actually increase the likelihood of engaging in new behaviors because encouraging clients to continue engaging in old behaviors "may operate as a paradoxical injunction and threaten the freedom to engage in the new behavior, thus making the new behavior more attractive and increasing the probability of its occurrence" (p. 55). Sharon Brehm also suggests that countertherapeutic reactance effects may be minimized by offering clients new adaptive behaviors that are highly similar to old ones. In this regard, recall our example of the client who resisted making decisions in advance of his actions, but who agreed to accept the assignment of making decisions only 3 seconds prior to having to act.

Concluding Comments on Dealing with Excuse-Bolstered Resistance

In summary, our goal in this section on dealing with excuse-bolstered resistance to therapeutic change has been to point out that the enterprise of therapy, just like the enterprise of life itself, presents many potential threats. As in other areas of life, people in therapy will use excuses to defend against challenges to their sense of well-being and self-esteem. The clinician who is sensitive to this fact can be prepared for the likelihood that certain changes, depending on the individual, will represent threats and will be resisted—often to the accompanying harmonies of a chorus of excuses. The techniques and strategies that we presented are based on a long tradition of clinical experience. As we suggested, however, such strategies may also prove to have a firm foundation in contemporary social-psychological theory. It somehow seems appropriate to end this section with two quotes from Alfred Adler, who described using many strategies that we would now call paradoxical in his own work:

> The so-called *resistance* is only lack of courage to return to the useful side of life. This causes the patient to put up a defense against treatment, for fear that his relation with the psychologist should force him into some useful activity in which he will be defeated. For this reason, we must never force a patient, but guide him very gently towards his easiest approach to usefulness. If we apply force he is certain to escape. (Adler, in Ansbacher & Ansbacher, 1967, p. 338)

> The consultee must under all circumstances get the conviction that in relation to the treatment he is absolutely free. He can do, or not do, as he pleases. (Adler, in Ansbacher & Ansbacher, 1967, p. 341)

SUMMARY AND CONCLUSIONS

In this chapter we attempted to provide a framework for thinking productively about the problem of excuse-making as a therapeutic issue. We also presented a variety of ideas about the types of intervention strategies that may be helpful in the treatment of excuse-making and excuse-related problems. There is no need to reiterate the many points made throughout this chapter. However, there are several themes that warrant repetition.

First, we believe that it is essential that excuse-making be viewed as highly idiosyncratic. Although there are many commonalities in the types of excuses that people use and in the issues and dynamics that motivate them, effective interventions must be based on an appreciation of each individual's unique circumstances. This was the fundamental point of our discussion of assessment. Our many suggestions regarding intervention strategies presuppose that the clinician has achieved a conceptual understanding of the role and function of the excuse-making behavior in the individual's life. Only such an understanding will prevent misguided and counterproductive treatment plans.

A related point is that we have deliberately avoided looking at excuse-making behavior as an isolated problem. The reader will, for example, find no place in this chapter where we imply that excuses should be directly eliminated without attending to the motivating circumstances. In only rare instances are excuses likely to occur in a nonmotivated (i.e., purely habitual) fashion, although this is possible. Consequently, effective interventions for excuses will nearly always be directed at the motivating causes rather than the excuse-making behavior itself. Our presumption here is that, once the motivating factors behind excuses are satisfactorily "resolved," excuse-making will cease to be a problematic issue. In those instances where this does not occur, the clinician should satisfy himself or herself that the motivating causes have been properly addressed and then give some consideration to our discussion of resistance in the preceding section of this chapter.

Finally, our devotion of an entire chapter to the matter of therapeutic interventions for excuse-making does not imply that we believe that excuses are inherently bad. We stand by our often-stated view that they play a useful and valid role in our efforts to maintain an affirmative view of ourselves as well as to sustain our ties to others in our lives. When used appropriately and in moderation, excuses rarely are a cause for concern. As our previous comments imply, we believe that, in those instances where excuses do become self-defeating, it is because they are used excessively or because they have "outlived" their usefulness.

We began this chapter with a quote from Alfred Adler making the point that neurosis and psychosis are expressions of a loss of courage. This generally fits our view of excuses. Perhaps the therapeutic techniques and strategies we have outlined in this chapter can best be thought of as means by which to enhance the excuse-maker's courage and confidence in his or her ability to face life's challenges and to emerge intact and even enhanced by the struggle. Until a realistic basis for such courage exists, however, we can expect excuse-making to persist *because it helps the individual to maintain faith in his or her ability to survive and to control destiny.* We are prompted to recall a quote from Maslow (1968) that we used in Chapter 8: Ultimately, *"all* choices are in fact wise, if we grant two kinds of wisdom, defensive-wisdom and growth-wisdom" (p. 54).

REFERENCES

Ansbacher, H. L., & Ansbacher, R. R. *The individual psychology of Alfred Adler.* New York: Harper & Row, 1967. (Originally published by Basic Books, New York, 1956.)

Ascher, L. M., & Efran, J. S. Use of paradoxical intention in a behavioral program for sleep onset insomnia. *Journal of Consulting and Clinical Psychology,* 1978, **46,** 547-550.

Bandura, A. Self-efficacy: Toward a unifying theory of behavioral change. *Psychological Review*, 1977, **84,** 191–215. (a)

Bandura, A. *Social learning theory.* Englewood Cliffs, N.J.: Prentice-Hall, 1977. (b)

Bandura, A., & Barab, P. G. Processes governing disinhibitory effects through symbolic modeling. *Journal of Abnormal Psychology,* 1973, **82,** 1–9.

Bandura, A., Jeffery, R. W., & Gajdos, E. Generalizing change through participant modeling with self-directed mastery. *Behaviour Research and Therapy,* 1975, **13,** 141–152.

Bandura, A., Jeffery, R. W., & Wright, C. L. Efficacy of participant modeling as a function of response induction aids. *Journal of Abnormal Psychology,* 1974, **83,** 56–64.

Beck, A. T. *Depression: Causes and treatment.* Philadelphia: University of Pennsylvania Press, 1967.

Becker, E. *The denial of death.* New York: Free Press, 1975. (Originally published by Free Press, New York, 1973.)

Berne, E. *Principles of group treatment.* New York: Grove Press, 1966.

Brehm, J. W. *A theory of psychological reactance.* New York: Academic Press, 1966.

Brehm, S. S. *The application of social psychology to clinical practice.* New York: Wiley, 1976.

Brehm, S. S., & Brehm, J. W. *Psychological reactance: A theory of freedom and control.* New York: Academic Press, 1981.

Bugental, J. F. T. *The search for authenticity: An existential-analytic approach to psychotherapy.* New York: Holt, Rinehart & Winston, 1965.

Cacioppo, J., Glass, C., & Merluzzi, T. Self-statements and self-evaluations: A cognitive-response analysis of heterosocial anxiety. *Cognitive Therapy and Research,* 1979, **3,** 249–262.

Clark, J. V., & Arkowitz, H. Social anxiety and self-evaluation of interpersonal performance. *Psychological Reports,* 1975, **36,** 211–221.

Colletti, G., & Kopel, S. A. Maintaining behavior change: An investigation of three maintenance strategies and the relationship of self-attribution to the long-term reduction of cigarette smoking. *Journal of Consulting and Clinical Psychology,* 1979, **47,** 614–617.

Coopersmith, S. *The antecedents of self-esteem.* San Francisco: Freeman, 1967.

Coyne, J. C., & Segal, L. A brief, strategic interactional approach to psychotherapy. In J. C. Anchin & D. J. Kiesler (Eds.), *Handbook of interpersonal psychotherapy.* New York: Pergamon, 1982.

Curran, J. P., & Wallander, J. L. The importance of behavioral and cognitive factors in heterosexual-social anxiety. Unpublished manuscript. Brown University Medical School/ Veterans Administration Hospital, 1979.

Davison, G. C., Tsujimoto, R. N., & Glaros, A. G. Attribution and the maintenance of behavior change in falling asleep. *Journal of Abnormal Psychology,* 1973, **82,** 124–133.

Davison, G., & Valins, S. Maintenance of self-attributed and drug-attributed behavior change. *Journal of Personality and Social Psychology,* 1969, **11,** 25–33.

Denney, D. R. Self-control approaches to the treatment of test anxiety. In I. G. Sarason

(Ed.), *Test anxiety: Theory, research, and applications.* Hillsdale, N.J.: Lawrence Erlbaum Associates, 1980.

Duval, S., & Wicklund, R. A. *A theory of objective self awareness.* New York: Academic Press, 1972.

Dweck, C. S. The role of expectations and attributions in the alleviation of learned helplessness. *Journal of Personality and Social Psychology,* 1975, **31,** 674–685.

Eisler, R. M., Frederiksen, L. W., & Peterson, G. L. The relationship of cognitive variables to the expression of assertiveness. *Behavior Therapy,* 1978, **9,** 419–427.

Ellis, A. Rational psychotherapy. *Journal of Genetic Psychology,* 1958, **59,** 35–49.

Ellis, A. *Reason and emotion in psychotherapy.* New York: Lyle Stuart, 1962.

Farrelly, F., & Brandsma, J. *Provocative therapy.* Cupertino, Calif.: Meta Publications, 1974.

Fiedler, D., & Beach, L. R. On the decision to be assertive. *Journal of Consulting and Clinical Psychology,* 1978, **46,** 537–546.

Frankl, V. E. *Man's search for meaning.* New York: Washington Square Press, 1963.

Freud, S. *Civilization and its discontents.* New York: Norton, 1930.

Girodo, M., & Roehl, J. Cognitive preparation and coping self-talk: Anxiety management during the stress of flying. *Journal of Consulting and Clinical Psychology,* 1978, **46,** 978–989.

Goldfried, M. R. Systematic desensitization as training in self-control. *Journal of Consulting and Clinical Psychology,* 1971, **37,** 229–234.

Goldsmith, J. B., & McFall, R. M. Development and evaluation of an interpersonal skill-training program for psychiatric inpatients. *Journal of Abnormal Psychology,* 1975, **84,** 51–58.

Haley, J. *Strategies of psychotherapy.* New York: Grune & Stratton, 1963.

Haley, J. *Advanced techniques of hypnosis and therapy.* New York: Grune & Stratton, 1967.

Haley, J. *Uncommon therapy.* New York: Norton, 1973.

Hammen, C. L., & Krantz, S. Effect of success and failure on depressive cognitions. *Journal of Abnormal Psychology,* 1976, **85,** 577–586.

Harvey, J. H., & Weary, G. *Perspectives on attributional processes.* Dubuque, Iowa: Wm. C. Brown, 1981.

Hollon, S. D., & Beck, A. T. Cognitive therapy of depression. In P. C. Kendall & S. D. Hollon (Eds.), *Cognitive-behavioral interventions: Theory, research, and procedures.* New York: Academic Press, 1979.

Holroyd, K., Westbrook, T., Wolf, M., & Badhorn, E. Performance, cognition, and physiological responding in test anxiety. *Journal of Abnormal Psychology,* 1978, **87,** 442–451.

Horney, K. *Neurosis and human growth.* New York: Norton, 1950.

Hussian, R. A., & Lawrence, P. S. The reduction of test, state, and trait anxiety by test-specific and generalized stress innoculation training. *Cognitive Therapy and Research,* 1978, **2,** 25–37.

Ickes, W. J., Wicklund, R. A., & Ferris, C. B. Objective self-awareness and self-esteem. *Journal of Experimental Social Psychology,* 1973, **9,** 202–219.

Jacobsen, E. *Progressive relaxation.* Chicago: University of Chicago Press, 1938.

Kazdin, A. E. Self-monitoring and behavior change. In M. J. Mahoney & C. E. Thoresen (Eds.), *Self-control: Power to the person.* Monterey, Calif.: Brooks/ Cole, 1974.

Kendall, P. C., & Hollon, S. D. *Cognitive-behavioral interventions: Theory, research, and procedures.* New York: Academic Press, 1979.

Leary, M. R., & Schlenker, B. R. The social psychology of shyness: A self-presentation model. In J. T. Tedeschi (Ed.), *Impression management theory and social psychological research.* New York: Academic Press, 1981.

Levitsky, A., & Perls, F. The rules and games of gestalt therapy. In J. Fagan & I. L. Shepherd (Eds.), *Gestalt therapy now.* Palo Alto, Calif.: Science and Behavior Books, 1973.

Lewinsohn, P. M., Mischel, W., Chaplin, W., & Barton, R. Social competence and depression: The role of illusory self-perceptions. *Journal of Abnormal Psychology,* 1980, **89,** 203–212.

Lewinsohn, P. M., & Shaffer, M. Use of home observations as an integral part of the treatment of depression. Preliminary report and case studies. *Journal of Consulting and Clinical Psychology,* 1971, **37,** 87–94.

Linehan, M. M., Goldfried, M. R., & Goldfried, A. P. Assertion therapy: Skill training or cognitive restructuring. *Behavior Therapy,* 1979, **10,** 372–388.

Maddi, S. R. *Personality theories: A comparative analysis.* Homewood, Ill.: Dorsey, 1972.

Malleson, N. Panic and phobia. A possible method of treatment. *Lancet,* 1959, **1,** 225–227.

Maslow, A. H. *Toward a psychology of being.* New York: Van Nostrand-Reinhold, 1968.

McFall, R. M. Effects of self-monitoring on normal smoking behavior. *Journal of Consulting and Clinical Psychology,* 1970, **35,** 135–142.

McFall, R. M., & Lillesand, D. Behavior rehearsal with modeling and coaching in assertion training. *Journal of Abnormal Psychology,* 1971, **77,** 313–323.

McFall, R. M., & Twentyman, C. T. Four experiments on the relative contributions of rehearsal, modeling, and coaching to assertion training. *Journal of Abnormal Psychology,* 1973, **81,** 199–218.

Meichenbaum, D. *Cognitive-behavior modification:* New York: Plenum, 1977.

Mowrer, O. H. *The crisis in psychiatry and religion.* Princeton, N.J.: Van Nostrand, 1961.

Nelson, R. E., & Craighead, W. E. Selective recall of positive and negative feedback, self-control behaviors, and depression. *Journal of Abnormal Psychology,* 1977, **86,** 379–388.

Newton, J. R. Considerations for the psychotherapeutic technique of symptom scheduling. *Psychotherapy: Theory, research and practice,* 1968, **5,** 95–103. (a)

Newton, J. R. Therapeutic paradoxes. *American Journal of Psychotherapy,* 1968, **22,** 68–81. (b)

Oliver, J. M., & Williams, G. The psychology of depression as revealed by attribution of causality in college students. *Cognitive Therapy and Research,* 1979, **3,** 355–360.

Pendleton, M. G. Negative practice and desensitization in the treatment of acrophobia. Unpublished doctoral dissertation, University of Kansas, 1979.

Pendleton, M. G., & Higgins, R. L. A comparison of negative practice and systematic desensitization in the treatment of acrophobia. *Journal of Behavior Therapy & Experimental Psychiatry*, in press.

Perls, F., & Baumgardner, P. *Legacy from Fritz*. Palo Alto, Calif.: Science and Behavior Books, 1975.

Rachman, S. J., & Wilson, G. T. *The effects of psychological therapy* (2nd ed.). Oxford: Pergamon Press, 1980.

Raskin, D. E., & Klein, Z. E. Losing a symptom through keeping it: A review of paradoxical treatment techniques and rationale. *Archives of General Psychiatry*, 1976, **33**, 548–555.

Rogers, C. R. *Client-centered therapy*. Boston: Houghton Mifflin, 1965. (Originally published by the Riverside Press, Cambridge, Mass., 1951.)

Rotter, J. B. Generalized expectancies for internal versus external control of reinforcement. *Psychological Monographs*, 1966, **80**, (1, Whole No. 609).

Schlenker, B. R., & Leary, M. Social anxiety and self-representation: A conceptualization and model. *Psychological Bulletin*, 1982, **92**, 641–669.

Schwartz, R. D., & Higgins, R. L. Differential outcome from automated assertion training as a function of locus of control. *Journal of Consulting and Clinical Psychology*, 1979, **47**, 686–694.

Schwartz, R. M., & Gottman, J. M. Toward a task analysis of assertive behavior. *Journal of Consulting and Clinical Psychology*, 1976, **44**, 910–920.

Smith, T. W., Snyder, C. R., & Handelsman, M. M. On the self-serving function of an academic wooden leg: Test anxiety as a self-handicapping strategy. *Journal of Personality and Social Psychology*, 1982, **42**, 314–321.

Smith, T. W., Snyder, C. R., & Perkins, S. The self-serving function of hypochondria: Physical symptoms as self-handicapping strategies. *Journal of Personality and Social Psychology*, 1983, **44**, 787–797.

Snyder, C. R., Augelli, R., & Smith, T. W. Shyness as a self-handicapping strategy. Paper presented at the American Psychological Association Convention, Anaheim, Calif., 1983.

Snyder, C. R., & Ingram, R. E. "Company motivates the miserable": The impact of consensus information upon help-seeking for psychological problems. *Journal of Personality and Social Psychology*, in press.

Snyder, C. R., & Smith, T. W. Symptoms as self-handicapping strategies: The virtues of old wine in a new bottle. In G. Weary & H. L. Mirels (Eds.), *Integrations of clinical and social psychology*. New York: Oxford University Press, 1982.

Stampfl, T. G., & Levis, D. J. Essentials of implosive therapy: A learning theory-based psychodynamic behavioral therapy. *Journal of Abnormal Psychology*, 1967, **72**, 496–503.

Storms, M. D., & McCaul, K. D. Attribution processes and emotional exacerbation of dysfunctional behavior. In J. H. Harvey, W. J. Ickes, & R. F. Kidd (Eds.), *New directions in attribution research* (Vol. 1). Hillsdale, N.J.: Lawrence Erlbaum Associates, 1976.

Suinn, R. M., & Richardson, F. Anxiety management training: A nonspecific behavior therapy program for anxiety control. *Behavior Therapy*, 1971, **4**, 498–510.

Sundberg, N. D. *Assessment of persons.* Englewood Cliffs, N.J.: Prentice-Hall, 1977.

Tharp, R. G., & Wetzel, R. J. *Behavior modification in the natural environment.* New York: Academic Press, 1969.

Ullmann, L. P., & Krasner, L. *A psychological approach to abnormal behavior.* Englewood Cliffs, N.J.: Prentice-Hall, 1969.

Vasta, R., & Brockner, J. Self-esteem and self-evaluative covert statements. *Journal of Consulting and Clinical Psychology,* 1979, **47,** 776–777.

Wahlroos, S. *Excuses: How to spot them, deal with them, and stop using them.* New York: Macmillan, 1981.

Warren, N. T. Self-esteem and sources of cognitive bias in the evaluation of past performance. *Journal of Consulting and Clinical Psychology,* 1976, **44,** 966–975.

Weintraub, M., Segal, R., & Beck, A. An investigation of cognition and affect in the depressive experience of normal men. *Journal of Consulting and Clinical Psychology,* 1974, **42,** 911.

Wilson, T. D., & Linville, P. W. Improving the academic performance of college freshman: Attribution therapy revisited. *Journal of Personality and Social Psychology,* 1982, **42,** 367–376.

Wolpe, J. *Psychotherapy by reciprocal inhibition.* Stanford, Calif.: Stanford University Press, 1958.

Wright, B. A. *Physical disability: A psychological approach.* New York: Harper & Row, 1960. (revision in press)

Yalom, I. D. *Existential psychotherapy.* New York: Basic Books, 1980.

Zimbardo, P. G., & Radl, S. *The shy child.* New York: McGraw-Hill, 1981.

CHAPTER 10

The Values of Excuse-Making

In previous chapters we attempted to demonstrate how and why people make a variety of excuses for their bad performances. Our conclusion is that excuse-making is a commonly practiced method for dealing with the sometimes frightening implications of responsibility, and that it is rooted in the individual's inherent motivation to maintain a sense of self-esteem. In this analysis, we described excuses coming after and before bad performances, and we looked at those people who may be especially prone to excuse-making. Our parents, teachers, and peers have been portrayed as facilitating the acquisition of excuse-making skills par excellence. Further, we have explored some of the ways in which excuses can be both harmful and beneficial for individuals as they play out their lines upon the stage of life.

In this final chapter we provide a brief and selective treatment of topics that we believe are important in understanding the excuse masquerade. We first look at two of our social institutions and explore excuse-making within the well-established structure of our society. Then we briefly entertain the question of what a world without excuses might be like. Finally, we summarize some of our ideas about the ills and benefits of excuse-making.

INSTITUTIONS AND EXCUSE-MAKING

The idea that excuses are more than an individual phenomenon has been noted throughout the chapters of this book. It has also been suggested that excuses are supported and fostered by the institutions that our society creates. We have argued that the behaviors and labels of "mental illness" are a prime example of excuse-making on an individual scale, and have alluded to the notion that the excuse-making functions of psychological symptoms are, at the least, not circumvented but rather supported by institutions devised to treat people with psychological problems. In addition, the educational system has been portrayed as a facilitator and teacher of excuse-making in the young. Now we would like to extend our thinking to assert that institutions are not only tacit but *active* supporters of excuse-making. In this latter sense, institutions serve both as vendors and makers of excuses.

Mental Health Institutions as Excuse Vendors

Mental health institutions have been criticized for providing individuals with ready-made ways to avoid responsibility for their behavior. Central to this alleviation of individual responsibility is the use of diagnostic labels implying that individuals have diseases. Also, basic to most mental health practice is the assumption that the diseases in question are "caused" by identifiable etiological agents. For example, individuals admitted to a mental hospital for violent and irrational displays of emotion toward family members quickly learn that they did not become violent because they chose to become violent. Rather, as far as the professionals are concerned, their behavior is a "symptom" (much like having a fever, pain, or upset stomach) of some underlying illness. They learn that they are not simply angry, but are suffering from a disorder that must be identified or, more appropriately, "diagnosed" and, finally, "treated." People quickly learn that it is not *truly* they who have committed the act of violence; their "mental disorders" are the cause of their violent symptoms. Given an ironclad excuse in the form of a psychiatric diagnosis, people are freed to rely upon their condition as a buffer to personal responsibility taking in a vast array of situations beyond the originally precipitating ones.

Similar to the person who has a physical disability, the "mentally ill" person's incompetence in a particular area of functioning spreads to an assumption that he or she is generally incompetent and incapable of taking responsibility for even the most mundane aspects of living (Wright, 1960). The mental hospital, then, as a giver of psychiatric diagnosis and medically oriented treatment, arms the person with an excuse that may be used liberally both inside and outside the hospital. The diagnosis is such an integral part of the treatment of people with psychological problems in our culture that most requests for payment from third parties (i.e., insurance companies) must be accompanied by the psychiatric diagnosis. These requirements apply not only to inpatients but also to outpatients. From the perspective of the excuse-making model, this is tantamount to requiring the therapist to act the part of priest, in many ways absolving individuals of responsibility for their actions.

The magical absolution power of the diagnosis is, as may be expected, not inherent in the term selected. Schizophrenia, for example, does not literally mean "not responsible." In fact, it is a term that may greatly aid in providing proper treatment to the individual. Rather than being inherent in the psychiatric label, the responsibility absolving quality of a diagnosis is tied to an attitude on the part of mental health professionals and the general public that "mental illness" is just that—an illness over which the suffering individual has little or no personal control. Thus bearers of a diagnostic title are not only able to use their symptoms as excuses, but they also may find it difficult to take responsibility when they wish.

Although mental health professionals are not, as a group, oblivious to the long-term detrimental effects of psychiatric diagnoses, the mental health system is constructed in such a way as to make it difficult for the individual professional to avoid dispensing them. Some professionals counter the problem by giving their clients the least "severe" diagnosis possible. Others even go so far as to suggest that their clients take part in selecting the most livable diagnosis. Both of these methods are inadequate because mere affiliation with and participation in the mental health system, irrespective of diagnosis, can be used as an explanation for socially unacceptable behavior both by the client and by others so long as the medical model of psychological problems holds sway over people's imaginations.

Just how responsible for their behavior and for their symptoms people should be held is a matter which is currently unresolved. Some, like Szasz (1961), proclaim that the person becomes the victim of large-scale mental health services. Others, like Glasser (1965), take a "tougher" stance and suggest that individuals are responsible for themselves and for managing their illnesses. Tennov (1976) even suggests that the mental health system has become a sort of excuse strategy for society. That is, by labeling people who deviate from acceptable standards as "mentally ill," society can avoid for prolonged periods the social transformation that might prevent the prevalence or occurrence of many psychological problems. Society as a whole, then, does not have to come to terms with its own "bad performances"—that is, its production of disturbed, overstressed, and unhappy individuals.

Tennov (1976) further suggests: "Psychotherapy, which originally functioned to provide a rationale for changes in social mores and values, particularly concerning sexuality, became a 'handmaiden of oppression' by providing an even stronger rationale for not examining poverty, crime, social protest, or racial prejudice as social issues" (p. 64). That psychological institutions very easily lend themselves to the role of social oppression is obvious in the Soviet Union, where failure to accept the party line is viewed as a psychological disturbance. Mental health institutions, then, can be seen as vendors of excuses both to individuals and to society more generally.

The Courts as Excuse Vendors

Mental health institutions are far from alone in their role as excuse vendors. Another social institution that provides excuses for individuals is the court system. Persons faced with prosecution for an act may defend themselves by making a case that they are not guilty by reason of insanity or, far more frequently, that they committed the act but with "extenuating circumstances," "in self defense," or "in the heat of passion." In recent decades, many defendants have appealed to the courts to dispense sentences aimed at ameliorating past injustices done to them rather than to dispense sentences that are aimed at delivering punishment. The current controversy over the insanity plea is a reflection of the ambivalence of the public and lawmakers alike with regard to continuing to allow the court system to deliver absolution for crimes committed.

Even the structure of the legal process helps to reinforce the notion that bad performances should be faced by the performer with some sort of excuse. Lawyers quickly learn that it is helpful to emphasize the distinctiveness of the crime in the context of the accused person's overall character. Character witnesses are called to verify that the accused is a typically responsible, productive member of society. The best legal defense can even be viewed as the most simplistic of excuses, such as outright denial that the individual could possibly have committed the crime. Or, at the very least, the defense lawyer will attempt to demonstrate that the accused, with a sense of true regret, never intended to do the act. Premeditated crimes are viewed as being far worse than spontaneous ones and are punished accordingly. If individuals refuse legal counsel and defenses and openly state a desire for punishment, they are viewed as being "masochistic," attention seeking, and perhaps "mentally ill."

Seen from the excuse-making model, the legal system is in the business of asking for and evaluating the merits of the excuses provided by defense attorneys. Despite the general position of the judicial system that the individual has free will, it is also in a position to decide, on the merits of the individual case, whether the individual has freely chosen evil (for the courts are ultimately moralistic). The court system embodies our basic human ambivalence over free will and determination and attempts to provide for the case in which the individual acts without choice. A recent article suggests that this flexibility is not so much for the benefit of the individual as it is for society:

> It is not psychiatrists, it is not criminals, it is not the insane who need the insanity defense. The insanity defense is the exception that "proves" the rule of free will. It is required by the law itself . . . It is the law's own deeply social and cultural choice. (Stone, 1982, p. 640)

The legal and psychological institutions of our society are examples of the way that excuses have become institutionalized, required, and often unavoidable for the modern person. Any attempts at reforming the incidence of excuse-making in society would of necessity have to consider the social structure, our deeply embedded and codified attitudes, and even the ways in which society uses the excuses provided by its institutions.

Organizational Excuse-Making

Social institutions have a larger role in excuse-making than simply as vendors of excuses to individuals and to society. In addition to vending excuses, our social and corporate institutions also make them. To understand this dynamic, it is helpful to think of institutions as systems. The beauty of systems is that when they function effectively, they can produce effects or products on a much larger scale than the individual. The oddity of systems is that, once constructed, they seem to take on a life of their own (Gall, 1975), with clear tendencies toward self-preservation and a loose approximation of self-esteem.

That systems act with intentionality and even free will is reflected in terms such as "corporate responsibility." One of the basic tenets of systems theory is "that the whole is greater than the sum of its parts" (e.g., Bertalanffy, 1975), and systems do indeed appear to be comprised of far more than the individuals they count as their members. The "self" of a system is physically and conceptually elusive so that, when a system is called upon to take responsibility for itself, what often results is a massive game of finger pointing, better known as "passing the buck." Responsibility in systems often resembles a hot potato being passed around a circle of players; no one person can ever be said to "have" it. The board of directors blames government policies or top-level management, who blame middle management, who blame line workers, who blame middle management, and so on. "Administrative hassles," often experienced as being switched from one department to another (none of whom will actually deliver the necessary goods, services, information, or explanation), are common experiences for individuals in our society.

The point is that systems are structurally evasive when it comes to responsibility taking. Ogilvey (1977, p. 24) states the problem in terms of power:

> Given an energistic picture of power it will be natural to assume that if those on the periphery feel impotent, then those at the center must be powerful. But empirical studies of perception of power in corporate structures reveal just the opposite: when those in lower management feel powerless, more often than not, those who are supposedly in control feel powerless as well.

A supporting statement was made by Czar Alexander on his deathbed: "I never ruled Russia. Ten thousand clerks ruled Russia" (cited in Gall, 1975, p. 77).

This elusiveness of responsibility appears to be inherent in systems, but it becomes a problem only when the system or an individual therein is somehow asked to account for itself. What then becomes clear is that individuals involved in the system do not know how it all works. Again, to borrow Ogilvey's (1977, p. 24) words:

> If parts of complex organizations are beyond the control of the people tending those parts, then chances are the system as a whole is beyond the control of anyone. Everyone then perceives the system as being controlled by someone else and the hallowed institution of buck passing sets in.

The gothic horror myth of Frankenstein's monster is reenacted in modern life by the creation of systems so large, complex, and powerful that we do not understand how they work, why they do not work, or who or what should be responsible when they do not work. Excuse-making with institutions operates in much the same way as it does with individuals. The self-esteem of the institution, often referred to as its "viability," is maintained when it can successfully evade taking responsibility for its bad actions. While institutions may not experience a negative sense of self-esteem for unexcused bad performances, they may instead be faced with structural revisions or elimination.

TWO WORLDS WITHOUT EXCUSES

A view of the world as being full of excuses and excuse-makers can be maddening, frightening, and disappointing. At the macro level of society, the notion that no one person or group is in control can lead to apocalyptic predictions about the fate of our society and the world. Lest we become overly pessimistic about excuse-making, however, it is important to remember that people have been bumbling along without a clear vision and employing excuses for quite some time now. Nevertheless, it is probably true that our growing abilities, along with the mere fact of "bigness" in the scale of our society and its potential acts, make responsibility taking more important. As Zbinden (1970, p. 13) puts it:

> The fundamentally different and disquieting thing about our situation is the growing disproportion between outer progress in the Western world, its overwhelming material and technical resources, on the one hand, and the stagnation or insufficient advancement of the inner powers, particularly ethical ones, on the other.

It is the rare individual who appears to be a blend of both ethical and technical genius. Given our current social situation, with its sense of urgency and import, it is easy to think that a massive revisioning is required. This leads us to ponder what a world without excuses might be like. Two extreme views are offered here for the reader's consideration.

Everything Not Forbidden Is Compulsory

Our first view of a world without excuse-making is of a rather cold place. It is a world that requires strict adherence to the rules of society and tolerates no deviance. Here we conjure up pictures of George Orwell's *1984*, where the problems inherent in human choice and freedom are remedied by taking choice away. The individual is not expected to make decisions or author free acts. Mistakes, mishaps, and errors in judgment are not possible for individuals who do not make decisions about their own vocations, avocations, spouses, children, or even thoughts. All areas of human existence would have to be strictly controlled and enforcement would be, to our emotional minds, brutal. In fact, there would be no room for our emotional minds. Humankind would need to operate, much like machines, in a mode of blind rationality.

Societies of this nature are possible, we discover, by examining the interactions of insects, notably termites, ants, and bees. If we were to enter their culture, as King Arthur does in T. H. White's (1965) *The Once and Future King,* we would be likely to find a sign that proclaims "EVERYTHING NOT FORBIDDEN IS COMPULSORY" (p. 122). In this world, there are no words for "happy" or "free" or for their opposites. There are not even words for right or wrong because it is a society that is amoral. Ethical issues do not come into play; the closest one comes to valuation in this world is through the terms "Done" and "Not done." Anyone caught thinking (beyond what is required for achievement of their tasks), loving, or questioning would have to be "altered" or, more likely, eliminated.

In this world, either there would be no excuses or none would ever be accepted. The interior life of the mind would be irrelevant and all judgments about efficacy or acceptability would be based on the objective facts of one's behavior. It is a world that is stark in its simplicity and cold in its lack of appreciation for those things that we call human: creativity, passion, fear, and freedom. It is a world that is superior to ours only in its neatness—everything is accounted for. There are no sloppy unresolved issues, no serendipitous findings, and no mysteries. It is, obviously, an impossible world for, being based upon blind rationality, it denies major aspects of our human nature. In fact, it appears that, even for its superior organizational qualities, such a world would be an extreme regression along evolutionary lines and would require a major stifling of the level of consciousness that human beings now possess.

Selflessness

A second, and perhaps equally untenable view of a world without excuses, is a world in which each person is fully aware and accepting of his or her freedom and responsibility. It is a world view that relies upon and calls for the perfectability of human beings. There may be a few people in our world who are able to accept the full responsibility for their acts and who simply do not make excuses, but these fully aware individuals would have to know and continuously accept the existential aspects of ontology. They would be individuals who, Bodhisattva-fashion, have lost all sense of simple self-consciousness and who have ascended from the bounds of individual existence to a communion with a larger consciousness. Einstein, Gandhi, the Dalai Lama, Christ, and a small number of mystics and shaman have been described as experiencing such an existence. There is, for example, no evidence of Christ's ever making an excuse. Even the idea seems absurd.

What appears to be required of these worlds without excuses is that they be made up of people without selves. This is either because self-consciousness has been squashed and eliminated in a dramatic step backward in evolution, or because self-consciousness has been transcended for a more global consciousness. In recent times growing numbers of people believe that this latter leap of consciousness is upon us; there are those who talk of the "New Age," and who write about such things as the "Aquarian Conspiracy" (Ferguson, 1981). It is a grand view, but it is something to which we may currently only aspire. Any individual attempting such a leap quickly finds just how difficult it is to be impeccable. And so, in the meantime, we are left in a world of individuals who have imperfect selves that they are motivated to protect. This is a messy world where excuses find their home.

IN SEARCH OF GRACE

If we are unwilling to give up our individual consciousness and unable to transcend our needs for individual self-esteem, we are left in our own world, excuses included. We are of the opinion that excuses are inherently two-sided, that is, both beneficial and harmful to us as individuals and as a society. The practical issue is not so much to decide whether excuses should exist, but rather to understand all that we can about them. As a basic guideline for living with excuses, we can advocate the proverbial "Golden Mean." That is, excuses, as all things, should be used in moderation.

Our advocacy of the Golden Mean implicitly conveys our belief that the art of adaptive excuse-making involves a balancing act that is similar to an acrobat walking a high wire. The acrobat's success is dependent upon his or her ability to use the balancing rod to maintain a safe center of gravity. Overcompensating the balance too much in one direction or the other can lead to an inevitable plunge. Like the acrobat's balancing rod, excuses provide the everyday high-wire artist important leverage against falls from "grace." Overcompensating the balance in either the direction of too much or too little excuse-making can lead to adverse consequences. In moderation, however, the excuse serves most of us very well.

Recognizing Limits

Just as it is not realistic for us to pretend that we are not free when we are (see Chapter 2), it is also not realistic to pretend that we are free when we are not. Being realistically responsible involves recognizing one's limitations. In this context, excuses may become a valuable tool for reevaluating the degree of our freedom and limitedness. With an examination of our own excuses, we may ask ourselves just how free we were to select some other course. Reevaluating what parts of our lives we can control may move us to accept responsibility for and to change things that we previously accepted as "givens." A reevaluation of this sort can also help us launch a more creative set of possibilities. Alternatively, we may discover that we are frustrating ourselves with an overblown sense of responsibility and that we are harming ourselves by refusing to recognize and account for very real limitations. Excuses used in this way are not fallacious or sneaky means to avoid negative self-implications; rather, they can operate in a freeing fashion. Thus excuses generated in the context of actual limitations can become a method of accepting our human imperfection.

Providing Social Ease

The area of social comfort applies not only to individual excuse-making but to institutional excuse-making as well. The advantage of excuses from the social perspective is that they make life "nicer." We expect excuses for social improprieties and are comforted when they are forthcoming. With excuses, social interactions run more smoothly and the rules of social discourse remain intact. When individuals or institutions excuse themselves they are recognizing the continued validity of the "rule" or "standard" that they violated. In much the same way that excuses allow the errant individual to continue without drastic revisioning, excuses allow society the flexibility to accept exceptions.

Facilitating Risk-Taking

Excuses enable us to sometimes have the courage to live lives and be people who are not safe. They help us to test our limits in a world where we know that we will occasionally engage in bad performances. Lacking excuses, we might spend most of our energies avoiding risks and situations where there is a possibility that we could make mistakes or even fail.

Saving Esteem

Probably the most fundamental benefit of most excuses is that they successfully cover. They hide, from others and from ourselves, the painful, the unseemly, and, more generally, the negative sides of our personal and social selves. Without the excuse-making cover, we would often be left exposed and vulnerable. With excuses, our sense of personal esteem may be preserved. Indeed, one could think of excuses in the following words: "Amazing grace! how sweet the sound, That saved a wretch like me!" (Opening lines to "Grace," by John Newton, 1779, Hymn No. 41.)

REFERENCES

Bertalanffy, L. V. *Perspectives on general systems theory.* New York: Braziller, 1975.

Ferguson, M. *The aquarian conspiracy: Personal and social transformation in the 1980's.* Los Angeles: Tarcher, 1981.

Gall, J. *Systemantics*. New York: Simon & Schuster (published by arrangement with Quadrangle/ The New York Times Book Co.), 1975.

Glasser, W. *Reality therapy: A new approach to psychiatry*. New York: Harper & Row, 1965.

Newton, J. Grace of Faith's Review and Expectation. In *Olney hymns*. London: Printed and sold by W. Oliver, # 12 Bartholomew Close, 1779, Hymn #41, Book i.

Ogilvey, J. *Many dimensional man*. New York: Oxford University Press, 1977.

Stone, A. The insanity defense on trial. *Hospital and Community Psychiatry* (monthly publication of the American Psychiatric Association), 1982, **33,** 636–640.

Szasz, T. *The myth of mental illness*. New York: Harper & Row, 1961.

Tennov, D. *Psychotherapy: The hazardous cure*. New York: Doubleday, 1976.

White, T. H. *The once and future king*. New York: Berkley (published by arrangement with G. P. Putnam), 1965.

Wright, B. A. *Physical disability: A psychological approach*. New York: Harper & Row, 1960. (revision in press)

Zbinden, H. *Conscience*. Edited by the Curatorium of the C. G. Jung Institute, Zurich. Evanston, Ill.: Northwestern University Press, 1970. (Translated by R. F. C. Hull and Ruth Horine.)

Author Index

Subject Index